Cicero

The Life and Times of Rome's Greatest Politician

CICERO

ANTHONY EVERITT

RANDOM HOUSE
NEW YORK

Published in the United States by Random House, Inc., New York,
and simultaneously in Canada by Random House of Canada Limited, Toronto.

Random House and colophon are registered trademarks of Random House, Inc.

This work was originally published in Great Britain by John Murray (Publishers) Ltd. in 2001.

LIBRARY OF CONGRESS CATALOGING-IN-PUBLICATION DATA
Everitt, Anthony.
Cicero: the life and times of Rome's greatest politician / Anthony Everitt.
p. cm.
Includes bibliographical references and index.
ISBN 0-375-50746-9 (alk. paper)
1. Cicero, Marcus Tullius. 2. Statesmen—Rome—Biography. 3. Orators—Rome—Biography. 4. Rome—Politics and government—265–30 B.C. I. Title.

DG260.C5 E94 2002
937′.05′092—dc21
[B] 2001048531

Random House website address: www.atrandom.com

Printed in the United States of America on acid-free paper

89

Book design by Casey Hampton

For Dolores and Simone

PREFACE

With the disappearance of Latin from the schoolroom, the greatest statesman of ancient Rome, Marcus Tullius Cicero, is now a dimly remembered figure. He does not deserve this fate and it is time to restore him to his proper place in the pantheon of our common past.

One powerful motive for doing so is that, nearly two thousand years after his time, he became an unknowing architect of constitutions that still govern our lives. For the founding fathers of the United States and their political counterparts in Great Britain, the writings of Tully (as his name was Anglicized) were the foundation of their education. John Adams's first book and proudest possession was his Cicero.

Cicero wrote about how a state should best be organized and decision-makers of the eighteenth century read and digested what he had to say. His big idea, which he tirelessly publicized, was that of a mixed or balanced constitution. He favored not monarchy nor oligarchy nor democracy, but a combination of all three. His model was Rome itself, but improved. Its executive had quasi-royal powers. It was restrained partly by the widespread use of vetoes and partly by a Senate, dominated by great political families. Politicians were elected to office by the People.

This model is not so very distant from the original constitution of the United States with the careful balance it set between the executive and the legislature, and the constraints, now largely vanished, which it placed on pure, untrammeled democracy. When George Washington, meditating on the difficulty of ensuring stable government, said, "What a triumph for the advocates of despotism, to find that we are incapable of governing ourselves, and that systems on the basis of equal liberty are merely ideal and fallacious," he could have been quoting Cicero.

Towards the end of his life Cicero distinguished himself in his battle to save the Roman Republic. Through sheer force of character he took charge of the state during the months following Julius Caesar's assassination, despite the fact that he held no public office, and organized a war against the dead Dictator's friend and supporter, Mark Antony. Cicero came to stand for future generations as a model of defiance against tyranny—an inspiration first to the American and then the French revolutionaries.

The triumphs and catastrophes of Cicero's stormy career were not the end of his story, for he has enjoyed a long life after death. His speeches and philosophical writings have had an incalculable influence on western civilization throughout its history, as his great contemporary Julius Caesar foresaw.

For the Christian Fathers he was a model of the good pagan. St. Jerome, ashamed of what he felt was an excessive partiality for a heathen author, would undertake a fast, so that he could study Cicero afterwards. Petrarch's rediscovery of his works gave a powerful steer to the Renaissance and by the age of sixteen Queen Elizabeth had read nearly all his works. Cicero's prose style left its mark on Dr. Johnson and Edward Gibbon. The cadences of his oratory can be heard in the speeches of Thomas Jefferson and William Pitt (not to mention Abraham Lincoln and, only half a century ago, Winston Churchill).

Cicero merits our attention not just for his influence, but because he was a fascinating man who lived through extraordinary times. One reason why he still speaks to us across a vast interval of time is that we know so much about him. Uniquely in the classical world, hundreds of his letters survive, many written to his dear friend Atticus. I challenge anyone who reads them not to warm to his nervous, self-regarding, generous personality. He was an introvert who led the most public of lives, a thinker and intellectual who committed himself to a life of action. We see him live his life from day to day and sometimes from hour to hour. We follow the spectacular narrative of the fall of the Roman Republic through the excited, anxious eyes of a participant who twice held the reins of power and who did not know how the story would end. Here is someone who dined with Julius Caesar, detected the incorruptible Marcus Brutus in a financial scam and helped put a stop to a sexual escapade of the teenage Mark Antony. In Cicero's correspondence, noble Romans are flesh and blood, not marble.

The last years of the Republic present particular difficulties for the biographer. Events come into sharp, close focus and then suddenly pull back into a fuzzy long shot. There are years about which little is known and all there is to go on are books or summaries of books by late and only variably reliable historians. Then all at once we are in the company of Cicero and his *bête noire* Publius Clodius Pulcher as they stroll down to the Forum together one morning; we listen to their conversation and hear Cicero making a tasteless joke at Clodius's expense. The letters to Atticus are a unique repository of firsthand information, but when Atticus is with Cicero in Rome the picture breaks up. Posterity should be grateful that he spent as much time as he did in Athens or on his estates in Epirus. It has often been possible to smooth the lumpiness in the historical record, but where the detail is missing there is no point in trying to conceal the fact.

I have referred to all those who appear in this book, other than Pompey, Mark Antony and Octavian, by their Latin names (except for passing references to writers such as Livy, Horace, Plutarch and Sallust). So far as places are concerned, I take a more relaxed line; it would sound odd to talk of Roma or Athenae rather than Rome or Athens. Other places' names retain their Latin forms to avoid giving too anachronistic an impression (so, for example, I prefer Antium to Anzio and Massilia to Marseille). One of the complications of the history of this period is the large number of bit players. This is compounded by the fact that the Romans tended to call firstborn males by the same given name as their own; I have sometimes not identified people who make only a single appearance.

Some Latin terms have been retained on the grounds that there are no reasonably close English equivalents. These include *imperium,* the official political authority to rule and to raise troops; *equites,* the wealthy social class below Senators, which included businessmen, Italian provincial gentry and aristocrats, usually young, who had not yet entered on a political career (the singular form is *eques*); *amicitia,* which could mean more, or less, than friendship, being a form of mutual indebtedness among equals; *clientela,* the mutual indebtedness between social superiors and inferiors; *optimates,* a common term for the aristocratic constitutionalists in the Senate; and *populares* for their radical, populist opponents.

Some guidance on the value of money may be helpful, although it is a vexed and difficult topic. The Roman unit of account was the *sestertius* or *sesterce.* Four *sesterces* equaled one denarius, a silver coin. A bronze coin, the *as,* was worth one tenth of a denarius (the word means a "tenner"). A *talentum,* talent, was worth 24,000 *sesterces.* It is almost impossible today to ascertain the real worth of Roman money and its relation to the standard of living. As a very rough-and-ready estimate, one might say that 1 *sesterce* would be worth about $1.50, or perhaps a little more.

My greatest anachronism has been to use the Christian chronology. Until the late Republic the Romans dated years according to the names of Consuls. Atticus and other antiquarian scholars established, or at least decided, that the city had been founded by Romulus in 753 BC and thenceforward that year was used as the point of departure for chronology. So Cicero was born in AUC (*ab urbe condita* or "from the City's foundation") 648, not 106 BC, and Caesar's assassination took place in AUC 710, not 44 BC. It seemed to me, though, that the reader would find this more confusing than helpful.

Wherever possible I allow Cicero to tell his own story, often quoting from letters, speeches and books. Scattered through them are characterizations of his contemporaries, memories of his youth and political analysis. His courtroom addresses bring back to life the social and moral attitudes of ordinary Romans.

Sadly, what cannot be conveyed is the quality and contemporary impact of his Latin; not only do his melodious periods, which have the grandeur of classical architecture, fail to translate well, but his style of oratory is a vanished art. When quoting from Cicero's letters or other ancient texts I have been guided by published translations and am grateful for permission to quote them. They are listed at the end of this book under *Sources.* However, I have translated a few texts myself. Cicero peppered his correspondence with Greek phrases; these are usually rendered in French.

There have been so many biographies of Cicero that it would be tedious to list them all. They range from Plutarch in the first century AD to Gaston Boissier's charming *Cicéron et ses amis* of 1865 and the 1939 study by Matthias Gelzer, one of the twentieth century's greatest scholars of the late Republic. The most recent full-length lives by English authors are by the indefatigable editor of Cicero's correspondence, D. R. Shackleton Bailey (1971) and Elizabeth Rawson (1975). Much indebted to my predecessors, I enter the lists only because I believe that each generation should have a chance to see a giant figure of the past from the perspective of its own time and circumstances.

This book is an exercise in rehabilitation. Many writers from ancient times to the present day have seriously undervalued Cicero's consistency and effectiveness as a politician. Too often tactical suppleness has been judged to be indecisiveness. His perspective was narrower and less imaginative than that of Julius Caesar, but Cicero had clear aims and very nearly realized them. He was unlucky, a defect for which history has no mercy but for which historians are entitled to offer a discount.

More generally, I shall be happy if I have succeeded in showing, first, how unrecognizably different a world the Roman Republic was from ours and, second, that the motives of human behavior do not change. Concepts such as honor and *dignitas,* the dependence on slavery, the fact that the Romans ran a sophisticated and complex state with practically none of the public institutions we take for granted (a civil service, a police force and so forth) and the impact of religious ritual on the conduct of public affairs make ancient Rome a very strange place to modern eyes. But, as we feel the texture of their daily lives, we can see that its inhabitants are not alien beings but our neighbors.

CHRONOLOGY

BC	
109	Birth of Titus Pomponius Atticus
106	Birth of Marcus Tullius Cicero. Birth of Cnaeus Pompeius
ca. 103	Birth of Quintus Tullius Cicero
100	Birth of Caius Julius Caesar
91–89	War of the Allies
89–85	First War against Mithridates, King of Pontus
88–82	Civil war
82–79	Sulla's Dictatorship
before 81	Cicero writes *Topics for Speeches (De inventione)*
81	Cicero opens his career as an advocate
79	Defense of Sextus Roscius Amerinus
ca. 79	Cicero marries Terentia
79–77	Cicero tours Greece and Asia Minor
ca. 76–75	Birth of Cicero's daughter, Tullia
75	Cicero Quaestor in Sicily. He joins the Senate
70	Consulship of Pompey and Marcus Licinius Crassus. Cicero prosecutes Verres
ca. 70	Quintus marries Pomponia
69	Cicero Aedile
67	Pompey's campaign against Mediterranean pirates. Birth of Cicero's nephew, Quintus Tullius Cicero. Tullia engaged to Caius Calpurnius Piso Frugi
66	Cicero Praetor

66–62	Pompey campaigns against Mithridates
65	Birth of Cicero's son, Marcus Tullius Cicero
63	Cicero Consul. He puts down the conspiracy of Catilina. Birth of Caius Octavius, later Caius Julius Caesar Octavius (Octavian)
62	Quintus Praetor. Tullia marries Calpurnius Piso
61–59	Quintus governor of Asia
60	Alliance among Caesar, Pompey and Crassus (the First Triumvirate)
59	Julius Caesar Consul
58	Publius Clodius Pulcher Tribune
58–49	Caesar governor of Gaul. The Gallic War
58–57	Cicero in exile in Greece
57	Death of Calpurnius Piso
56	Caesar meets Pompey in Luca and renews the First Triumvirate
55	Second Consulship of Pompey and Crassus. Tullia marries Furius Crassipes. Cicero writes *The Ideal Orator (De oratore)*
54–52	Quintus with Caesar in Gaul
54	Cicero starts writing *On the State (De re publica;* published 51)
53	Crassus campaigns against the Parthians. Death of Crassus at Carrhae. Cicero frees his slave Tiro
52	Murder of Publius Clodius Pulcher. Pompey sole Consul
52/51	Tullia and Crassipes are divorced
52–43	Cicero writes *On Law (De legibus)*
51–50	Cicero governor of Cilicia
50	Tullia marries Publius Cornelius Dolabella
49–45	Civil war
49–48	Cicero at Pompey's headquarters in Greece
48	Defeat of Pompey at the battle of Pharsalus. Murder of Pompey. Cicero returns to Italy. Death of Marcus Caelius Rufus
48–44	Dictatorship of Julius Caesar
47	Cicero pardoned by Caesar
46	Suicide of Marcus Porcius Cato. Cicero divorces Terentia. He marries Publilia
45	Death of Tullia. Cicero divorces Publilia. Divorce of Quintus and Pomponia. Cicero writes *Hortensius; Academic Treatises (Academica); On Supreme Good and Evil (De finibus bonorum et malorum); Conversations at Tusculum (Tusculanae disputationes); The Nature of the Gods (De natura deorum)*

44	Assassination of Julius Caesar. Cicero writes *Foretelling the Future (De divinatione); Destiny (De fato); Duties (De officiis)*
44–43	Siege of Mutina
44/43	Suicide of Dolabella
43	Battles at Mutina. Alliance among Mark Antony, Octavian (Caius Julius Caesar Octavianus, later the Emperor Augustus) and Marcus Aemilius Lepidus. Quintus and his son put to death. Cicero put to death
42	Suicides of Caius Cassius Longinus and Marcus Junius Brutus at Philippi
32	Death of Atticus
31	Octavian's victory over Antony at Actium
30	Suicides of Mark Antony and Cleopatra
27	Title of Augustus conferred on Octavian

AD

14	Death of Augustus

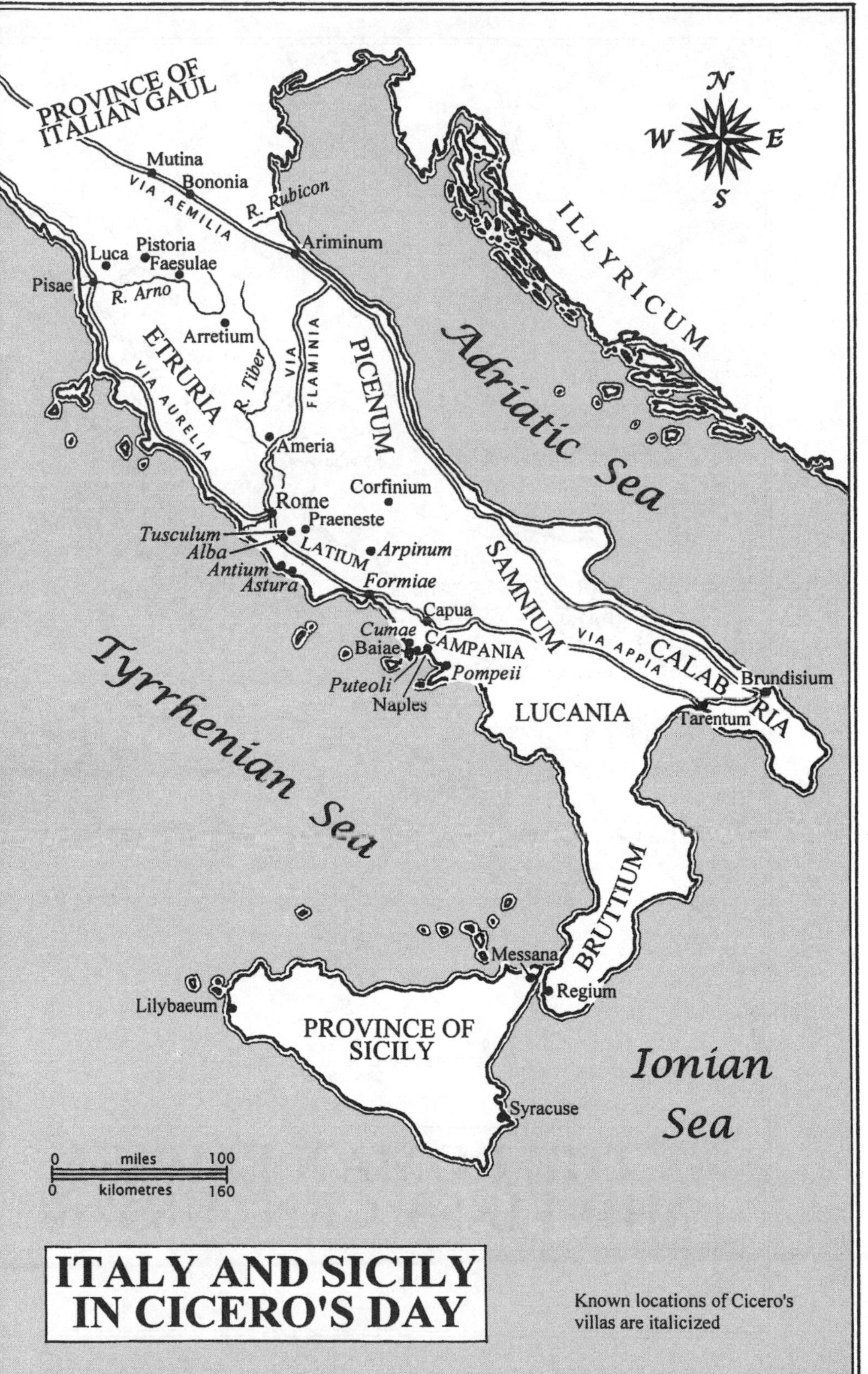

ITALY AND SICILY IN CICERO'S DAY

THE ROMAN EMPIRE MID-FIRST CENTURY BC

Black Sea
RICUM
rrhachium
MACEDONIA
undisium
Apollonia
rentum
Thessalonica
Propontis
Epirus
Pharsalus
Corcyra
Patrae
Corinth
Athens
Ilium
ASIA
Ephesus
CILICIA
Rhodes
CRETE
BITHYNIA AND PONTUS
Sinope
Galatia
Zela
Cappadocia
Armenia
Carrhae
Tarsus
Antioch
SYRIA
Parthia
Cyprus
Tyre
CYRENAICA
Alexandria
Memphis
Egypt
Boundary of province where known

CONTENTS

CICERO

The spring weather was unsettled in Rome. The fifteenth of March was a public holiday, marking the end of winter. From the early morning, crowds of people had been streaming out of the city. It was almost as if Rome were being evacuated. Families abandoned the busy streets and huddled houses and crossed the River Tiber. In the countryside, in huts made of branches or makeshift tents, they would set up picnics and consume large amounts of alcohol. It was said that the drinkers would live for as many years as they downed cups (in that case, as one wit had it, everyone ought to live for as long as Nestor, the classical equivalent of Methuselah).

The Senate, however, had more serious business at hand—its last meeting under the Dictator before he departed from Rome on a military expedition to Parthia. It was due to be held not as usual in the Senate House in the Forum but in one of Rome's most spectacular buildings, the 340-meter-long Theater of Pompeius just outside the city on the Field of Mars. During the first half of the morning, the Senators gathered in a ceremonial hall in the center of the complex.

Among the leading figures arriving at the theater was Marcus Tullius Cicero, now in his early sixties and by Roman standards an old man but still handsome, with full lips, a decisive nose and beetling brows. Rome's most famous orator and one of the pillars of the Republican tradition, he was in theory in political retirement. Having sided against Julius Caesar in the recent civil war, he had reluctantly come to terms with the new regime. He still kept abreast of events. A witty man, he could seldom resist making topical jokes, often at the most inopportune moments. At the moment he was worrying about what new flattering honor the Senate might be preparing to award Caesar.

When Cicero got out of his litter, surrounded by hangers-on waiting for his latest *bon mot,* he noticed leading members of the government mingling with the crowd. There was Marcus Junius Brutus, a member of one of Rome's oldest families and a favorite of Caesar's. He was joined by Caius Cassius Longinus, who had just arrived after being delayed by his son's coming-of-age ceremony. They were soon deep in a private conversation. An acquaintance interrupted them, whom Cicero heard to say mysteriously that he hoped they would accomplish what they had in mind, but that they should hurry. Brutus and Cassius reacted nervously and seemed ill at ease.

A rumor suddenly went round the gathering dignitaries that Caesar would not be attending the sitting after all. He and his wife had passed a restless night and both had had bad dreams. His doctors were advising him to stay at home, fearing a recurrence of the dizzy fits from which he suffered. Furthermore, the omens from the morning's animal sacrifice were discouraging.

Nevertheless, the great man at last arrived at about eleven o'clock, wearing the gold-bordered purple toga and high red boots that generals wore at their victory ceremonies. Fifty-six years old, he was tall, fair and well-built, with a broad face and keen, dark brown eyes. Years of ceaseless campaigning had left their mark on his constitution and he looked older than his years. Known for his personal vanity, he kept his thinning hair neatly trimmed and his face shaved. (According to gossip, he was also in the habit of depilating his pubic hair.)

The Senators, who had been standing around talking, walked into the hall ahead of Caesar, but one of them came up to him and engaged him briefly in animated conversation. Meanwhile, Mark Antony, the Dictator's right-hand man, was detained in an anteroom by someone with urgent business.

Caesar was moving away from his litter when a teacher of public speaking whom he knew, a certain Artemidorus, confronted him. He handed over a note which he said should be read immediately. The Dictator was struck by the urgency in the man's voice and kept the letter in his hand, though the pressure of the occasion put the document out of his mind and he was never to read it.

Most Senators settled down on their benches, but a number stood around Caesar's gilded ceremonial chair. As an elder statesman, Cicero had a place of honor on a front bench. Meanwhile, outside the theater, further sacrifices were being conducted. Once more the slaughtered victims revealed unfavorable signs and more animals had to be brought forward, one after another, to see if better omens could be found. Caesar, losing patience, turned away and faced west, supposedly an unlucky direction.

A religious official who had previously warned him that the Ides of March would bring danger caught Caesar's eye. Caesar remarked jokingly: "Where are your predictions now? The day you were afraid of has come and I'm still alive." "Yes, come, but not yet gone," was the dry reply.

The Dictator was again on the point of calling off the sitting when attendants announced that the Senate was ready. One of his staff intervened. "Come on, my dear fellow, there's no time for this nonsense. Don't put off the important business which you and this great assembly need to deal with. Make your own power an auspicious omen." He led Caesar by the hand into the crowded chamber. On the Dictator's appearance everyone stood up. The men gathered round his chair closed in on him as he sat down.

Cicero had a perfect view of what happened next.

A Senator called Tillius Cimber grabbed Caesar's purple toga like a suppliant, preventing him from standing up or using his hands. Caesar was furious. "Why, this is violence!" he shouted.

"What are you waiting for, friends?" cried Tillius, pulling the toga away from Caesar's neck.

Publius Servilius Casca, who was standing behind the chair, aimed a blow at Caesar's throat, but Caesar, well-known for his lightning reactions, wrenched his toga from Tillius's grasp and the blow miscarried, only wounding him in the chest. Then, springing from his seat, he whirled round to grab Casca's hand and rammed his writing stylus into his arm. The man yelled in Greek to his brother, standing nearby, who drove a dagger into Caesar's side, which was exposed in the act of turning.

The Senators in the body of the hall were in a state of shock. Only two of them tried to intervene, but they were driven off. No one else moved to help the stricken man.

Given no forewarning of what was to happen, Cicero saw to his astonishment that one of his closest friends, Marcus Brutus, was leading the bloodstained throng as it hacked and thrust at its victim. Cassius, who gave Caesar a glancing blow across the face, was in the melee too. Clearly, there had been a conspiracy and, equally clearly and hurtfully, Cicero had not been invited to join it.

Caesar kept twisting from side to side, bellowing like a wild animal. He was cut in the face and deep under one flank. The assassins accidentally stabbed one another rather than their target and it almost looked as if they were fighting among themselves. Then Brutus wounded Caesar in the groin. The dying man gasped: "You too, my son?" Either in response to this culminating betrayal or because he saw he had no hope of survival, he wound himself in his toga, unfastening the lower part to cover his legs, and fell neatly at the base of Pompey's statue. No one would be allowed to see him defenseless. The conspirators went on savaging the body.

The audience of Senators had no idea whether or not they too were under threat and they were not waiting to find out. There was a scuffle at the door as everyone pushed to leave.

Then Brutus walked to the center of the hall. He brandished his dagger, shouted for Cicero by name and congratulated him on the recovery of freedom. The retired statesman, who had apparently made his peace with the tyrant, was suddenly pushed to center stage. Hitherto scarcely able to believe his eyes, he could now scarcely believe his ears. It was almost as if the assassination had been staged especially for him—as a particularly savage benefit performance.

What had happened was a mystery to him. Even in the terror of the moment he actually had no regrets for Caesar. Quite the opposite. . . . But he could not begin to understand why a superannuated statesman, a self-confessed collaborator, was now being hailed as a symbol of Republican values and traditional liberties by the very man, Brutus, who had not trusted him enough in the first place to let him join the conspiracy to rid Rome of its tyrant.

Cicero did not linger in the empty hall but made his way back to his house on Palatine Hill, while a thunderstorm burst overhead. One thing at least was clear to him. His shouted name meant that he was forgiven, and that after all his compromises and disappointed hopes, the steps for which he had been bitterly censured and even accused of cowardice, he was no longer peripheral to the future of Rome.

Later, when he had time to reflect, Cicero thought back to the heyday of his political career nearly twenty years previously. During his Consulship he had put down an attempted coup by a dissolute nobleman, Lucius Sergius Catilina, a friend of Caesar's but a much less talented politician, and had enforced the execution of his leading followers. Although he had been a member of the Senatorial oligarchy, Catilina had wanted to pull it down. Where he had tried and failed, Caesar had succeeded. But now he too had been destroyed and the Republic had been saved again. Brutus's cry linked the past with the present and was an implicit invitation to Cicero to return to active politics.

Giving the lie to his critics, the old orator was happy to respond. In the days and months that followed, he stepped back eagerly into the dangerous limelight.

I

FAULT LINES

The Empire in Crisis: First Century BC

To understand Cicero's life, which spanned the first two thirds of the first century BC, it is necessary to picture the world in which he lived, and especially the nature of Roman politics.

Rome in Cicero's day was a complex and sophisticated city, with up to a million inhabitants, and much of its pattern of life is recognizably familiar, even at a distance of two millennia. There were shopping malls and bars and a lively cultural scene with theater and sport. Poetry and literature thrived and new books were much talked about. Leading actors were household names. The affluent led a busy social round of dinner parties and gossip, and they owned country homes to which they could retreat from the pressures of urban living. Politics was conducted with a familiar blend of private affability and public invective. Speech was free. Everyone complained about the traffic.

The little city-state, hardly more than a village when it was founded (according to tradition) in 753 BC, gradually annexed the numerous tribes and statelets in the Italian peninsula and Sicily. The Romans were tough, aggressive and, to reverse von Clausewitz, inclined to see politics as a continuation of war by other means. They came to dominate the western Mediterranean. First, they gained a small foothold in the Maghreb, the province of Africa which covered roughly the territory of modern Tunisia.

From here the great city of Carthage ruled its empire, until it was twice defeated by Rome and later razed to the ground in the second century BC. Spain was another prize of these wars and was divided into two provinces, Near Spain and Far Spain. In what is now Provence, Rome established Transalpine Gaul (*Gallia Transalpina*), but the rest of France was an unconquered and mysterious mélange of jostling tribes. Northern Italy was not merged into the home nation but was administered as a separate province, Italian Gaul (*Gallia Cisalpina*).

Then Rome invaded Greece and the kingdoms of Asia Minor, enfeebled inheritors of the conquests of Alexander the Great. In the first century BC, along the eastern seaboard of the Mediterranean, now named with literal-minded accuracy "our sea" (*Mare Nostrum*), Rome directly governed a chain of territories: Macedonia (which included Greece), Asia (in western Turkey), Cilicia (in southern Turkey) and Syria (broadly, today's Syria and Lebanon). Beyond them, client monarchies stood as buffers between Rome's possessions and the unpredictable Parthian Empire, which lay beyond the River Euphrates. Pharaohs still ruled Egypt, but their independence was precarious.

This empire, the largest the western world had so far seen, was created more through inadvertence than design and presented Rome with a heavy and complicated administrative burden. This was partly because communications were slow and unreliable. Although a network of well-engineered roads was constructed, travel was limited to the speed of a horse. The rich would often travel by litter or coach, and so proceeded at walking pace or not much faster. Sailing ships before the age of the compass tended to hug the coast and seldom ventured beyond sight of land.

There being no public postal service, letters (which were scratched on waxed tablets or written on pieces of papyrus and sealed) were sent at considerable cost by messengers. The state employed couriers, as did commercial enterprises, and the trick for a private correspondent was to persuade them, or friendly travelers going in the right direction, to take his or her post with them and deliver it.

The greatest underlying problem facing the Republic, however, lay at home in its system of governance. Rome was a state without most of the institutions needed to run a state. There was no permanent civil service except for a handful of officials at the Treasury; when politicians took office or went to govern a province they had to bring in their own people to help them conduct business. The concept of a police force did not exist, which meant that the public spaces of the capital city were often hijacked by gangs of hooligans in the service of one interest or another. Soldiers in arms were absolutely forbidden to enter Rome, so all the authorities could do to enforce law and order was to hire their own ruffians.

The Republic was governed by the rule of law but did not operate a public prosecution service, and elected politicians acted as judges. Both in civil and criminal cases it was left to private individuals to bring suits. Usually litigants delegated this task to professional advocates, who acted as private detectives, assembling evidence and witnesses, as well as speaking at trials. Officially these advocates were unpaid, but in practice they could expect to receive favors, gifts and legacies in return for their services.

There was no penal system, and prisons were used for emergencies rather than for housing convicts. (Distinguished foreign captives and state hostages were exceptions and could be kept under lock and key or house arrest for years.) Penalties were usually exile or a fine and capital punishment was rare: no Roman citizen could be put to death without trial, although some argued that this was permissible during an official state of emergency.

The Republic became enormously rich on the spoils of empire, so much so that from 167 BC Roman citizens in Italy no longer paid any personal taxes. However, banking was in its infancy, and there were no major commercial financial institutions. Moneylenders (silversmiths and goldsmiths) laid cash out at interest and it was even possible to hold private accounts with them; but most people felt it safer to borrow from and lend to their family and friends. Without a bureaucracy the government was not in a position to collect taxes, selling the right to do so to the highest bidder. Tax farmers and provincial governors often colluded to make exorbitant profits.

All these things, in their various ways, were obstacles to effective administration. However, the constitution, which controlled the conduct of politics, was the Republic's greatest weakness.

Rome was an evolutionary society, not a revolutionary one. Constitutional crises tended to lead not to the abolition of previous arrangements but to the accretion of new layers of governance. For two and a half centuries Rome was a monarchy that was very much under the thumb of neighboring Etruria (today's Tuscany). In 510 BC King Tarquin was expelled in circumstances of great bitterness; according to legend he had raped a leading Roman's daughter, Lucretia. Whatever really happened, the citizenry was determined that never again would any single man be allowed to obtain supreme power. This was the main principle that underpinned constitutional arrangements which, by Cicero's time, were of a baffling complexity.

For generations the system worked well. It created a sense of community. To be a Roman citizen did not confer equality, but it did mean that one lived under the rule of law and felt a personal stake in the Republic's future. Rights, of course, were accompanied by duties and one of the secrets of Rome's strength was that even in moments of military catastrophe the state could call on all its citizens to come to its rescue. Another was pragmatism: for most of its history Rome's leaders showed a remarkable talent for imaginative improvisation when they met intractable problems. These were the qualities that assured the triumph of the Republic's legions and the creation of its empire.

After the fall of the monarchy, royal authority was transferred to two Consuls who alternated in executive seniority month by month. They were elected by the people (that is, all male Roman citizens within reach of the capital city, where elections took place) and held office for one year only. There was a ladder of other annual posts (called the *cursus honorum,* the Honors Race) up which aspiring politicians had to climb before they became eligible for the top job, the Consulship. The most junior of these brought with it life membership of a committee called the Senate and led on to glittering privileges: in Cicero's words, "rank, position, magnificence at home, reputation and influence abroad, the embroidered robe, the chair of state, the lictors' rods, armies, commands, provinces." The number of Senators varied; at one point, in Cicero's youth, there were only 300, but half a century later Julius Caesar packed the Senate with his supporters, and the membership reached 900.

On the first rung of the ladder were twenty Quaestors, who were responsible for the receipt of taxes and payments. The next stage for an aspiring young Roman was to become one of four Aediles, who handled—at their own expense—various civic matters in the capital: the upkeep of temples, buildings, markets and public games. Lucky for those with limited means or generosity, the Aedileship was optional, and it was possible to move directly to the Praetorship.

The eight Praetors, like the two Consuls, stood above the other officeholders, for they held *imperium*—that is to say, the temporary exercise of the old power of royal sovereignty. *Imperium* was symbolized by an official escort of attendants, called lictors, each of whom carried *fasces*, an ax and rods signifying the power of life and death. Praetors acted as judges in the courts or administered law in the provinces. Only after he had been a Praetor might a man stand for the Consulship.

The constitution had a safety valve. In the event of a dire military or political emergency, a Dictator could be appointed on the nomination of the Consuls. He was given supreme authority and no one could call him to account for his actions. However, unlike modern dictators, his powers were strictly time-limited: he held office for a maximum of six months. Before Cicero's lifetime, the last Dictator had been Quintus Fabius Maximus in 217, whose delaying tactics had helped to drive the great Carthaginian general Hannibal out of Italy. The post then fell into disuse.

Life after the high point of the Consulship could be something of a disappointment. Former Consuls and Praetors were appointed governors of provinces (they were called Proconsuls or Propraetors), where many of them used extortion to recoup the high cost, mostly incurred by bribing voters, of competing in the Honors Race—and, indeed, of holding office, for the state paid no salaries to those placed in charge of it. After this point, for most of them, their active careers were to all intents and purposes over. They became elder statesmen and wielded influence rather than power through their contribution to debates in the Senate. The only political job open to them was the Censorship: every five years two former Consuls were appointed Censors, whose main task was to review the membership of the Senate and remove any thought to be unworthy. Circumstance or ambition allowed a few to win the Consulship again, but this was unusual.

In theory the Senate was an advisory committee for the Consuls, but in practice, largely because it was permanent and officeholders were not, it became the Republic's ruling instrument. It usually met in the Senate House in the Forum (*Curia Hostilia*, named after its legendary founder king, Tullus Hostilius) but was also convened in temples and other public buildings, sometimes to ensure the Senators' safety. It gained important powers, especially over foreign affairs and money supply. The Senate could not pass laws; it usually considered legislation before it was approved by the People at the General Assembly. But to all intents and purposes it decided policy and expected it to be implemented. The proud wielders of *imperium* knew that they would soon have to hand it back and as a rule thought twice before irritating the one body in the state that represented continuity.

Another remarkable device inhibited overmighty citizens. This was the widespread use of the veto. One Consul could veto any of his colleagues' proposals and those of junior officeholders. Praetors and the other officeholders could veto their colleagues' proposals.

At bottom, politics was a hullabaloo of equal and individual competitors who would only be guaranteed to cooperate for one cause: the elimination of anybody who threatened to step out of line and grab too much power for himself. It follows that there was nothing resembling today's political parties. Governments did not rise and fall and the notion of a loyal opposition would have been received with incredulity.

However, there were two broad interest groups: the aristocracy, the oldest families of which were called Patricians, and the broad mass of the People, or the *plebs.* Their political supporters were known respectively as *optimates,* the "best people," and *populares,* those who favored the People. The high offices of state were largely in the hands of the former and, in practice, were the prerogative of twenty or fewer families. With the passage of time, some plebeian families were admitted to the nobility. But only occasionally did a New Man, without the appropriate blue-blooded pedigree, penetrate the upper reaches of government. Cicero was one of these few.

Since the fall of the monarchy in 510 BC, Roman domestic politics had been a long, inconclusive class struggle, suspended for long periods by foreign wars. During one never-to-be-forgotten confrontation over a debt crisis in 493 BC, the entire population withdrew its labor. The *plebs* evacuated Rome and encamped on a neighboring hill. It was an inspired tactic. The Patricians were left in charge—but of empty streets. They quickly admitted defeat and allowed the creation of new officials, Tribunes of the People, whose sole purpose was to protect the interests of the *plebs.* In Cicero's day there were twelve of these. While everybody else's term of office ran till December 31, theirs ended on December 12.

Tribunes could propose legislation and convene meetings of the Senate, of which they were ex officio members, but they had no executive authority and their basic role was negative. Just as the Consuls had a universal power of veto, so a Tribune could forbid any use of power that he judged to be high-handed and against the popular will. Tribunes could even veto one anothers' vetoes. No doubt because their purpose in life was to annoy people, their persons were sacrosanct.

Different kinds of popular assembly ensured a degree of democratic control. The Military Assembly (*comitia centuriata*) elected Consuls and Praetors through voting blocs called "centuries" (the word for an army platoon), membership of which was weighted according to citizens' wealth. The more important Tribal or General Assembly (*comitia tributa*) voted by *tribes,* which were territorial in composition rather than socioeconomic. It had the exclusive power to declare peace or war and it approved bills, usually after consideration by the Senate. The General Assembly could only accept or reject motions and, except for speeches invited by the officeholder who convened the meeting, debate was forbidden. Despite these restrictions, the General Assembly was a crucial mechanism for enforcing change against the Senate's wishes. An informal assembly meeting *(contio)* could also be called, at which reports could be given but no decisions taken.

A serious problem of unfairness arose as Roman citizenship was increasingly conferred on Italian communities at a distance from Rome. Democratic participation in Roman political life was direct and not based on the representative principle: the General Assembly was not a parliament. Those who lived more than a few hours' travel from the city (say, twenty miles or so) were effectively disfranchised and "rural" communities were often represented by a handful of voters, who therefore exerted considerably more influence than members of city wards. Well-targeted bribes could easily swing bloc votes.

Widespread corruption was not the only obstacle to orderly process. Meetings were often convened at the Assembly Ground (*Comitium*), a circular open space looking like a gigantic sundial, in the Forum, Rome's central square, although elections were held on the Field of Mars, a stretch of open land just outside the city limits, also the venue for military exercises. This was a matter of some tactical importance. The Assembly Ground had limited space and it was easy for the authorities or armed groups of toughs to take control of a meeting—or, for that matter, of the entire Forum. Public opinion as expressed through the medium of a General Assembly often represented no more and no less than the view of a particular faction.

The main trouble with the Roman constitution was that it contained too many checks and balances, whether to restrain ambitious power-seekers or to protect ordinary citizens from the executive. It is somewhat surprising that anything was ever decided. However, so long as the different forces in the Republic were prepared to resolve disputes through compromise, the system worked well enough. As far as it could, the Senate allowed events to take their course, intervening only when absolutely necessary.

Most Romans believed that their system of government was the finest political invention of the human mind. Change was inconceivable. Indeed, the constitution's various parts were so mutually interdependent that reform within the rules was next to impossible. As a result, radicals found that they had little choice other than to set themselves beyond and against the law. This inflexibility had disastrous consequences as it became increasingly clear that the Roman state was incapable of responding adequately to the challenges it faced. Political debate became polarized into bitter conflicts, with radical outsiders trying to press change on conservative insiders who, in the teeth of all the evidence, believed that all was for the best under the best of all possible constitutions.

Towards the end of the second century BC, disputes led to bloodshed, and, unprecedentedly, leading personalities found themselves at personal risk. The long crisis that destabilized and eventually destroyed the Republic opened in the 130s, about two decades before Cicero's birth. A repetitive pattern emerged of civilian reformers (mostly dissident members of the ruling class), who argued for reform and were usually assassinated for their pains, and successful generals, who imposed it.

The problem was twofold: an agricultural crisis and the changing role of the army. In Rome's early days the army was a militia composed of citizen-farmers who went back to their fields as soon as a campaign was over. However, the responsibilities of empire meant that soldiers could no longer be demobilized at the end of each fighting season. Standing forces were required, with soldiers on long-term contracts. In Cicero's childhood the great general Caius Marius supplemented and largely replaced the old conscript army with a professional body of long-service volunteers. When their contracts expired, they wanted to be granted farms where they could settle and make livings for themselves and their families. Their loyalty was to their commanders, whom they expected to make the necessary arrangements, and not to the Republic.

Unfortunately, land was in short supply. As the second century BC proceeded, a rural economy of arable smallholdings gave way to large sheep and cattle ranches, owned by the rich and serviced largely by slave labor. Many peasants were forced off the countryside and swelled Rome's population; jobs were scarce and they soon became dependent on supplies of subsidized, cut-price grain. The state owned a good deal of public land (*ager publicus*) throughout Italy and in theory this could be distributed to returning soldiers or the urban unemployed, but much of it had been quietly appropriated by wealthy landowners. These eminent squatters were extremely difficult to dislodge. Many of them were Senators and they fiercely resisted any proposals for land reform.

Wiser heads in the Senate realized that this was a shortsighted attitude and backed a leading aristocrat, Tiberius Sempronius Gracchus, who was elected Tribune in 133 BC, to introduce a land-redistribution scheme. During riots in and around the Forum, a group of Senators lynched him. A Roman historian wrote in the following century: "This was the first time in Rome's history that citizens were killed and recourse had to brute force—in both cases without fear of punishment. . . . From now onwards, political disagreements which had previously been resolved by agreement were settled by the sword."

Ten years later Tiberius's brother, Caius, returned to the fray. In addition to land reform, he tried to address another challenge facing the Republic, to which diehards in the Senate were turning blind eyes. The conquered and partly assimilated communities in Italy were becoming more and more envious of the rising tide of wealth flowing exclusively into Rome from its imperial possessions.

Italy was a patchwork quilt of communities and ethnic groups. Many of them had their own non-Latin languages—among them the civilized Etruscans, who had once dominated Rome when it was little more than a village, the fiercely independent Samnites in the impregnable Apennines, and the Volscians to the south of Rome. In the heel of Italy there were a number of well-established city-states founded by Greeks in the preceding four centuries. Some communities were granted Roman citizenship, but this was a comparatively rare privilege; others were given only what were called Latin Rights, a package of legal entitlements and duties which allowed a limited degree of involvement in the political process. Certain city-states or tribes kept a theoretical independence and were honored as Allies but exercised only a local autonomy. As a security measure, a network of citizen settlements, *coloniae,* peopled by army veterans, was established across the peninsula.

The Italian communities were obliged to supply soldiers to fight the Republic's wars, but they received nothing in return. The peninsula was becoming increasingly Romanized, but most of its inhabitants were not allowed to be Roman. Unless they were soon granted full rights of citizenship, an armed showdown was going to be unavoidable. Caius Gracchus's attempt to give them what they wanted was a sensible move but deeply unpopular with public opinion in Rome. Suspecting that his brother's fate awaited him, he armed a bodyguard and turned to violence. The Senate declared a state of emergency and he and some of his followers were summarily killed in a skirmish.

Now an external threat intervened. From 113 BC word filtered south that two huge Germanic tribes, the Cimbri and the Teutones, were on the move, traveling slowly from their homes in the Jutland area with their wives and children and without any ascertainable destination. It was feared that they intended to invade Italy.

A hero came forward to meet the hour: Caius Marius, who not only professionalized the army but also transformed its tactics. The basic unit was the legion, a body of between 4,000 and 5,000 men. It had traditionally fought in a formation of three lines; Marius changed that, dividing the legion into ten subgroups or cohorts. These were more mobile than the lines and could be deployed flexibly to meet threats on the battlefield as they arose. In 102 BC, when Cicero was still only a four-year-old child, Marius broke the Germanic threat in two colossal battles at Aquae Sextiae in southern France and Vercellae in northern Italy so completely that it was centuries before migrating tribes again dared to threaten Rome.

The savior of the day won the Consulship a record seven times, but, for all that, he was a clumsy politician. He made sure that his demobilizing veterans were given allotments of land by founding colonies in various parts of the Mediterranean. He was helped by an unscrupulous and radical Tribune, Lucius Appuleius Saturninus. Marius's popularity with the chauvinistic Roman mob fell sharply when it emerged that some of the colonies were to be for people from the Allied communities as well as for Roman citizens. In an illegal action that had bleak implications for the future, Marius brought soldiers into the Forum to put down a disturbance against the reforms.

In 99 BC Saturninus, bidding for a third year as Tribune, overreached himself and his chief rival in the election campaign was killed in a riot. Marius, who was in the last resort a constitutionalist, abandoned his ally. The Senate declared a state of emergency and Saturninus holed himself up on the Capitol Hill overlooking the Forum. Marius cut off the rebels' water supply and forced their surrender. To protect them from being lynched, he locked them inside the Senate House. Probably without his sanction, some youths climbed up onto the roof and killed the prisoners by hurling roof tiles down on them.

Although he had not been directly involved in the killings, a young man called Caius Rabirius was reported to have gotten hold of Saturninus's head and carried it around the table at a dinner party as a joke. It was an incident he would come to regret bitterly more than thirty-five years later when a new generation of radical politicians sought belated revenge. It would also cast a shadow across Cicero's path.

The Senate, back in control, repealed Saturninus's reforming legislation and a discredited Marius, out of favor both with the People and the ruling elite, withdrew into private life. The Republic subsided into an uneasy calm, which lasted from 99 to 91. The great political and constitutional issues of the time remained unsolved. The agricultural question had not been permanently answered: where would the land be found for the superannuated soldiers of Rome's next war? The disgruntled Allied communities in Italy continued to agitate for their rights. Rome's swollen population of unemployed immigrants from the countryside was a bonfire waiting to be lit. The ruling class resisted giving its most talented members long-term commands or postings for fear of creating overmighty citizens; as a result, deep-seated problems at home and abroad were left untended.

To the uninstructed eye, Rome was at the height of its power and wealth. It controlled a vast empire that stretched from Spain to Asia Minor. No external threat was in sight or could be imagined. However, behind the facade of this magnificent edifice the internal structure was unsound. The walls could not bear the weight they were carrying. Collapse was imminent.

This was the self-defeating political system that Cicero and his contemporaries inherited. As boys and young men they witnessed the demolition gangs move in.

2

"ALWAYS BE THE BEST, MY BOY, THE BRAVEST"

From Arpinum to Rome: 106–82 BC

Looking back towards the end of his life, Marcus Tullius Cicero recalled the scenes of his childhood in the countryside near the town of Arpinum with much affection. "Whenever I can get out of Rome for a few days, especially during the summer, I come to this lovely and healthful spot, although I can't often manage it," he tells a friend in one of the fictional dialogues he wrote on philosophical themes. "This is really *my* country, and my brother's, for we come from a very old local family. It is here we have our sacred rituals, it is here our people came from, it is here you can detect our ancestors' footprints."

Cicero could not claim to be a native Roman. In fact, he did not want to. He held Roman citizenship and owed Rome his primary loyalty, but his origins lay in a Volscian tribe that had fought for many wars with the fledgling city-state on the Tiber before accepting defeat, assimilation and ultimately full civic rights: "We consider both the place where we were born and the city that has adopted us as our fatherland." His dual nationality is central to an understanding of Cicero's personality. He had that passionate affection for Rome and its traditions which many newcomers feel when they join an exclusive club and was deeply hurt when the feeling was not invariably reciprocated. But he could always recharge his self-confidence with a trip to the place of his birth.

Arpinum was (and, now called Arpino, still is) a picturesque hill town some seventy miles or so south of Rome. It was an out-of-the-way spot, and it took up to three days to journey to the capital in comfort. Cicero's family was part of the local aristocracy; they were landowners and farmers and may also have run a fulling business. Fullers were the Roman equivalents of laundry and dry-cleaning firms: soap had not been invented and clothes were bleached with human and animal urine and various easily found chemicals, such as potash and carbonate of soda, before being washed thoroughly in water and dried. It was an unpleasant job and not one to boast about—just the kind of detail in his past that anyone who was upwardly mobile would wish to forget and an unfriendly critic to expose.

Cicero's paternal grandfather was a civic worthy and played a leading part in local politics. He was obviously not much of a democrat, for he opposed a motion to adopt secret ballots on the town council. But he had a gift for public administration which a leading Roman statesman of the day recognized: "With your courage and ability, Marcus Cicero, I wish that you had preferred to be active at the political center rather than at the municipal level." However, like his ancestors, he had no ambitions for a national career and kept his distance from the busy, competitive hub of the Republic's political life. There was no pressing need to do otherwise, for the central authorities interfered as little as possible in provincial life. Arpinum carried on more or less as it had always done with little fear of external busybodies.

Marcus Cicero had two sons. They both seem to have reacted against his stuffy provincialism and political conservatism. The younger, Lucius, had progressive ideas and was, his nephew said, a *humanissimus homo*—a most cultivated man. Apparently he aimed to make a mark on the national stage and accompanied the distinguished Roman orator and politician Marcus Antonius (grandfather of the man we know as Mark Antony) on a campaign against pirates in the eastern Mediterranean. His ambitions came to nothing, for he probably died soon after his return.

Lucius's brief career is an illustration of the importance of connections for anyone wanting to rise up the political ladder. A glance at the Cicero family tree shows how even a relatively undistinguished provincial family far from the center of events was linked by marriage to leading aristocratic clans and ultimately to senior personalities in Rome. Lucius probably got his posting through the good offices of his maternal uncle, Marcus Gratidius, who was a senior officer on Antonius's staff. Gratidius was a member of another leading local family, but its political leanings (unlike those of the Ciceros) were left-wing and *popularis.* He married a sister of Arpinum's most celebrated son, Caius Marius, hammer of the German tribes and a gate-crasher into Roman politics without a drop of noble blood in his veins. Marius himself married a certain Julia, a noblewoman whose later claim to fame was that she was Julius Caesar's aunt.

Lucius's elder brother Marcus, our Cicero's father, was held back from greater things by poor health and was something of a scholar. He lived on the family estate near Arpinum on the River Liris, where he spent much of his time in retirement and enlarged the rather poky house into a grand villa. It was a beautiful spot with poplars and alders lining the river and plenty of opportunity for pleasant walks. Promenades were laid out with seats where, "strolling or taking our ease among these stately poplars on the green and shady riverbank," family and friends could exchange political gossip or engage in philosophical debates. The Liris had a tributary, the Fibrenus, with an island in the middle which was a quiet retreat for thinking, writing and reading.

We do not know what crops were grown on the estate, but for wealthier landowners olives and grapevines were popular. Grain would have been sown on the plain below Arpinum, and grass fields would have supported sheep, goats and oxen. Timber was a valuable commodity and it is likely that willows were cultivated by the river to provide baskets and panniers for transporting agricultural products. Oak was a useful source of acorns for pigs. Doubtless, there would have been an orchard and a vegetable garden near the house.

The Ciceros lived out a grand version of the Roman ideal of the good life, although, with the arrival of empire, untold wealth and urbanization, it was more honored in the breach than the observance. This ideal consisted of a small farm which a man could manage himself or with the help of a steward and which would provide most of his family's food. For the well-to-do, of course, the hard work of tilling the land and bringing in the harvest was done by slaves and local farm laborers. But the myth was a tenacious plant and, half a century after Cicero's death, the poet Horace showed that it still exerted a persuasive force. "This is what I prayed for!" he wrote. "A piece of land not so very large, with a garden, and near the house a spring of ever-flowing water, and up above these a bit of woodland."

It was in such easy, calm surroundings that Marcus Tullius Cicero was born on January 3, 106 BC. His arrival was easy and quick and apparently his mother, Helvia, suffered few labor pains. About two years later he was joined by a younger brother, called Quintus.

Roman names conveyed in quite a complicated way a good deal of information about their bearers. First came the *praenomen,* or personal name. There were only a few in general currency: Marcus was one of the most popular, but so were Caius or Gaius, Lucius, Quintus, Sextus and Publius. Annoyingly for historians, eldest sons usually bore the same first names as their fathers. Next came the *nomen* or family name: Tullius was an ancient name borne by Rome's sixth king; a legendary leader of the Volscians, familiar from the story of Coriolanus, was called Attius Tullus.

Finally, the *cognomen,* a personal surname, was particular to its holder or his branch of the family. It often had a jokey or down-to-earth ring: so, for example, "Cicero" is Latin for "chickpea" and it was supposed that some ancestor had had a wart of that shape on the end of his nose. When Marcus was about to launch his career as an advocate and politician, friends advised him to change his name to something less ridiculous. "No," he replied firmly, "I am going to make my *cognomen* more famous than those of men like Scaurus and Catulus." These were two leading Romans of the day, and the point of the remark was that "Catulus" was the Latin for "whelp" or "puppy," and "Scaurus" meant "with large or projecting ankles."

Sometimes individuals were granted additional *cognomina* to mark a military success. So the famous Publius Cornelius Scipio was given the additional appellation of "Africanus" after he defeated Hannibal at the battle of Zama in Africa.

As the young Cicero grew up he gradually learned the realities of the Roman world. In the first place, he was fairly lucky to survive; as many as one in five children died in their infancy and only about two thirds of those born reached maturity. By another stroke of good fortune, he was one of about 400,000 Roman citizens. He found himself near the top of the socioeconomic pyramid. Aristocrats stood at the apex. Rural gentry (like the Ciceros), businessmen and merchants, made up the second tier in

Roman society; they tended to avoid entering national politics, for members of the Senate were not allowed to accept public contracts or to engage in overseas trade. Originally a military class, they were called *equites* or knights—that is, men who were rich enough to buy a horse for a military campaign.

Beneath them were the mass of the people: shopkeepers, artisans, smallholders and, at the bottom of the pile, landless farmworkers. Living standards could be low and uncertain and the struggle against poverty was unremitting. Competition for jobs was fierce.

However, there was one group even less fortunate than the *plebs:* the slaves. Slavery was endemic in the classical world and huge numbers of men, women and children, the captives of Rome's ceaseless wars, flooded into Italy. Slaves provided a cheap workforce, contributing significantly to unemployment among free-born citizens. In the city of Rome it is estimated that slaves amounted to about a quarter of the population in Cicero's day. Many household servants were slaves. In the case of the Cicero family, the surviving evidence suggests that they were treated kindly.

Both Cicero and his brother followed the common practice of freeing domestic slaves as a reward for good service or allowing them to buy their freedom. This automatically gave them Roman citizenship and the sons of freedmen were eligible for public office. Most ex-slaves continued to work for their former owners, for whom emancipation had a number of advantages. The hope of eventual freedom helped to discourage slave revolts; and allowing a slave to purchase his liberty either from his savings or by mortgaging his future labor ensured a return on the owner's investment, which would not be forthcoming in the event of the slave's (perhaps costly) illness and death.

The dominant figure in the lives of Marcus and Quintus was their father. By tradition the *paterfamilias* was the absolute master of his family. On his own property he could act as he pleased. He was entitled to torture or kill his slaves and to put his wife or children to death. His word went and there was no right of appeal.

By contrast, women were cast as demure, silent and usually unseen helpmeets. They managed the household and devoted much time to spinning or weaving (the classical equivalent of knitting). They were not given personal names and even sisters were known simply by their *nomen*—not only demeaning but extremely confusing. Their essential function was to find a husband and they could be married off as young as twelve years of age (although consummation was usually delayed for a couple of years or so). Most marriages were arranged and in the upper classes were a means of forging political and economic alliances.

Romantic attachment was felt to be beside the point. If a wife was seen in public with her husband, any display of affection was universally felt to be indecent. Less than a century before Cicero's birth, Cato the Censor, self-appointed guardian of traditional Roman values, expelled a candidate for the Consulship from the Senate on the grounds that he had kissed his wife in broad daylight and in front of their daughter.

Unsurprisingly, Helvia is a shadowy figure, although she seems to have been a sharp-eyed housewife. Quintus recalled "how our mother in the old days used to seal up the empty bottles, so that bottles drained on the sly could not be included in the empties." It is curious that throughout his copious writings Cicero himself never once mentions her: this may simply be a consequence of the low status of women, but perhaps his silence reflects some unhappiness in his childhood, which may in turn have helped to create the adult man with all his multiple insecurities.

In practice, Roman society was not exactly as it seemed on the surface. In the final years of the Roman Republic old conventions were decaying and bonds were loosening. Young men were more rebellious than their fathers had been; those who lived in Rome increasingly left home before marriage and set up house in small apartments in the city center, where they learned how to have a good time on little money.

Women were much more influential than their formal position would suggest. In the upper classes they were expected to be cultivated and could study with tutors at home; and it was possible for girls to attend primary school. They did not invariably assume their husbands' names. Crucially, they were able to retain their own property on marriage and so did not fall completely under their husbands' sway. In fact, men were often absent on public duties in the army or in the provinces, and wives were expected to take on the management of the family estate and financial affairs. Some of them acted as political brokers behind the scenes. Cato, who was as blunt as he was censorious, reportedly remarked, "We rule the world and our wives rule us."

We do not know exactly where the Cicero boys spent their preschool years; presumably for most of the time they stayed in the villa outside Arpinum. But the family had a house in Rome in the respectable but not very fashionable quarter of Carinae on the Esquiline Hill, not far from the center. Marcus and Quintus may well have been taken on visits to the big city, perhaps for extended stays.

The better type of Roman house, such as the Ciceros', had a small courtyard at the back. It was usually a garden with a colonnade running around it. This part of the building was reserved for the family and contained bedrooms, a kitchen (usually tiny), a larder and a bathhouse with a steam room. There were no nurseries or special spaces for children and, when they were not out playing in the fields of Arpinum or being shown the sights of Rome, little Marcus and Quintus must have spent a good deal of their time in the garden under the watchful eyes of slaves.

Cicero's father had high ambitions for his two sons and made sure they were given a good schooling. Like other upper-class children, they may have been taught by a tutor at home, but what evidence we have suggests that they were sent to school. Roman education in the late Republic typically fell into three distinct phases. From seven to twelve years boys and girls could attend a *ludus litterarius,* where they learned reading, writing and elementary arithmetic.

Cicero's schoolmates seem to have admired him for his academic ability. He was always in the middle of the group when out walking and was the focus of attention. Some fathers visited the school to witness the infant prodigy at work, although others were irritated by his dominance over their children. Brains are seldom liked and this popularity may have been the product of hindsight. However, it is possible that Cicero had already developed the strong sense of humor he showed as an adult. He could well have won friends through laughter rather than cleverness.

A household slave, the *paedagogus,* would accompany his young master (or mistress) to school and carry his satchel. Classes were often held on an open porch or shop, which was protected from the noise of traffic and the inquisitive stares of passersby by only a sheet of tent cloth stretched between pillars at the front. The pupils sat on benches and wrote on wax tablets placed on their knees, with the teacher presiding on a dais. They learned the names of letters before their shapes, singing them in order backwards and forwards; they then graduated to combinations of two or three letters and finally to syllables and words. Knowledge was acquired through imitation and repetition, as when learning fencing or some other sport. Hence the Latin word for school, *ludus,* also means "game."

Classes began at dawn, without breakfast, and went on into the afternoon. There were no physical sports, although the day ended with a steam bath. Summer holidays lasted from the end of July to the middle of October, but otherwise the school year was interrupted only by public holidays.

At twelve, a boy graduated to a secondary school. The curriculum was narrowly confined to the study of grammar and literature. Both Latin and Greek were taught. In Latin the archaic epic and dramatic poets (now lost to us except for fragments) were on the curriculum and in Greek the emphasis was mainly on Homer and the Athenian tragedians, especially Euripides. Another key document for study was the Twelve Tables, Rome's primary code of laws established in about 450 BC. This "germ of jurisprudence" has not survived, but was the basis of civil law: one of its provisions suggests its down-to-earth, practical flavor. This was that each piece of land should include an untilled five-foot strip for the turning of the plow, but that no squatter could settle on it on the grounds that it was uncultivated.

At the best schools lessons were given in rhetoric, or the art of public speaking. The Romans and the Greeks before them believed that it was possible to establish a system of oratory that could be taught. They spoke of training public speakers under five traditional headings: *inventio,* seeking out ideas or lines of argument; *collocatio,* structure and organization; *elocutio,* diction and style; *actio,* physical delivery; and *memoria,* memory (speeches could last for hours and as they were spoken not read they had to be learned by heart). There were different opinions as to the best form of *elocutio.* Some advocated an elaborate, ornate style and others plainness and simplicity. There was a middle way, grand but not exaggerated, which the adult Cicero came to favor.

The good public speaker recognized that he had to be a performer, like an actor. Later in his life Cicero wrote books on oratory and in them he underscored the point:

> A leading speaker will vary and modulate his voice, raising and lowering it and deploying the full scale of tones. He will avoid extravagant gestures and stand impressively erect. He will not pace about and when he does so not for any distance. He should not dart forward except in moderation with strict control. There should be no effeminate bending of the neck or twiddling of his fingers or beating out the rhythm of his cadences on his knuckles. He should control himself by the way he holds and moves his entire body. He should extend his arm at moments of high dispute and lower it during calmer passages. . . . Once he has made sure he does not have a stupid expression on his face and or a grimace, he should control his eyes with great care, for as the face is the image of the soul the eyes are its translators. Depending on the subject at hand they can express grief or hilarity.

Students were taught how to turn fables and other kinds of stories into simple narrative; to develop arguments from quotations from famous poets; and to compose speeches inspired by actual or fictional situations and events. They would declaim them to the class. Although by Cicero's day the teaching of rhetoric had been reduced to a complicated and arid system of rules, it lay at the heart of the curriculum. At one level rhetoric was a vocational subject, for it was the key to a political career, to which all men of good birth should aspire. They would be able to do so only if they acquired the necessary skills to persuade people of the rightness of their point of view. In Rome reputations were made not only at public meetings and in the Senate but also in the law courts. Ambitious young men in their early twenties often appeared as prosecutors in criminal trials in order to make a name for themselves, not just as lawyers but as potential future politicians.

Both rhetoric and the study of literature were also intended to give students an ethical grounding, a moral education which inculcated the virtues of fortitude, justice and prudence.

Public speaking in this complex sense is extinct and it is difficult now to conceive of its power, immediacy and charm. Just as Samuel Pepys in seventeenth-century England would spend a Sunday going from sermon to sermon for the sheer pleasure of it, so crowds of Romans would pack the Forum, where trials were held in the open air, to listen to and applaud the great advocates of the day as they presented their cases. The "Friends, Romans, countrymen" speech in Shakespeare's *Julius Caesar* gives a hint of how the real thing must have been.

In 90 Cicero reached the age of sixteen, the Roman age of majority, by which time his secondary schooling ended. A special rite of passage marked the moment when a boy became a man, not on his birthday but on or around March 17, the feast day of Liber, the god of growth and vegetation. We do not know where the ceremony took place in Cicero's case, but bearing in mind his family's ambitions for him, it would most likely have been in Rome.

About the time Marcus came of age, his father decided that his sons should complete their training in public speaking and study law in the capital. Higher education was exclusively devoted to debate and declamation and was in the hands of a *rhetor,* a specialist teacher of public speaking. He and other learned men, philosophers or scholars, had much the same status as university professors. However, as academic institutions such as universities did not exist, such men were freelance and often lived in the household of a leading political figure, where they acted as advisers and added to their employers' prestige. Elder statesmen were also willing to impart their experience and legal and constitutional knowledge to the younger generation.

Access for a couple of provincial teenagers to these informal and exclusive finishing schools was difficult. It could be achieved only through the web of personal connections called clientship (*clientela*). Society was a pyramid of matching rights and obligations; the basic principle was summed up in the phrase "*do ut des*"—"I give so that you give." A wealthy and powerful man acted as a "patron" for many hundreds or even thousands of "clients." He guaranteed to look after their interests. He welcomed them to his home and occasionally gave them meals and provided very needy followers with food handouts. He was a source of advice and of business and political contacts. If a client got into trouble with the law his patron would offer his support. In return, a client (if he lived in Rome) would regularly pay a morning call and accompany his patron as he went about his business in the town. He could be recruited as a bodyguard or even a soldier in his army. Neither party could go to law or vote in elections against the other. These networks of mutual aid cut across the social classes and linked the local elites in the various Italian communities, not to mention those in the Empire as a whole, to the center. Clientship was a binding contract and, for lack of other administrative instruments, it was an essential means of holding the Empire together. A family's client list survived from one generation to the next. Durable bonds could, of course, also be established between equals. *Amicitia* or "friendly alliance" meant more than personal affection and referred to formal networks between superiors and inferiors.

To get on in society, indeed to survive in it at all, a Roman had to be an effective member not only of his family but also of his town and village, his guild (if he was an artisan or tradesman) or his district. Each of these institutions had a patron, through whom a man was locked into the highest reaches of authority and power. In an age without a welfare state, a banking system and most public services, he had no alternative but to assure his future in these ways. This was why politics was largely conducted on a personal basis and was seen in moral rather than collective terms. The client-list system was not compatible with alliances based on political programs or manifestos of common action.

Like all provincial clients of good social status, the Ciceros had patrons in Rome and they made use of them when finding good teachers for Marcus and Quintus. They were connected in particular to the Leader of the Senate, Marcus Aemilius Scaurus; Marcus Antonius, a distinguished lawyer and politician (who had taken Cicero's uncle Lucius with him on the expedition against the pirates); and an even more celebrated orator and statesman, Lucius Licinius Crassus, a conservative who understood the need for reform.

Strings were successfully pulled. One of Marcus and Quintus's maternal uncles, Caius Visellius Aculeo, a legal expert, knew Crassus well and arranged a placement for them. The boys spent a good deal of time at the great orator's house, an elegant building at an excellent address on the Palatine Hill, where there were columns of Hymettan marble and shade-giving trees—rare features in this city of tufa and brick. They often listened to him discussing contemporary politics and studied with his scholars-in-residence. Marcus was also much impressed by the pure, traditional Latin spoken by Crassus's wife. In return, the brothers would doubtless have been expected to join the daily crowd of *clientes* who accompanied leading men when they appeared in public. The larger the following, the greater the prestige.

Cicero also became a pupil of Crassus's father-in-law, Quintus Mucius Scaevola, then in his eighties and one of the earliest and greatest of Roman jurists. On Scaevola's death Cicero transferred to a younger cousin of the same name, who was Chief Pontiff, the leading official of the state religion, and had shared the Consulship with Crassus in 95.

His father entrusted him to the care of an older fellow student, Marcus Pupius Piso, who acted as a kind of mentor and kept an eye on him. Later the historian Sallust, a near contemporary, presented this arrangement as a homosexual affair in a lampoon against Cicero: "Didn't you learn your unbridled loquacity from Marcus Piso at the cost of your virginity?" But this was the kind of insult that Roman public figures routinely exchanged with one another and while something of the sort may have briefly occurred, it is just as likely that it did not.

It was during these years that Cicero's ambition to become a famous advocate crystallized. He found he had a gift for writing and public speaking. He was swept along by the almost unbearable excitement of the trials in the Forum and the glamour of the lawyer's job, very much like that of a leading actor.

There were a number of jury courts, specializing in different kinds of crime—treason, murder, extortion and so on. Temporary stands and seating were set up to accommodate those taking part in the proceedings. A Praetor usually presided and between thirty and sixty jurors were appointed by lot for each case, who voted in secret. They were originally Senators, but one of Caius Gracchus's reforms transferred the right of jury service to *equites.* This was a highly disputatious issue, especially in cases where Senatorial or commercial interests were in any way at stake. Jurors voted by rubbing off either an A (for *absolvo*) or a C (for *condemno*) on either side of voting tablets. Verdicts were often biased and bribery of jurors was common.

Court procedures in ancient Rome are known only in broad outline. Prosecutors opened with a long speech, which the defense sought to rebut, at equal length. Addresses by supporting counsel followed. A water clock ensured that everyone kept to time. Witnesses for either side were then cross-examined. At some stage, the opposing advocates entered into a debate between themselves (*altercatio*). The case was then adjourned, probably resuming after a day's interval. There were further speeches by either side and the calling of additional evidence was allowed. The verdict then followed.

Civil cases were heard in two parts; the first before a Praetor who defined the issues in question, and the second, for decision, before a judge or a jury to whom the Praetor had passed his opinion.

Cicero was amazed by the sensational impact a leading advocate could have on his hearers and looked upon his skills as being akin to those of an actor. Despite the fact that the theater was not regarded as a respectable profession, Cicero was fascinated by it and later became a close friend of the best-known actor of his day, Quintus Roscius Gallus. Although he always insisted that oratory and drama were different arts, he modeled his style on Roscius's performances and those of another actor he knew, Clodius Aesopus (who once became so involved in the part he was playing—that of King Agamemnon, overlord of the Greeks—that he ran through and killed a stagehand who happened to cross the stage).

The attitudes Cicero acquired as a serious-minded, bookish boy lasted him all his life. He always loathed and feared physical aggression. He recalled, a little priggishly: "The time which others spend in advancing their own personal affairs, taking holidays and attending games, indulging in pleasures of various kinds or even enjoying mental relaxation and bodily recreation, the time they spend on protracted parties and gambling and playing ball, proves in my case to have been taken up with returning over and over again to . . . literary pursuits."

Cicero wrote poetry in his adolescence and as early as the age of fourteen completed a work in Latin tetrameters called *Pontius Glaucus*. Although it has not survived, we know that it told the story of a Boeotian fisherman who eats a magic herb and is turned into a fabulous sea divinity with a gift of prophecy. It was an apt subject for someone who had dreams of making his way in the world by means of his chief talent, a strikingly persuasive way with words.

As a young man Cicero was as well known for his verse as for his oratory. His style was fluent and technically accomplished. He wrote quickly and easily, as many as 500 lines a night, and could turn his hand to unpromising subjects such as a translation of a Greek work on astronomy by Aratus. However, he did not really have a poetic imagination and readers found that verbal virtuosity was not enough. His reputation as a poet declined sharply and permanently with the arrival a generation later of a new, more personal and lyrical style of verse writing, pioneered by Catullus and his circle. Tacitus, the imperial historian of the following century, noted: "Caesar and Brutus also wrote poetry—no better than Cicero, but with better luck, for fewer people know that they did."

As his education proceeded, Cicero met the full force of an inherent schizophrenia in Roman culture. There was a widespread belief that traditional values were being undermined by foreign immigrants. The decadence that was perceived to permeate the Republic was attributed largely to slippery and corrupt Greeks and Asiatics who had come to Rome from the hellenized Orient. Cicero's paternal grandfather, for one, would have nothing to do with them and deplored falling standards of Roman morality. "Our people are like Syrian slaves: the better they speak Greek, the more shiftless they are." When speaking in public, senior Philhellenes such as Crassus and Antonius sometimes felt obliged to conceal their true beliefs.

But the fact is that while the ferocious city-state on the Tiber was able to defeat them in war, it had nothing to rival the Greeks culturally. Greek literature, philosophy and science were a revelation to people who had little more than ballads and primitive annals as their literary heritage. They immediately started borrowing what they found and the history of Roman literature in the third and second centuries BC is essentially one of plagiarism. Even in Cicero's day there was a good deal of catching up to be done.

Cicero's father seems to have reacted against his own father's anti-Greek views. Like many other *bien-pensants* of the time, he believed that the future for his sons lay in a grounding of Greek literature, philosophy and rhetoric. So it is no wonder that the young Cicero was given access to a well-known Greek poet of the day, Archias, from whom he gained much of his knowledge of the theory and practice of rhetoric. Archias was a fashionable figure in leading circles and mixed with many of the best families in Rome. Cicero recognized the debt: "For as far as I can cast my mind back into times gone by, as far as I can recollect the earliest years of my boyhood, the picture of the past that takes shape reveals that it was [Archias] who first inspired my determination to embark on these studies, and who started me on their methodical pursuit."

Cicero became so addicted to all things Greek that he was nicknamed "the little Greek boy." However, he also made sure that he learned about Rome and its history. To this end he cultivated the acquaintance of Lucius Aelius Stilo. Rome's first native-born grammarian and antiquarian, Aelius was a fund of knowledge about the history of the Republic, which he made available to his friends for use in their political speeches. His patriotism rubbed off on the precocious adolescent from Arpinum, who developed a lifelong fascination with the details of Rome's inadequately recorded past.

It was while studying with Scaevola at the house of Crassus that Cicero met other contemporaries in the little world of upper-class Roman society. Two boys in particular stood out from the crowd. Caius Julius Caesar was six years younger than Cicero, but both he and Quintus knew him personally. Through Marius's marriage to Caesar's aunt Julia they were, after all, distant relatives. Cicero also struck up a friendship that would last a lifetime with a boy named Titus Pomponius, who came from an old but not strictly noble family. They met at the Scaevolas' and found that they shared a passion for literature and Roman history. Cicero's friendship with Atticus, as he later called himself, was to be central to his life. Years later when he was adult, he wrote: "I love Pomponius . . . as a second brother."

The three youngsters were not allowed to pursue their education without interruption. The few years of relative calm that had followed the assassination of the radical Tribune Saturninus came to end when Cicero was fifteen. The Republic was now battered by a succession of crises that set the scene for the politics of the boys' adult lives. Cicero, Caesar and Pomponius watched events in the Forum and on the streets.

While most of the Senate was unwilling to countenance any constitutional change, a few of its more farsighted members realized that the status quo could not last and that it was wiser to anticipate events than react to them. It fell to yet another aristocrat to pick up the battered baton of reform. Marcus Livius Drusus was a wealthy and ambitious nobleman who became Tribune in 91. He was a friend of Cicero's mentors, Scaurus and Crassus, and we can presume that the young student witnessed some of the events that followed at firsthand. Drusus's main project was a renewal of the plan to extend Roman citizenship to the Italians, but the Senate, with typical shortsightedness, threw out his legislation. They were profoundly suspicious of him from the most self-interested of motives: if the Italians were enfranchised, they would join Drusus's *clientela* in huge numbers and that would make him far too powerful.

The outcome was predictable. The Allied communities lost all hope that the Republic would ever share the profits of empire with them. The mood in the countryside became tense and feverish. Drusus was known to have entertained one of the Allied leaders at his house in Rome and public opinion suspected him of disloyalty. There were reports that the Italians had vowed allegiance to Drusus.

It was about this time that Crassus made his last contribution to a Senatorial debate. Cicero left a detailed account of what took place. Furious with one of the Consuls, Lucius Marcius Philippus, for criticizing the Senate, Crassus launched a tirade against him. The Consul lost his temper and threatened to fine him. The old man refused to back down: "Do you imagine that I can be deterred by the forfeit of any of my property?" The Senate unanimously passed a motion in his support. Crassus had made a fine speech, but the effort had weakened his strength and he was taken ill while delivering it; he contracted pneumonia and died a few days later. Cicero and the other boys were probably at Crassus's house when the great orator was brought home. They were deeply upset, and Cicero describes them as going later to the Senate House to look at the spot where that last "swan song" (a phrase of his coining) had been heard.

The incident illustrates an attractive aspect of Cicero's personality: his predisposition to admire. He was not a cynic and, although he was much concerned with his own glory and had a fair share of hatreds and dislikes, he was appreciative of the achievements of others and liked to praise them if he could.

It was another death soon after that caused the conflagration that set Italy alight. Drusus knew that he was at personal risk and seldom went out of doors, conducting business from a poorly lit portico at his house on the Palatine Hill. One evening as he was dismissing the gathering he suddenly screamed that he had been stabbed and fell with the words on his lips. A leather worker's knife was found driven into his hip, but the assassin was never caught.

Drusus's murder was the final blow to Italian aspirations. Communities across the peninsula rose in revolt. The struggle, called the War of the Allies, was bloody and bitter. Young, well-connected and ambitious Romans were expected to serve on military campaigns; although Cicero seldom showed any interest in soldiering, the war was too close to home for him to ignore. He temporarily abandoned his studies to serve in the army of Cnaeus Pompeius Strabo as a member of his general staff. He met the commander's son for the first time, young Cnaeus Pompeius (whom we know as Pompey). Exact contemporaries, they were about sixteen or seventeen years old—and of course without an inkling of how closely their destinies were to be interlinked in future years.

Rome sustained some serious defeats and there was a distinct risk that the rebellion, which was centered on the Adriatic side of Italy, might spread. The neighboring Etruscans and the Umbrians seemed on the point of secession. So in 90 the Senate, facing disaster, gave way. They awarded Roman citizenship to all those Allies who stayed loyal and, it seems, also to those who surrendered. This was decisive, and, although fighting continued for some time at a terrible cost in human lives and suffering, Rome emerged the military victor—and the political loser.

Italy was now united and very gradually the old cultural divisions and languages of the peninsula gave way to an overall Latinity. In the short run, the shock to the Republic's stability and to the self-confidence of its ruling class was great. And there was worse to come. The War of the Allies signaled a new bloodier spiral into social and political chaos. Soldiers in the Forum, elder statesmen massacred, half the Empire in revolt—nothing like it had been seen in the history of the Republic. It was nearly ten years before something approaching normality returned, in 82; during this period, according to a modern estimate, 200,000 lost their lives from a free population in Rome and Italy of about 4,500,000.

With typical, tricky mean-mindedness, the Senate corralled the new Italian citizens into a small number of the *tribes,* or voting groups, into which the General Assembly was divided, thus reducing their electoral impact. A radical Tribune, Publius Sulpicius Rufus, now intervened; he had been a friend of the dead Drusus and promoted a policy of fair play for the newly enfranchised Italians. In 88, he brought forward a proposal to distribute the new citizens across the complete range of the *tribes.* Uproar ensued among the *optimates* and Sulpicius, the latest in the line of civilian reformers, recruited 600 young *equites* as bodyguards; they were nicknamed the "anti-Senators."

One of the Consuls in 87 was Lucius Cornelius Sulla Felix, a descendant of an old but impoverished family who had arrived comparatively late on the political scene. Sulla had misspent his youth among a demimonde of actors and hustlers and first made a name for himself on the battlefield when he was thirty-one. His appearance was remarkable, for his face was disfigured by a birthmark which people said looked like a mulberry with oatmeal sprinkled on it. A conservative, he aimed to restore the Senate's traditional authority. His Consulship was a reward for signal achievements in the War of the Allies. He was given a military command once his Consular year was over to deal with a serious crisis that had overtaken Rome's territorial possessions in Asia Minor.

Mithridates, King of Pontus, on the southern coast of the Black Sea, had been scheming for years to free the entire region from Roman control. He was an able and ambitious man, of remarkable physical strength and mental stamina. Fearful of the plots endemic in an oriental court, he was reputed to consume small regular doses of poison to build up his resistance. The War of the Allies gave him a one-time opportunity to act while Rome's back was turned, and he seized it. His army invaded the region and his fleet sailed into the Aegean. Democrats in Athens invited him to liberate Greece.

Mithridates' advance was so swift and total that about 80,000 Roman and Italian businessmen and their families found themselves unexpectedly marooned in enemy territory. Mithridates' solution to the problem of what to do with them was final. He sent secret instructions to local authorities in every town to kill all strangers who spoke Latin. In general the order was obeyed with enthusiasm, clear evidence of the unpopularity of Roman rule. In one town, the executioners planned their work with sadistic ingenuity: children were killed in front of their parents, then wives in front of their husbands and lastly the men. All Italian property was confiscated and handed over to the king.

The massacre was a terrible blow to the Republic's authority and added greatly to its economic difficulties, because a regular flow of tax and trading revenues was abruptly cut off. Bankruptcies became common and indebtedness in every social class reached very high levels. Senators, much of whose wealth was locked up in land, found themselves with few liquid assets; the aftermath of the War of the Allies was no time to sell real estate to raise cash. Everyone agreed that it was crucial to retrieve Asia Minor. The future of the Empire was in the balance and, whatever Rome's internal problems, dealing with the threat in the east came first.

At this point, Marius, the great general who had saved Rome from the Gauls, unexpectedly reappeared. He had served in the War of the Allies but had spent a number of years out of public view. Now nearly seventy, he was old and embittered by what he saw as the Republic's ingratitude and was out for vengeance. The Tribune Sulpicius unwisely turned to him for support. In return, he arranged for Sulla's eastern command to be taken from him and given to Marius. The Consuls tried to stop Sulpicius by suspending public business and in the riots that followed Sulla was forced to take refuge in Marius's house.

This was an unbearable humiliation. Sulla decided to rejoin his army not far from the city, where it was waiting for him to lead them eastwards. But he had a score to settle and did not set off at once. Instead he turned his legions on Rome, which he captured after a few hours of street fighting. Sulpicius was hunted down and killed, but Marius, after a series of hair-raising adventures, made his escape to Africa where many of his old troops had been settled. Sulla quickly passed laws which invalidated Sulpicius's legislation and would make it difficult for reformers to have their way during his absence. He then marched off to fight the King of Pontus, who would not wait.

Sulla's entry into Rome was a watershed. He had broken one of the Republic's greatest taboos by marching soldiers inside the city limits. Worse than that, the army had shown decisively that its loyalty was to its leader, not to the state. The rule of law had been overturned, and a legally elected Tribune, whose person was meant to be sacrosanct, had been put to death. Others would lose little time in exploiting these fatal precedents.

Sulla's plans to contain the situation in Rome fell apart almost as soon as his back was turned. One of the Consuls for 87, Lucius Cornelius Cinna, a ruthless *popularis,* promptly proceeded to repeal Sulla's measures. Marius, deranged and in poor health, staged his own invasion of Rome and let his men run amok during five days of slaughter and looting. The victims included friends of the Cicero family, among them one of his mentors, the orator and elder statesman Marcus Antonius.

Marius did not survive to enjoy his triumph for long. Bad news from abroad brought on an illness, perhaps a stroke, and he died in 86 at the beginning of his seventh Consulship. Cinna was left in charge; he brought the killings to an end and retained the Consulship for two more years, until he was killed in 84 by mutinous troops.

Meanwhile, Sulla won his war with Mithridates despite also having had to cope with a Roman army sent out against him. Anxious to return to Rome, he did not have time to insist on an unconditional surrender. He met the king near the ruins of Troy and signed a peace treaty. Mithridates got off quite lightly, merely agreeing to evacuate Asia and pay a moderate indemnity. In return he was confirmed as King of Pontus and recognized as an Ally—in today's terms, he was awarded "most favored nation status."

In 83 Sulla was back at last after an absence of three years. He landed in Brundisium (modern-day Brindisi) and marched inexorably up Italy like an avenging angel. The *popularis* regime that had been governing the Republic fought back. However, having brushed aside one army in the north, Sulla resoundingly defeated another outside one of the gates of Rome and, in 82, entered the city. He regulated his position by reviving the disused post of Dictator, which gave him supreme authority in the government. He had himself appointed for an indefinite period, instead of the traditional six months, and set himself the task of reforming and restoring the institutions of the Republic.

Another massacre of the ruling class now took place. Under Marius, men of the political right had been struck down. Now it was the turn of the left. After a period of indiscriminate slaughter, a young Senator complained to Sulla, "We are not asking you to pardon those you have decided to kill; all we ask is that you free from suspense those you have decided not to kill."

The Dictator took the point and agreed to put some order into the mayhem. He posted proscription lists on white tablets in the Forum, which gave the names of those he wanted dead. Anybody was legally entitled to kill a proscribed person and on the presentation of convincing evidence (usually a head) could claim a substantial reward of 1,200 denarii. As a rule, the heads of those killed were displayed in the Forum.

A cousin of Cicero's, the Praetor Marcus Marius Gratidianus, was one of those who suffered. He was handed over to Quintus Lutatius Catulus, a leading conservative, because he had been implicated in the forced suicide of Catulus's father during Marius's reign of terror. With the help of a young aristocrat named Lucius Sergius Catilina, Catulus flogged Gratidianus through the streets to the tomb of the Catulus clan. There his arms and legs were smashed with rods, his ears cut off, his tongue wrenched from his mouth and his eyes gouged out. He was then beheaded and his corpse was offered as a sacrifice to the spirit of Catulus's dead father. In a grim postscript, an officer fainted at the horror of what he was seeing and was himself executed for disloyalty. Catilina was then said to have carried Gratidianus's severed head "still alive and breathing" (according to Cicero in one of his more fanciful flights of rhetoric) into Rome to present to Sulla.

Many of the most senior figures of the day were liquidated. Forty Senators were proscribed at the outset and 1,600 *equites,* but the final death toll was far higher. According to one estimate there were 9,000 victims in all. The sons of those killed were sent into exile, their descendants barred forever from holding public office. One consequence of these massacres was that the Senate became seriously depleted. There were fewer than 200 survivors, not enough to run an empire.

At the time of the proscriptions, Cicero was twenty-four and his friend Pomponius was three years older. Julius Caesar was only eighteen. The terrible events of the War of the Allies and the bloodlettings of Marius and Sulla had taken place during their formative years. Their reactions to what they saw hardened over the years into mature political positions which, as it happened, covered the whole spectrum of the possible. Defense of Republican traditions, withdrawal from direct political activity, and commitment to radical reform—these were the various ways in which three very different personalities came to terms with the breakdown of the constitution and the decimation of the ruling class.

Of the trio, Caesar was in the greatest personal danger during this period. His family, although highly born, was not well-off and lived in the densely populated working-class district of Subura. He was fiercely proud of his Patrician ancestry, but Romans saw public life very much in personal terms; his aunt Julia's marriage to Marius placed Caesar in the thick of revolutionary politics and made him an enemy of Sulla.

Caesar was only fourteen in 86 when, under the Consulship of Cinna, he was chosen to be a Priest of Jupiter (*flamen dialis*), a religious post reserved for Patricians; the previous incumbent had been forced to commit suicide during the troubles. It was not unusual for Priests to be appointed when they were young, fresh enough to learn all they had to about religious rules and procedures. Perhaps, too, Cinna's government found it hard to find a more prominent Patrician willing to take the job.

In any event, Caesar would not be able to assume office until he reached his majority and, perhaps thanks to the fact that in due course Sulla annulled all Cinna's acts, it seems he never had to do so. This was a stroke of luck, for, theoretically at least, the appointment would have prevented him from ever leading a political career. The Priest of Jupiter, who held office for life, was forbidden to mount a horse, set eyes on armed soldiers or spend more than two nights in succession outside Rome. But nominated as he was to the post, Caesar was now obliged to marry a Patrician; so he broke off his engagement with the daughter of a rich equestrian family and married Cinna's daughter, Cornelia.

Caesar did not take part in the civil war that broke out after Sulla's return from Asia Minor. The victorious Dictator did not harm him, insisting only on one point—that he divorce his wife, perhaps because he had someone more suitable in mind. The young man rejected out of hand this apparent sign of goodwill. Fearful of Sulla's anger, Caesar slipped out of Rome and, he hoped, out of sight, but he fell seriously ill with malaria and was picked up by a Sullan patrol. He managed to buy his way out of trouble for the sum of 3,000 sesterces and eventually well-connected relatives persuaded a reluctant Sulla to leave him alone. Relieved, Caesar set off for Asia Minor to do some soldiering.

Why was he so steadfast in his resistance? It is hard to be sure, but his actions anticipate what we know of the mature man. He would not be bullied. He was loyal even when it was inconvenient to be so. (He stayed faithful to Cornelia until her death in 69.) He was energetic and coolheaded in a crisis. Caesar's views were governed by a profound impatience with the aristocracy, not just for its selfishness but for its incompetence. He had been brought up a *popularis* and would remain one for the rest of his life. While he held his first political position ten years or so later, a Quaestorship, his aunt Julia died. The Sullan constitution was still in place and the Senate very much in charge. Nevertheless, Caesar delivered the funeral oration and, in defiance of the law and with some personal courage, brought out effigies of Julia's husband, Marius, and his son to display in the procession. No action was taken against him, but he had nailed his radical flag to the mast for all to see.

The second young man of the trio, Titus Pomponius, also had *popularis* connections, but he did not share Caesar's flamboyant temerity. In fact, he turned his back on politics, throwing in his cards before they had even been dealt. Born in Rome into a wealthy and cultivated equestrian family, he was related to Sulpicius, and when the Tribune came to grief in 88 he saw he was in serious danger. Realizing that Sulla's bloodletting was not just designed to eliminate opposition but was also a form of fund-raising, he decided to leave Italy and settled in Athens, taking good care to transfer all his assets to Greece at the same time. He may have heard the story of the rich man who, although having nothing to do with politics, read his name on the proscription lists in the Forum and remarked: "Things are bad for me: I am being hunted down by my Alban estate." Pomponius had no more intention of losing his fortune than his life.

In fact, he wanted to become richer. He had inherited about 2 million sesterces and set about making his money grow. He bought a large amount of land in Epirus at a time when Mithridates had just ravaged Greece and prices were low. Noting the popularity of gladiatorial shows, he invested in fighters whom he kept on his estate and trained in the art of dying gracefully. He lent money at interest but on the quiet, as it was not felt to be a trade fit for a gentleman. He shared his father's literary tastes and by collecting a large staff of skillful copyists in his house became, in due course, a successful publisher. He was a distinguished scholar, writing a summary of Roman history from the earliest times to his day and genealogical studies of some aristocratic Roman families.

In Athens, Pomponius went to great lengths to be popular. He learned to speak Greek fluently and soon acquired the *cognomen* Atticus—after Attica, the territory of which Athens was the capital. From now on this was the name by which he was known and is how he will be referred to in this book. He was generous to local charities and took the trouble to develop the common touch. His biographer, Cornelius Nepos, a younger contemporary whom he knew personally, wrote that Atticus "behaved so as to seem at one with the poorest and on a level with the powerful."

Atticus had a nasty fright when Sulla called at Athens on his way back to Rome in 83. The general was sufficiently impressed by the young man to ask him to go back to Italy with him. His back to the wall, Atticus for once in his life refused to do a powerful man's bidding. "No, please, I beg you," he replied. "I left Italy to avoid fighting you alongside those you want to lead me against." Sulla liked his candor and let the matter drop.

Atticus always came back to Rome for elections and he made a profession of friendship. In his personal relationships, he was a kind and affectionate man and an excellent conversationalist. He insisted on high standards of personal behavior: according to Cornelius Nepos, "he never told a lie and could not tolerate lying in others." He cultivated politicians of every persuasion, doing them favors and steering clear of any overt ideological commitment. He was often used as a go-between and could be relied on to carry messages discreetly hither and thither. Like Caesar, he was loyal but with this difference: he liked to do good by stealth, behind the scenes. Posterity is greatly in his debt, for his friendship with Cicero was maintained by a constant exchange of correspondence, much of which survives.

For all his excellent personal qualities, Atticus had an unerring instinct for the protection of his own interests. It is hard to warm to him. Gaston Boissier, who wrote in the mid-nineteenth century what is still one of the most charming and witty books on Cicero, observed:

> He always belonged to the best party [i.e., the *optimates*] . . . only he made it a rule not to serve his party; he was contented with giving it his good wishes. But these good wishes were the warmest imaginable. . . . His reserve only began when it was necessary to act. . . . The more we think about it, the less we can imagine the reasons he could give [his friends] to justify his conduct.

Cicero agreed neither with Caesar nor with Atticus about the conclusions to be drawn from the years of bloodshed and confusion. In his eyes, the breakdown of civilized values was inexcusable. Physical timidity may have had something to do with it, but his deepest instincts were for the rule of law. What was needed, in his view, was a recall to order.

As a fellow Arpinate, he had mixed feelings about Marius, whom he saw during his last agonized years. He wrote a poetic eulogy of Marius in epic hexameters and admired the superhuman achievements of the general who had destroyed the Cimbri and the Teutones and the tenacity that had raised him to the head of affairs, but he was not at all tempted by his *popularis* politics. He despised Cinna, whose reign he regarded as a black interlude of criminality. The time spent in the company of senior statesmen and jurists, two of whom, Antonius and Scaevola, had perished in the chaos, gave him a love of tradition he never lost. If only the good old ways could be restored, he thought, all would again be well.

At the same time, although he was on Sulla's side ideologically, the memory of the Dictator's vengefulness never left him. In a book published in the 40s he referred, one senses almost with a physical shudder, to "the proscriptions of the rich, the destruction of the townships of Italy, the well-known 'harvest' of Sulla's time." Cicero detested Roman militarism and came to the view that his old civilian patron, Scaurus, the Leader of the Senate and a forceful defender of the Senate's authority, was in no way inferior to a general like Marius. "Victories in the field," he commented, "count for little if the right decisions are not taken at home."

While in the last resort he could be brave and decisive, Cicero did not have Caesar's flamboyant coolness under fire. His brief military experience during the War of the Allies had not recommended a soldier's life to him. So, not for the last time in his career, when confronted by brute force, he retreated from the bloodshed into his books. He feared that he would never realize his ambition to become a lawyer, for, as he recalled, "it appeared that the whole institution of the courts had vanished forever." As Plutarch, his biographer, who wrote around the turn of the first century AD, put it: "Seeing that the whole state was splitting up into factions and that the result of this would be the unlimited power of one man, he retired into the life of a scholar and philosopher, going on with his studies and associating with Greek scholars."

An uncovenanted benefit of the war with Mithridates was that many intellectuals and thinkers fled to Rome. One of these was Philo of Larisa, head of the Academy in Athens, founded by Plato three hundred years before. He inspired Cicero with a passion for philosophy, and in particular for the theories of Skepticism, which asserted that knowledge of the nature of things is in the nature of things unattainable. Such ideas were well judged to appeal to a student of rhetoric who had learned to argue all sides of a case. In his early twenties Cicero wrote the first volume of a work on "invention"—that is to say, the technique of finding ideas and arguments for a speech; in it he noted that the most important thing was "that we do not recklessly and presumptuously assume something to be true." This resolute uncertainty was to be a permanent feature of his thought.

He learned about the doctrines of Stoicism from the philosopher Diodotus, who was a member of his *clientela* and, until his death in about 60, lived in Cicero's house. Diodotus seems to have been an indomitable old man; when he became blind in his declining years, he took up geometry and played the lyre. His young employer was impressed by what he learned of a school of thought that saw the universe as an organic whole consisting of two indivisible aspects: an active principle (God) and that which it acts on (matter). Man's duty was to live an active life in harmony with nature; that was the way to be virtuous, because virtue was the active principle that infused nature. It followed that the wise man was indifferent to fortune and suspicious of emotion. Cicero could not go this far, but he appreciated the modified Stoicism of his day, which sought to reconcile the notion of a divine spirit in the universe with conventional Greco-Roman religious ideas.

Cicero's withdrawal into literary pursuits was temporary; he had every intention of entering the law and politics once circumstances permitted. If he was out of sympathy with the more aggressive, military aspirations of his peers, he did share with them an unquenchable thirst for personal fame. This found its classic expression in Homer's *Iliad,* in which Glaucus says to Diomedes that he still hears his father's urgings ringing in his ears:

Always be the best, my boy, the bravest,
and hold your head high above the others.

It was a text that had inspired Alexander the Great and, once Homer appeared on their curriculum, many Roman boys were equally impressed, among them Marcus Tullius Cicero. Years later he told his brother that the lines had expressed his "childhood dream." He was determined to be the best and the bravest, to join the ranks of the Republic's greatest heroes. He planned to excel, however, not on the battlefield, but in Rome's sacred center, the Forum.

3

THE FORUM AND THE FRAY

The Birth of an Orator: 81–77 BC

Almost all the main incidents in Cicero's career unfolded in a space hardly larger than two football fields, a square in the center of Rome. This was the Forum, where advocates addressed juries and politicians the People. In contemporary British terms, it combined the functions of Westminster Abbey, the Houses of Parliament, Trafalgar Square, the City of London and a shopping mall. All the personal services of urban life could be found there, from food stores to rent boys.

Rome itself had a profound impact on a teenager who had spent his early years in a small provincial town. It was by far the largest city in the ancient world. Time-travelers from the present day who had only the gift of sight would be at home in a townscape recognizably like the ancient cities of the Maghreb—say, Marrakesh or Fez or the *casbah* of Algiers. But if they could hear and understand Latin, they would quickly realize that Rome was a city without any of the public facilities which today we take for granted (except for the water supply, channeled into the city on aqueducts and underground sewers). Life was lived in the daylight hours. There was no street lighting: when night fell, the only illumination came from individual torches carried by pedestrians or their servants. Most Romans found it safer to be indoors in the evening.

Town planning was an art in its infancy and Rome had no wide thoroughfares or avenues. It was a web of lanes and alleys. Cicero referred to the city as "planted in mountains and deep valleys, its garrets hanging up above, its roads far from good, merely narrow byways." An urban district was, in effect, defined by a single street running through it. (The Latin word *vicus* meant both a quarter and a street.) The law required it to be at least five meters wide. At the end of each one there was a crossroads from which other roads and quarters led off. These central streets were the only ones that strangers were wise to visit. They were public spaces, but the urban hinterland beyond was essentially private and outside state control.

Different quarters specialized in particular industries or trades. So, for example, leather goods—books and sandals—could be found in the Argiletum. The Subura was known for its lowlife and brothels. The Aventine Hill, with its temple of Minerva, goddess of wisdom and the arts and sciences, on the summit, was an artists' quarter, like the Left Bank in Paris or London's Soho. Many playwrights and actors were based there, as was a community of poets. A self-help corporation of artists who lived and worked on the Aventine afforded a degree of mutual protection in what were, then as now, precarious professions. This was also a part of the city that attracted social misfits and victims of exclusion: foreigners, widows and prostitutes.

Rome was seriously overcrowded and, in an attempt to solve the chronic housing problem, blocks of apartments or *insulae* (literally, "islands") were constructed. These high-rise buildings, usually with shops on the ground floor, had about five or six stories and could be as tall as twenty meters. They were usually jerry-built and frequently collapsed. Other risks that citizens, and especially the poor, faced were fires and periodic floods when the Tiber overflowed its banks. The state took little or no interest in such events and the only social intervention it made was to insure and subsidize the corn supply. Anything might happen to urban Romans, but at least they would not starve.

Cicero was to become a landlord and developer, once he had made his fortune and become a man of means; he wrote to Atticus with that combination of insouciance and greed that has marked the upper-class rentier throughout the ages: "Two of my shops have collapsed and the others are showing cracks, so that even the mice have moved elsewhere, to say nothing of the tenants. Other people call this a disaster, I don't even call it a nuisance. . . . Heavens above, how utterly trivial such things appear to me!

However, there is a building scheme under way . . . which should turn this loss into a source of profit."

The smartest addresses were on the Palatine and Velia Hills, although the pressure on space was so great that the mansions of the rich were built on tiny plots of land with minuscule gardens. In his heyday Cicero was hugely proud to own one of the largest houses on the Palatine. Two winding streets, Victory Rise (*Clivus Victoriae*) and Palatine Rise (*Clivus Palatinus*), could accommodate carriages and led up from the valley below, from the Forum and the hurly-burly of urban life.

Although the Romans were a practical people, they believed that the foundation of a built community was a sacred act. The city's boundary, the *pomoerium,* was holy and inviolable. According to legend, this was a furrow which a plow drawn by a white heifer and ox had traced at the time of Rome's foundation and it was forbidden to cross it. Entrance was restricted to the gates or *ianua* where the plow had been lifted. Soldiers were denied access and became civilians when they came inside the ritual enclosure. Likewise burials were not allowed inside the *pomoerium.*

The Forum was the city's political, commercial and legal heart, but it was also its spiritual center, a space even more sacred than the city itself. A rectangular piazza, approaching 200 meters long by 75 meters wide, and flagged with stones, it lay in what had once been a marsh between the hills of the Capitol, the citadel where the great Temple of Jupiter stood, and the Palatine. Today it is a jumble of grass and stone rubble, where a few lucky pillars survive to recall the days of ancient Rome. However, with imagination and a guidebook, it is not very difficult to reconstruct in the mind's eye the scene as it was when the young Cicero presented his first case as a counsel for the defense in 81 BC.

At one end, the tall facade of the national archive, the Tabularium, lined the steep cliff of the Capitol. In front, from the point of view of an observer facing it, stood the Temple of Concord (*Concordia*) and on its left the Temple of Saturn with its large forecourt, which functioned as the State Treasury. Religion and daily life were not separated in the Roman mind and temples were regularly used for business and state purposes.

On the right, the Senate House and the Assembly Ground (*Comitium*) provided the setting for political activity. A Speakers' Platform stood on the outer edge of the Comitium. It was decorated with ships' prows captured in a sea battle in 338 and their name in Latin, *Rostra*, was applied to the platform as a whole.

The long sides of the square were bordered by two colonnaded halls, the Basilica Fulvia Aemilia and the Basilica Sempronia. Maintained and refurbished by the great families that had had them built, they contained shops and meeting rooms. Farther down just past the Basilica Sempronia, the Temple of Castor and Pollux (or Temple of the Castors) stood on a high podium under which were two rows of moneylenders' booths—the nearest equivalents to modern banks. The building, which had a large speaker's platform in front of the temple porch, also served as a political meeting place and the Senate was often convened there. Nearby, judicial proceedings were held at the Tribunal Aurelium, a stone dais surrounded by steps from the top of which Cicero was to harangue juries. Cases were conducted out-of-doors in various parts of the Forum and advocates had to speak in rain or shine, summer heat or winter cold.

Underneath the flagstones of the square itself was (and still is) a network of underground tunnels. These were where gladiators waited before emerging to fight in a temporary wooden arena where various kinds of spectacle were staged during festivals and on holidays.

The Forum was closed at its far end by a group of religious buildings—among them the circular Temple of Vesta, goddess of the hearth. Here an eternal flame was tended by a team of six free-born women dedicated to chastity, the Vestal Virgins, who lived in a large house beyond the Temple. They were appointed between the ages of six and ten and served for thirty years. If they broke their vows (happily, a rare event), they were buried alive outside the *pomoerium*, and their lovers were whipped to death on the Assembly Ground. The Vestal Virgins were symbolically married to the Chief Pontiff (*pontifex maximus*, a title later expropriated by the pope).

The Chief Pontiff chaired the highest religious council, the College of Pontiffs, and was responsible for the organization of the state religion. The College in turn was in charge of the calendar and decided the dates of festivals and public holidays. It also kept a record of the principal events of each year, the Annals. Overall, its task was to regulate the relations between gods and men. The Chief Pontiff lived next door to the Vestal Virgins in the State House (*domus publica*). Nearby was the somewhat extravagantly named Palace (*regia*), a poky little structure built centuries before, when kings still ruled the city. It contained a variety of sacred objects and housed the Annals and the official calendar.

Politics in the late Republic was grounded in a profound sense of what it was to be a Roman, a commitment to the *mos maiorum,* ancestral customs. This sense was, quite literally, embodied in the Forum's layout and structures. There was hardly a spot that had not been the scene of some great event in the city's legendary past as well as more recent, historical times.

At the center of the Forum a low wall surrounded a water hole near a cluster of three plants: a vine, a fig tree and an olive bush. This was the Pool of Curtius, where in Rome's early years a chasm had suddenly appeared. The prophetic Sibylline Books, an antique collection of oracular utterances in Greek hexameters which the Romans consulted in times of national crisis, advised that the gap in the ground would close only when it received what the Roman people valued most highly. From that day forward the earth would produce an abundance of what it had taken in. People threw cakes and silver into the hole, but it stayed open. Then a young cavalryman, one Marcus Curtius, told the Senate that he had worked out the answer to the riddle: it was its soldiers' courage that Rome held most dear. Fully armed astride his warhorse, he galloped down into the chasm and the crowd hurled animals, precious fabrics and other valuables after him. Finally, the earth closed. According to another version, Curtius was an enemy Sabine whose horse drowned in what was then a swamp. The most plausible (and least exotic) account claimed that a Consul named Curtius fenced the Pool off and consecrated it after the area had been struck by lightning. But for the average Roman, the historical truth was neither here nor there. What mattered was that the Pool was a holy emblem of the city's past.

Beside the Basilica Fulvia Aemilia stood a little shrine to Venus Cloacina, just above the spot where a great subterranean drain, the Cloaca Maxima, ran beneath the Forum (the Cloaca survives to this day). Here in the dim past Roman and Sabine soldiers, about to do battle, had laid down their arms and purified themselves with sprigs of myrtle: they had quarreled after the Romans, facing a population crisis, had kidnapped some women of the neighboring Sabine tribe to provide themselves with more wives. A few yards away was the Navel of the Globe (*umbilicus orbis*); this was considered to be the center of the city and the point at

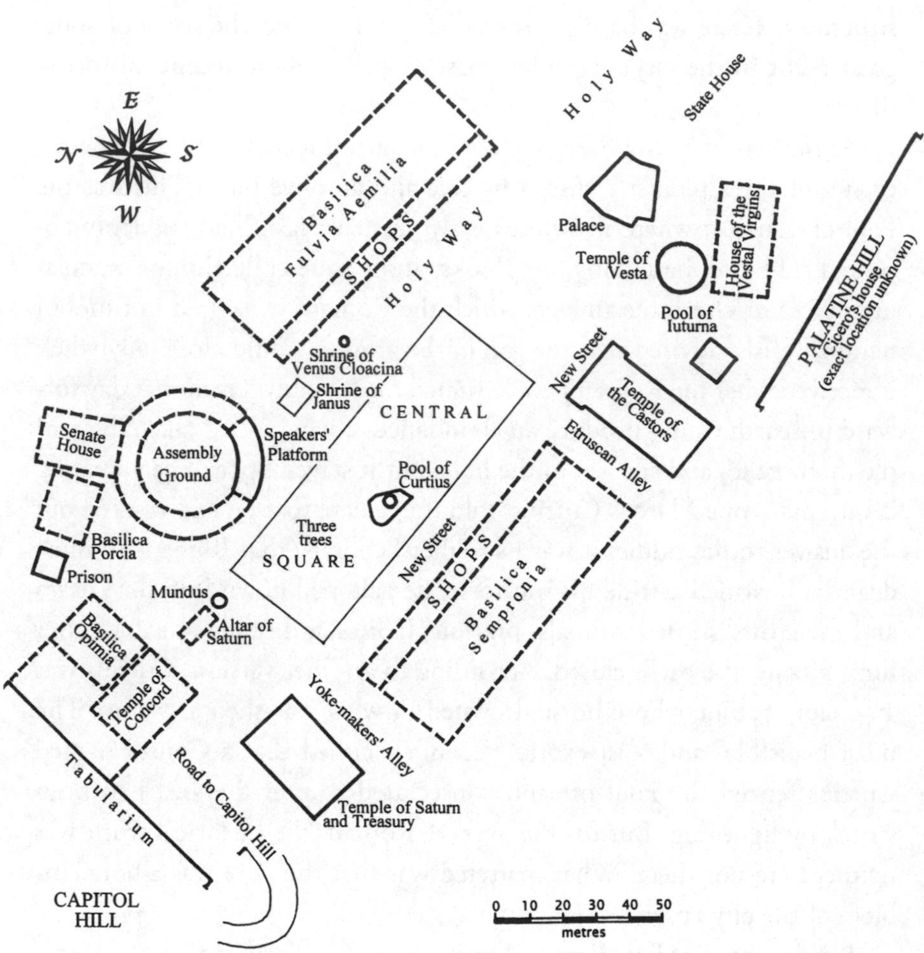

Plan of the Roman Forum, Cicero's workplace as a lawyer, as it was from the mid-second to the mid-first century BC. The positioning of buildings indicated by broken lines is different from that of the present day. Trials were held in the open air with the presiding judge on a platform and jury seated nearby.

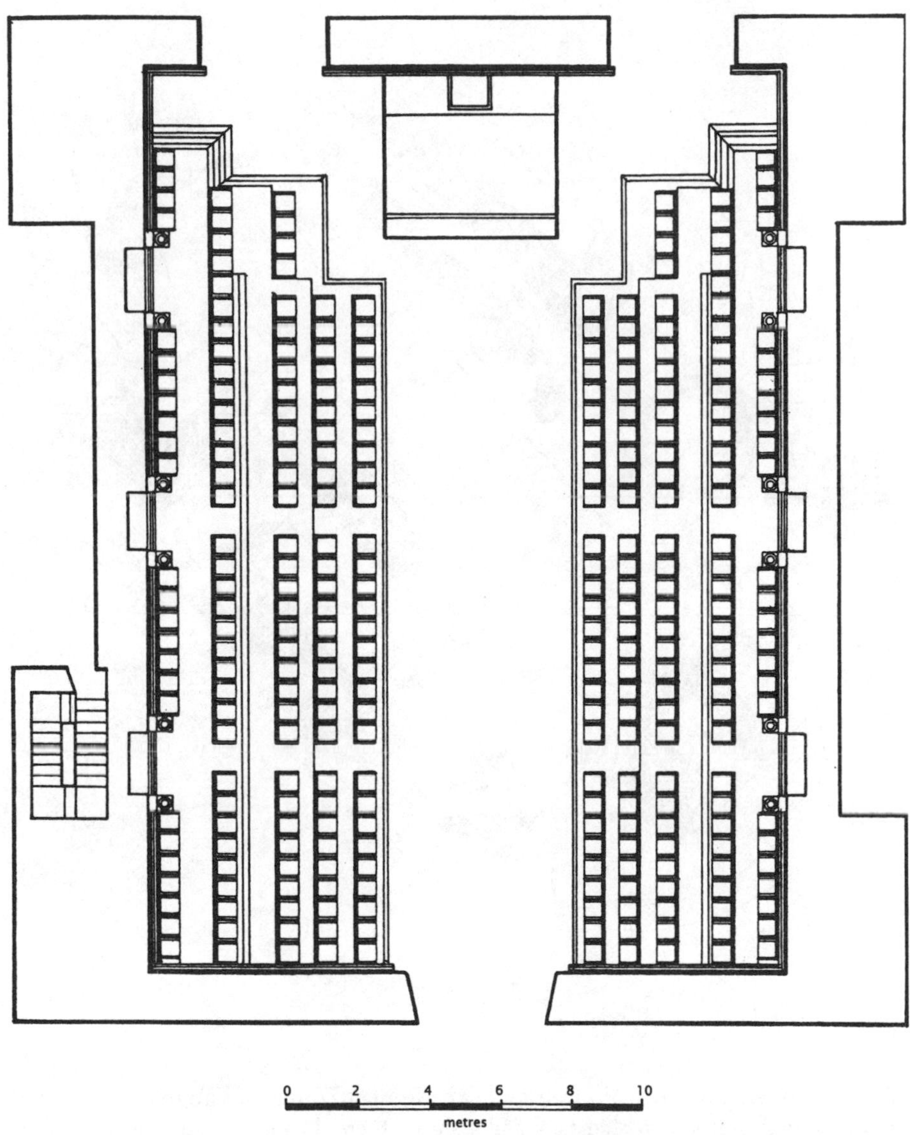

Speculative plan of the Senate House. The presiding Consul chaired meetings from the dais opposite the main door. Former Consuls sat in the front rows.

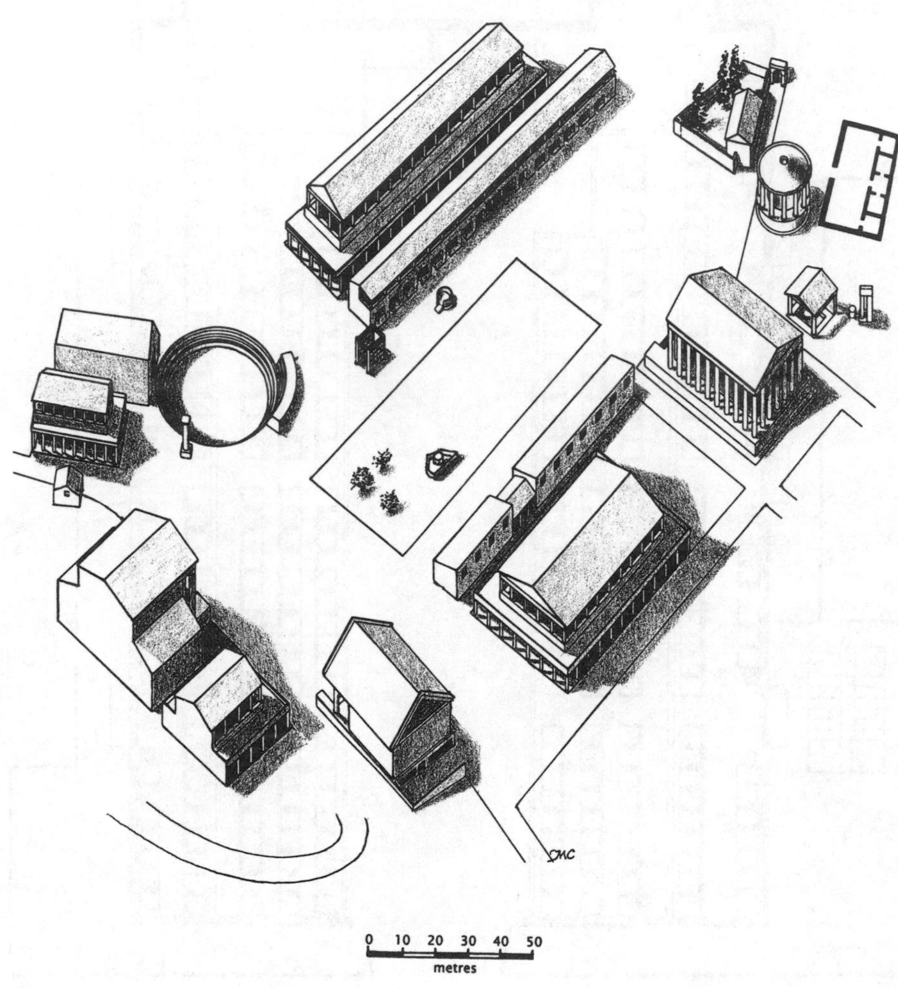

A reconstruction of the main features of the Roman Forum in Cicero's day. It was crowded with statues, an altar here and a shrine there, historical paintings near the Assembly Ground, a stone lawyers' platform, and the impedimenta of temporary stands and notice boards.

which the living world was in contact, through a deep cleft in the ground, with the underworld. The site that combined the historical and the sacred at their most vital was the Black Stone (*niger lapis*) next to the Assembly Ground. This was a sanctuary of great antiquity dedicated to the god Vulcan and nearby was the legendary site of the assassination of Rome's founder, Romulus.

It was not only the Forum that was sacred but also most of the activities that were conducted there. Political and indeed private life was governed by a web of religious rules and procedures, predictions and omens. Religion was not so much a set of personal beliefs as precisely laid-down ways of living in harmony with the expectations of the gods. In fact, by the end of the Republic educated men believed less in the literal truth of the apparatus of religious doctrine than in a vaguer notion of the validity of tradition.

The basic proposition was that no human enterprise could be undertaken without divine sanction. This applied to domestic households as well as to state affairs. The gods worked through natural phenomena to reveal their wishes or intentions. Signs included the flight or songs of birds, the activities of animals and thunder and lightning. It was also possible to attach significance to words or phrases casually spoken.

The College of Augurs had the sole right of interpreting the auspices. (Like the College of Pontiffs, it comprised leading personalities of the Roman establishment and Cicero became a member towards the end of his career.) An Augur would mark off a rectangular space, called a *templum* (the origin of the word "temple"), from which he would conduct his observations. In some places permanent *templa* were identified, one of which was on the citadel on the Capitol Hill. Signs from the east (usually on the Augur's left) were held to be favorable and those from the west unfavorable. In addition, Etruscan soothsayers, or *haruspices,* were often called to Rome to explain apparently supernatural events and gave judgments based on an examination of the entrails of sacrificed animals.

Sanctity permeated the annual calendar, which controlled political and legal processes according to a religious framework. The calendar was divided into twelve columns and each day was marked with an F or an N, depending on whether it was *fastus* or *nefastus*—lucky or unlucky, lawful or unlawful. On the former days, business could be conducted, the law courts could sit, farmers could begin plowing or harvesting crops. Especially fortunate days were marked with a C (for *comitialis*), which meant that popular assemblies could meet. Some days were thought to be so unlucky that it was not even permissible to hold religious ceremonies: these included the days following the Kalends (first of a month), Nones (the ninth day before the Ides), the Ides (the thirteenth or fifteenth of the month) and the anniversaries of national disasters.

If a day was *nefastus,* the gods frowned on human exertion (although one was allowed to continue a task already started). An added complication was that some days were partly lucky and partly unlucky. According to a stone-carved calendar discovered at Antium, 109 days were *nefasti,* 192 *comitiales,* and 11 were mixed. The Roman year was also punctuated by numerous festivals or public holidays (some of which were one-time events caused, say, by the need to expiate some offense or sacrilege). For certain public holidays the dates were not fixed until the last minute by the priests and officeholders who managed the calendar.

The interfusion of church and state gave plenty of leeway for manipulation and chicanery by the colleges and by politicians. Julius Caesar's colleague during his first Consulship, Marcus Calpurnius Bibulus, tried to invalidate all Caesar's legislation by withdrawing to his house to "scrutinize the heavens," a step that theoretically brought all political activity to a halt. Popular assemblies were sometimes prevented from meeting by the simple expedient of declaring *nefastus* the day when they were to be called.

Public and religious ceremonies were conducted according to precise forms of words and any mistake by the officiant was held to be so unlucky that the entire ritual had to be repeated. Men in public life did their best to avoid accidental events or actions from being seen as unlucky. On a famous occasion during the civil war, Caesar tripped when disembarking from a ship on the shores of Africa and fell flat on his face. With his talent for improvisation, he spread out his arms and embraced the earth as a symbol of conquest. By quick thinking he turned a terrible omen of failure into one of victory.

Cicero came to know the Forum well during his student years. But then, alarmed by the turbulent reigns of Marius and Sulla, he stayed clear of public life. During the latter part of the 80s, he read and wrote, studied literature and philosophy and improved his knowledge and practice of public speaking. His aim was "not (as most do) to learn my trade in the Forum, but so far as possible to enter the Forum already trained." Other ambitious young upper-class Romans were trying their hands as advocates in their early twenties, building political support and generally getting noticed; but for the time being Cicero was silent and invisible.

In the summer of 81 the proscription came to an end, and life began to return to normal. Sulla turned his attention to political reform. His basic idea was to prevent the dominance of two classes of politician who, he believed, had come near to destroying the Republic. The first was the radical Tribune, like the Gracchus brothers with their dangerous obsession with land reform. The second was the powerful general willing to lead his loyal army on Rome—in other words, someone very like himself. He was determined to stop another Sulla from expropriating the state.

He increased the powers and size of the depleted Senate. Between 300 and 400 new members were appointed. He also raised the quota of Quaestors and introduced the rule that they became Senators ex officio. In order to prevent inexperienced young men from gaining power too early, he set strict age limits for officeholders. Although there were scandalous exceptions, this was the basic pattern to which the younger generation, including Cicero and Caesar, had to conform.

Tribunes lost much of their authority: their right to present legislation to the General Assembly, thus bypassing the Senate, was withdrawn. More seriously, they were debarred from holding any other public office. The Tribuneship could no longer fast-forward a political career.

New rules were introduced to control elected officials abroad. The Senate allocated provincial appointments and was expected to ensure that the most dangerously ambitious politicians were kept from the most sensitive governorships. Postings were usually to be for one year only and a new treason law regulated governors' behavior. They were not allowed to start wars without permission, leave their provinces or take their troops into someone else's. With a few spectacular exceptions, governors adhered to these rules.

Cicero warmly approved of Sulla's ends but not his means; he believed that the Dictator had won "a disreputable victory in a reputable cause." He was greatly relieved when order was restored. It meant not only that the constitution had survived but that at long last it was safe to return to the Forum and launch his career at the bar. He was twenty-five years old.

We do not know how the inexperienced advocate won his first briefs. Almost certainly his family's *clientela* network was put to work and cases were found that for one reason or another were unattractive to more senior lawyers. His first extant speech dates from 81; it was a defense of a certain Publius Quinctius, who had become embroiled in a complicated dispute with his dead brother's business partner about the ownership of a cattle farm in Transalpine Gaul. Cicero was noticed as a promising newcomer; but while his voice was powerful, it was harsh and untrained and he strained it from overuse.

All his life he suffered from first-night nerves. He acknowledged:

> Personally, I am always very nervous when I begin to speak. Every time I make a speech I feel I am submitting to judgment, not only about my ability but my character and honor. I am afraid of seeming either to promise more than I can perform, which suggests complete irresponsibility, or to perform less than I can, which suggests bad faith and indifference.

On at least one occasion he is known to have broken down completely. He would work up and polish his speeches after delivery and publish them in a form which may sometimes have been substantially different from the original versions. A few times he published speeches that had never been delivered at all.

Malicious critics drew an unkinder picture. A contemporary attack on Cicero's method in 43 (as reported, perhaps invented, by an imperial historian) is knockabout invective and not to be taken too seriously, but it has a ring of truth.

> Why, you always come to the courts trembling, as if you were about to fight as a gladiator, and after uttering a few words in a meek and half-dead voice you take your leave. . . . Do you think anyone is ignorant of the fact that you never delivered those wonderful orations of yours that you have published but wrote them all out afterwards, like craftsmen who mold generals and cavalry leaders out of clay?

In 80 the case arose that made Cicero's reputation. He must have hesitated before taking it on, for it touched on corruption in the Dictator's entourage. Famous legal names had declined to have anything to do with it, fearful of Sulla's well-known vengefulness. It took some courage for the timid young orator to accept the brief.

His client was one Sextus Roscius, who was accused of having murdered his father. It was the first trial of a capital offense since the proscription. The story Cicero presented to the jury threw a sharp light on the impact that high events in the capital had had on the lives of ordinary people. Roscius's father, a well-to-do farmer, had paid a visit to Rome during the previous summer or autumn. One night, walking back from a dinner party, he was set upon and killed near some public baths. His son, meantime, was at their home at Ameria, a hill town to the north of Rome, looking after the family estate.

A long-standing feud existed between the victim and two fellow Amerians. According to Cicero, one of the pair happened to be in Rome and immediately sent a messenger to the other with the news of Roscius's father's death. This man passed the information to Chrysogonus, a powerful freedman and favorite of Sulla, then encamped with his army a hundred miles north of Ameria. A simple but effective plot was devised to get hold of the substantial Roscius estate.

The proscription lists had been closed on June 1, 81 BC, but Chrysogonus arranged for Roscius's father's name to be entered on it retrospectively, despite the fact that he was a well-known conservative. As a result, all his property was confiscated and publicly auctioned. Although valued at 6,000,000 sesterces, it was knocked down to Chrysogonus for a trifling 2,000 sesterces. As his share of the spoils, one of the Amerians was given some of Roscius's father's land. The remainder went to Chrysogonus, who appointed the other Amerian as his agent and business manager.

The affair caused a great deal of bad blood in Ameria, where Roscius's father had been a respected figure, and a civic delegation was dispatched to Sulla to lay a complaint. One of the alleged conspirators was appointed to the group and he made sure that it failed to obtain a personal audience with the Dictator. Instead, the Amerians met Chrysogonus, who gave them the assurances they asked for: he would have Roscius's father's name removed from the proscription list and would help the son to regain possession of the dead man's estate.

This bought the conspirators some time, but obviously their promises would have to be delivered sooner or later—and seen to be delivered. If young Roscius were somehow to come by a nasty accident in the meantime, the problem would be solved. This would not be difficult, for he was now isolated, penniless and vulnerable. After more than one attempt on his life, he realized it would be sensible to leave town and he made his way south to the comparative safety of Rome.

Foiled, Chrysogonus and his partners in crime decided on a bold course of action. In fact, if they wanted to preserve their gains, they had little other choice. Father and son had been on poor terms (even Cicero acknowledged this) and it was arranged for the young man to be accused of parricide. This was among the most serious offenses in the charge book and was one of the few crimes to attract the death penalty under Roman law. The method of execution was extremely unpleasant. An ancient legal authority described what took place: "According to the custom of our ancestors it was established that the parricide should be beaten with blood-red rods, sewn in a leather sack together with a dog [an animal despised by Greeks and Romans], a cock [like the parricide devoid of all feelings of affection], a viper [whose mother was supposed to die when it was born], and an ape [a caricature of a man], and the sack thrown into the depths of the sea or a river."

It is difficult to judge how convincing the case against Roscius was. As with all Cicero's speeches at the bar, the arguments of the other side have not survived—sometimes (albeit not on this occasion) even the verdict is lost. Taken as a whole, the story Cicero tells is internally consistent. The likeliest explanation of the murder is either that Roscius was the victim of a late-night mugging, plausible enough in a city without police and street lighting, which his enemies in Ameria then opportunistically exploited—or alternatively that they arranged his assassination themselves.

Cicero's speech appears to have been soundly based on meticulous research, but its dramatic effect derived more from its daring structure than from the evidence. He opened with a refutation of the charge of parricide. Then he shifted gear and took the offensive: his aim was to destroy the character of the two Amerians and pin the murder charge on them. Finally, and one can only imagine the gasps of surprise around the courtroom, he launched into a full-frontal assault on the Dictator's favorite, Chrysogonus and the un-Roman excesses of his lifestyle. He, the argument went, was the real villain of the piece.

"He comes down from his mansion on the Palatine Hill," Cicero intoned with a measured flourish before swooping in for the kill. "For his enjoyment he owns a delightful country place in the suburbs as well as some fine farms close to the city. His home is crammed with costly gold, silver and copper Corinthian and Delian dishes, including that famous pressure cooker which he recently bought at auction at so high a price that when people heard the bids called they thought a landed estate was up for sale. And that is not all. How much embossed silver, carpets and coverlets, pictures, statues, marble do you think he owns? As much, of course, as he could pile up in one house, taken from many famous families during this age of riot and pillage." Cicero was nothing if not a genius at character assassination. "And just look at the man himself," he concluded, "gentlemen of the jury. You see how, with his elegantly styled hair and reeking with perfume, he floats around the Forum, an ex-slave surrounded by a crowd of citizens of Rome, you see how superior he feels himself to be to everyone else, that he alone is wealthy and powerful."

The court burst into loud applause and Roscius was acquitted. (Unfortunately, the future fate of the players in the drama is unknown.) Cicero had scored a brilliant victory and in one bound joined the front rank of Roman orators. However, the achievement was not without risk.

Cicero insisted that he was not attacking Sulla, who (he claimed) knew nothing about the case, but it was hard to read the speech other than as a critique of the regime. The Dictator was in a position to take revenge on an impertinent young advocate if he wanted to do so. Soon after Cicero compounded the offense by taking on another case with political overtones, that of a woman from Arretium who challenged Sulla's withdrawal of her Roman citizenship.

In any event, the Dictator took no action against Cicero. Perhaps he could not be bothered to intervene in a minor matter of this kind; he was beginning to lose interest in the exercise of power and withdrew into private life in the following year.

The chief result of Cicero's defense of Roscius was a flood of briefs. In the months that followed he brought a rapid succession of cases to court—as he recalled, "smelling somewhat of midnight oil." He was soon suffering severely from overwork.

He did, however, make time to find a wife. This would help him stabilize and enhance his finances and, if he chose well, extend his political connections. It seems that in or around 79, at the age of twenty-seven, Cicero married Terentia. Apparently much younger than he was, she came from a wealthy, perhaps aristocratic family and brought with her a dowry of 480,000 sesterces. This was a substantial fortune, well beyond the sum of 400,000 sesterces required for entry into the equestrian order. She owned woods and pastureland, probably near Cicero's villa at Tusculum. Little is known about her background, except that her half-sister, Fabia, was a Vestal Virgin. She had a strong character, as Plutarch observed: "Terentia was never at any time a shrinking type of woman; she was bold and energetic by nature, ambitious, and, as Cicero says himself, was more inclined to take a part in his public life than to share with him any of her domestic responsibilities."

The traditional Roman wedding was a splendid affair designed to dramatize the bride's transfer from the protection of her father's household gods to those of her husband. Originally, this literally meant that she passed from the authority of her father to her husband, but at the end of the Republic women achieved a greater degree of independence, and the bride remained formally in the care of a guardian from her blood family. In the event of financial and other disagreements, this meant that her interests were more easily protected. Divorce was easy, frequent and often consensual, although husbands were obliged to repay their wives' dowries.

The bride was dressed at home in a white tunic, gathered by a special belt which her husband would later have to untie. Over this she wore a flame-colored veil. Her hair was carefully dressed with pads of artificial hair into six tufts and held together by ribbons. The groom went to her father's house and, taking her right hand in his, confirmed his vow of fidelity. An animal (usually a ewe or a pig) was sacrificed in the *atrium* or a nearby shrine and an Augur was appointed to examine the entrails and declare the auspices favorable. The couple exchanged vows after this and the marriage was complete. A wedding banquet, attended by the two families, concluded with a ritual attempt to drag the bride from her mother's arms in a pretended abduction.

A procession was then formed which led the bride to her husband's house, holding the symbols of housewifely duty, a spindle and distaff. She took the hand of a child whose parents were living, while another child, waving a hawthorn torch, walked in front to clear the way. All those in the procession laughed and made obscene jokes at the happy couple's expense.

When the bride arrived at her new home, she smeared the front door with oil and lard and decorated it with strands of wool. Her husband, who had already arrived, was waiting inside and asked for her *praenomen* or first name. Because Roman women did not have one and were called only by their family name, she replied in a set phrase: "Wherever you are Caius, I will be Caia." She was then lifted over the threshold. The husband undid the girdle of his wife's tunic, at which point the guests discreetly withdrew. On the following morning she dressed in the traditional costume of married women and made a sacrifice to her new household gods.

By the late Republic this complicated ritual had lost its appeal for sophisticated Romans and could be replaced by a much simpler ceremony, much as today many people marry in a registry office. The man asked the woman if she wished to become the mistress of a household *(materfamilias),* to which she answered yes. In turn, she asked him if he wished to become *paterfamilias,* and on his saying he did the couple became husband and wife.

Just as the exact date of Cicero's marriage to Terentia is uncertain, so the style of their wedding is unknown. Perhaps the young provincial, the New Man from Arpinum with his feeling for the Roman past and his eagerness to be socially accepted, opted for tradition. On the other hand the skeptical Philhellene might well have resisted meaningless flummery. Unfortunately, there is not a scintilla of hard evidence pointing in one direction or the other. By the same token, the birth date of their first child, Tullia, is unknown. Although she came to be the apple of her father's eye, the arrival of a girl was no great cause for celebration or even notice in a male-oriented society. She was born probably in 75 or 76 but possibly earlier.

In 79 Cicero went abroad with a group of friends for an extended tour of the eastern Mediterranean and, as it would appear that the wedding took place that year, left his bride behind. Evidently at this stage in their relationship the couple was not close. Cicero's emotional life was still centered on the male friendships he had made in his student years.

On the face of it, Cicero's decision to leave Rome just when his career had taken off was mysterious. People whispered that he was afraid of reprisals from Sulla, or perhaps more plausibly Chrysogonus, because of Roscius's acquittal. But on balance this seems unlikely. Having completed his work of reform, Sulla was now approaching retirement; reliving his debauched youth, he survived, if Plutarch is to be believed, only for a few more disreputably entertaining months.

Cicero's true motive for his foreign travels was the need to recover his health, which suddenly collapsed. Physically he was not robust. He was thin and underweight and had such a poor digestion that he could manage to swallow only something light at the end of the day. Success had come at a high price and he needed time to recoup his forces. Such in any case was his own explanation and there is little reason to doubt it. He recalled:

> I was at that time very slender and not strong in body, with a long, thin neck; and such a constitution and appearance, if combined with hard work and strain on the lungs, were thought to be almost life-threatening. Those who loved me were all the more alarmed, in that I always spoke without pause or variation, using all the strength of my voice and the effort of my whole body. When friends and doctors begged me to give up speaking in the courts, I felt I would run any risk rather than abandon my hope of fame as a speaker. I thought that by a more restrained and moderate use of the voice and a different way of speaking I could both avoid the danger and acquire more variety in my style; and the reason for my going to Asia was to change my method of speaking. And so, when I had two years' experience of taking cases and my name was already well-known in the Forum, I left Rome.

If recuperation was the primary reason for his travels, he also grasped the chance to deepen his professional training. For all his years of study, Cicero was unsatisfied with his technique; he lacked ease of delivery and his oratorical effects were sometimes strained and artificial. He visited various celebrated or fashionable teachers of rhetoric and, never forgetting what he saw as the moral dimension of rhetoric, also spent time on fundamental philosophical studies.

His brother Quintus, a small, choleric man, and his much younger cousin Lucius Cicero, son of the uncle whose early death cut short a promising career, went with him on this classical equivalent of an eighteenth-century grand tour. Two former fellow students, Titus Pomponius

Atticus and Marcus Pupius Piso, were welcome additions to a congenial party. They spent six months in Athens and did a good deal of sightseeing.

Not long after their arrival the group was initiated into the secret religious mysteries of Eleusis, a few miles from Athens, which must have come as a shock to Romans brought up to see religion as a set of rules and social rituals. The mysteries were at the heart of a festival of purification and fertility; those taking part witnessed some kind of spiritual reenactment of death and rebirth, involving a descent into the underworld and a vision of the future life. Cicero was profoundly stirred by the experience and believed that of all Athenian contributions to civilization, these transcendental ceremonies were the greatest. Writing near the end of his life in his book *On Law,* he claimed: "we have learned from them the beginnings of life and have gained the power not only to live happily but also to die with a better hope."

But what really interested him was Greek philosophy and, as he saw it, its essential interconnection with the art of public speaking. His book *On Supreme Good and Evil (De finibus),* written more than three decades later, is a series of philosophical dialogues, one of which recalls his stay in Athens. The speakers are the companions of his grand tour and the setting is the Academy, the grove of olive trees containing a gymnasium or exercise ground where Plato had taught and which became a kind of university for the study of philosophy and rhetoric. In the morning the young men attend a class given by the head of the Academy, Antiochus of Ascalon, and in the afternoon they take a stroll in the gardens to enjoy the quiet calm of the place.

According to Plutarch, Cicero "planned that, if he were finally deprived of the chance of following a public career, he would retire to Athens, away from the law and politics, and spend his life here in the quiet pursuit of philosophy." In fact, although from time to time over the years he was indeed forced into periods of retirement, this never happened. But if he did not go to Athens he made Athens come to him. At his house at Tusculum he would later re-create the Academy, with halls and walks for intellectual debate and meditation, and build a version of Aristotle's base in Athens, the Lyceum.

In the autumn of 79, Cicero left Athens for Asia Minor. In Rhodes, he sat briefly at the feet of a well-known Stoic philosopher and historian,

Posidonius. More important, he consulted a distinguished rhetorician, Apollonius Molon, whom he had heard twice in Rome and whose style was rather more restrained than that of his florid rivals on the Asian mainland. He provided the technical retraining Cicero needed. Molon was, Cicero later recalled,

> not only a pleader in real cases [as distinct from theoretical exercises] and an admirable writer but excellent as a judge and critic of faults and a very wise teacher and adviser. . . . And so I came home after two years not only more experienced but almost another man; the excessive strain of voice had gone, my style had so to speak simmered down, my lungs were stronger and I was not so thin.

In 78 news came of Sulla's death and any residual anxieties Cicero may have had for his personal safety disappeared. In two years he would be old enough, under the new rules, to put a foot on the first rung of the political ladder and run for Quaestor. He was determined to stand at the earliest legal opportunity. If elected he would hold office the following year, when he would be thirty. By 77 he was back in Rome rebuilding his legal career in the Forum and planning his first political campaign.

4

POLITICS AND FOREIGN POSTINGS

Cicero Enters the Ring: 77–63 BC

During his childhood and youth Cicero had watched with horror as Rome set about dismantling itself. If he had a mission as an adult, it was to recall the Republic to order. The image that came to his mind when describing its constitution was of a musical concert.

> Just as in the music of harps and flutes or in the voices of singers a certain harmony of the different tones must be maintained . . . so also a state is made harmonious by agreement among dissimilar elements. This is brought about by a fair and reasonable blending of the upper, middle and lower classes, just as if they were musical tones. What musicians call harmony in song is concord in a state.

These words were written late in life, but, even if his political thinking as a young man was not yet fully formed, Cicero's experience of Roman politics and his philosophical explorations would already have confirmed his conservative cast of mind. It became his self-ordained duty to conduct the orchestra of all the classes and train it to play in tune again.

Cicero campaigned vigorously and won his election as Quaestor for 75 without apparent difficulty. It may be imagined that he and his family called in every favor and exploited every connection in order to ensure a good turnout. Doubtless many citizens of Arpinum took the trouble to travel to Rome to vote for their local boy. The fact that he was a New Man meant that the outcome would not have looked at all certain.

A Quaestor had no political or military authority. He and his colleagues assisted the Consuls by supervising the collection of taxes and authorizing payments. They were responsible for the management of the Treasury in the Temple of Saturn and had a small, permanent staff to conduct day-to-day business. Since Sulla's recent reforms the really important feature of the post was that it gave the holder automatic membership in the Senate.

Some Quaestors were given foreign postings and Cicero was allocated one of the two Quaestorships based in Sicily, reporting directly to the governor. Wives did not accompany Romans on official business abroad, and so, once again, Terentia was left behind in Italy, where she doubtless spent much of her time with little Tullia.

With the decline of Italian agriculture and the provision of subsidized corn for the urban masses in the capital, Sicily was Rome's most important provider of cereals and it was essential to ensure stability of its supply and price. The oldest of Rome's provinces, the island had been won from the Carthaginians in 241 and, as tribute, its communities were required to export gratis 10 percent of their corn harvest to Rome. If more was needed, it could be acquired by compulsory purchase. It was the Quaestors' job to calculate the price and the quantity of extra corn to be bought.

In carrying out this task Cicero showed a talent for competent and fair administration. To counteract an inflation of the corn price in Rome, he made an assessment of additional need and negotiated a fair rate with the suppliers. When the Sicilians received payment, he made sure that his office did not deduct the usual, but illegal, commission. This behavior made him very popular.

Cicero believed in honesty in public affairs, but it was also in his personal interest to win over local opinion. If his career was to progress, he would have to build up political support and his stay in Sicily was an excellent opportunity to expand his client list. Cicero won the backing of many *equites,* some of whom he represented in court in front of the governor. This class included Roman tax farmers and traders and also, since the enfranchisement of Italy and Sicily after the War of the Allies ten years earlier, local aristocracies across the peninsula. It was a substantial new constituency of Roman citizens, still largely untapped, and someone like Cicero whose roots were non-Roman and provincial was well placed to appeal to it. Although his ambition was to join the ruling elite in Rome, he never forgot where his political backing really lay—among the Italian middle classes.

In his leisure hours Cicero was an indefatigable tourist. Sicily had a long and colorful history: originally colonized by the Greek states during their heyday, it contained many wealthy and beautiful cities, with fine temples and works of art by great sculptors and painters. Carthage had dominated the west of the island for many years and, although that was now long in the past, something of the exotic character of her culture survived. Cicero's headquarters were at Lilybaeum (now Marsala), a wealthy town at Sicily's western extremity.

The Roman heritage attracted Cicero's prime loyalty and his deepest feelings, but he was also fascinated by the legacy of other people's pasts. He sought out and rediscovered the lost grave of Archimedes, the great scientist and geometer, a citizen of Syracuse who had been killed during the Roman siege more than one hundred years before. The exploit demonstrated detective skills and inquisitiveness which he put to good use in his legal career, and he recalled it with pride:

> When I was Quaestor, I tracked down his grave; the Syracusans not only had no idea where it was, they denied it even existed. I found it surrounded and covered by brambles and thickets. I remembered that some lines of doggerel I had heard were inscribed on his tomb to the effect that a sphere and a cylinder had been placed on its top. So I took a good look around (for there are a lot of graves at the Agrigentine Gate cemetery) and noticed a small column rising a little way above some bushes, on which stood a sphere and a cylinder. I immediately told the Syracusans (some of their leading men were with me) that I thought I had found what I was looking for. Slaves were sent in with scythes to clear the ground and once a path had been opened up we approached the pedestal. About half the lines of the epigram were still legible although the rest had worn away. So, you see, one of the most celebrated cities of Greece, once upon a time a great seat of learning too, would have been ignorant of the

grave of one of its most intellectually gifted citizens—had it not been for a man from Arpinum who pointed it out to them.

When Cicero's Quaestorship came to an end in 74, he made his way back to Rome. He was feeling very pleased with himself. He had proved his worth as a public official. He had been able to practice and perfect his advocacy techniques in a more relaxed setting than the Forum. He had begun the process of attracting a political following. Above all, he seems to have had a good time. Nevertheless, the episode was a distraction from his true vocation and he avoided further foreign postings. For him, the real point of the Quaestorship was that it gave him entry to the Senate. After years of preparation the serious work of his life was, at last, beginning.

He told an amusing story against himself about an incident on his journey home, a reminder that his thirst for recognition was redeemed by an endearing sense of the ridiculous. "I was filled with the notion that the Roman People would fall over themselves to honor and promote me," he recalled. He arrived at the seaside resort of Puteoli at the height of the tourist season and had his nose put out of joint when an acquaintance asked if he'd just come from Rome and what was the news. No, Cicero replied, he was on his way back from his province. "Of course," said the man, "you've been in Africa." No, Cicero observed huffily, Sicily.

Another member of the group, trying to show off his knowledge while smoothing over the misunderstanding, intervened. "Don't you know that our friend was Quaestor in Syracuse?" With this final inaccuracy (for his headquarters in Lilybaeum had been at the other end of the island), Cicero gave up and decided to act as if he were a holidaymaker like everybody else and had gone only for the bathing.

On reflection he thought he had learned a useful lesson. "Once I had realized that the Roman People was rather deaf, but sharp-eyed, I stopped worrying about what the world *heard* about me. From that day on, I took care to be seen *in person* every day. I lived in the public eye and was always in the Forum. I would not allow my *concierge,* nor the lateness of the hour, to close the door on any visitor." He trained himself to remember names and liked as far as possible to do without the services of a *nomenclator,* a slave with a good memory who accompanied a public figure when he went out and whispered in his ear the name of anyone important he was about to meet. Cicero made sure he knew exactly where well-known people lived, where they had their country houses, who their friends and neighbors were. On whatever road he happened to be traveling he could name the owners of the estates he was passing.

Cicero returned to Rome with a growing fortune, a wife and daughter and a bright future. He resumed the pattern of life common to all upper-class Romans of the period. Although he seldom troubled to describe the daily round in his correspondence, there is no reason to suppose that he deviated from the habits and conventions of his friends and peers.

The waking day lasted little longer than the hours of daylight. At dawn Cicero would have risen from his bed in a tiny, barely furnished bedroom and dressed. Traditionalists wore only a loincloth under their togas, but by the first century BC many also put on a tunic, no doubt especially during the winter months. The toga, a remarkably incommodious garment, was a large length of unbleached woolen cloth, cut in a rough circle as much as three meters in diameter. Putting it on was an art and the rich employed a trained slave to arrange its complicated folds. It was draped over the body in such a way that the right arm was free but the left covered. Drafty in winter and stickily hot in summer, it had few practical advantages to recommend it and took continual care and attention to keep in place. But, however uncomfortable, the toga was a Roman's uniform and a powerful visual symbol of citizenship.

The day's work began at once. Breakfast was a glass of water or, at most, bread dunked in wine and served with cheese, honey or olives. Cicero's front door was opened to all comers but especially his clients or followers, who came to pay their respects and accompany him to the Forum when political or legal business took him there. Otherwise, the first half of the day was devoted to work in his study.

As a rule Romans were clean-shaven. They paid a visit every day or so to a barber's shop, a center of gossip and chatter, unless they owned a domestic slave who had the necessary skill with a razor. In the absence of soap, barbers used only water and considerable dexterity was required if the customer was to survive the experience without smarting eyes and cut skin. Young men delayed as long as possible before removing the down on their faces (as so often with the Romans, this was the occasion for a religious ceremony, the *depositio barbae*).

The afternoon was a time for a siesta or at least for winding down. There might be a public entertainment to attend; holidays were frequent and often marked by gladiatorial shows, chariot races, boxing matches or theatrical spectacles. Going to the public baths was the most important, or at least the most regular, of a Roman's relaxations. These were similar to today's Turkish baths, with steam rooms for washing and scraping the body, *tepidaria* for cooling off and cold plunges. The wealthy built small bathhouses in their own homes.

Cicero would take a light lunch or snack if he wished but did not have to wait long for the main meal of the day, dinner, which was taken in the mid- to late afternoon. For a man who liked company, as he did, this was the ideal occasion for entertainment and, witty and well-informed, he was at the top of many guest lists. The food served was as sumptuous as could be afforded and laws were passed in unavailing attempts to limit extravagance. Meals would begin with a *gustatio* or taster—honeyed wine and canapés. The main courses featured a varied diet of meats—chicken, turbot, boar and (a special delicacy) sows' udders and vulvas. Fattened game, fowl and pigs were the height of luxury. Finally came dessert, for which only the lightest food was served—not only fruit but also shellfish.

During the late Republic a fashion grew for collecting fish, which sold for very high prices in the markets. Well-heeled gourmets had fishponds of their own where they bred eels, bream and lampreys. One was sold by a contemporary of Cicero for the astonishingly high price of 40,000 sesterces and the mentor of his adolescence, Crassus, was supposed to have gone into mourning when a lamprey of his died.

Diners, lying on couches, were provided with knives, spoons and toothpicks; forks were unknown and much use was made of fingers. Slaves went around with water jugs and towels so that guests could wash their hands course by course. Wine was served during the meal (rich and heavy, it was usually diluted with water), but the real drinking began once the food had been cleared away. This was the *commissatio*—a ceremonial drinking competition at which goblets had to be drained in a single gulp. Healths were drunk. This was the time for conversation and debate, which might last well into the evening, and was the Roman equivalent to the Greek symposium.

Unless out at a late-night party, most people were safely back at home by sunset, when public life shut down; at this hour Senate meetings were adjourned and the baths closed. For most people bedtime was early, although Cicero admitted to writing speeches or books and reading papers at night (there was a Latin word for it, *lucubrare*—to work by lamplight).

Sulla's reforms promised a return to order. Traditionalists were back in charge and, despite a brief, unsuccessful insurrection by a *popularis* ex-Consul in 77, the Senate's authority had been greatly enhanced. But two major new threats called for urgent attention. Spain, in the hands of a general who had fought under Marius, was in revolt. Then, in 73, a small band of gladiators escaped from their barracks in Padua, set up camp for a time on the slopes of Mount Vesuvius, marched to the cattle ranches of the south and freed thousands of slaves. The gladiators were led by a Thracian named Spartacus, who not only was physically brave and aggressive but was an educated and cultured man. He also had an instinct for generalship and defeated four Roman armies sent out to dispose of him.

Two of Sulla's former *protégés* rose to the occasion. The first was thirty-three-year-old Cnaeus Pompeius (our Pompey), who put down the Spanish rebellion with some difficulty. He was a delightful man to look at. According to Plutarch, "his hair swept back in a kind of wave from the forehead, and the configuration of his face around the eyes gave him a melting look, so that he was supposed (although the resemblance was not a close one) to resemble statues of Alexander the Great." His appearance belied a vigorous organizational energy. A decade previously, on Sulla's return from his eastern wars, he had raised (entirely against the law) an army of his own from the district of Picenum, northeast of Rome, where his family had estates. At the scandalously early age of twenty-three he had appointed himself its commander and been active in wiping out opposition from the defeated *popularis* regime. He had acted so ruthlessly that he had been nicknamed the Butcher Boy (*adulescens carnifex*). It was in these early campaigns that he won the formal, and much politer, *cognomen* of Magnus, the Great—a not altogether deserved compliment, but another link with the memory of Alexander.

Sulla, duly grateful and impressed, promoted Pompey and married him to his stepdaughter. But he soon grew alarmed by his young general's growing prestige and their relationship cooled. In fact, success failed to go to the young man's head. He enjoyed recognition and liked to be busy, but he had no intention of following in his patron's footsteps and taking over the state.

The second of Sulla's former lieutenants to distinguish himself was Marcus Licinius Crassus, a distant relative of the old orator under whom Cicero had trained in his student days. Probably about forty, Crassus was able, affable and unscrupulous. His father and brother had been killed by *populares* when Marius was in power and Crassus had escaped to Spain, where his family had connections. He spent eight months hiding in a cave (friends supplied him with food and a couple of attractive slave girls to while away the time) and came out only on Sulla's return to Rome. However, despite his experiences he developed no particular political convictions and was happy to support *populares* in the future whenever it suited him.

Crassus made his fortune from the proscription, buying up on the cheap the property of those who had been killed. Like Chrysogonus, he was rumored to have inserted an innocent man into the list in order to get hold of his money. He noticed that jerry-built apartment blocks had a tendency to collapse or catch fire and, whenever this happened, he purchased adjacent buildings at knockdown prices—sometimes even while fires were still blazing. He trained teams of slaves as architects and builders and became one of the wealthiest property developers in Rome. He owned silver mines and landed estates and would say that no one could claim to be rich unless he could afford to pay an army's wages.

Crassus lived modestly but his house was open to everyone; guests at his dinner parties were usually ordinary people rather than members of the great families. He lent freely to all and sundry, although he was pitiless when it came to repayment. In the street he was polite and unaffected and was good at flattering people and getting them on his side. He liked to be well-liked and generally was.

Crassus was given the command against Spartacus. The former slave had turned out to be a first-rate general and posed a growing threat. He was in negotiation with the Republic's great opponent in the eastern provinces, Mithridates, King of Pontus, and it was feared he might even march on Rome. But Crassus too was an effective campaigner and in 71 he defeated the slave army in a decisive and bloody battle, during which Spartacus and more than twelve thousand of his companions lost their lives.

Crassus crucified six thousand of the survivors in rows along the Appian Way all the way from Capua, where the revolt had started, to the walls of Rome. He won his victory in the nick of time. Pompey had been recalled from Spain to help dispose of the slaves and arrived with his army just as the battle was coming to an end. There was nothing more to do than help mop up the fugitives, but much to Crassus's irritation, his rival managed to gain a good deal of the credit for a success in which he had played only a minor role.

In fact, the one thing that most upset Crassus throughout his life was Pompey's predominance. Once when someone said, "Pompey the Great is coming," he laughed and asked, "As great as what?" As a rule Crassus did not bear grudges. This was not because he had a good heart but because other people rarely engaged his emotions. He had little difficulty in dropping friends or making up quarrels as occasion served. Cicero, whose view of friendship was different, had a very low opinion of him.

The two generals deserved the state's gratitude for their military accomplishments, but the Senate regarded them as serious threats to the status quo. Yet despite the fact that Pompey was underage, had not yet become a Senator nor yet been elected to any of the magistracies, it proved impossible to stop him from standing as candidate with Crassus for the Consulship in 70. They stood out from the common run of their contemporaries, and had no trouble getting elected.

Pompey and Crassus were on very poor personal terms, and neither wished to be put at a disadvantage vis-à-vis the other. As a result, they hesitated for some time before disbanding their armies; but they could see that if they did not hold firm as partners in the face of Senatorial opposition, they would be picked off separately. Pompey's glamour made him popular with the voters and there was general relief at the winding up of the slave revolt. The candidates added to their appeal by announcing a program of reforms that did away with many of the key components of Sulla's constitution; in particular, they revived the powers of the Tribunes. This was not a disinterested measure, for it gave powerful generals a handy mechanism for bullying or bypassing the Senate.

Another reform under consideration at this time was of particular interest to Cicero. Sulla had transferred the right to sit on juries from the *equites* to the Senate. The result had been judgment by peers at its most debased.

Senators were often charged with corruption and there had been a long line of scandalous acquittals, due to bribery and the unwillingness of jurors to condemn their friends and colleagues. In extortion cases in particular it seemed next to impossible to secure a conviction.

The problem came into sharp focus when a group of leading Sicilians decided to sue their former governor, Caius Verres, who had served an unusually long term of three years, thanks to the demands that Spartacus had made on the time of his appointed successor. During this period Verres had behaved with a greed and ruthlessness that was unusual even by Roman standards.

The chain of events that led to the complaint went back a couple of years. Verres got to know Sthenius, a distinguished Sicilian from the town of Thermae. Both men were art lovers and collectors and for a while they had been on good terms. The governor had persuaded his new friend to part with much of his collection. But when he also demanded some of the city's unique heritage of Greek sculpture (including a sixth-century BC statue of the poet Stesichorus), it was too much for Sthenius, who convinced the local council to say no.

An enraged Verres contrived to have Sthenius taken to court to face a false accusation of forgery. Deeming discretion the better part of valor, the Sicilian fled abroad and was given a heavy fine of 500,000 sesterces *in absentia.* This was not good enough for Verres, who then arranged to have a capital charge laid against him. Sthenius soon appeared in Rome, where he had many connections, to air his grievance. An official complaint was to be put before the Senate, but Verres's father arranged for it to be withdrawn after giving assurances that his son would be persuaded to relent. In spite of this, Verres went ahead with his case and brought in a conviction.

Such was the situation in late 71 when the delegation from Sicily called on Pompey, then Consul-Elect, to ask for his help. They also made contact with Cicero, who now counted Sicilians on his client list, and asked him to bring a case of extortion against Verres. This was the only legal remedy available to them, for they were not allowed to plead in court themselves and were obliged to find a Roman lawyer to act on their behalf. The young Quaestor's friendliness and lack of bias were not forgotten—nor the forensic skills he had demonstrated during his Sicilian posting. Although not yet acknowledged as the leader of his profession, he was an obviously rising star and seemed a sound choice.

Throughout his career Cicero usually represented the defense; this was one of the rare occasions when he prosecuted. The conventions of clientship gave him little option but to agree to do so. He may have calculated that his involvement in such a high-profile event would do no harm to his chances when he stood for Aedile in the summer of 70, the next lap in the Honors Race. Aediles reported to the Consuls, on whose behalf they exercised various administrative duties in Rome; these included looking after the grain supply, the control of markets, streets and traffic and the prosecution of offenders against moneylending laws. They were also responsible for staging public shows and games. (There were two kinds of Aedile: Plebeian, open only to the popular classes, and Curule, for which both Plebeians and Patricians were entitled to stand; Cicero probably ran for the former.)

Verres and his friends in the Senate were uneasy. His counsel was the best that could be found: Quintus Hortensius Hortalus. Eight years older than Cicero, he was a virtuoso of an elaborate "Asiatic" (as it was called) style of oratory, and the most celebrated member of the Roman bar. In case this was not enough to win an acquittal, steps were taken to sabotage the proceedings in various ways. First, an attempt was made to prevent Cicero from appearing at all. There being no state prosecution service, anyone could bid to take on a case; a friend of Verres, who had once been his Quaestor, volunteered to prosecute him—with the clear intention of pulling his punches and so reducing the risk of conviction. Also, if possible, he would drag out the trial till the following year, when a number of Verres's friends would probably be assuming important official positions. (Hortensius, for example, was running for Consul.)

So a preliminary hearing had to be held to determine which of the competing advocates had priority. Cicero won the decision and then asked for a stay of trial for 110 days so that he could collect evidence and recruit witnesses. He traveled to Sicily with his cousin Lucius in the depths of an unusually harsh winter and began his investigations. The current governor of Sicily was Lucius Caecilius Metellus, a friend of Verres and a member of one of Rome's most aristocratic clans. His good offices, supplemented by the recycling of some of Verres's ill-gotten gains back to Sicily in the form of bribes, hindered Cicero's detective work. Local communities were unexpectedly reluctant to appoint delegations to attend the trial. Although Cicero was entitled to ask for documents, they were not always produced. Witnesses became mysteriously unavailable for questioning.

Cicero was undeterred, tracking people down to remote cottages or fields where they were working at the plow. He completed his inquiries in fifty days and, after a trying, storm-tossed voyage in a small boat, was back in Rome for the summer well before his deadline was up.

An unpleasant surprise awaited him. The case had been delayed by the specious interposition of another trial and was now unlikely to take place before August. This was a serious blow, for there were very few *fasti* days between August and mid-November when trials could be heard. This was partly because of the large number of regular holidays and festivals, but also because Pompey was planning some additional games to celebrate his Spanish victory.

Worse was to come. Hortensius and Quintus Caecilius Metellus Creticus, Verres's patron, won the Consular elections for the following year, 69, and a few days later yet another Metellus was elected Praetor, with responsibility for the extortion court before which Cicero would be appearing. On top of that, a fourth Metellus was appointed to follow his brother as governor of Sicily. The only good news was that an attempt to prevent Cicero from being elected as Aedile was decisively thwarted. In fact, he scored a notable success, leading his competitors by a large majority.

From Verres's point of view, the battle seemed to be won before it started. Taken overall, the election results were almost as good as an acquittal and congratulations began to pour in. Of course, it would be necessary to put up with the formality of trial, but a formality was all it was expected to be. When proceedings opened in the Forum on August 4, the accused man had reason to feel optimistic.

Cicero thought hard about the tactics he should use in court. He knew that the evidence he had assembled was detailed and robust, but he had to find a way of preventing the case from trickling desultorily through the autumn into the new year. He decided to launch a surprise attack. Roman trials usually began with long addresses by the advocates. With permission from the presiding Praetor, Cicero gave up the opportunity for time-consuming oratorical display and, after a brief introduction detailing Verres's delaying tactics, proceeded directly to the evidence itself. He showed methodically, and with full reference to witnesses and documents, that during his three years in Sicily Verres had amassed the enormous sum of 40 million sesterces.

"Today the eyes of the world are upon you," Cicero told the jurors, fearing that they would allow themselves to be suborned. "This man's case will establish whether a jury composed exclusively of Senators can possibly convict someone who is very guilty—and very rich. Let me add that because the defendant is the kind of man who is distinguished by nothing except his criminality and his wealth, the only imaginable explanation for an acquittal will be the one that brings the greatest discredit to you. No one will believe that anybody likes Verres, or that he is related to any of you, or that he has behaved well in other aspects of his life, no, nor even that he is moderate in his faults. No such excuses can extenuate the number and scale of his offenses."

It was crucial that Cicero finish his presentation before the court went into recess with the opening of Pompey's games on August 16. In the event, he managed to set out his material expeditiously as well as comprehensively. On August 13 he rested his case.

Cicero's coup was devastating for the defense and had immediate consequences. Clearly, it was no longer feasible for Verres and his friends to try to keep the trial going indefinitely. Far more serious, though, was Hortensius's reaction. He was appalled by what he had heard and his sense of having been ambushed by Cicero magnified the impact of the evidence. He withdrew from the case without saying a word in response. Verres drew the inevitable conclusion and left at once for Massilia (in Transalpine Gaul) and a lifetime of exile. He was able to take his fortune with him, for he was as yet unconvicted, and so did not have to sacrifice his extorted comforts.

On the following day the jury, despite having been heavily bribed, had no choice but to bring in a guilty verdict. A fine of 3 million sesterces was levied—a derisory figure but probably the maximum that could be legally claimed. Hortensius was persuaded to return to court and speak in mitigation. As a reward Verres gave him an ivory figurine of a sphinx. In the course of his own address, Cicero made some enigmatic remark and Hortensius interrupted: "I am afraid I'm no good at solving riddles." "Oh, really," snapped Cicero. "In spite of having a sphinx at home?"

Although Cicero had done little more than call witnesses and examine them, he had been able to display his eloquence, or at least his wit, in a number of heated exchanges. He had no hesitation in delivering brutal and sometimes tasteless put-downs. When a Jewish freedman named Caecilius (his name suggests he was an ex-slave of the Metelli) tried to push himself forward instead of the Sicilian witnesses, Cicero remarked scornfully: "What can a Jew have to do with a pig?"—"Verres" meaning "castrated boar" in Latin. At another point in the proceedings, when Verres attacked Cicero for not having the most virile or healthy of constitutions, he replied: "Virility is something you would do better to discuss with your boys at home." (One of Verres's sons was supposed to be promiscuously homosexual.)

Even though their property was not restored, the Sicilians were delighted by the verdict. Cicero's routing of Hortensius was a professional turning point. He was now beyond dispute the leading advocate of his day. Not wanting to waste the results of his researches, he worked up the documentation he had gathered on Verres into a series of speeches which he might have delivered had he had the chance.

These made a powerful case for reform of the courts and the jury system and also allowed Cicero to demonstrate his mastery of presentation. He spoke explicitly on the subject. "Gentlemen of the jury, you must take thought and make provision for your public credit, for your good name, for your common interest in self-preservation. Your spotless characters make it impossible for you to behave badly, save at the cost of damaging and endangering the state. For if you are unable to arrive at a correct judgment in this case, the Roman People cannot expect that there will be other Senators who can. It will despair of the Senatorial Order as a whole and look around for some other type of man and some other method of administering justice." Later in the autumn the Senatorial monopoly of juries was rescinded and their share of the membership reduced to one third, the remainder being allocated to *equites.*

On January 1, 69, Cicero took up his duties as Aedile and addressed the task of staging various festivals—that of Ceres with its circus games on or about April 19; ten days or so later, the celebrations in honor of Flora, goddess of flowers, with its program of popular plays and striptease shows; and from September 4 to 19 the great Roman Games (*Ludi Romani*), which featured drama performances and chariot races. Aediles were expected to supplement the official budget from their own pockets and there was fierce competition to stage the most splendid and extravagant events. Cicero's resources were limited and he could not afford the kind of conspicuous expenditure with which Julius Caesar would cut a dash when he was Aedile later in the decade. However, his *clientela* in Sicily apparently made up for any deficiencies by flooding Rome with foodstuffs and so keeping the cost of living artificially low. This won Cicero golden opinions among the urban masses.

He continued to be very busy in the law courts, where his dominance was confirmed by Hortensius's gradual withdrawal into a luxurious private life. He undertook no further prosecutions. Cicero led the defense in the trial of a provincial governor who faced corruption charges. Although probably a Verres on a small scale, he was presented as being completely innocent, beyond the shadow of a doubt. Cicero's conscience was clear; he took the view that an advocate's task was to win, not to uncover the truth. As he observed towards the end of his life: "It is the judge's responsibility always to seek the truth in trials; while it is the advocate's to make out a case for what is probable, even if it doesn't precisely correspond to the truth."

In 68 the surviving correspondence with his old school friend Atticus begins. For the first few years only a handful of letters survives (the flood starts in 61), but they provide our first direct insight into Cicero's personal life. Although Quintus, his younger brother, made no attempt to compete with him as a public speaker, he too set his sights on a political career and served as Quaestor. With Cicero playing matchmaker, Quintus had married Atticus's sister, Pomponia, a couple of years earlier. Both husband and wife were hot tempered and the relationship was stormy. Sexual chemistry seems to have been lacking. In November 68, Cicero reported to Atticus his attempts to act as marriage counselor. He was anxious that "my brother, Quintus, should feel towards her as a husband ought. Thinking that he was rather out of temper I sent him a letter designed to mollify him as a brother, advise him as my junior and scold him as a man on the wrong track." His efforts seem to have had some success, for in the following year he reported that Pomponia was pregnant. She gave birth to a son, who, following Roman custom, was named after his father.

In the same letter we meet other members of the family for the first time: Cicero's wife, Terentia, who "has a bad attack of rheumatism," and his daughter, "my darling little Tullia," perhaps now seven or eight years old. In the following year, she was formally engaged to Caius Calpurnius Piso Frugi, great-grandson of a distinguished historian and Consul. This aristocratic link was an important aspect of Cicero's plan to establish himself as a rising man in public life. The wedding took place some years later, in 62.

In 65 Cicero's second and last child, Marcus, was born. Cicero's father probably died at about this time, and so did his dearly loved cousin, Lucius, who had been with him in Greece and had helped him collect evidence against Verres. They had been very close. Cicero was deeply upset and told Atticus: "All the pleasure that one human being's kindness and charm can give another I had from him."

The letters between the two friends show a growing interest in property investment. Atticus bought an estate near the town of Buthrotum in Epirus, across the strait from the island of Corcyra. Here he raised sheep, cattle and horses on a large scale. Cicero was not interested in farming; what he wanted was a country retreat, or more precisely a growing number of them, where he could refresh himself and renew his energies away from the noise and ceaseless social demands of Rome. He acquired a villa at Formiae, a fashionable seaside resort, and another at Tusculum, in the Alban Hills southeast of the city, which had once belonged to Sulla. Although the exact number is uncertain, Cicero ultimately owned at least nine villas and other real estate.

Of all his properties Tusculum was, and remained, his favorite. "I am delighted with my place at Tusculum, so much so that I feel content with myself when, and only when, I get there." He spent large amounts of money on decoration and sculpture; he knew he was being extravagant, but could not stop himself. A hundred years later a citrus table of his was still in existence, which was reputed to have cost him the fabulous sum of 500,000 sesterces. He was always pestering Atticus in Greece to look out for any suitable *objets d'art,* and he used his uncomplaining friend as purchaser, shipping agent and artistic adviser. Contemporary taste favored the masterpieces of Greek art, whether copies or, more expensively, originals.

It is an interesting question how Cicero made his money. He inherited land and property from his father and Terentia's dowry had been handsome. But, as a Senator, he was not allowed to engage in trade or to invest money for interest; although many of his colleagues cheated or bent the rules, there is no evidence he did so. It was not the done thing to profit from book sales and his record as a public administrator suggests that he resisted bribes. He was not allowed to charge legal fees. However, those whom he defended in the courts were expected to find ways of expressing their gratitude and many named him in their wills. Looking back at the end of his career, Cicero estimated that he had grossed 20 million sesterces in legacies, a very substantial sum, which would make him a multimillionaire by today's standards.

Cicero was becoming a man to reckon with in the Senate, as well as in the law courts. His provincial origins remained an obstacle in aristocratic circles, where he was looked down on as a pushy nobody. The time was approaching when he would be eligible for senior office and he could count on opposition from the great families. However, Cicero was not to be deterred. His dominance as a public speaker made him a household name and he could depend on support from his growing *clientela* among the commercial and mercantile class.

In the first permissible year he was elected at the age of forty to the Praetorship, taking office in 66. There was nothing to prevent public officials from accepting briefs in the courts and Cicero remained much in demand as an advocate. From this time on he stopped appearing in civil suits and specialized exclusively in the criminal law; he developed a particular expertise in two offenses which had political implications: improper influencing of voters *(ambitus)* and extortion in government *(crimen repetundarum).*

During his year as Praetor, Cicero appeared in an extraordinarily complicated multiple murder case, which threw a lurid light on vice and corruption in provincial society. He defended Aulus Cluentius Habitus, who was accused of poisoning his stepfather, Statius Albius Oppianicus. Most of his speech concentrated on a series of trials eight years earlier, when Cluentius had successfully prosecuted Oppianicus for attempting to murder *him.* Public opinion was on Oppianicus's side and Cicero had to show that the original verdict had been right. He took the jury step by step through Oppianicus's bizarre career, showing how, for personal gain, he had systematically killed eleven members either of his own family or of others into which he had married. Cicero made no effort to simplify the narrative and was happy to concede that, in the interests of his client, he had "wrapped the jury in darkness."

The case also gave Cicero the opportunity to score a political point. During his defense of Cluentius he reinforced his reputation as a supporter of the *equites* by making flattering references to their importance as a class. Now that he was within sight of the Consulship, the apex of government, it was important to assure himself of their backing. A newcomer to the charmed circle of Roman politics, he had to maximize his support across the political spectrum if his candidacy was to have a chance of success. This meant somehow keeping on good terms with both the *populares* and the *optimates,* the radicals in the Assembly Ground and the diehards in the Senate. "You know the game I am playing," he confided to Atticus, "and how vital I think it not only to keep old friends but to win new ones."

The most sensitive issue of the hour concerned the future role of Pompey, whose name was being put forward to take over the command of the Roman army in Asia Minor. In the years following Sulla's death, Mithridates of Pontus had gradually rebuilt his forces and raised the standard of revolt for a second time.

Cicero had to decide what line he was going to take about the proposed appointment. The *optimates* in the Senate were vehemently opposed. They had not forgiven Pompey for dismantling Sulla's reforms during his Consulship. It was not only this that annoyed traditionalists but his unstoppable subsequent progress as a general and administrator. In 67, in the face of furious Senatorial opposition, Pompey had been given a special command with wide-ranging powers covering all coastal regions to rid the Mediterranean of the growing scourge of piracy. The appointment had been so popular that the price of corn in Rome had immediately fallen. The operation had been expected to take some time, but through efficient organization Pompey had accomplished the task in three months.

Everyone could see that the crisis in Asia Minor called for military talent of the highest order. Since 74, an able general, Lucius Licinius Lucullus, had been campaigning against Mithridates with considerable success. Unfortunately, Lucullus had infuriated the Roman tax farmers by lowering taxation and now his soldiers, losing patience after eight years in the field, were in a state of mutiny. Despite his achievements, Lucullus clearly had to be replaced and Pompey was the obvious successor. With the victory over the pirates still ringing in everyone's ears, the Senate would be hard put to resist yet another special commission. But this was unlikely to stop it from trying.

Cicero decided to support Pompey. In 66, making the first political speech of his career, he addressed the General Assembly in favor of the appointment. His tone was fawning. Listing Pompey's achievements, he said: "Such is his unbelievable, superhuman genius as a commander. A little while back I was beginning to speak of his other qualities as well; and they too are as superlative as they are numerous." The Praetor and would-be Consul was walking a tricky line. His fundamental position was conservative, but, in light of growing social and political divisions, he recognized the urgent need for reconciliation. His real opinion of Pompey at this point is uncertain. The great commander had been often abroad and, although the two men were of the same age, Cicero had been too junior a figure until recently to have been worth cultivating.

The special command against Mithridates was not something Cicero would have cared much about in itself. Rather, the controversy gave him an opportunity to do two things: first, to establish himself as a man who could bring the different classes together and resolve their differences or, to use his musical metaphor, make the orchestra of Roman society play in tune; and second, to attract a broad base of support for his eventual candidacy for the Consulship. This meant winning the attention and the approval of the People while at the same time not unduly offending the Senate. At this point it was in his interest to present himself as something of a *popularis,* but he took great care to be polite to leading *optimates.* The speech was an early, unacknowledged opening of his election campaign.

The sincerity of Cicero's populism at this stage in his political development is hard to gauge. He was perfectly willing to support reforms but tended to see them as concessions to avert discontent rather than as desirable in their own right. Like many politicians before and after him, he was rather more open to radical ideas when campaigning for votes than he was when he no longer had to run for office.

Cicero's attempts to keep all sides happy nearly went adrift. It so happened that a number of *populares* appeared on various charges before his Praetorian court, and he did not want to spoil his credentials with the People by presiding over guilty verdicts. In one case that we know of, he managed to effect a condemnation without offending public opinion. He commented to Atticus: "My handling of C. Macer's case has won popular approval to a really quite extraordinary degree. Though I was favorably disposed to him, I gained far more from popular sentiment by his conviction than I should have gained from his gratitude if he had been acquitted."

He found himself in more serious trouble at the end of his year as Praetor. Cicero decided to postpone the trial of a Tribune who had recruited street gangs and intimidated the courts until after he left office. From his point of view, acquittal or conviction would be equally dangerous. The former would infuriate the Senate and the latter the People. However, the postponement backfired. At a public meeting voices from the crowd called him a "turncoat." Taken aback, Cicero promised that he would defend the Tribune himself. Luckily, for some reason, the trial never took place.

In 65 he again braved Senatorial disapproval when he agreed to defend a former Tribune, Caius Cornelius, on a charge of treason—no doubt largely because he was a supporter of Pompey, whom Cicero wished to please. The trial was a *cause célèbre* and attracted much attention. Cicero's speech on Cornelius's behalf was a success and he was acquitted by a decisive majority. With great skill Cicero managed to ensure, as he told Atticus, "both that he did not assault the standing of his distinguished opponents and that he did not let the defendant be undermined by their influence."

The Senate was not greatly perturbed. Cornelius was essentially a moderate and Cicero had few serious worries about helping him. However, he was openly suspicious of extremists and he took care to make this clear. Pompey and his supporters were one thing, the unscrupulous circle of radical politicians that had gathered around the multimillionaire Crassus was quite another. Cicero sided firmly with the *optimates* when Crassus proposed the annexation of Egypt, which had been left to Rome by the will of its last king. The richest man in Rome was also the greediest and had his eye on the fabulous riches of the Pharaohs. Cicero agreed with his fellow Senators that Crassus had to be stopped and spoke out vigorously against his insatiable pursuit of wealth. No action was taken to claim a bequest the Egyptians were certain to resist.

Cicero distrusted and disliked Crassus and his criticism of him was sincere; but it also conveniently enabled him to demonstrate that there was a point beyond which he would not go in his flirtation with *popularis* sentiment. He wanted the Senate to know that he could be trusted and that he was a conservative at heart.

5

AGAINST CATILINA

Campaign and Conspiracy: 63 BC

Cicero aimed to scale the summit of Roman political life at the first possible opportunity or, as the phrase went, "in his year." A two-year interval was required by law between a Praetorship and a Consulship and when he left office as Praetor in December 66, Cicero laid down his powers completely, forgoing the customary provincial governorship, and at once began planning his campaign for the Consulship in 63. The election would be held in the summer of the preceding year.

Quintus wrote a "Short Guide to Electioneering" (*Commentariolum petitionis*) for his brother, in which he set out a comprehensive campaign strategy. (Some scholars regard the document as a rhetorical exercise of the imperial age, but, with its good sense and knowledge of the period, it is to all appearances authentic.) There is a good deal in it which today's politicians would find instructive, as when Quintus observed that candidates should not hesitate to be generous with pledges and assurances. "People naturally prefer you to lie to them rather than refuse them your help," he writes. There is advice about the specific obstacles Cicero was facing, chief of which was his status as a New Man. "You must cultivate [the aristocrats] diligently. You must call upon them, persuade them that politically we have always been in sympathy with the *optimates* and have never in the least been supporters of the *populares*."

Of Cicero's six rivals, four were hopeless electoral prospects, respectable but dull—and in one case probably dull-witted. The other two raised very different considerations. Caius Antonius was the son of the great orator, Marcus Antonius; he was corrupt, often insolvent and with little native ability or pluck. He had been disgraced in 70 and expelled from the Senate but managed all the same to be reelected to the Praetorship. Although unimpressive, he was acceptable to the political establishment and for that reason had to be taken seriously.

Lucius Sergius Catilina was an altogether more formidable opponent. He was one of a line of able and rebellious young aristocrats during the declining years of the Roman Republic who refused to settle down after early indiscretions and enter respectable politics as defenders of the status quo. They usually joined the *populares.* Sometimes they did so out of youthful idealism and intellectual conviction, but others were simply rebelling against family discipline. They often badly needed money.

In recent years the failure of agriculture and the sudden block in trade with, and tax revenues from, the eastern provinces following the resurgence of Mithridates had created a cash-flow crisis for the state of Rome and for many citizens. So far as we can make it out, the main plank of Catilina's political program was a general cancellation of debts. This thoroughly frightened the propertied classes. How much popular support the policy attracted is harder to say. In the absence of a proper banking system, the web of credit spread through every level of society. While debt cancellation would to some extent benefit the poor more than the rich, in many respects it would simply shift the problem of financial liquidity around the system rather than get rid of it, replacing one set of bankrupts with another.

Whatever Catilina's precise policies, he stood for, or was part of, the wider *popularis* movement, which step by step was dismantling Sulla's reforms and was set on weakening the Senate's hold on the levers of government. The radicals seem not to have had a clear set of proposals and seized opportunities as they came along.

The Senate had no answer to Rome's problems and indeed sought none. Its aim was simply to maintain the constitution and resist the continual attacks on its authority. Above all, it needed to conserve its forces for the day of Pompey's return. On the likely assumption that he would defeat Mithridates and bring Asia Minor back under Roman control, he would acquire immense prestige and would overshadow all his peers. Not only that, he would come back to Italy at the head of a victorious army and would be in a position to control, or even take over, the government.

Born into an old but impoverished family, Catilina was about the same age as Cicero. Their paths had first crossed during the War of the Allies, when they both served as very young men on Cnaeus Pompeius Strabo's military staff. Later, during the civil war between Sulla and Marius, Catilina had taken part in the horrifying murder of Cicero's cousin and Marius's nephew, the Praetor Marcus Marius Gratidianus. He had been accused, with what truth we do not know, of having had sex with a Vestal Virgin, Fabia, the half-sister of Cicero's wife, Terentia. He was also believed to have killed his own son because he was in love with a certain Aurelia Orestilla, who would not agree to marry a man with a child. Despite a pervading smell of scandal, he rose steadily up the political ladder and was Praetor in 68. He then spent a year as governor of the province of Africa and was back in Rome in mid-66.

It was at this point that he began to flirt with revolutionary illegality. Like other reformers before him, Catilina found it advisable to surround himself with bodyguards. Hostile contemporaries put a sexual gloss on this. "No one has ever had such a talent for seducing young men," Cicero remarked. Sallust claimed that Catilina recruited "debauchees, adulterers and gamblers, who have squandered their inheritances in gaming dens, pot houses and brothels."

Like every Roman politician Catilina needed to create a coterie of supporters on the basis of favors provided. What was unusual about him was his focus on the young; this may reflect his social and personal tastes or, alternatively, hostility in respectable circles, where alarmist stories deterred mature and experienced citizens from joining his cause. His following was said to include criminals and informers alongside members of his own class. He was reported to reward his youthful supporters handsomely for their loyalty, procuring mistresses for some and dogs and horses for others. Cicero gave an account of a party attended by a certain Quintus Gallius, a friend of Catilina, which evokes the raffish atmosphere of his circle.

> There are shouts and screams, screeching females, there is deafening music. I thought I could make out some people entering and others leaving, some of them staggering from the effects of the wine, some

> of them still yawning from yesterday's boozing. Among them was Gallius, perfumed and wreathed with flowers; the floor was filthy, soiled with wine and covered with withered garlands and fish bones.

The picture classical historians give of Catilina is a garish one and there is evidence that it may be exaggerated. Some years later, in 56, Cicero found himself obliged, to his clear embarrassment, to put in a good word for Catilina when he was representing one of his former followers on trial for murder. He offered a less diabolic likeness of a complex and many-sided personality, and one that is both more plausible and more attractive. He said:

> Catilina had many excellent qualities, not indeed maturely developed, but at least sketched out roughly in outline. . . . There was a good deal about him that exercised a corrupting effect on other people; and yet he also undeniably possessed a gift for stimulating his associates into vigorous activity. Catilina was at one and the same time a furnace of inordinate sensual passions and a serious student of military affairs. I do not believe that the world has ever seen such a portent of divergent, contrary, contradictory tastes and appetites.

Whatever the truth about his personality, Catilina now began to get into serious trouble. He was put on notice of trial for extortion in Africa. At about the same time, during the summer of 66, the two Consuls-elect for 65 were disqualified for bribery. Catilina would have liked to stand for one of the vacancies but, because of the legal threat hanging over his own head, was debarred. Furious, he is said to have colluded with the two disgraced men and a bankrupt young noble in a plot to assassinate the replacement Consuls when they took up office on January 1, 65, kill as many Senators as possible and seize one of the Consulships for himself. The plot, if it existed at all, failed and the moment passed.

Some have argued that Cicero had a hand in making up or greatly embellishing the story (he referred to it in an election speech, for which a politician is not on oath). It is impossible to deduce what really happened from the available evidence. But it is probably true that at worst Catilina was beginning angrily to flex his conspiratorial muscles. This confused business is known as the first Catilinarian conspiracy, but the above version of events may simply have been black propaganda devised against Catilina a couple of years later.

Two more substantial figures can be detected in the shadows of this mysterious affair. Caius Julius Caesar was now a mature politician in his mid-thirties. Working with Crassus, who provided generous subsidies, he quietly supported Catilina's endeavors from the wings. Indeed, according to another version of the story, it was not Catilina (who does not even receive a mention) who conceived the massacre of Rome's political establishment, but Crassus and Caesar, who planned to become Dictator and his deputy, the Master of Horse, respectively. A different denouement was offered to this story: Crassus, through nervousness or scruple, failed to turn up at the appointed hour. So Caesar decided that discretion was the better part of valor and failed to give the agreed signal for the assassination.

It is an unlikely tale, but, if some kind of *coup d'état* was being attempted, the key player would surely have been Crassus rather than Caesar. The accusations implicating Caesar can be traced to imaginative attacks by his opponents. Crassus, by contrast, had both the means and a powerful motive for trying to assert himself as the leading man in the state—namely, the continuing, maddening dominance of Pompey. He would have been irritated by the fact that the two men who won the by-elections for the Consulship of 65 were known adherents of Pompey. However, having helped Catilina financially, he may have gone on to ask himself whether, on reflection, it was in his interest as a multimillionaire to support a man who proposed to abolish debts. Massively rich but politically cautious, he was willing to wound but afraid to strike.

Caesar was beginning to move center stage. Throughout his career he was always a high spender, on both his pleasures and his politics. When he was Aedile in 65, he borrowed himself almost into bankruptcy to create the most exciting and magnificent spectacles and gladiatorial shows that money could buy, which he piously dedicated to the memory of his dead father. He set up stands in the Forum to create an arena into which gladiators emerged from the network of tunnels below the pavement. But he went further: building temporary colonnades, he took over most of the rest of the square and the neighboring halls as well as the Capitol Hill and crammed them with exhibitions. He wanted to make sure that his year as Aedile was not soon forgotten.

In the eyes of his contemporaries, Caesar was cast in the mold of a Catilina: bright, radical and scandalous. He had already acquired an exotic reputation. His adventures during his teens when he had been on the run from Sulla had been only the start. In his twenties, like many young upper-class Romans, he had gone soldiering in Asia and won the Civic Crown—an award analogous to the Medal of Honor—for conspicuous gallantry in action. He may also have had a brief love affair with the King of Bithynia, but it did not inhibit his vigorous sex life among the wives of his contemporaries back in Rome. A Senator once referred to him in a speech as "every woman's man and every man's woman" and for the rest of Caesar's career he had to endure much heavy-handed jocularity about the incident.

A few years later Caesar was captured by pirates, who were endemic in the Mediterranean; while waiting for his ransom to arrive he got onto friendly terms with his captors, but warned them that he would return and have them crucified. They thought he was joking. They were not the last to underestimate Caesar's determination and regret it. As soon as he was free, he raised a squadron on his own initiative, tracked down the pirates and executed them, just as he had promised.

The fact that he was a nephew of Marius impeded his political progress under the Sullan constitution and the dominant Senatorial establishment. However, he had displayed traits which seemed clearly to promise future success: courage, rapidity of reaction, a refusal to let emotion control his decisions, absolute loyalty to friends, pride in race and an easy sociability which gave way, when necessary, to an equally easy ruthlessness.

Above all, his powers of observation and analysis enabled him to see more quickly than other politicians what was possible and what was not. Caesar pulled away from the impulsive Catilina, who plunged down a path that was bound to lead to disaster. Even if he did succeed in overthrowing the Senate with the help of his scented youngsters, it would be a brief victory: Catilina was hardly likely to survive Pompey's return to Italy. Caesar realized that the *popularis* cause would succeed only if the great general was won over or at least neutralized. It was to this purpose that he turned his mind in the coming years.

As spring turned into summer and the election for the following year's Consulship approached, there was a concentration of minds among the governing classes in Rome. After careful consideration and despite their distaste for New Men, the *optimates* decided to back Cicero as the best of the evils on offer. In fact, the more observant of them could see that the Senate's obstinate passivity was counterproductive and that Cicero would take a thoughtful and active approach to promoting its interests. However, an awkward matter presented itself. Cicero had neither the means nor the will to buy victory. So it may have been no accident that shortly before the vote the Senate decided to tighten up the rules against corruption at the polls; this would be necessary if Cicero was to compete effectively with Catilina and Antonius, both of whose campaigns were apparently being bankrolled by Crassus.

Cicero was particularly uneasy about Catilina. At one point he thought of taking on his defense against the impending extortion charges in return for cooperation over his candidacy. "We have the jury we want," he told Atticus sardonically, "with the full cooperation of the prosecution. If he is acquitted, I hope he will be more inclined to work with me in the campaign." This is one of the very few occasions when we see Cicero on record as willing to aid and abet corruption, a sign of his desperation to win. In the end, though, he gave up the idea and Catilina proceeded to secure a rigged acquittal without Cicero's help.

Cicero's other main rival, Antonius, was a much more malleable character. He had little aptitude for leadership in any direction, good or bad; Quintus said that "he was frightened of his own shadow." However, he was happy enough to give additional support to someone who took the lead, a quality Cicero was to make the most of later.

Cicero decided to play to his own strength: he would use his skills as a public speaker to blacken his opponents. This would be a safer tactic than setting out policies which would be bound to offend the People whose votes he needed or the Senate on whose patronage he depended. He delivered a ferocious speech against Catilina and Antonius, citing the possibly nonexistent conspiracy of the previous year and attacking their political and private records. Both men had dirtied their hands during the proscription. Of Catilina, Cicero asked: "Can any man be a friend of someone who has murdered so many citizens?" He continued in that rip-roaring vein. "He has fouled himself in all manner of vice and crime. He is soaked in the blood of those he has impiously slaughtered. He has robbed the provincials. He has violated the laws and the courts." He categorized Antonius as "this ruffian in Sulla's army, this cut-throat at the entrance to Rome." He also dropped some dark hints about their secret backers. "I assert, gentlemen, that last night Catilina and Antonius, with their attendants, met at the house of a certain nobleman well known to investigations of extravagance." He had to mean either Crassus or Caesar, one of whom had the money and the other the flair for spending it.

Cicero claimed that a new plot was brewing and there is evidence that something sinister was afoot. Before the Consular election, which took place in June, Catilina called a meeting of friends and dissidents. A list of those present survives: it includes the rejected Consular candidates of 65; Lucius Cassius Longinus, brother of the Cassius who would conspire against Caesar many years later; an old blue-blooded reprobate, P. Cornelius Lentulus Sura, who had already been Consul but, like Antonius, had been expelled from the Senate and was running for Praetorship in 63 in order to gain reentry. A man of no great note was also present, a certain Quintus Curius, who had been expelled from the Senate in 70. His importance was to lie in the fact that he had a talkative mistress named Fulvia. Members of the local nobility from the Italian colonies and municipalities visited Rome in order to attend the gathering. Finally, according to one first-century account, Crassus or Caesar was involved. If true, they were playing for very high stakes. By now they must have been questioning Catilina's political judgment: the charge is best seen as guesswork by hostile contemporaries.

In the event, Cicero won the election by a wide margin, heading the vote in all the wards. Admittedly, he had been lucky in his rivals, but he had succeeded without bribery or violence. For a New Man to win the Consulship was a remarkable accomplishment. In less than twenty years, Cicero had risen from being a little-known lawyer from the provinces to being joint head of state of the greatest empire in the known world. His triumphs in the law courts and his successful ascent up the honors ladder were due to his own abilities and native talent.

The election was a great day for Terentia as well as her husband. She had taken a risk when she married the newcomer from Arpinum, but now it seemed she or her relatives had chosen well and she joined the band of powerful matriarchs who exercised considerable influence behind the scenes. The record of the Consulship suggests that this strong-willed woman showed little hesitation in offering her husband political advice and support.

Cicero had lived through terrible times and his fundamental aim was to make sure that they never returned. He stood for the rule of law and the maintenance of a constitution in which all social groups could play a part, but where the Senate took the lead according to ancestral tradition. His colleague was the feeble Antonius, with whom he struck an astute deal. Cicero, not wanting the usual governorship that followed a Consulship, agreed to give up the rich province he had been allocated, Macedonia, and pass it to Antonius. This would enable Antonius to recoup his debts (or more precisely, his election "expenses") by the normal techniques of extortion. In return he would give Cicero a free hand during their Consular year and withdraw his support from Catilina, from whom trouble could be expected. This meant in effect that Cicero would be sole Consul.

Catilina was enraged by his defeat. Some time during the following months, Crassus and Caesar reviewed their options; they concluded that Catilina might become dangerously unreliable after this disappointment and began to scale down their support. They would have been reassured by Catilina's decision to be patient and stand again for Consulship in 63. But if he could not win the first time around, would he be likely to do so a second time, with the Senatorial cause now in the capable hands of Cicero? Probably not. In future he would not be able to rely on their backing.

When Cicero entered office on January 1, 63 BC, the economic situation was bleak. Although the signs were that Pompey would defeat the King of Pontus, reopen the trade routes, set up the tax farmers in business again and come home loaded with booty, that still lay in the future. Victory was in sight, but for the time being Italy was suffering.

One consequence was that levels of unemployment in Rome were high. This was serious, for in the absence of a police force or any security services, it was easy for mob rule to flourish. So far as poor free-born citizens were concerned, life was precarious and many survived on jobs in the building trade or at the docks. Freedmen usually had the backing of their former owners and a wider range of specialist skills at their disposal; they probably dominated the retail trade and small-scale industrial enterprises. Both groups were suffering under the recession.

Meanwhile the endemic crisis of the countryside worsened. The south of Italy was still suffering from the after-effects of the Slave War. Also, many of Sulla's veterans had been settled in Etruria fifteen years previously, within striking distance of the capital: they had either been allocated poor-quality agricultural land or turned out to be unlucky farmers. Either way they were in trouble, and of a mind to make their unhappiness known.

The rich were in some difficulty too. When the recession hit them, their finances were already strained by various forms of conspicuous expenditure—in particular, the fashion for building *horti,* large and expensive villas with gardens outside the city, or holiday homes on the coast at resorts like Baiae. The costs of public life were high, with increasing pressure on candidates to spend a fortune in bribes or on theatrical shows and gladiatorial games. Some great families were running the shameful risk of insolvency.

The *populares* immediately threw down a challenge to the new regime. In January 63 a Tribune tabled the first land-reform bill for years. It was generally thought that, once again, Crassus and Caesar were behind the move. This presented Cicero with a ticklish problem. He was indebted to the *optimates,* who were as hostile to the redistribution of state land as their fathers and grandfathers had been, and indeed shared their conservative instincts. But if he could, Cicero wanted to be a Consul for all, believing that Rome would not have a future without what he called the *concordia ordinum,* the "concord of the classes."

On the face of it, the bill's contents were sensible and moderate. Colonies were to be established by selling public land in Italy and the provinces and by buying additional privately owned land on a voluntary basis. Nevertheless, Cicero opposed the legislation both in the Senate and at the General Assembly, thus opening his Consulship on a negative note.

The proposed law was probably less contentious than the means of implementing it—a powerful commission with ten members and a life of five years. This was too much for a political culture that disapproved of power being handed for a substantial period of time to any individual or group. Cicero derisively nicknamed the commissioners the "ten kings." It is not entirely clear what ensued, but in all likelihood the bill never came to the vote at the General Assembly.

Crassus and Caesar were probably not too put out by this setback. They had made some gains. The debate had cast doubt on the sincerity of Cicero's promise to be a Consul for all. It had also inserted a wedge between him and Pompey, who would soon have an army to resettle.

Meanwhile, Cicero maintained his oratorical predominance in the courts. He successfully defended a former Consul on a charge of extortion, a case in which Caesar gave evidence for the prosecution.

Caesar and his friends now staged a remarkable coup, a real-life agitprop drama with an unfriendly lesson for the Senate. Titus Labienus, a member of Caesar's circle and later one of his most able military commanders, unexpectedly indicted an elderly and inconspicuous Senator, Caius Rabirius, on a charge of high treason for a murder committed thirty-six years previously, when Saturninus had surrendered to Marius, then Consul, and been locked up with his followers in the Senate House. According to Labienus, Rabirius was one of the young men who had climbed on the roof and killed Saturninus with a rain of tiles.

This was no ordinary prosecution. The old man was to be tried under an archaic and brutal procedure called *perduellio.* The punishment, if he was found guilty, was scourging and crucifixion. A court was appointed according to the antiquated rules and Caesar and his cousin cleverly managed to get themselves chosen as its two judges. An execution post was erected in the Field of Mars in anticipation of a conviction.

What was the point of this bizarre rigmarole? Apparently the identity of Saturninus's killer had long been known: a slave who had won his freedom as a reward. What Labienus and, behind him, Caesar wanted to do was deliver a political warning. In times of crisis the Senate had the authority to call a state of emergency, through a special decree known as the Final Act (*senatusconsultum ultimum*). Its terms were broadly drawn: "The Consuls should see to it that the state comes to no harm." This, some said, allowed the Consuls to override a Roman citizen's basic rights not to be executed without trial. According to this view, Saturninus's death had been legal because the Senate had passed the Final Act—despite the fact that he had been no ordinary citizen but a Tribune whose person was meant to be inviolable. *Populares* never accepted this interpretation of the law and argued that nothing could cancel a fundamental civic liberty. Legally they appear to have been correct; the power under the Final Act to condemn citizens to death without due process had only become accepted through time and custom.

The reason for the timing of the attack on Rabirius is obscure. In general terms, it was in the interest of the *populares* continually to find ways of seizing the initiative from the *optimates.* This was especially the case now that the Senate, in Cicero's capable hands, looked as if it would recover lost ground. Rabirius's trial may then have simply been an episode in the ongoing campaign against the forces of conservatism. But there is another possibility. Caesar knew that Catilina had not yet run his full political course. If rejection at the polls drove him to act illegally, as appeared not unlikely, he might need protection from an extreme interpretation of the Final Act. In this case, the affair shows Caesar at his most prescient and most loyal.

Unsurprisingly, the judges found Rabirius guilty and passed a sentence of death. As expected, he appealed to the People against the verdict. Hortensius spoke on Rabirius's behalf, arguing that he did not in fact commit the crime. He was followed by Cicero, who spent little time on the facts of the case. This was a political show trial and he went straight to the constitutional point. "What I assert with all the emphasis at my command, what I proclaim, what I publish to the world is identical with the stated opinions of the prosecutor [Caesar or Labienus]. No king remains, no tribe, no nation who can cause you any alarm. No external or foreign threat can infiltrate our Republic. If you wish Rome to live forever and our empire to be without end, if you wish that our glory never fade, we must be on our guard against our own passions, against men of violence, against the enemy within, against domestic plots. But against these evils your forefathers left you a great protection [in the Final Act]. Cherish this pronouncement."

A vote on the appeal never took place and sources disagree about which way it looked as if it would go. After fruitlessly remonstrating with the judges, a Praetor, Quintus Caecilius Metellus Celer, used one of Rome's many obstructive constitutional devices to halt the proceedings. He ran up to the fort on top of the Janiculan Hill on the other side of the Tiber and pulled down the military flag flying there. In the city's early history this flag was raised during assembly meetings; if lowered, it warned of an enemy attack and led automatically to the immediate suspension of public business. The rule was still in force and so the assembly dispersed.

How serious had Caesar been? It is hard to say. It may be that the trial was a neat and painless way of twisting the Senate's tail. If that were so, Caesar had presumably prompted Metellus Celer to abort the project before the old man was crucified. On the other hand, it is possible that Caesar really did want a guilty verdict and, one must suppose, an execution. Either way, he had made his point and he did not attempt to reconvene the court.

In 63 Caesar stood for the senior religious post of Chief Pontiff, chairman of the college of *pontifices,* the most important political function of which was to decide the annual calendar of lucky and unlucky days for the conduct of public business. It was usually the preserve of ex-Consuls and elder statesmen and Caesar contracted enormous debts to bribe the necessary voters. Success brought him little power but great prestige and an official residence in the Forum. If Caesar had lost, his credit would have collapsed and he would have been bankrupt. He told his mother, as she kissed him good-bye on the morning of the poll, that if he did not return as Chief Pontiff, he would not return at all.

Meanwhile Catilina was pursuing his schemes and the well-informed Cicero went on keeping an eye on him. Support for Catilina was more broadly based than at the time of his putative first conspiracy. Many Senators who had spent or gambled away their wealth saw nothing to be lost and much to be gained by joining him. A general cancellation of debts, the central plank of his policies, would solve all their problems. Unsurprisingly, this was a program unlikely to appeal to the propertied classes and indeed to the middling sort of people—shopkeepers and small traders. The revolutionary leader was under growing pressure from his supporters in Rome, and from the discontented Sullan veterans in the countryside to seize power by fair means or foul.

At the instigation of a friend from his youth, Servius Sulpicius Rufus, now a distinguished legal expert and candidate for the Consulship of 62, Cicero superintended the passage of a law increasing the penalty for electoral bribery to ten years' exile. Sulpicius was in fact aiming at one of his rivals, Lucius Licinius Murena, whom he intended to prosecute under the new legislation. However, Catilina believed that he was the target. Infuriated, he decided to have Cicero and other leading figures assassinated. The plan was to attack them on the day in July when elections for next year's officeholders were to be held.

Cicero learned about the plot from Fulvia, mistress of Catilina's fellow plotter, Quintus Curius. Curius, who was in financial difficulties, had become less generous to Fulvia than previously and she had pulled away from the liaison. In an attempt to regain her affection, Curius boasted in mysterious terms about his future prospects. Fulvia wheedled the truth out of him. She immediately contacted Terentia, with whom she happened to be acquainted, and told her all she knew. Thereafter, Cicero used Fulvia as a regular informer and, in due course, Curius was himself persuaded to betray his fellow conspirators. Unfortunately, there was no other evidence to corroborate the allegation of conspiracy, and it was not easy to identify specific plans from a welter of wild talk.

Cicero was sufficiently alarmed to persuade the Senate to postpone the forthcoming elections. He questioned Catilina publicly in the Senate about his intentions. Catilina responded with a sinister metaphor: "I see two bodies, one thin and wasted, but with a head, the other headless, but big and strong. What is so dreadful if I myself become the head of the body which needs one?" The first body was the Senate and the second the People. The remark was a bold and threatening claim to leadership of the masses.

The Senate was not convinced of Catilina's seriousness and took no action. Many *optimates* still thought of Cicero as a parvenu and felt that he was getting above himself by creating an atmosphere of crisis on the basis of very few facts. This left the Consul in a distinctly awkward position. He had revealed his hand to no avail. Catilina was now alerted to his investigations and, given his personality, might well be provoked into a violent response. Cicero appointed a bodyguard and was careful to let people see that he had started wearing a breastplate under his toga.

When the postponed elections eventually took place, Cicero insured himself against the risk of violence by assembling a large number of armed followers. This and all the publicity preempted Catilina's plans and there were no assassinations. The voting proceeded without any trouble. Quintus, following in his brother's footsteps in the Honors Race, was elected Praetor, as was Caesar, who won by a strong margin.

Catilina failed for a second time to secure the Consulship. So far as he was concerned, this was the final insult. During the two years that he had been running for Consul, Catilina's second "conspiracy" had probably been more a secret alliance around a radical program (land redistribution and debt cancellation) than a revolutionary plot, but now, enraged by Sulpicius's antibribery law and his electoral defeat, he abandoned legality. Against his better instincts, he had stuck by the rules, and look where it had gotten him. His aim was personal—to claim what he saw as his right and to take revenge on everyone who had prevented him from obtaining it. This included Cicero and most of the Senate. He set his mind on a *coup d'état.*

His closest partners were Praetor Lentulus in Rome and Caius Manlius, one of Sulla's old centurions, who was gathering a military force in northern Etruria at Faesulae. Catilina was reported to have insisted on a "monstrous" oath of loyalty, which even his friend the Consul Antonius swore. According to Dio (and Plutarch): "He sacrificed a boy and, after administering the oath over his entrails, ate them in company with others." This sounds far-fetched and was probably another example of black propaganda, but there was a half-submerged tradition of occasional human sacrifice. The last recorded case had taken place after the battle of Cannae, when Hannibal had scored one of his most decisive victories. Two Gauls and two Greeks had been buried alive. The great Greek historian Polybius, writing in the previous century, noted that in times of extreme danger the Romans would go to any lengths to propitiate the gods and thought no ritual inappropriate or beneath their dignity.

Seeing what Catilina had in mind, Crassus, who was not a revolutionary at heart, and Caesar, doubtless as disturbed by Catilina's poor judgment as by his intentions, definitively abandoned him. For all his difficulties with a skeptical Senate, Cicero was clearly receiving good intelligence, and he looked forward to assembling enough evidence to be able to take action against Catilina.

There was a lull for a time as summer gave way to autumn. Then, at about midnight on October 20, Cicero received an unannounced visit from Crassus and two leading Senators. They had an alarming tale to tell. After dinner earlier the same evening Crassus's doorkeeper had taken delivery of some letters for various senior Romans. Crassus read the one addressed to him, which was unsigned. It claimed that Catilina was organizing a massacre and warned him to slip away from the city as soon as possible. Crassus said that he had left the other letters unopened and come at once to Cicero—"quite overcome by the news," as Plutarch puts it, "and wishing to do something to clear himself from the suspicion that he lay under because of his friendship with Catilina."

Having thought the matter over, Cicero convened a meeting of the Senate early the next morning. It may have occurred to him that Crassus, rattled by Catilina's behavior and to avoid being implicated in some wild adventure, had himself arranged for the mysterious letters to be written and "delivered." That did not matter; the important thing was that he at last had something that looked like proof. Once the Senate had assembled, Cicero handed the letters to their recipients, who read them aloud to the meeting. They all contained information about a plot. Next a report was given on the formation of regular bands of soldiers in Etruria; it was claimed that Manlius would take the field on October 28. The Consul asked to be given emergency powers.

So far, the Senate had been treating Cicero as something of a joke and the words "I have been informed that," which opened his constant announcements that the state was in peril, had become a catchphrase. However, the Senators had no choice now but to give him, through the Final Act, the authority he had been asking for. For a few days nothing happened and there was no news. Perhaps the Consul had got his facts wrong. A week or so later, a relieved Cicero was able to announce that, just as predicted, Manlius had risen.

Military countermeasures were taken and troops levied to put down disturbances. An attempt to capture Praeneste, a town only about 20 miles from Rome, was foiled. Catilina, at his best in a crisis, kept his nerve. No direct links had been discovered between him and Manlius and he stayed in town, behaving normally. Seeing that a prosecution was being threatened, Catilina offered to surrender himself into custody, cheekily suggesting that he be kept under arrest at Cicero's house. The Consul declined the ambiguous honor and Catilina took up residence in the house of the Praetor Metellus Celer. Metellus was married to a sophisticated and promiscuous noblewoman, Clodia, sister of Publius Clodius Pulcher, who at the time was one of Cicero's supporters and joined his bodyguard.

On the night of November 6 Catilina somehow managed to leave

Metellus's house and attended an important planning meeting with the other conspirators. Evidently morale was low, and he did his best to raise everyone's spirits. His absence seems to have escaped the Praetor's notice, but the indispensable Fulvia, briefed by her lover, was on hand to tell Cicero later in the evening what had been discussed.

Cicero's growing confidence is illustrated by the fact that he waited until November 8, two days later, before summoning the Senate to meet at the temple of Jupiter the Stayer near the Palatine Hill, which was easier to guard than the Senate House. He had extraordinary news to impart and the occasion was all the more dramatic in that Catilina, although he must have known or guessed that his cover was blown, put in an appearance. The Senate's mood had hardened and few members spoke to him or sat beside him. At the meeting, the Consul addressed Catilina directly:

> I am able to report how [on November 6] you came into Scythemakers' Street (I will be perfectly specific) and entered the house of Marcus Laeca: and many of your accomplices in this lunatic, criminal enterprise joined you there. Do you dare to deny it? . . . You parceled out the regions of Italy. You decided where you wanted each of your agents to go. You divided up the city for the benefit of the incendiaries. You confirmed that you yourself would be leaving and added that the only thing that held you back for a little was the fact that I was still alive.

Cicero reported that two of those at the meeting had agreed to go to his house in the early hours, somehow gain entry and murder him in his bed. Forewarned, he had increased his guard and arranged that the men, ostensibly presenting themselves to convey "the morning's greetings," were refused admission.

A heated exchange between the two protagonists in the drama followed. According to Sallust, Catilina reacted fiercely to the speech, calling Cicero an "immigrant" and refusing to go into voluntary exile without a trial. Cicero asked the Senators if they wished to banish Catilina. This was an ill-judged intervention. Embarrassed by Catilina's presence, the majority said nothing. Cleverly retrieving the situation, Cicero then asked if they would order him to banish Quintus Lutatius Catulus, one of the House's most respected members. They roared back, "No." This allowed the Consul to claim that, by its silence, the Senate had in fact consigned the revolutionary to exile.

Catilina said he would think over what he had heard and left the meeting freely. He understood that all was up for him in Rome: only the military option remained. He slipped out of the city that night, accompanied by 300 armed men, and made his way north to Manlius's troops. Before he left he wrote an explanatory letter to the elder statesman Catulus. If it is genuine, and it reads so, it almost touchingly reveals a man, self-centered yet sincere, who had nothing left to hope for.

> I do not intend . . . to make any formal defense of my new policy. I will however explain my point of view; what I am going to say implies no consciousness of guilt, and on my word of honor you can accept it as the truth. I was provoked by wrongs and insults and robbed of the fruits of my painstaking industry, and I found myself unable to maintain a position of dignity. So I openly undertook the championship of the oppressed, as I had often done before. . . . I saw unworthy men promoted to honorable positions [and] felt myself treated as an outcast on account of unjust suspicions. That is why I have adopted a course of action, amply justified in my present circumstances, which offers a hope of saving what is left of my honor. I intended to write at greater length, but news has come that they are preparing to use force against me. So for the present I commend Orestilla [his wife] to you and entrust her to your protection. Shield her from wrong, I beg in the name of your own children. Farewell.

Claiming the office of which he believed he had been robbed, Catilina assumed a Consul's rods and axes. He also took with him a silver eagle, a military standard that had belonged to Marius and which he kept in a shrine at his house. He took his time to reach Faesulae, arriving in mid-November. As soon as the Senate heard the news of his departure/defection, he and Manlius were declared public enemies.

In Rome the management of the conspiracy devolved to the middle-aged Lentulus. It is strange that he and his colleagues did not abandon their plans. Perhaps they were still under the influence of Catilina's outsize personality. Perhaps they feared to break their oaths. Perhaps they felt they were on a vehicle careering out of control and that it was marginally safer to stay on board than jump off. Whatever their reasons, they held to their course.

Although Lentulus had a contemptuous attitude toward the proprieties of public life, he was a superstitious man and was apparently encouraged by some forged prophecies predicting that he would achieve absolute power (from which it may be inferred that he was not averse to supplanting Catilina). He decided on a wholesale massacre of the Senate and timed it for one of the nights of the Saturnalia in mid-December. This festival of misrule (a distant original of Christmas) would provide cover for the preparations. It was the custom for clients to bring their patrons presents, and houses were kept open all night for the purpose. About 400 men, carrying concealed swords, were detailed to kill Senators individually in their homes. Lentulus devised a solution to the problem of the returning Pompey; his children would be taken as hostages against his good behavior. The plan had a frivolous kind of ingenuity, but, as ever, Fulvia was able to pass on the details to Cicero.

The Consul was now interrupted by a legal matter. As he had promised he would, Sulpicius prosecuted Murena for handing out bribes during his election campaign. Cicero defended him and, although exhausted, produced one of his most entertaining speeches. He poked fun at legal terminology and scoffed at Marcus Porcius Cato, a leading conservative who was a member of the prosecution team, for his extravagant commitment to the doctrines of Stoicism. "But I must change my tone," he said coyly,

> for Cato argues with me on rigid and Stoical principles. He says that it is not right for goodwill to be enticed by food. He says that men's judgments, in the important business of electing men to office, ought not to be corrupted by pleasures. So, if a candidate invites a man to supper, he commits an offense. "Do you," he asks, "seek to obtain supreme power, supreme authority, and the helm of the Republic, by encouraging men's sensual appetites, by soothing their minds, by offering them luxuries? Are you seeking employment as a pimp from a band of lecherous young men, or the sovereignty of the world from the Roman people?" What an extraordinary thing to say! For our customs, our way of living, our manners, and the constitution itself reject it. Consider the Spartans, the inventors of that

> lifestyle and of that sort of language, men who lie down at mealtime on hard oak benches, and the Cretans, none of whom ever lies down at all to eat. Neither of *them* has preserved their political constitutions or their power better than the Romans, who set aside times for pleasure as well as times for work. One of those nations was destroyed by a single invasion of our army, the other only maintains its discipline and its laws thanks to our imperial protection.

Cato sourly observed: "What a comical Consul we've got!" Murena was acquitted.

It was time to deal with Lentulus. With almost incredible stupidity, the conspirators played into Cicero's hands. It so happened that a delegation from the Allobroges, a Gallic tribe with a grievance, was in Rome. Lentulus thought it would be a good idea to let them into the conspiracy and encourage them to stir up a revolt in Gaul. The Allobroges were uncertain how to react and consulted their patron in Rome, one Fabius Sanga (a forebear of whom had conquered the Allobroges in 121 BC). He brought them at once to Cicero, who instructed them to negotiate with the conspirators.

An elaborate sting was devised. The Allobroges were asked to obtain documentary proof of the conspiracy by persuading the conspirators to write letters to the tribe's Senate. They did so, also sending along a messenger, a man from Croton, with an unsigned communication for Catilina, whom the Allobroges were invited to visit on their way home. In addition, the messenger was given a word-of-mouth recommendation that Catilina should commit one of the most heinous offenses in the Roman catalog: the freeing of slaves to take up arms against the Republic.

The Allobroges left Rome on the night of December 2 and ran into an ambush, led by the Praetor Caius Pomptinus, which Cicero had laid at the Milvian Bridge across the Tiber just outside the city. Everyone was arrested and brought back to the city. Here, at last, was all the evidence that could be desired. Cicero convened the Senate early the following morning, aptly enough at the Temple of Concord at the foot of the Capitoline Hill.

Most of the day was taken up with hearing the evidence and receiving reports. The man from Croton was given immunity, and he testified. Four Senators took down verbatim notes at the Consul's request, so that a full and accurate record of the debate would be available. (Cicero arranged for clerks with shorthand skills to attend future sessions.) The house of one of the conspirators, Caius Cornelius Cethegus, was found to be stacked with weapons, spears, armor and a large number of knives and swords. Lentulus, as a senior magistrate, underwent some sort of cross-examination. He resigned his office as Praetor, taking off his purple-bordered toga on the floor of the Senate and putting on other clothes more in keeping with his new situation.

It was a cut-and-dried case. The leading conspirators were handed over to the Praetors to keep them under arrest, although not in chains, and there was a scare when slaves and freedmen of Lentulus and Cethegus came around by back streets to the Praetors' houses and tried, unsuccessfully, to rescue them. Cicero left the debate briefly to station guards in appropriate places in the city.

In the evening dense crowds gathered outside the Temple of Concord and, when the Senate adjourned, Cicero came outside to make a short speech to the crowd: he made the most of the horror stories about firing the city, freeing the slaves and inviting a Gallic invasion. Large numbers of people then escorted him to a friend's house where he spent the night. He was unable to go home, for Terentia was presiding, as the Consul's wife, over a secret ceremony in honor of the Good Goddess in the presence of the Vestal Virgins, from which men were forbidden. Those attending the ceremony were well aware of what was happening outside; when a flame suddenly shot up from a dying fire on the altar, it was immediately interpreted as a portent and a message was sent out to Cicero advising him to take action against the conspirators.

What should be done with the prisoners? In principle, as Roman citizens, they should receive a trial, but that would entail a dangerous delay while Catilina was in the field. The mood in the city was volatile, and the likelihood of bribery would make the outcome of any court proceedings uncertain, however strong the prosecution's case. The alternative was to execute the men without delay. This was both legally and politically problematic. The trial of Rabirius was still fresh in everybody's mind. Caesar had used the case to limit the force of the Final Act. As Cicero was well aware, Caesar could well organize a backlash if citizens were killed without a proper hearing. While a Consul had power over life and death when in office, he could be called to account in the courts after the end of his term.

It could, of course, be argued that the conspirators had abrogated their citizenship by taking up arms against the state. This would self-evidently be the case with Catilina, who was at the head of a hostile army. But as for Lentulus and the others, the position was less clear-cut. They had not been caught in the act of rebellion, although the cache of weapons was damning evidence of their intentions.

Cicero decided to cover his back by asking the Senate, which met again two days later, for its opinion. He indicated that he would implement whatever they decided, although he implied that he favored execution. He called on the Consul-designate, Junius Silanus, to speak first. Silanus argued for the "extreme penalty," which everybody took to mean death. The other Consul-designate, Murena, agreed, as did the bench of ex-Consuls. It looked as if there would be no argument. But then the Praetors-Elect were invited to speak and Caesar stood up to address the meeting.

He spoke with great severity. No form of punishment could be too harsh for the crime, he said. But the death penalty would be a mistake. The accused were men of distinction. Death without trial would create a disastrous precedent and, although he had "no fear of Marcus Tullius," another Consul might use his power despotically. The text of his speech has not come down to us, but Cicero's response has. In the published version Cicero is recorded as saying, "Imprisonment, [Caesar] says, was unmistakably devised as the special penalty for atrocious crimes. He moves, therefore, that the defendants should be imprisoned, and distributed among the municipalities for their incarceration." If Caesar had indeed argued for long-term, perhaps life imprisonment, his suggestion would have been hard to take seriously in a country that did not have residential jails. How would the conspirators be looked after? Surely there would be a high risk of escape. (The previous day, after all, had seen an attempt to free the prisoners.)

According to later sources, Caesar in fact proposed that Cicero "ought to distribute the accused around the towns of Italy, as he thought best, until Catilina had been suppressed and they could be brought back for trial." No doubt, he had in mind house arrest at the homes of local worthies. This was a more rational and practical proposition and one far more difficult to oppose. It is probably what was actually said, in which case Cicero distorted Caesar's position in his published address. He would have had good reason for doing so, for it was not long before he needed every argument he could muster to defend the decision that was actually taken.

It would help him if he could show, or suggest, that Caesar's alternative was unrealistic.

One way or another, Caesar's speech was a courageous and clever act. It had a decisive impact, and opinion turned against execution. Silanus recanted, saying he had meant not death but imprisonment. Only one ex-Consul, Catulus, spoke against Caesar's proposal.

Then Marcus Porcius Cato, an influential figure still only in his early thirties, took the floor. Cato was one of the most remarkable and idiosyncratic personalities of the age. An uncompromising Republican, he was a ferocious opponent of the *populares* and of anyone who breached the constitution. From his childhood on he had had an obstinate nature and his name became a byword for virtue and truthfulness. "That's incredible, even if Cato says so," was a common expression.

As a boy he had been "sluggish of comprehension and slow, but what he comprehended he held fast in his memory." He had loved a half-brother, who died young, with the same almost monomaniac excess with which he adhered to his opinions. Cato had rigid views of right and wrong, and he had no sense of humor. He was impervious to physical discomfort. Apart from the fact that he was a heavy drinker, he lived austerely, sometimes not troubling to wear shoes. Although not averse to making money, he was ferociously opposed to bribery and corruption in public life. As Quaestor in 65, he was responsible for the management of the Treasury: he reformed the lax financial procedures he found there, upsetting the civil servants and his Senatorial friends. Cicero admired him, but found him difficult to handle, mainly because he had no aptitude whatever for compromise.

Cato was a good public speaker with a loud, penetrating voice, although, unusually for the age, he did not practice rhetorical exercises or rehearse his speeches in public. Once he was on his feet he could speak for hours and was an indomitable filibusterer. On this occasion he was blunt. He attacked Silanus for changing his mind but reserved most of his scorn for Caesar. Under a popular pretext and with humane words, he said, Caesar was trying to subvert the state. He wanted to frighten the Senate about a situation from which he had a good deal to fear himself. Why was the Senate hesitating? The conspirators had confessed to planning massacres and arson. "If we could afford to risk the consequences of making a mistake," Cato said (according to Sallust), "I would be quite willing to let experience convince you of your folly, since you scorn advice. But we are completely encircled. Catilina and his army are ready to grip us by the throat, and there are other foes within the walls, in the very heart of our city." He concluded by putting a motion to the house: "Having admitted their criminal intention, they should be put to death as if they had been caught in the actual commission of capital offenses, in accordance with ancient custom."

An incident occurred while Cato was speaking which caused much amusement at his expense. A letter was brought in for Caesar, and Cato immediately accused him of being in touch with the conspirators. He challenged him to read the note out loud. Caesar simply passed it across: it was a love letter from Servilia, Caesar's mistress at the time and Cato's half-sister. Cato threw it back angrily with the words: "Take it, you drunken idiot."

The speech was the only one of Cato's ever to be published and is a good example of his ability, when he fixed his mind on something, to see it with exceptional clarity. He was one of the first to recognize the seriousness of the threat Caesar posed to conservative interests. The Senate was impressed and shifted its ground again, endorsing Cato's motion for the death penalty. Picking up a suggestion of Caesar's, they also ordered the confiscation of the conspirators' property. Caesar protested that it was unfair for the Senate to endorse the severest element in his proposal while rejecting his recommendation for mercy. Cicero acknowledged the point and remitted the confiscation.

Caesar now appears to have lost his temper. According to Suetonius, he tried to block the proceedings. A body of *equites* outside, serving as a defense force for the House and presumably listening through open doors, threatened to kill him unless he desisted. They unsheathed their swords and made passes at him. Some friends huddled around him and protected him with their arms and togas. The guards looked at Cicero, who shook his head. Daunted, Caesar left the meeting and did not attend the Senate for the rest of the year.

What were the legal rights and wrongs of the argument? In the absence of a complete knowledge of the Roman legal system, it is hard to be sure. The *populares* may have been correct to argue that the Final Act did not override citizens' basic rights. Cicero's insistence on consulting the Senate before deciding what to do with the prisoners suggests that he was aware of the possible validity of their view. However, it is interesting that in his intervention Caesar did not raise the question of the legality of summary executions. The facts that Lentulus and his friends had admitted their guilty intent and that weapons had been found in their possession may have been enough to place them outside the protection of the law. However, unlike Catilina, the conspirators had not yet put their armory to any use. So the issue came down to whether plotting to commit treason could be equated with the act of treason itself. Cato was in no doubt that this was so, but he was arguing in the heat of the moment. In the final analysis, he and the other Senators were behaving not as legal experts but as politicians forced to come to a quick decision in an emergency. Nobody at the time challenged their right to do so.

Leaving the Senate in session, Cicero, surrounded by leading Senators, went to collect the prisoners one by one from the Praetors' houses. There was no announcement, but the crowds in the Forum sensed that, after the noise and drama of debate, something real and irreversible was under way. Most observers thought that at this stage the men were simply being taken to prison. Apparently no one expected that there would be immediate executions.

A frightened silence descended as the Consul brought Lentulus from the Palatine Hill and led him down the Holy Way to the far corner of the Forum, where the state prison stood. Prisoners were thrown into the dungeon, originally built as a cistern, which was entered through a hole in the roof, and usually left to starve or to await the executioners. According to Sallust, "its filthy condition, darkness and foul smell give it a loathsome and terrifying air." Lentulus was lowered inside and strangled with a noose. The Praetors went to collect the other four prisoners and they too were led down to the dungeon and executed in turn.

For the time being few people knew what was going on. Cicero decided not to make any announcements at this stage, for he noticed groups of people standing here and there in the Forum who had played minor roles in the conspiracy. They were waiting for nightfall when they hoped to make a rescue bid. Once the executions were over, though, there was no further need for silence. The Consul walked into the Forum and shouted in a loud voice: "They have lived," avoiding a direct and unlucky mention of death.

Night began to fall and the mood of the crowd changed. As often happens after the relief of tension, there was an explosion of hysterical high spirits. Still accompanied by Senators, the Consul made his way home across the Forum and up the Sacred Way. He was cheered along streets brightly lit by lamps and torches in doorways and on roofs. The Senate had conferred on him the title "Father of His Country," and when Cato repeated the compliment outside, doubtless at the top of his voice, everyone applauded. It was the proudest moment in the life of Marcus Tullius Cicero. Here he was, center stage in his chosen arena, the Forum, the hero of the hour and the first man in Rome. Nothing again in the years that lay ahead would happen quite like it.

As for Catilina, the dreadful news from Rome soon reached his troops and they began to melt away. He was said to have recruited 20,000 soldiers, but in a little while he had only one quarter of that number. His old friend Antonius was given the task of tracking him down. On the day in February 62 when the two armies met, the reluctant general, no doubt diplomatically, pleaded gout and left the battle to his deputy. It was an easy but bloody victory. Catilina fell beside Marius's standard—we are told, fighting hand-to-hand to the last. The encounter was probably little more than a messy one-sided skirmish. But Catilina was dead.

For all the jibes of the *optimates,* Cicero had averted a danger to the state. In contrast with his later reputation for vanity and indecision, he had acted with intelligence, patience and firmness. He had amply fulfilled the administrative promise of his Quaestorship in Sicily and shown that he was better able to govern than many of his peers. The conspiracy was perhaps less of a threat than Cicero claimed. Nevertheless, Catilina represented, if only in caricature, the continuing challenge from the *populares* and a new model of politician. His defeat was likely to have serious implications for activists like Caesar.

The outgoing Consul had reason to be proud of his stewardship of the Republic, but success had come with a cost. His efforts before he took office to be all things to all men, to please the radical as well as the conservative interest, had failed. His refusal to countenance the land-reform bill in January and his decision to execute the conspirators without trial (especially after the warning of the Rabirius affair) placed him firmly on the side of the *optimates.* Cicero's cover was blown.

6

PRETTY-BOY'S REVENGE

The Good Goddess Affair and the Return of Pompey: 62–58 BC

The Father of His Country believed that, thanks to him, the Republic was safe. There were, to be sure, troubles ahead. Pompey and his legions would soon return from Asia Minor and the victorious general would expect to play a leading role in the state; just conceivably, if given an excuse, he might act like Sulla, march on Rome and establish an autocracy. The *populares* had lost decisively with the defeat of Catilina, but the snake was only stunned. Caesar, who had been plotting against the Senatorial interest behind the scenes, was rising up the political ladder and, barring accidents, would be Consul in a few years' time. It would be Cicero's task, which he felt to be well within his abilities, to hold the balance between the competing parties.

Overelated by his Consulship, he refused to stop talking about it. His listeners soon grew tired of him. "One could not attend the Senate or a public meeting nor a session of the law courts without having to listen to endless repetitions of the story of Catilina and Lentulus," Plutarch writes. "This unpleasing habit of his clung to him like fate."

Cicero's boastfulness was not simply an expression of conceit, although that played a part. Privately, he mocked himself for "a certain foolish vanity to which I am somewhat prone." However, the prestige, or *dignitas,* which was the essential political and social attribute of a leading Roman rested on a combination of his own achievements and those of his ancestors. Cicero had only the former to maintain his status, and so he felt obliged to keep himself firmly and prominently in the public eye by ostentation and constant self-praise. He also encouraged his friends and acquaintances to write about him and his achievements.

Cicero's position was not nearly so preeminent, nor so secure, as he supposed. As it turned out, a reaction against him was under way even before his triumph ended. Pompey, who had been watching events from afar, saw in the military threat from Catilina an opportunity for his recall as the only man able to meet it. This would strengthen his position vis-à-vis the Senate, from which he expected trouble back in Rome. He asked his brother-in-law, Quintus Caecilius Metellus Nepos, who was a Tribune, to obtain a special command for him against Catilina and to do his best to remove the gloss from Cicero's Consulship.

Metellus Nepos launched his attack on the last day of the year. It was the custom that, just before leaving office, Consuls gave a public account of their stewardship to the People gathered at the Assembly Ground in the Forum. Cicero was looking forward to his first major opportunity to publicize his record, but Metellus Nepos put a stop to the festivities. Accompanied by a fellow Tribune, he used his power of veto and refused to let Cicero speak. Seated on benches in front of the Speakers' Platform, they told Cicero that he could only make the traditional oath on leaving office and then had to step down.

Cicero agreed to do as asked, but he was determined to have the last word. Instead of the usual formula, he improvised a new oath. He said: "I swear to you that I have saved my country and maintained her supremacy." Later in the day he appealed to Metellus Nepos through intermediaries to soften his hostile attitude. Metellus Nepos replied that his hands were tied, for he could not go back on his public statement. He had insisted that someone "who had punished others without a hearing should not be given the right to speak himself."

The message was sinister and unmistakable. Metellus Nepos, and so presumably Pompey, was in alliance with *populares* like Caesar. The Tribune went on to promote a bill commissioning Pompey to restore order in Italy, but by then Catilina was dead and his army destroyed. So another decree was laid before the People, allowing Pompey to stand for the Consulship in his absence. Caesar, now Praetor, was on hand to help and seated himself with Metellus Nepos on the platform in front of the Temple of the Castors in the Forum to superintend the vote.

As expected, Cato, also a Tribune that year, entered a veto. But Metellus Nepos had assembled a troop of gladiators and other fighters, who were waiting in the side streets. He now unleashed them on the crowd, and most of the Senatorial party withdrew under a hail of blows—except, to no one's surprise, for Cato, who obstinately held his ground until one of the Consuls, fearing for his safety, pulled him inside the Temple. Yet despite these strong-arm measures, there was too much opposition from the assembled crowd to proceed with the vote, and the proposal was abandoned.

The Senate sensed that Metellus Nepos had overplayed his hand and suspended both him and Caesar from their official functions. Caesar knew when to recognize defeat: he dismissed his lictors, changed out of his purple-edged toga and went home. However, with typical tactical brilliance, he quickly retrieved the situation. When noisy crowds shouted for his reinstatement, he went out into the Forum and persuaded them to disperse. It is hard to avoid wondering whether this was improvisation or a cleverly scripted piece of street theater. In any event, the Senate was so surprised and gratified by his good behavior that it pardoned him and he returned to his duties as Praetor. As for Metellus Nepos, he made his way back to Pompey to report the failure of his mission.

Undaunted by the attempt to undermine him, the former Consul decided that he needed a new, more opulent house to match his prestige. Towards the end of 62, he purchased one of the grandest mansions in the city's grandest quarter, the Palatine Hill, overlooking the Forum. It belonged, unsurprisingly, to Crassus. The house stood on a northeastern spur of the Palatine and had a magnificent view of the city. Its location could not have been more convenient; the Forum was only a few minutes' walk—or litter ride—down Victory Rise. Cicero's visitors and hangers-on did not have far to go to pay their morning calls. Space in the city center was in short supply and the house was one of the few with a substantial garden. It contained a fine walk of poplar trees together with an exercise ground (*palaestra*), which, following the Greek custom, was also used for philosophical debates.

The purchase price was high, some 3.5 million sesterces, and Cicero had to borrow heavily to find the money. It was awkward that just at this juncture he found himself short of ready cash. Part of his arrangement with Antonius, his fellow Consul, had been a large loan financed by Antonius's expected profits as governor of Macedonia. He was also rumored to have negotiated another loan with one of the conspirators, whom he had successfully defended on a bribery charge. Unfortunately, he found it difficult to get the cash out of Antonius and had to send a freedman to Macedonia to look after "our joint profits."

Cicero greatly enjoyed buying houses—he called his collection of eight or so villas the "gems of Italy." In addition to the palace on the Palatine, there was his family home in Carinae, which he had inherited from his father and now passed on to Quintus, and others in Argiletum and on the Aventine Hill, which were rented out and brought in an income of 80,000 sesterces. There was the family estate at Arpinum, and he owned two small farms near Naples and Pompeii (where he also had a house); he also acquired a number of small lodges or *diversaria,* which wealthy Romans used as private wayside stops along the main roads in the absence of comfortable hotels. Some of his properties he bought, but others were legacies or presents from clients he had represented in the courts.

He had his preferences. The house at Formiae, on the Campanian border about 50 miles north of Pompeii, was "not a villa—it is a public lounge." As ever, his pride and joy was the place at Tusculum, within easy reach of Rome, where he continued to spend money on improvements. Writing about another property (acquired towards the end of his life) on the tiny wooded peninsula of Astura on the coast near Antium, he observed to Atticus: "This district, let me tell you, is charming; at any rate it's secluded and free from observers if one wants to do some writing. And yet, somehow or other, 'home's best'; so my feet are soon carrying me back to Tusculum. After all, I think one would soon get tired of the picture scenery of this scrap of wooded coast."

Now that he no longer had official duties, Cicero kept himself busy as an advocate, but he also had to appear occasionally in court as a witness. One trial at which he gave evidence followed a sensational scandal that took place at the end of 62. He broke the alibi of the unruly young aristocrat Publius Clodius Pulcher, who was accused of sacrilege. Clodius was a member of the patrician Claudius family, although he used a popular version of the name. The Claudii had produced Consuls in every generation since the foundation of the Republic and over the centuries had built up a well-deserved reputation for high-handedness and violence. In one typical incident, a Claudius was leading a Roman fleet into battle. The sacred chickens refused to give a favorable omen by feeding on some corn that was put out for them. So Claudius had them flung into the sea, with the words: "If they won't eat, then let them drink."

Clodius possessed a full share of ancestral genes. When serving in Asia Minor during his youth, he had helped foment a mutiny against his commander and later got himself kidnapped by pirates. On his return to Rome he had unsuccessfully prosecuted Catilina on a charge of extortion—with no very serious intent, one guesses, other than to extort money from Catilina's rich protector, Crassus. He had joined Cicero's bodyguard in 63, perhaps as much for the fun of it as from political conviction. Now, as Quaestor-designate, he was on the point of starting his political career in earnest. At present he was known as little more than a young roisterer and it would be a year or two before he revealed himself as a serious and ruthless *popularis.*

The festival of the women's deity, the Good Goddess, was celebrated in early December every year in the house of a senior government official. Secret mystical ceremonies in the presence of the Vestal Virgins took place which only women were permitted to attend. Little is known about them except that the most important rituals took place at night. Music was played and there was a sacrifice of some kind. The previous year it had been Cicero's turn—or, more precisely, Terentia's—and this time the ritual took place at the State House, Julius Caesar's official residence as Chief Pontiff. Clodius, who had fallen for Caesar's wife, Pompeia, decided to infiltrate the event in drag. He came dressed as a lute player but lost his way in the corridors of the house. He came across a maid who asked him his name. His masculine voice gave him away, and he ran off. The alarm was given and a search conducted until he was found hiding under a bed. Somehow he managed to escape. Most people thought he was lucky to have survived the incident without injury.

When Cicero wrote to Atticus about the affair, his excited amusement is palpable. "I imagine you have heard that P. Clodius, the son of Appius, was caught dressed up as a woman in C. Caesar's house at the national sacrifice and that he owed his escape alive to the hands of a servant girl—a spectacular scandal. I am sure you will be deeply distressed!" It was, in fact, as Cicero knew, a serious business. Religious ritual accompanied almost every public event, and to breach it was unforgivable. Clodius would almost certainly face grave charges. Caesar himself was embarrassed and immediately divorced Pompeia, making the famous point that, whether or not she was innocent, his wife had to be above suspicion.

It is difficult to know what to make of the Good Goddess affair. As far as one can tell, there were no political overtones. But a house crowded with visitors was hardly a convenient rendezvous point for clandestine lovers. Probably all that Clodius had in mind was a dare. It was exactly the kind of practical joke that would amuse Rome's fashionable younger generation. These young men and women had plenty of money and were socially and sexually liberated. They turned their backs on the severe tradition of public duty. No longer defining themselves exclusively in terms of community—family, *gens,* patrician or noble status—and rebelling against authority, they lived for the moment.

Many of them had been sympathizers with Catilina (although for some reason Clodius had had little to do with the failed revolutionary) and, even if they had no time for politics now, they emerged later as supporters of Caesar during the civil war. Some became his key associates during his years of supreme power: able, unscrupulous and with huge debts to settle, they had no objection to aiding and abetting the death throes of the Republic, provided that Caesar paid them generously. Although most of them knew one another, they were not a coherent movement. Friendships were made and broken; cliques formed, melted away and re-formed. Respectable opinion deeply disapproved of them. The contemporary historian Sallust claimed they had a

> passion for fornication, guzzling and other forms of sensuality. Men prostituted themselves like women, and women sold their chastity at every corner. To please their palates they ransacked land and sea. They went to bed before they needed sleep, and instead of waiting until they felt hungry, thirsty, cold or tired, they forestalled their bodies' needs by self-indulgence. Such practices incited young men who had run through their property to have recourse to crime.

The great poet Caius Valerius Catullus, a member of Clodius's circle, fell in love with the eldest of Clodius's three sisters. After she threw him over, Catullus wrote memorably, with all the rage of discarded passion, of Clodia's loose way of life. In a poem to Marcus Caelius Rufus, another of her lovers, he described her as loitering "at the crossroads and in the back streets / ready to toss off the 'magnanimous' sons of Rome." She had a house on the fashionable Palatine Hill and gardens on the Tiber conveniently near a public bathing area, where she was accused of picking up young men. Clodia and her sisters were widely supposed to have slept with their brother and, although these kinds of accusations were part of the cut-and-thrust of political life, the rumors of incest were persistent and were confirmed under oath by one of their ex-husbands.

As a bachelor Caelius lived in a block of apartments owned by Clodius, but eventually relations with his friend's sister became strained. In 56 Clodia accused Caelius, who shared with Catullus the status of rejected lover, of attempting to poison her. Cicero successfully defended him with one of his most entertaining speeches, in which he gave a devastating exposé of the "Medea of the Palatine" or, in Caelius's phrase, "that ten-cent Clytemnestra."

Other members of the young circle included Mark Antony, grandson of the great orator of Cicero's childhood and stepson of the conspirator Lentulus, and Caius Scribonius Curio. The two were close friends and, according to Cicero, lovers. Curio encouraged his young *protégé* to run up huge debts for which he stood surety. In one of the Philippics, the sequence of great speeches against Antony which Cicero gave nearly two decades later, this relationship is subjected to lively (perhaps overlively) scrutiny.

> You [Mark Antony] assumed a man's toga and at once turned it into a prostitute's frock. At first you were a common rent boy; you charged a fixed fee, and a steep one at that. Curio soon turned up, though, and took you off the game. You were as firmly wedded to Curio as if he had given you a married woman's dress. No boy bought for lust was ever as much in his master's power as you were in Curio's. How many times did his father throw you out of his house? How many times did he set watchmen to make sure you did not

cross his front door? And yet under cover of night, driven by lust and money, you were let in through the roof tiles.

This sounds exaggerated, but Cicero should have known what he was talking about, for he was brought in as mediator and persuaded Curio's father to pay off his son's debts. Antony was barred from the house and for a while latched himself on to Clodius. Their relationship did not last, perhaps because Antony had an affair with Clodius's wife, Fulvia, whom he was later to marry. Also he grew uneasy with Clodius's extremist politics and the opposition they were arousing. Deciding it was time for a fresh start, he went to Greece for military training and to study public speaking.

In fact, although Cicero deeply disapproved of such goings-on, he knew many of the younger generation quite well. For a time he was friendly with Clodius, who had been a member of his consular bodyguard, until Terentia began to worry that he was attracted to Clodia. (It is hard to imagine a more implausible romance.) He became very fond of the brilliant but volatile Caelius, whom he first met in 66, when he took him on as an informal pupil to study public speaking. Caelius became a sharp-eyed observer of the Roman scene, delighted in gossip and had an excellent sense of humor; ten years on he kept Cicero, who would forgive a lot for a good joke, up-to-date on the latest events in the city when the reluctant elder statesman was in Asia Minor on a foreign posting.

Catullus knew Cicero too and respected him enough to write him a charming poem:

Silver-tongued among the sons of Rome,
the dead, the living and the yet unborn,
Catullus, least of poets, sends
Marcus Tullius his warmest thanks:
—as much the least of poets
as he a prince of lawyers.

It seems odd that Cicero was on such good terms with people whose behavior he found morally objectionable. The fact is that he liked young men and, as he grew older, took much pleasure in bringing them on, developing their talents and promoting their careers. He enjoyed the liveliness of their company. Caelius was the first in a succession of youthful friends—the last and trickiest of whom was to be Caesar's adopted son, the young Octavian, later the Emperor Augustus.

None of this is to suggest that Cicero was homosexual. He explicitly disapproved of same-sex relationships. In an age when politicians hurled every conceivable accusation of sexual malpractice against their opponents, this charge was very seldom laid at his door. Apart from the probably abusive suggestion that he lost his virginity to an older classmate in his youth, the only direct piece of evidence on the matter is a flirtatiously erotic ode he penned to a young slave of his, Tiro. But this is best seen as a playful imitation of Greek love poetry.

The Senate was uncertain how to handle the Good Goddess scandal. A trial would only cause trouble and might ignite the *populares,* but it seemed that there was no alternative. A bill to set up a special tribunal was agreed on by the Senate and the proposal was then considered by the People. Cicero was there and described the scene: "When the day came for the bill to be put to the assembly under the terms of the Senatorial decree, there was a flocking together of our goateed young bloods, the whole Catilinarian gang with little Miss Curio at their head, to plead for its rejection. Clodius's roughs had taken possession of the gangways." It seems to have been impossible to take a vote and the matter went back to the Senate. Eventually, in July 61, a court was established, but on terms favorable to Clodius. Crassus, Catilina's shadowy financier, happy as ever to make trouble for the Senate, came forward with funds to bribe the jurors.

Clodius pleaded that he could not have been the intruder, for he had been out of Rome at the Etruscan town of Interamna (where he wielded considerable political influence and, according to Cicero, employed gangs to harass the countryside). Terentia, still irritated by the visits she believed her husband to be paying Clodia, goaded Cicero to take the witness stand and break Clodius's alibi by reporting that he had seen him in Rome on the day in question. The trial started well, the jury asked for a guard (which suggested honesty), and it looked as if it was an open-and-shut case. But then Crassus's cash began to do its work.

Cicero reported to Atticus:

> Inside a couple of days, with a single slave (an ex-gladiator at that) for go-between, [Crassus] settled the whole business—called them to

his house, made promises, backed bills or paid cash down. On top of that (it's really too shocking!), some jurors actually received a bonus in the form of assignations with certain ladies or introductions to youths of noble families. Yet even so, with the [*optimates*] making themselves very scarce, 25 jurors had the courage to take the risk, no small one, preferring to sacrifice their lives rather than the whole community. As for the other 31, they were more worried about their empty purses than their empty reputations.

Clodius was acquitted, but he was a vindictive man and made up his mind to punish Cicero for having testified against him. For a while, though, nothing happened and Cicero could not help amusing himself at his expense. He liked to call him Pretty-Boy (making a play on his *cognomen* Pulcher, the Latin word for "beautiful"). There were a number of barbed exchanges at Senate meetings and elsewhere over the next year or so.

"You bought a mansion," Clodius sneered.

"One might think he was saying I had bought a jury," Cicero riposted.

On another occasion, the two men happened to be taking a candidate for political office down to the Forum together and entered into conversation. Clodius asked if Cicero was in the habit of giving Sicilians who were in his *clientela* seats at gladiatorial shows. Cicero said he was not.

"Ah," replied Clodius. "But I'm a new patron of theirs and I'm going to institute the practice. But my sister, with all that free space at her disposal as an ex-Consul's wife, only gives me one wretched foot."

Unable to resist referring to the gossip about their relationship, Cicero remarked: "Oh, don't grumble about *one* foot in your sister's case. You can always hoist the other."

This kind of jibe was not overlooked. As so often in his career, Cicero let his sense of humor do serious damage to his prospects.

Sometime towards the end of 62 or perhaps in early 61, Pompey returned to Italy after nearly six years of campaigning. He had swept the seas clear of pirates, the war against Mithridates, King of Pontus, had been won, and Syria from the Euphrates to the frontiers of Egypt had been annexed to the Empire. Trade with Asia Minor could now resume and money flooded back into Rome.

Pompey was an able rather than a great general, but he was an administrator of the first order. The campaign against Mithridates had been long and hard fought, for the king was a wily foe. Hostilities opened after he invaded Bithynia, a new Roman province, thirteen years previously. When Pompey arrived to take over command of the Roman forces in the east from his able predecessor, Lucullus, he found that final victory was close at hand. The groundwork had been done for him and he had only to stamp out the final flames of resistance. Pompey persuaded the King of Parthia to invade Armenia, which was ruled by an ally of Mithridates, while he himself marched into the enemy's homeland, Pontus. With overwhelming superiority of numbers, the Romans won a crushing victory.

The indomitable old king tried to keep going, seized the territories of a treacherous son, raised fresh troops and meditated an invasion of Italy. But his much put-upon subjects had had enough and revolts ensued. The great game was finally over. Holed up inside a remote citadel, Mithridates tried to poison himself, without success thanks to the physical immunity he had laboriously built up, and was forced to get a slave to stab him.

After some mopping-up operations, Pompey marched south to deal with a civil war in Palestine and visited the Holy of Holies in the Temple in Jerusalem. He dreamed of advancing Roman arms to the Red Sea, but when the news of Mithridates' death reached him he moved from military to organizational matters. His task was to reorder the eastern empire in such a way that its long-term security was assured. His settlement of the eastern provinces was so well judged that it was to remain in place mostly unchanged until the next century. A chain of directly governed Roman provinces was established along the Mediterranean seaboard, stretching from Pontus in the Black Sea to Syria in the south. Their eastern frontiers were protected by a series of quasi-independent kingdoms which were allowed to manage their internal affairs without interference but whose foreign policy was in Roman hands.

Pompey was only forty-four years old, but it must have seemed to him that there was little left in life for him to do. As soon as he landed at Brundisium he disbanded his forces, much to everyone's relief. The sight of the famous general traveling unarmed and in the company of only a few friends, "as if he were coming back from a foreign holiday" (as Plutarch put it), made a huge impression on public opinion. On his leisurely journey along the Via Appia to Rome, where he arrived in February, large crowds came out to watch him pass by.

He felt no need to establish a military autocracy, as some had feared, for he was self-evidently the first man in Rome. But the Senate, envious of his preeminence, could not see that he was at heart a conservative and had no desire for monarchical powers. In any case, if he did ever come under threat, he knew that he had the public support, as well as the financial resources, to raise a new army.

Pompey had two main aims in mind. The first was to persuade the Senate to ratify his eastern settlement, and the second was to arrange for a land-distribution law, which would grant farms to his veterans. His attempted deployment of Metellus Nepos showed that he foresaw trouble and, without making his views entirely clear, he positioned himself alongside the *populares* in order to gain leverage over the Senate.

Cicero saw an opening. As a distinguished backbencher in the Senate, he had influence rather than power, but he was still in a position to guide change. His aim as ever was to get the constitution to work better. This could be achieved only by persuading the different interest groups—the aristocracy with its stranglehold over the Senate, the *equites* with their commercial concerns and the People (and that meant, to all intents and purposes, the urban masses)—to work together more cooperatively. At present things were badly out of balance. The *populares* were constantly on the attack and the *optimates* refused, blindly, to have anything to do with them.

If Cicero could only find a way of drawing Pompey towards the conservative cause and detaching him from the radicals, the ship of state might return to an even keel. This would mean gaining the general's confidence. The going was more difficult than he expected. Cicero sent Pompey a long self-congratulatory letter about his Consulship during the general's journey home but received only a perfunctory reply. Cicero's boastfulness irritated Pompey and, more to the point, he knew that the orator had no real power base.

Cicero saw he was making little progress and began to lose heart. On January 25 he gave Atticus a telling description of Pompey's character: "He professes the highest regard for me and makes a parade of warm affection, praising on the surface while below it, well, not so far below that it's difficult to see, he's jealous. Awkward, tortuous, politically paltry, shabby, timid, disingenuous—but I shall go into more detail on another occasion."

In fact, Pompey *was* privately considering a rapprochement with the

Senate. He hinted at his intentions by divorcing his wife, Mucia. Whatever personal reasons there were for this (Plutarch tells us that she was widely whispered to have been unfaithful), it was a political act; for the two Metelli, her half-brothers, were prominent *populares.* To make sure that everyone understood the message that he was thinking of shifting his ground in the direction of the *optimates,* Pompey opened negotiations for the hand of Cato's niece. However, the Senate's unyielding and self-appointed conscience dismissed the idea out of hand, calling the offer a kind of bribery. This left Pompey awkwardly placed, having abandoned one faction and been rebuffed by the other. His return to civilian life was off to a bad start.

"Life out of uniform can have the dangerous effect of weakening the reputation of famous generals," Plutarch noted in his biography of Pompey. "They are poorly adapted to the equality of democratic politics. Such men claim the same precedence in civilian life that they enjoy on the battlefield. . . . So when people find a man with a brilliant military record playing an active part in public life they undermine and humiliate him. But if he renounces and withdraws from politics, they maintain his reputation and ability and no longer envy him."

The trouble was that Pompey was a poor political tactician and an uninspiring public speaker. He found the grubby business of politicking in the Forum distasteful and embarrassing. He tended not to express his intentions clearly and was criticized for being misleading or even hypocritical. Proud of his achievements, he wanted to receive without having to ask and had no real idea how to handle the Senate. Crassus remained jealous of him and did little to be helpful. Only Caesar seemed happy to give him any assistance, but his Praetorship was now over and he would soon be leaving for a governorship in Spain. He was as ever hugely in debt and creditors delayed his departure. He remarked dryly: "I need 25 million sesterces just to own nothing."

Soon after his arrival in Rome in early February 61, Pompey addressed a meeting of the Senate. He commented politely but noncommittally on the sacrilege scandal and said in general terms that he approved of the Senate's decrees. He was given a poor reception. Cicero said the speech was a "frost." As for his own contribution to the debate, he was of the opinion that he had given a vintage performance, which, he confessed wryly to Atticus, contained more than a degree of self-parody.

> I brought the house down. And why not, on such a theme—the dignity of our order, concord between Senate and *equites,* unison of Italy, remnants of the conspiracy in their death throes, reduced price of grain, internal peace? You should know by now how I can boom away on such topics. I think you must have caught the reverberations in Epirus [Atticus was on his estate there], and for that reason I won't dwell on the subject.

For the time being Pompey proceeded with caution. He decided to leave his bid to secure ratification of his provincial settlement and land for his soldiers until the following year. In an effort to improve his chances, he laid out large sums of money to ensure the election as Consul of his supporter, Lucius Afranius, an unimpressive man who was known for little more than being a good dancer. (This probably meant that he performed publicly on the stage, an unrespectable activity for an upper-class Roman citizen.)

In the autumn of 61 Pompey finally celebrated his Triumph. A Triumph was a victory procession awarded to generals after important campaigns. It was the most splendid ceremony in the Roman calendar. Pompey was celebrating not just victory over Mithridates and his campaigns in Armenia, Syria and Arabia, but also his subjugation of the Mediterranean pirates, and two days were set aside: September 28 and, his birthday, September 29.

Temporary stands were set up in the Forum and at the city's racecourses. Crowds of people, all wearing white clothes, filled them and any other vantage point they could find along the processional route. All the temples were opened to the public and were filled with flowers and incense. Lictors and other attendants did their best to hold onlookers back and keep the streets open and clear.

The procession set off from outside the city, crossed the *pomoerium* and wound its way towards the center. At its head placards displayed the names of all the countries over which the great general was triumphing: Pontus, Armenia, Cappadocia, Paphlagonia, Media, Colchis (mythical home of Medea and the Golden Fleece), Iberia, Albania, Syria, Cilicia, Mesopotamia, Phoenicia and Palestine, Judaea and Arabia. They claimed that Pompey had captured no fewer than 1,000 fortified places, nearly 900 cities and 800 pirate ships; and had founded 39 new cities. Even more spectacular were the resources now flowing into the city. Inscriptions boasted that Rome's tax revenues had jumped from 200 million sesterces every year to 340 million thanks to Pompey's annexation of new territories. He was also bringing to the Treasury a vast quantity of coined money and gold and silver plate. Captured weapons, shields, armor, swords and spears were carried on wagons. There were trophies for every engagement in which Pompey or his lieutenants had been victorious. The polished bronze and steel would have glinted in the sunlight and clattered together, adding a counterpoint to the harsh military music of bands. The crowds would have wished to see Rome's great bogeyman, Mithridates, in chains. His suicide had made that impossible, but in his place a monumental statue of the king was included in the parade.

On the second day of the Triumph the most distinguished prisoners of war were put on show. This was one of the high points of the ceremony, with the packed citizenry booing the Republic's humiliated enemies as they walked past only a few feet away. Five of Mithridates' children were in the procession, and one of his sisters. They were accompanied by the King of Armenia's wife and son and the King of the Jews, together with captured pirate chiefs. Following them came a huge portrait of Pompey fashioned from pearls.

Finally, Pompey himself appeared in a gem-encrusted chariot; he had a wreath of bay leaves on his head and was dressed in a purple toga decorated with golden stars. A cloak belonging to Alexander the Great hung from his shoulders. His face was covered in red lead, for the victor was supposed to represent Jupiter, king of the gods. A slave also stood in the chariot and whispered in his ear: "Remember that you are human." Behind the chariot marched columns of soldiers who held sprays of laurel and chanted triumphal songs: they also sang, by ancient tradition, obscene lyrics satirizing their general.

When he reached the end of the processional route, the Capitol Hill, Pompey dedicated 8 million sesterces to the goddess Minerva and promised a shrine in honor of Venus the Victorious at the new theater he was to build on the Field of Mars. Surely, he may reasonably have felt, his glorious deeds would win him the gratitude of the Senate and People of Rome.

Towards the end of the year Cicero, powerless, witnessed a serious blow to his ideal of an "alliance of all the classes." The *equites,* mainly traders and businessmen, on whom Cicero relied for much of his political support, were annoyed by a Senatorial decree which removed their immunity from prosecution when sitting as jurors. The effect was simply to put them on an equal footing with Senators, but, while they kept their feelings to themselves, they resented the reform.

Not long afterwards a delegation of *equites* asked the Senate to review their tax-farming concessions in the provinces of Asia Minor. On reflection, they felt that they had bid too high for the contracts and that their profit margins were at risk. Crassus was behind the move. His support for the tax farmers was in part a bid to counterbalance Pompey's huge new power base in Asia Minor. Plutarch writes: "Giving up all attempts to equal Pompey in military matters, Crassus devoted himself to politics. Here by taking pains, by helping people in the law courts or with loans . . . he acquired an influence and a reputation equal to that which Pompeius had won by all his great military expeditions."

Cicero was furious but had no choice but to support the claim. "The demand was disgraceful," he wrote to Atticus on December 5, "a confession of recklessness. But there was the gravest danger of a complete break between Senate and *equites* if it had been turned down altogether." Cato was his usual obstructive self and made sure that the Senate resisted the request. The *equites* began to think that if Cicero could not get them what they wanted, they would have to look elsewhere for favors.

Early in 60 a Tribune, Lucius Flavius, brought forward a comprehensive bill to distribute land to Pompey's soldiers. It was carefully and unprovocatively framed and, after proposing some amendments, Cicero supported it. Private interests were to be protected and he welcomed the prospect that, if properly organized, "the dregs of the urban population can be cleared out and Italy repeopled." To critics who argued that he was abandoning his constitutionalist position, he replied that Pompey "has become more constitutionally minded and less inclined to court popularity with the masses." In other words, if Pompey's wishes were granted, he might be persuaded to abandon the radicals and join the conservative interest.

The *optimates* saw things in a very different light and opposed the measure from start to finish. This had little to do with its intrinsic merits. They were thinking in exclusively competitive terms; anything that enhanced Pompey's standing would diminish theirs. It would not be long before this ill-conceived attack brought about the exact opposite of what was intended.

Had there been more conservative politicians of real ability, the history of these years might have been quite different. The bloodlettings earlier in the century under Marius and Sulla had depopulated the ruling class and, with the deaths of senior figures (including, recently, that of that elderly pillar of the political establishment Catulus), the talent on the Senate's benches was much reduced. The increasing wealth that flowed from the provinces had reduced the appeal of, and the necessity for, a political career. Major personalities such as Hortensius and Lucullus (the able general who had preceded Pompey in the east) had withdrawn into a private life of, in Cicero's opinion, scandalous luxury.

Of course, Cato did not fall into this category. But his inability to compromise made him as fatal to his cause, Cicero believed, as the moral dereliction of the others did. "As for our dear friend Cato," he observed to Atticus while the land bill was being debated, "I have as warm a regard for him as you do. The fact remains that with all his patriotism, he can be a political liability. He speaks in the Senate as if he were living in Plato's Republic instead of Romulus's cesspool."

By June the political atmosphere was overheating. The Consul, Metellus Celer, placed all kinds of obstacles in the way of Flavius, who eventually lost his temper and dragged him off to the prison not far from the rear of the Senate House. The Consul preserved his sangfroid and resisted offers of help from other Tribunes. (They could, for example, have vetoed the arrest.) Instead he called a Senate meeting at the prison. Flavius, undaunted, placed himself across the entry to prevent the Senators from going in. The Consul, however, countered this move by having a hole knocked through the wall. As he had doubtless calculated, public opinion swung decisively in his support. An embarrassed Pompey intervened and called Flavius off. He did not proceed with the bill. This incident marked the end of any possible rapprochement between him and the Senate.

Cicero was not enjoying the situation in which he found himself. His efforts to keep in favor with all sides meant that he had to behave with unaccustomed circumspection and keep his emotions—and his tongue—under control. The only advantage that accrued from his support for the land bill and his growing closeness to Pompey was popularity in an unexpected quarter: as he wrote to Atticus, "those conspirators of the wine table, our goateed young bloods." Curio, Caelius and other budding *populares* were pleased with him. He was cheered at the Games and gladiatorial shows "without a single wolf whistle." Otherwise he took what consolation he could in spending more time with his family and in literary pursuits.

Increasingly aware of the need to bolster his fading influence, Cicero decided that more propaganda about his Consulship was called for. He produced an epic in three books, furnished with all the apparatus of gods and muses. He told Atticus that he "had used up the entire perfume cabinet of Isocrates [a famous Greek orator] along with all his pupils' scent boxes and some of Aristotle's rouge too." His tone of voice is ironic, as if he knew perfectly well that what he was doing was not to be taken too seriously. Nor was it: Cicero's readers ridiculed the poem's pretensions and had a good laugh at his expense.

At the end of January 60, Cicero let Atticus know of his unhappiness.

> What I most badly need at the moment is a confidant. . . . And you whose talk and advice has so often lightened my worry and vexation of spirit, the partner in my public life and intimate of all my private concerns, the sharer of all my talk and plans, where are you? I am so utterly forsaken that my only moments of relaxation are those I spend with my wife, my little daughter and my darling Marcus. My brilliant worldly friendships may make a fine show in public, but in the home they are barren things. My house is crammed of a morning, I go down to the Forum surrounded by droves of friends, but in all the crowds I cannot find one person with whom I can exchange an unguarded joke or let out a private sigh.

Later in the same letter he hinted that even family life was not all it might be. Apart from Terentia's futile jealousy of Clodia, there were worries about his brother, Quintus. For most of his life Quintus was overshadowed by his more celebrated older brother, and every now and again he kicked against his lot and revealed a sore and irascible inferiority complex. He had been Praetor in 62 and in the following year went out to govern the province of Asia. Cicero was anxious for him and hoped that Atticus might accompany him to exert a moderating influence. He was afraid that Quintus's behavior might damage his own interests, for Cicero tended, maddeningly for his brother, to regard both of them as a single political entity.

Quintus chose this moment to pick a quarrel with Atticus. Its cause is unknown. Perhaps Quintus sensed Atticus's and his brother's lack of confidence in him, or perhaps there was some dispute with his wife, Pomponia, Atticus's sister (heralding the marital difficulties of later years). In any event, Cicero was dismayed that two of the people closest to him were suddenly on bad terms. He did his best to pacify Atticus: "I trusted and indeed convinced myself that . . . a frank talk or even the mere meeting and sight of one another would set all to rights between you. I need not tell you, for you already know, what a kindly, amiable chap my brother is, how impressionable he is both in taking offense and laying it aside."

Quintus's performance as governor threatened to realize his brother's worst fears. He had two men found guilty of killing their father sewn up in a sack and drowned—the traditional Roman penalty. When an important provincial named Zeuxis was tried for murdering his mother, Quintus decided to display his evenhandedness by meting out the same punishment—despite the fact that Zeuxis had been acquitted. Zeuxis wisely made himself scarce and, although cross, the new governor then changed his mind, writing him a friendly letter and inviting him to return. On another occasion Quintus ordered one of his lieutenants to burn two embezzlers alive and threatened to have a Roman *eques* "suffocated one day in smoke, to the applause of the province." When criticized, he said that he had only been joking. His anxious relatives must have raised their eyebrows at his sense of humor.

Another of Quintus's weaknesses (according to Cicero) long outlasted his governorship. While outwardly decisive, he relied a great deal on the advice of those around him, and he preferred to listen to his slaves than to his social equals. His favorite was a certain Statius whom he soon freed and kept as a personal assistant and adviser for many years. Cicero could not stand him and resented his (as he saw it, thoroughly un-Roman) influence over his brother.

Partly as thanks for the election pamphlet of a few years earlier and partly as a kind of insurance policy, Cicero wrote Quintus a long letter, in effect an essay, on the duties of governorship and, while sugaring the pill, spoke his mind; his brother had to learn to control his temper.

In any case, perhaps because of the good advice of his brother, Quintus seems to have settled down and remained at his post until 59, an unusually long assignment. For all his faults, he was an honest and sophisticated man, who read Plato and Xenophon, spoke Greek fluently and even wrote tragedies in his spare time.

Back in Rome an uneasy interval was dragging on. After the defeat of the land-distribution bill, Pompey, disgruntled and moody, was considering his position. Meanwhile, in what is now Portugal and northwest Spain, Caesar was winning a lively little war against some rebellious tribes. It was not clear what Clodius's ambitions were, and where they might or might not lead, but he was busy building political support. The Senate was in a defensive and obstructionist mode.

By June of the year 60 Caesar had returned from Spain with a new reputation for generalship. Despite opposition from Cato and his friends, he was duly elected Consul for the next year. His colleague was Marcus Calpurnius Bibulus, an obstinate and not very astute conservative.

It may have been at this point that Caesar began to look beyond his policy of harrying the *optimates* as occasion arose and to think seriously of ways to break their power permanently. In any case, in the months before taking office, he took stock of the general situation. He saw that there were four senior personalities: himself, Pompey, Crassus and Cicero, each of whom was alienated in one way or another from the political process and unable to achieve his aims. Would it be possible, he wondered, to bring them together in a partnership that would bypass the obstructionist Cato and the Senate? As summer gave way to autumn, he began to assemble a deal that would give them what they wanted. Pompey's needs took priority; it was becoming urgent to settle his soldiers and confirm the arrangements he had made in Asia Minor. This was not just a question of satisfying the vanity of a great commander; it was in the public interest, although his opponents would not see it, to ensure that discontented and unemployed veterans were not allowed to add to social confusion in the countryside and in the city of Rome. And the prosperity and stability of the Empire depended on the pacification of the eastern provinces after years of war, massacre and destruction. Crassus was at loggerheads with the Senate too. The tax farmers were still waiting for a decision about their contracts. The problem would be to find a way of persuading him and Pompey to patch up their poor personal relations.

Then there was Cicero. Although his influence was in decline he still had an extensive network of clients and friends; he was at the height of his powers as an orator and could swing opinion; and he was the ablest politician on the right, a moderate who stood for social and political reconciliation. It is possible that at this stage Caesar had not altogether despaired of a consensual solution to the difficulties facing the Republic. Cicero might have a useful contribution to make; at the very least he would give any pact a degree of respectability—something that would appeal to Pompey.

Finally there were Caesar's own claims. If his forthcoming Consulship was to be a radical and reforming one, which he intended it to be, it would arouse great animosity and it would be essential to protect his personal position once it was over. This could be managed only if he obtained the governorship of a major province—better still, a province where he could further develop his military career. He was the junior partner of the quartet and doubtless perceived that his long-term future would be assured only if he could create the circumstances which would allow him to raise himself and his reputation to a level with that of Pompey.

In December Caesar quickly came to an understanding with Pompey, thoroughly disillusioned with the *optimates,* and, once he had been secured, sounded out the other two. Crassus presented no insuperable difficulties and sometime in the early new year he joined the alliance. The basic proposition was that all three would promise to take no political action of which one of them disapproved. Once Consul, Caesar would put through a land-reform act and get the eastern settlement confirmed, revise the tax farmers' contracts and arrange a five-year provincial command for himself. For all these measures he would receive Pompey's and Crassus's support.

Cicero, however, was a tougher nut to crack. He was approached towards the end of December and for a time could not make up his mind how to react. The go-between was a millionaire businessman from Gades in Spain, Lucius Cornelius Balbus, who had received Roman citizenship about ten years previously. Caesar had come across him during his recent governorship and brought him to Rome, where he acted as his confidential agent. He and an *eques,* Caius Oppius, became the subtle and ingenious fixers Caesar used to promote his interests during his frequent absences from the capital during the coming years. They wrote letters and published pamphlets. On good terms with all the leading politicians of the day, they wheedled and cajoled, or when necessary threatened, enemies and influential neutrals. They did favors and called them in later as and when the need arose. They were fiercely loyal to their employer.

Balbus told Cicero that Caesar would like him to support the land-reform bill with which he intended to launch his Consulship; in return Caesar would follow his and Pompey's advice in all things and try to draw Pompey and Crassus together. Cicero gave the proposition serious thought. The alliance would bring him closer to Pompey and would secure his position from his critics—and especially from Clodius, who had not forgotten his part in the Good Goddess trial: the word was that as soon as he won public office he would prosecute Cicero for the execution of the conspirators.

Then some lines from the poem on his Consulship came to Cicero's mind, in which the muse of epic poetry, Calliope, appears to him and gives him some advice:

> *Meantime the paths which you from earliest days did seek,*
> *Yes, and when Consul too, as mood and virtue called,*
> *These hold, and foster still your fame and good men's praise.*

Nobody else had taken the book very seriously, but, as he pointed out to Atticus, for Cicero the passage reminded him of his duty. As he thought about what he had written, it struck him how it was essentially a celebration of traditional, aristocratic values. They were where his deepest feelings lay, even if the Patricians of his day cold-shouldered him. His decision not to join the Caesarian alliance was at bottom an emotional one. It was beyond his imagination that the established order could not be saved.

Caesar, Pompey and Crassus went ahead without Cicero and sealed their secret agreement. With their money, their influence, their access to military force and their ruthlessness, they were in a position to act more or less as they wished. They could control the results of elections and arrange special commands or postings almost at will. A cabal was now in command of affairs, which was willing and able to bypass the Senate. When a later contemporary, Caius Asinius Pollio, wrote one of the first histories of the period, it was no accident that he opened his narrative with this alliance, which signaled the bankruptcy of the old order.

Caesar's success as a politician sprang not only from his capacity for rigorous analysis of a given situation and for decisive action but also from his charm and attention to detail. So, when softening up Pompey, he had appealed to the great man's vanity by getting the Senate to let him wear his triumphal insignia, including the special embroidered purple gown, at public shows. Few people saw the steel behind his agreeable, good-humored manners. He knew how to make himself liked by all and sundry. He was scrupulously polite: once when he was served asparagus dressed with myrrh instead of olive oil, he ate it without objecting and told off his friends when they objected to the dish (because it tasted bitter and was vulgarly expensive). "If you didn't like it, you didn't need to eat it. But if one reflects on one's host's lack of breeding it merely shows one is ill-bred oneself." His attitude towards money was strategic: it was not so much that he wanted it for himself, he sought it as a fund into which his friends and soldiers could dip, often providing them with cheap or interest-free loans. He was always giving people presents, whether or not they asked for them.

From his youth Caesar took a dandyish care of his appearance, once adding wrist-length sleeves to his purple-striped Senatorial tunic and wearing his belt fashionably loose. His dinner parties and entertainments were legendary; in Plutarch's phrase, he was known and admired for a "certain splendour in his life-style." Cicero observed: "When I notice how carefully arranged his hair is and when I watch him adjusting the parting with one finger, I cannot imagine that this man could conceive of such a wicked thing as to destroy the Roman constitution."

In January 59, the new Consul moved with speed, introducing his land-reform bill designed to resettle Pompey's soldiers. He was determined to proceed legally if at all possible. The legislation had been very carefully framed to avoid giving needless offense, and Senators could find little to say against it. After he had read the text aloud, Caesar said he was ready to make any improvements that might be suggested. But Cato was having none of it: he tried to talk the proposal out by filibustering until sunset, when Senate meetings automatically closed.

The strategy of the *optimates* was simple; to oppose Caesar's reforms lock, stock and barrel and to get his fellow Consul Marcus Calpurnius Bibulus, to veto them. This would have the effect either of neutralizing Caesar or of pushing him into illegality, for which he could be put on trial once he resigned.

The Forum now provided the setting for one of those decisive turning points in history. As recounted by Dio Cassius, Caesar seems to have been genuinely taken aback by the opposition of the diehards and, using his legal power of enforcement (*coercitio*), ordered an official to arrest Cato and take him to prison. This was too much for many Senators and, as in the recent case of Metellus Celer, they followed him to the prison.

"Why are you leaving the meeting early?" Caesar asked one of them.

"I prefer Cato's company in prison to yours in the Senate," came the reply.

Outmaneuvered, the Consul rescinded the arrest and announced that he would ignore the Senate from now on and take the bill directly to the People. An informal public meeting was held at which Caesar asked Bibulus if he had any objections to what was proposed. Bibulus replied that there would be no innovations during his term of office.

"You shall have the law," Caesar told the crowd, "only if he agrees to it."

"You shall not have this law this year, not even if you all want it," Bibulus shouted back. This incautiously undemocratic admission made the Senate's intransigence embarrassingly clear.

Pompey and Crassus were then brought forward to speak, an unusual step for they were private citizens and had no official status. They made the point that the law could well be afforded, seeing that the eastern campaign had filled the state's coffers. In fact, it would even be possible to acquire land for the veterans of an earlier war, a measure which the Senate had approved at the time but never acted on.

Bibulus now started to "watch the heavens daily"—a religious device for halting public business and, to make assurance double sure, declared all the remaining days of the year on which the General Assembly could be legally held to be holidays. This did not deter Caesar from formally convening the General Assembly to pass the bill—a good example of the Consul's sweeping powers, even when wielded against his coequal colleague. The result of the vote could not be in any doubt, but Caesar was taking no risks. Crowds of veterans occupied the Forum the night before it was to be taken. Bibulus, with a crowd of followers, turned up during the middle of a speech Caesar was giving from the Temple of the Castors. He was let through, partly out of respect for his office and partly because no one imagined he would continue to maintain his opposition. But that was just what he did. When he tried to announce a veto, he was thrown down the Temple steps. He was showered with filth, his *fasces*—the rods and axes of office—were smashed and he and some Tribunes who supported him were lucky to escape with their lives. After being beaten up and wounded, they made their escape as best they could.

The *optimates* had little choice but to give way under duress and the bill was passed. Insultingly it included a clause obliging Senators to sign a statement agreeing to abide by the legislation. Cato was persuaded only with the greatest difficulty to do so.

With every new development, each side raised the stakes. Not long afterwards, Caesar introduced a second land bill, this time much harsher in its terms. Its purpose was to redistribute publicly owned land in Campania (a fertile territory in the Naples area) to Roman citizens with more than three children. At present it was rented out, so the reform would severely reduce an important stream of state revenue. As Cicero noted, nothing could be better designed to inflame "better class sentiment." An ancient Senator, Lucius Gellius, declared that the bill would not be implemented for as long as he lived. "Let us wait then," said Cicero, "since Gellius is not asking us to postpone things for long." Despite Senatorial opposition, this measure too was pushed through the General Assembly.

Bibulus withdrew to his house, where he stayed for the rest of the year. He tried to halt all public business, including elections, by continually declaring bad omens. Because they had been unable to stop Caesar, the *optimates* were laying the ground for a move, after the Consulship was over, to declare all his measures unlawful. Powerless, Bibulus resorted to insult: dredging up the old story about King Nicomedes, he described Caesar in an edict as "the Queen of Bithynia . . . who once wanted to sleep with a king but now wants to be one." On the streets people laughingly spoke of the Consulship of Caius Caesar and Julius Caesar.

Cicero was not impressed by Bibulus's behavior. He became more and more depressed by the course of events and could only wait and watch from the sidelines as Pompey's settlement in the east was at last ratified, in the end with little trouble. Crassus's tax farmers had the price of their contracts reduced by a third, but he could not claim any of the credit.

In March Cicero defended his former fellow Consul, Antonius, on a corruption charge, without success. After Antonius's conviction, flowers were laid on Catilina's grave and a celebratory banquet was held. Audaciously Cicero used his speech for a strong attack on the First Triumvirate. He soon saw that this was a serious mistake. Caesar made no public comment, but he acted at once to bring Cicero into line by letting Clodius off his leash. On the afternoon of the day Cicero made his comments, Caesar approved an application by Clodius for a change in status from Patrician to Plebeian. This was no mere technicality: only a Plebeian could be elected Tribune—a post Clodius coveted, for (among other things) it would enable him to get his long meditated revenge. As part of the procedure to change his social status, Clodius had to be adopted by a Plebeian man; to show his disregard for social norms, he chose as his "father" a youth of twenty.

Alongside covert threats, various blandishments were offered to Cicero during the spring and summer, including a seat on the commission that had been set up to implement the land-reform laws and an assignment as special envoy to the Egyptian Pharaoh. He turned them all down. Seeing that Caesar would use fair means or foul to gag him, he silently admitted defeat and for the time being withdrew from public life, leaving Rome for a tour of his villas.

Cicero was planning to write a book on geography but could not concentrate on it. He preferred to work instead on a candid memoir of his life and times, in which he denounced his enemies and attacked the First Triumvirate. This *Secret History* (*De consiliis suis*) was well-known in antiquity but is now lost; it was unpublishable in Cicero's lifetime and he gave it to young Marcus with the instruction not to issue it until after his death. In April 59, he told Atticus: "I have taken so kindly to idleness that I can't tear myself away from it. So either I amuse myself with books, of which I have a good stock at Antium, or I count the waves—the weather is unsuitable for mackerel fishing. . . . And my sole form of political activity is to hate the rascals, and even that I do without anger." This did not mean he had lost his appetite for news and gossip. He depended on his friend for a reliable flow. "When I read a letter of yours I feel I am in Rome, hearing one thing one minute and another the next, as one does when big events are toward." At about the same time, he wrote: "I have so lost my manly spirit that I prefer to be tyrannized over in peace and quiet."

Curio paid an unexpected visit. No longer a "little Miss" but now "my young friend," he brought the welcome news that his circle was unhappy with the regime but also reported, less agreeably, that Clodius was definitely standing as Tribune for 58. Cicero could see this only as an ominous development.

In Rome matters went from bad to worse for the *optimates.* As the months passed, the existence of an explicit alliance among the three became public knowledge. Pompey's marriage in April to Caesar's dearly loved daughter, Julia, was a sign that it was not a temporary expedient but a permanent arrangement. Pompey's private life seems to have been remarkably free from scandal. Attractive to women, he had some affairs, but usually acted with great caution in questions of the heart. A courtesan, Flora, used to recall that she never left his bed without carrying the marks of his teeth and he is reported to have slept with the wife of a favorite freedman of his. In fact, he was uxorious by nature and tended to fall in love with his wives. This was certainly the case with Julia. He adored her and was criticized for spending too much time on holiday with her at Italian resorts when he should have been attending to public business. For her part, despite a considerable difference in age, she developed a genuine affection for her middle-aged husband and was a crucial, emollient and reconciling link between him and her father in Gaul.

Cicero told Atticus that "Sampsiceramus," his nickname for Pompey (after an oriental potentate), "is out for trouble. We can expect anything. He is confessedly working for absolute power. . . . They would never have come so far if they were not paving their way to other and disastrous objectives." He noticed that the uninhibited freedom of speech which marked political life in the Republic was giving way to caution at social gatherings and across dinner tables. Despite the fact that there was no official censorship, he agreed on a simple code with Atticus for sensitive parts of their correspondence.

Popular opinion began to move against the First Triumvirate and they were booed at a gladiatorial show in July. A contemporary commentator called them "the Beast with Three Heads." When an actor in a play spoke the line, "To our misfortune art thou Great," the audience took it as a reference to Pompey and called for a dozen encores.

Cicero began to detect a weakness in the alliance. He suspected that Pompey profoundly disliked the position he found himself in. He was right, up to a point. But although he knew better than to trust Pompey, with whose double-dealing he was familiar, he needed so much to believe that the former general could be detached from the "rascals" that he overinterpreted the evidence of his unease. There is no doubt that Pompey did feel uncomfortable, but at the same time there is every reason to suppose that his alliance with Caesar and Crassus remained as firm as ever. In fact, it was Cicero, the recipient of many melancholy private confidences, who would be discarded.

Cicero pretended to take Clodius's election as Tribune lightly, but he could not stop mentioning it. "Dear Publius is threatening me, most hostile. . . . I think I have very firm backing in my old Consular army of all honest men, including the moderately honest. Pompeius signifies goodwill to me out of the ordinary. He also assures me that Clodius will not say a word about me; in this he does not deceive me but is himself deceived."

Caesar's final task was to decide on the future once his Consulship came to an end. So far he had achieved all they could have hoped: Pompey had had his eastern settlement approved and his soldiers had been given land, and Crassus had had the tax farmers' contract renegotiated. The Consular elections, delayed from the summer by a decree of Bibulus, were eventually held on October 17. Two supporters of the Triumvirate, Aulus Gabinius and Lucius Calpurnius Piso Caesoninus, whose daughter Caesar had recently married, won the day. Caesar was allocated the governorships of Italian Gaul, Transalpine Gaul and Illyricum (today Dalmatia) for five years. His friend Sallust wrote: "For himself he wanted a high command, an army and a war in some field where his gifts could shine in all their brightness." This is what he had now obtained and over the coming years he methodically set about conquering what is now France and Belgium. Rome called these territories Long-haired Gaul (*Gallia Comata*).

On December 10, Clodius at last took office as Tribune. Unfortunately, as his great crisis approached, Cicero was joined in Rome by Atticus and their correspondence stops. He was still guardedly optimistic about his prospects and thought that the worst that could happen would be a trial before the Military Assembly, as had been the case with Rabirius. Because its voting system favored the affluent, his chances of acquittal would, he felt, be reasonably good. In any case, "all Italy" would come to his support.

It soon transpired that the new Tribune had more ambitious plans than anyone had expected. He produced a far-reaching program, well tailored to win the support of the urban proletariat. Grain distributions to citizens in Rome would, for the first time, be absolutely free; the right of association was restored and the veto on local clubs revoked; officeholders were prohibited from halting public business by reporting bad omens on days when the General Assembly was due to vote on a bill; a limitation on legislation brought in by Tribunes was removed; and a restriction on the Censors' powers to expel Senators (presumably this was to protect *popularis* members) was imposed. The importance of the clubs or *collegia* for Clodius was that they would allow him to organize support (in the form of well-organized street gangs) in Rome's poorer districts.

Clodius was a mysterious and in some senses a maligned figure, whose behavior was so bizarre that for some people rational explanations were unnecessary. So far as can be judged from the uniformly hostile sources, he was a serious politician with a loyal constituency among the urban masses. He had a coherent reform program designed to advance their interests. According to Cicero, the restoration of political clubs meant that he had inherited "all Catilina's forces with scarcely any change of leaders." However, unlike Catilina, Clodius saw that there was a distinction to be drawn between revolution and behavior that was merely illegal. Clodius observed the basic political norms, attending Senate meetings and standing for office. In the years ahead he stood for Aedile, successfully, and for Praetor. From the few scraps of evidence that remain, he maintained a client list both in the city and beyond.

Clodius's originality lay in his perception of what could be achieved by *consistent* violence on the streets and in the Forum. For half a century politicians of every persuasion had resorted to force from time to time. The scale of public spaces in the city center, the absence of wide streets or avenues and the facts that there was no police force and that soldiers were forbidden to cross the *pomoerium* meant that gangs could temporarily take over the seat of government, terrorize officeholders and force legislation through or impede it. Clodius saw that this could be turned into a permanent state of affairs. He developed the concept of the standing gang, equipped and ready to act at any time. Once his Tribuneship was over in December 58, this would become his power base. He realized that this private army would need an operational headquarters and, apparently, took over the Temple of the Castors in the Forum for a time, turning the building into a fortress by demolishing the steps that led down from its high podium. This was insurrection as a means of government rather than as a means of overthrowing a government.

What Clodius wanted to do with power, once he had achieved it, is uncertain. Unlike other radicals, whether of the left or right, he gave no indication that has come down to us of a serious interest in root-and-branch constitutional reform. He was happy enough to exploit the constitution or subvert it, but he had no idea of overthrowing it. Beneath the eccentricity of his politics probably lay a basically conventional ambition to climb the political ladder, reach the Consulship and make a fortune from misgoverning a province. In that sense, there was no material difference between him and his hot-tempered brother, Appius Claudius Pulcher, who stood on the other side of the political fence and was a leading conservative. Clodius was typical of his ancestors in his waywardness, volatile moods and disrespect for respectable opinion. He regarded the political scene in a highly personalized light and was not a man to be crossed lightly, as Cicero found out.

Wisely, Cicero had taken steps to protect his personal position by finding a friendly Tribune who agreed to veto all Clodius's reforms. In response, Clodius made a deal with Cicero: if Cicero would not block his legislation, he promised not to launch a prosecution. He made a point of being friendly with Cicero, saying that he wanted a reconciliation and blaming Terentia for their estrangement.

In late January or early February of 58, Clodius hurled his thunderbolt. He proposed two new bills, the first of which bought off the Consuls by allotting them rich provinces (Macedonia and Cilicia) for the following year with unusually generous financial allowances. The second cynically broke the assurance he had given Cicero. It punished with the denial of the traditional symbols of hospitality, fire and water (in other words exile), any public official who executed or *had* executed a citizen without due process of law. This was, in effect, a renewal or restatement of an existing law, but its target was obvious. It would be wrong, though, to see the bill simply as a question of revenge. From the point of view of his patron, Caesar, waiting outside the city limits in order to watch developments before he left for his provincial command, the indictment of Cicero for illegal acts as Consul would distract the Senate from examining the legality of his own legislation. More broadly, Clodius was exactly the weapon Caesar needed to keep the Senate cowed and on the defensive.

Cicero responded by going into mourning, wearing torn clothes and letting his beard and hair grow, and presented himself in public as a suppliant. This was recognized behavior when a Roman found himself in serious trouble and especially if facing prosecution in the courts. Many *equites* followed suit and held a protest meeting at the Capitol. According to Plutarch, "the Senate met to pass a vote that the people should go into mourning as at times of public calamity." The Consuls, one of whom was Caesar's father-in-law, were politely unsympathetic. They opposed the measure, although the Senate as a whole seems to have been on Cicero's side. When Clodius surrounded the Senate House with armed men, many Senators ran out of the building, tearing their clothes as a sign of grief.

Although they did not want their involvement to become known, the First Triumvirate was complicit with Clodius, who, in another ingenious initiative, managed to temporarily remove the obstructive Cato from the scene, sending him on a commission to annex Cyprus. Special commands were his bane, but, as a strict constitutionalist, Cato felt obliged to accept an officially conferred duty. He was absent from Rome for two years. Clodius's move had two purposes: to further weaken the *optimates* and to provide revenue to pay for his planned free distribution of corn.

Caesar and Pompey knew what was going on but posed as candid friends, giving Cicero cordial if conflicting advice. Caesar said he should accept a command with him in Gaul; in that case, he would be seen to be acting from a position of strength. Pompey criticized Caesar for his advice, remarking that to quit Rome precipitately would be cowardly; Cicero should defend himself openly and, naturally, his old friend would be on hand to help him.

As the crisis came to a head, Pompey became increasingly embarrassed by his own double-dealing and withdrew to his splendid villa in the Alban Hills outside Rome. Cicero went to seek him out and plead for assistance. According to Plutarch, when the great man heard of Cicero's arrival he

> could not face seeing him. He was bitterly ashamed when he remembered how in the past Cicero had fought his battles on many important occasions and had often taken a particular line in politics for his sake; but he was Caesar's son-in-law, and at his request betrayed his previous obligations. He slipped out of the house by another door and so avoided the interview.

Clodius shared with Cicero an inability to hold his tongue. He was indiscreet about Caesar's connivance and there were signs that public opinion was swinging to Cicero. Now that he had officially taken up his military command, Caesar was not allowed to enter the city. He was studiedly reasonable, assuring the crowd that, as everyone well knew, he had disapproved of Lentulus's execution—but he equally disapproved of retrospective legislation.

Wherever Cicero turned, support was lukewarm and he slowly came to realize that his position was untenable. He could hardly leave his house without being pelted with mud and stones by the Tribune's gangs. Even friends were counseling retreat. At a meeting in his house, senior *optimates,* led by Hortensius, advised him to leave the city, promising him an early return—advice he took but never forgave. Most people were sympathetic in principle (or appeared to be), but nobody in practice would act against Clodius.

Despairing, Cicero carried a little statue of Minerva down through the Forum and up to the summit of the Capitol, where he dedicated it with the inscription: "To Minerva, Guardian of Rome." *He* had once been Rome's guardian and now he asked the goddess to protect the Republic during his enforced absence. Then, escorted by friends, he slipped out of the city, on foot in dead of night in order to avoid detection.

As soon as Cicero's departure was discovered, a furious Clodius placed a new, bolder measure before the People, this time condemning Cicero by name and confiscating his goods. He was to be refused fire and water and was forbidden to live closer than 400 miles from Rome. It is a sign of the affection in which Cicero was widely held, of his fundamental likeability, that most people paid little attention to the new law and happily put up the exile on his journey from Italy. There were exceptions, though: the Praetor of Sicily asked him to avoid the island, so he made his way instead through Macedonia and settled in Thessalonica, where the Roman Quaestor, Cnaeus Plancius, generously and not uncourageously took him into his official residence.

Cicero was always prone to excessive mood swings. He easily became overconfident when his affairs went well and a setback could drive him into an exaggerated depression. The present crisis was unlike anything he had faced before. Even the most sanguine mind would have been daunted. If we are to believe what he writes in his letters, he may have suffered something like a mental breakdown and seems to have attempted, or at least considered, suicide.

Before too long, though, the exile returned to something approaching his old form, scheming and arguing for his recall. He decided that Terentia, probably now in her early forties, should not join him because she would be more useful to his interests in Rome. Atticus bore the brunt of his newfound agitations, receiving a constant flow of suggestions, instructions and criticisms without apparent complaint.

But if Cicero was determined that one day he would return to Italy, his enemy had different ideas. Clodius did all he could to ensure that his victim's disappearance was permanent. He had his house on the Palatine burned down, together with some if not all of his villas in the country and arranged for the site of the house to be consecrated and reserved for a Temple of Liberty.

7

EXILE

The Rise of Caesar: 58–52 BC

Cicero was shattered by his downfall; he reported to Atticus that he was losing weight and crying a lot. Expulsion from Rome, the world city, and its center, the Forum, seemed to annihilate all he was and stood for.

He longed for his family, which must have gone through a terrifying time when the house in Rome was demolished. Terentia, the "frailty" of whose health caused him anxiety, and the seven-year-old Marcus were now homeless. Perhaps Quintus and Pomponia put them up, but we do not know, for, in the surviving correspondence, Cicero, preoccupied with his own emotions, does not discuss the matter. Atticus was a tower of strength and Terentia repeatedly told her husband how grateful she was for his help as she tried to put some order into their domestic affairs.

Cicero's thoughts often turned to Tullia, his favorite child. "I miss my daughter, the most loving, modest and clever daughter a man ever had, the image of my face and speech and mind." She was living with her husband, Calpurnius Piso, a model son-in-law, who was a Quaestor in 58 but gave up his foreign posting to work for Cicero's return.

The exile indulged himself by translating his grief and shock into high rhetoric. "Has any man ever fallen from so fine a position, with so good a cause, so strong in resources of talent, prudence and influence, and in the support of all honest men? Can I forget what I was, or fail to feel what I am and what I have lost—rank, fame, children, fortune, brother?" One senses here less a broken man than an orator looking for an admiring audience.

When it came to the allocation of blame for what had been done to him, Cicero's resentment overmastered him. His paranoia enriched with plausibility, he blamed the aristocrats in the Senate who had never accepted him as one of them and, he felt, had taken pleasure in abandoning him. He was particularly angry with his old rival Hortensius, who (he believed) had never forgiven him for outdoing him in the law courts. It was about such people that he complained to Atticus: "I will only say this, and I believe you know I am right: it was not enemies but jealous friends who ruined me."

It was, of course, the First Triumvirate that was really to blame: the three had knowingly let Clodius engineer Cicero's ruin. Curiously, though, Cicero said little against them and never directly criticized Pompey. Did he not see the link between his refusal to join the alliance and his subsequent political destruction? With the benefit of hindsight, the connection seems inescapable.

As soon as he had settled down in Thessalonica, he sent off letters to various public figures, including one to Pompey. Although he was familiar with Pompey's faults, he may have become too fond of him to credit his duplicity. More probably, he knew he would need his support in the future. Cicero was sure that at heart Pompey was no radical; sooner or later he would make common cause with the Senate. And in the short run, Cicero needed Pompey for a more practical reason. Without his active backing it was clear that he would never be allowed to return to Rome.

Atticus came in for his share of criticism. If only he had loved Cicero enough he would have given him better advice; instead he had "looked on and done nothing." Atticus very sensibly paid no attention to this unfair jibe and went on doing all he could to help, even offering to place his personal fortune, now much augmented by the death of an "extremely difficult" but extremely wealthy uncle, at Cicero's disposal. This was a gesture of some significance for, with the confiscation of his property, Cicero's financial affairs were in a very poor state. Cicero's letters to Atticus are full of practical advice, complaints and queries.

In June 58 the Senate attempted to pass a motion reprieving him, but a

Tribune friendly to Clodius blocked it. In October eight Tribunes drafted a law to revoke the second of Clodius's two laws (the one naming Cicero). It failed too, but Cicero was not too disappointed, for he thought it "carelessly drafted." As the year drew to a close he expressed growing worries about the Tribunes-Elect and the likely attitudes of the incoming Consuls. One of these was his old enemy Metellus Nepos, who had opened the sniping against him on the last day of his Consulship five years before.

However, Metellus agreed (more or less) to a reconciliation and the senior Consul, Publius Cornelius Lentulus Spinther, turned out to be a strong supporter. The Tribunes were sympathetic too. Atticus was successful in his informal role as campaign manager for Cicero's recall. With his aptitude for networking and the freedom with which he could cross enemy lines, he gradually and discreetly pushed matters forward.

Even more helpful than Atticus was the deteriorating situation in Rome. Only a few weeks after Cicero's melancholy departure for Greece, Clodius turned his attentions to Pompey and a supporter of his, the Consul Aulus Gabinius (a onetime friend of Catilina's or, in Cicero's dismissive phrase, his "pet dancer"). With his gangs of supporters he made life so dangerous for Pompey that the former general shut himself up for much of the time in his villa outside the city.

It is possible that Clodius was being egged on by Caesar or Crassus, the idea being to keep Pompey's hands full and so reduce the chances of his coming to terms with the *optimates.* More probably, Clodius was simply asserting his independence from his patrons and putting himself beyond their reach. He was aware that the pressure for Cicero's recall would grow and may have guessed that the beleaguered Pompey, skulking helplessly at home, might be tempted to change his mind. There were repeated riots and disorder throughout the city, and it was becoming difficult to conduct public business. On January 1, 57, after the close of Clodius's term as Tribune, Consul Lentulus proposed a motion in the Senate allowing Cicero's return. It was passed with a good majority. Clodius deployed a troop of gladiators, already assembled for the funeral of a relative, to prevent the bill from being put to the People. Some Tribunes were wounded in the Forum—a scandalous development—and Cicero's brother, Quintus, only just escaped with his life. He was left lying unnoticed among the corpses in the square and for a time was presumed dead.

The only way to deal with Clodius was to fight fire with fire. Two Tribunes, Titus Annius Milo, a rich conservative who was popular with the urban masses because he had paid for sumptuous theatrical performances and gladiatorial shows, and Publius Sestius, a long-standing supporter of Cicero, recruited their own armed groups. Many weeks of street fighting ensued. In his defense of Sestius against charges of violence in 56, Cicero described in graphic terms the effects of this gang warfare: "The Tiber was full of citizens' corpses, the public sewers were choked with them and the blood that streamed from the Forum had to be mopped up with sponges." To begin with, the cure was worse than the disease and public business once more came to a standstill. However, by the summer Clodius, while by no means defeated, was at least being contained.

Pompey was now persuaded to back Cicero's recall, but Caesar's approval was more difficult to win. Although he was preoccupied with the conquest of Long-haired Gaul, he managed to devote much attention to monitoring and, so far as he could from a distance, managing the political situation in Rome. Cicero was no longer a major force either with his traditional constituency, the *equites,* or with the *optimates* in the Senate, but he was one of the few politicians of the day who could have an impact on events as an individual. As Rome's best-known advocate and with his mastery of the art of rhetoric, his opinions carried a certain weight. To some extent, his political isolation worked in his favor, for it contributed to a reputation for independence of mind. He was growing into an elder statesman.

Caesar finally gave his reluctant consent to Cicero's return, presumably realizing that it was pointless to resist what he could not prevent. But he insisted that, in return, Cicero promise not to attack the First Triumvirate openly. Quintus offered Pompey a guarantee, on his brother's behalf, of future good behavior.

Enthusiasm for Cicero's cause grew. He became, briefly, the focus for a coming together of almost every shade of political opinion. He had suffered at the hands of Clodius and his rehabilitation was an economical and elegant way of publicly rejecting mob rule. How this was to be achieved, though, required a degree of care. It was possible to mount a plausible case against the legality of all Clodius's acts as Tribune—on the grounds that his renunciation of patrician status had been handled improperly and, accordingly, his election was invalid. However, his reforms had attracted enthusiastic popular support and it would be unwise to disturb them. Even Cato took a lenient line on this topic, because he did not want to see his annexation of Cyprus nullified. It is disconcerting that the uncompromising constitutionalist was willing to bend his principles when *his* interests were at stake. Cicero was much put out by this, and for a while relations between the two men were icy.

Lentulus decided to proceed by stages. In May 57 the Senate endorsed his proposal that the various Roman officials and citizens who had helped Cicero during his banishment be formally thanked. It also agreed to convene a meeting of the Military Assembly later in the summer to consider his recall. This was a little odd because for many years this Assembly's main function had been the election of senior magistrates; its use on this occasion was probably due to the fact that its voting system was more manageable than that of the General Assembly. The meeting was extensively publicized throughout Italy, and citizens were encouraged to come to Rome and vote. The political establishment was taking no chances with the Roman mob, which was still largely under Clodius's thumb.

Then, in July, an unusually well-attended meeting of the Senate called on the Consuls and magistrates to prepare legislation for Cicero's recall. No Tribune vetoed the proposal and Clodius was the only one to speak against it. Except for Clodius's brother Appius and two Tribunes ("bought at auction," as the word went), the entire magistracy came together behind a motion to repeal the law that had banished Cicero. No reference was made to the general measure condemning the execution of Roman citizens without trial, which had in fact precipitated Cicero's hurried departure from Rome. The assumption now was that it simply did not apply to him.

The campaign accelerated. Thanks largely to lobbying by Pompey, all kinds of institutions—town councils, associations of tax farmers, craft guilds—passed resolutions in favor of recall. Pompey instructed his veterans to attend the Military Assembly, which was held in Rome on the Field of Mars in August. The most important men in the State, led by Pompey, addressed the meeting, which was guarded by Milo's gangs and teams of gladiators. Senior Senators superintended the voting. The bill was passed triumphantly.

Apart from his appearance at the Senate, there is no record of where

Clodius spent his time during these weeks. His career shows that he was no coward and he is likely to have made his presence felt in some way, if not directly on the Field of Mars. He had suffered a serious setback, but he soon demonstrated that he was by no means routed.

In Greece Cicero's moods had been seesawing between pessimism and elation. Some months earlier he had written to Atticus: "From your letter and from the facts themselves I see that I am utterly finished." Now he had every justification for euphoria. As the news improved, he decided it was safe to leave boring Thessalonica and stay somewhere closer to Italy. He moved to Dyrrachium, a port on the Adriatic Sea, which was only a few days' sail to Brundisium; he was "patron" of the town and had "warm friends" among the townsfolk. Confident enough to anticipate the outcome of events in Rome, he set sail before the vote was taken and arrived on Italian soil on the Nones of August. It was an auspicious day, for it happened to be the anniversary of Brundisium's foundation. The town was *en fête* and Cicero's arrival added an excitingly topical dimension to the civic celebrations. Even more joyfully, it was Tullia's birthday and she was there to greet him. In her early twenties and as always the apple of his eye, she was now a widow. Her first husband, Calpurnius Piso, had recently died—from what cause is unknown. Although it had been an arranged marriage, the union had been a happy one.

Cicero's journey up Italy and his reception in Rome were as close to a Triumph as a nonmilitary man could aspire to. There were massive demonstrations in his favor and he said later that Italy had taken him on its shoulders and carried him back to Rome. He described it all in a long, excited letter to Atticus. Official delegations came out to meet him from every township and gave him "the most flattering marks of regard." As usual he overreacted: speaking a few days later, he said that their decrees and votes of congratulation and confidence were like a ladder "by which I did not simply return home but climbed up to heaven." When he reached the outskirts of Rome on September 4, almost everybody on his list of VIPs turned out to welcome him. Only his enemies stayed away. At the Capena Gate the steps of the temples were packed with ordinary citizens who greeted Cicero with loud applause. The Forum and Capitol were filled with "spectacular" crowds.

It was a great moment, but Cicero already detected difficulties ahead.

He suspected disaffection among the aristocrats, whom he still blamed for his misfortunes. "It is a sort of second life I am beginning. Already, now that I am here, secret resentment and open jealousy are setting in among those who championed me when I was away."

The day after his arrival Cicero gave a speech in the Senate before later offering his thanks briefly to the People. It was not one of his most brilliant performances. The speech was little more than a list, larded with invective, of those whom he believed to have betrayed him, contrasted with praise for those who had helped secure his return. He described Gabinius, one of the two Consuls of 58 who had refused to lift a finger on his behalf, as "heavy with wine, somnolence and debauchery, with hair well-oiled and neatly braided, with drooping eyes and slobbering mouth." As for his colleague Calpurnius Piso, "talking with him is much the same as holding a discussion with a wooden post in the Forum . . . a dull and brutish clod . . . profligate, filthy and intemperate." On the credit side of the account, pride of place went to Pompey, "whose courage, fame and achievements are unparalleled in the records of any nation or any age." It was the first indication that, far from being an independent political operator as he had tried to be in the past, Cicero was now, in effect, a creature of the First Triumvirate.

Meanwhile, Clodius had been busy. He was not finished with Cicero. For some time there had been a growing food shortage, exacerbated by Clodius's extension of the free corn dole to the urban poor. He now spread it about that a sudden scarcity during the past few weeks was all Cicero's fault. There was a riot and stones were thrown at Consul Metellus Nepos. Cicero reacted firmly and immediately. In the Senate he proposed Pompey for a special commission to take charge of grain supplies. A decree authorizing the preparation of appropriate legislation was passed. Cicero was delighted at having outmaneuvered Clodius so quickly and comprehensively. "The decree was read out immediately," he told Atticus, "and the People applauded in the silly new fashion by chanting my name."

The following day the Consuls drafted a law giving Pompey control over grain supplies for five years. He asked for fifteen Lieutenant-Commissioners, one of whom was to be Cicero (who accepted, typically, on condition that he would not have to leave Rome). The special command was agreed and Pompey left Rome at once to relieve the shortage, which he did with his customary efficiency.

The Senate's position was becoming increasingly weak. This was almost entirely its own fault, even if its blunders were not exclusively the products of stupidity. In the eyes of the Senate, the integrity of the constitution was at stake, and in particular the fundamental principle that no single member of the ruling class should be allowed to predominate. This was the cause for which the *optimates* had driven Pompey into the arms of Caesar and Crassus. Although Cicero was not such a powerful figure, they were ill-advised to alienate him, for his intelligent and flexible conservatism could have helped them to resist radical outsiders like Caesar and to attract Pompey into their camp by judicious concessions. The Senate acted in ways that made its worst fears likely to come to pass. It lost control of the domestic security situation and now found itself compelled to do what it most wanted to avoid: give yet another special command to Pompey.

Having plunged more or less successfully into the political melee, Cicero had some domestic worries to exercise him. His property was to be returned to him, but the question arose of compensation for the demolition of his house on the Palatine and of his country villas. He had been unable to earn money at the bar for a year and a half and was in urgent need of funds. Also there was the problem of the temple that Clodius had erected on the site of his home; unless the consecration could be annulled, rebuilding would be out of the question. The matter was put before the relevant religious authority, the College of Pontiffs.

Like the Senate, the College of Pontiffs wanted to avoid a full-scale confrontation with Clodius. It came up with a clever formulation which invalidated the consecration without discrediting its originator. At a meeting of the Senate on October 1, the College's findings were discussed. Given the absence in Long-haired Gaul of the Chief Pontiff (who might well have taken a view less friendly to Cicero), a spokesman for the College emphasized that it saw its role as judge of the religious issue and that the Senate was judge of the law. Those Pontiffs who were also Senators then asked to speak in their latter capacity and did so on Cicero's behalf. Clodius was present; after some futile filibustering, he saw that further opposition in the Senate would be pointless. On the following day a decree was passed and the Consuls, with the help of surveyors, proceeded to agree to a financial valuation of the house and villas. To Cicero's annoyance, the house on the Palatine was estimated at 2 million sesterces (much less than the original purchase price of 3.5 million sesterces), the villa at Tusculum at 500,000 sesterces and the one at Formiae at 250,000 sesterces.

The affair confirmed Cicero's continuing resentment against fair-weather friends in the Senate, who he believed would never let slip an opportunity to harm his interests. He told Atticus: "Those same gentlemen (you don't need me to tell you their names) who formerly clipped my wings don't want to see them grow back to their old size. However, I hope they *are* growing already."

It turned out that Clodius had only appeared to accept defeat in the gang wars: he was running for Aedile in 56—an important venture, for, if successful, he would once again have a constitutional position. When the elections were postponed Clodius stepped up the pressure on the streets. He let it be known that if elections were not held soon, he would carry out reprisals against the city. In November he staged a series of riots. On November 3 an armed gang drove away the workmen who were rebuilding Cicero's house on the Palatine. From this vantage point they threw stones at Quintus's house nearby and set it on fire. A few days later Clodius mounted an attack on Cicero in person. Cicero wrote excitedly to Atticus:

> On November 11 as I was coming down the Holy Way, he came after me with his men. Uproar! Stones flying, cudgels and swords in evidence. And like a bolt from the blue! I retired into Tettius Damio's forecourt, and my companions had no difficulty keeping out the rowdies. Clodius himself could have been killed, but I am becoming a dietitian, I'm sick of surgery.

The next morning, in broad daylight, Clodius led a force armed with swords and shields to storm and burn the house of Milo, his competitor for mastery of the streets. A counterattack beat them off and a number of leading Clodians were killed. For the time being, this was a decisive encounter, and Clodius temporarily lost control of the situation.

In general, Cicero was in a remarkably good mood, considering the political disarray, his continuing money worries and the threats to his physical safety. "My heart is high," he wrote to Atticus, "higher even than in my palmy days, but my purse is low." We do not know the reason for his elation, because the surviving correspondence with Atticus is sparse for a number of months, but he may have been buoyed by signs of strain among the First Triumvirate. In December, apparently with Pompey's tacit support, a long-standing Senatorial grievance received a new airing: a Tribune criticized Caesar's second Land Reform Act, which had removed from state ownership the profitable Capuan Marches and had been a sore point with the *optimates* ever since. The Senate had been forced to authorize 40 million sesterces to pay for the corn supply and this new expenditure went to highlight the loss of state revenues that the law had brought about.

In the new year a problem with the Egyptian Pharaoh led to a falling out between Pompey and Crassus. Although nominally a freestanding kingdom, Egypt was effectively a Roman dependency. Its importance was not merely its legendary wealth but its grain production, which served as an increasingly valuable complement to Sicilian supplies. King Ptolemy had been expelled from his country by his subjects and the question arose of who should reinstall him. A stable Egypt was in Rome's interest and, what was more, the king could be counted on to pay a generous reward to his lucky savior. The Senate thought that the former Consul Lentulus, now governor of Cilicia, should be given the commission. However, as it promised to be an extremely lucrative operation, Pompey was understood not to be averse to accepting it himself.

This was most embarrassing to Cicero, who was indebted to both men for their help in ending his exile. He was seeing a good deal of Pompey at this time, who as usual failed to make his wishes explicit. For once, Cicero found this vagueness helpful, for it allowed him to press Lentulus's qualifications for the job without causing offense. He describes these attempts in laborious detail in a sequence of long letters to Lentulus. Reading between the lines, one senses that he knew he was fighting for a lost cause. The *optimates* were determined to prevent Pompey from winning the commission under any circumstances and, with breathtaking shortsightedness, allied themselves with Clodius to present a common front. Pompey strongly suspected that Crassus was behind this curious turn of events.

About this time an old prophecy was discovered in the Sibylline Books, stored in a vault in the temple of Jupiter on the Capitol Hill and consulted in times of emergency. Cicero had little faith in them, though he admired the ingenuity by which they avoided specific references to persons and place and so appeared to predict everything that happened. On this occasion, they conveniently but unconvincingly pronounced that the Egyptian king should not be restored "with a host." The point was that the Senate did not want to see the great commander in charge of another army. To their disappointment Pompey let it be known that he would be willing to restore Ptolemy without military assistance.

With typical impudence Clodius, who had by now won election as Aedile and was back in office, brought Milo to court in February 56 for the illegal use of force. Milo appeared with Pompey as his supporting counselor. The Forum was packed with supporters of both sides. Clodius's people tried to shout Pompey down when he got up to speak, but he plowed doggedly on. He concluded with some highly scabrous verses about Clodius and Clodia. Cicero described the scene in a letter to his brother, Quintus:

> Pale with fury, [Clodius] started a game of question and answer in the middle of the shouting:
>
> "Who's starving the people to death?"
>
> "Pompey," answered his gang.
>
> "Who wants to go to Alexandria?"
>
> "Pompey."
>
> "Who do you want to go?"
>
> "Crassus . . ."
>
> About quarter past two the Clodians started spitting at us, as though on a signal. Sharp rise in temperature! They made a push to dislodge us, our side countercharged. Flight of gang. Clodius was hurled from the Speakers' Platform, at which point I too made off for fear of what might happen in the free-for-all.

Pompey found it hard to handle this kind of abuse and, nervous, stayed away from the Forum. He eventually abandoned the idea of the Egyptian command (as did Lentulus, who had no intention of proceeding without an army behind him) and came to believe that there was a plot against his life. Soon after he decided to bring men to the city from his country estates in northern Italy to protect him.

Cicero continued to speak in the courts as and when the opportunity arose. Sometime in the spring of 56 he gave his entertaining (and successful) defense of young Marcus Caelius Rufus, his former pupil, against Clodia's charge of attempted murder. This allowed him plenty of opportunity to amuse himself and his listeners with jabs at her brother. As ever, he could not resist a joke. "My refutation would be framed in considerably more forcible terms," he said, "if I did not feel inhibited by the fact that the woman's husband—sorry, I mean brother, I *always* make that slip—is my personal enemy."

In February accusations of bribery and breach of the peace were laid against Sestius, the Tribune who had pressed for Cicero's recall. Cicero agreed at once to represent him. In the meantime, he was involved in a separate trial defending a former Aedile on a bribery charge. By a happy chance the man had saved Sestius's life in a riot in the Forum and Cicero was able to use the speech to lay down the outline of his defense of Sestius. This had the helpful effect of preparing public opinion.

By the time the case against Sestius came to court in early March, political observers in Rome were convinced that the First Triumvirate was in serious trouble. There were rumors that it was teetering and might even collapse. Now that Pompey had broken with Clodius and Crassus, perhaps he could be persuaded to distance himself from Caesar, preoccupied in Gaul. Cicero judged the moment right to set out a viable political alternative. In his defense of Sestius he restated his political philosophy. Although he showed little sign of understanding the true balance of forces, he offered a rational and civilized alternative to the policies of the reactionaries in the Senate. Rome no longer faced any foreign dangers, Cicero claimed; the threat now came from within. Radicals like Clodius were not true friends of the People and, by the same token, the term *optimates* should not be restricted to a small backwards-looking circle of aristocrats. All men of goodwill were *optimates* now.

To summarize his message he invented a famous but almost untranslatable slogan: *otium cum dignitate.* By *otium* he meant "peace" as distinct not only from war but also from engagement in public affairs. This is what Cicero promised the People, security at the price of minimum involvement in the political process. Peace could be achieved only if respect was given to the traditional political establishment. In other words, social harmony could be achieved only if the balance of power was shifted from the People back to the Senate. Cicero was presenting himself as a Sulla without blood and tears—but also, unfortunately, a Sulla without a method, for he had little idea how reconciliation and reform might be attained in practice.

One of the witnesses for the prosecution of Sestius was Publius Vatinius, who as Tribune in 59 had helped Caesar with his legislation and had proposed the law giving him his special five-year command. In cross-examination Cicero "cut him up to the applause of gods and men" with extraordinary, but probably calculated, fury. There was growing talk that the Gallic command was unconstitutional and an attack on Vatinius was a good way to soften up the terrain for a later assault.

This was playing a dangerous game. Quintus was worried and told his brother that he might be going too far for Caesar's comfort. Cicero did his best to reassure him. In April, flush with his victory in the case against Sestius, who was acquitted unanimously, he felt bold enough to place the question of Caesar's second Land Reform Act on the agenda of a Senate meeting in May. Its repeal would be an open attack on Caesar. Cicero's move was received with unusual warmth. His confidence was at its height and he was sure that his political career was back on track. He had regained his lost prestige and was delighted to see that his house was as full of visitors and petitioners as it had been in his heyday.

One evening in early April Cicero called on Pompey, who informed him he was leaving shortly for Sardinia to buy grain. Pompey was being more than ordinarily economical with the truth. When he left the city he in fact made a detour before setting sail for Sardinia and first made his way to Luca, a town at the extreme limit of Italian Gaul, where Caesar had secretly summoned him for emergency talks. Taking time off from his operations in Gaul, Caesar had already met Crassus in Ravenna and was planning a counterstroke which would silence his opponents in Rome.

Caesar had spent the last two years in a series of brilliantly conducted military campaigns. When taking up his governorship, he hoped for an opportunity to build on the military reputation he had won three years previously during his governorship in Spain. He was in luck, for long-standing hostilities between two Germanic tribes led one of them to invade Gaul from what is now Switzerland. Caesar claimed to see a potential threat to Italy from barbarian hordes and reacted vigorously. He routed the enemy with ease and then turned his attention to the other tribe, led by a charismatic chieftain who had incautiously reminded him when they once met that Caesar's death would not be unwelcome in certain circles in Rome. This accurately aimed insult was not left unavenged. A victory, this time hard won, ensued.

"The Germans' left was routed," Caesar wrote, "but their right began to press our troops hard by weight of numbers. Their perilous position attracted the attention of young Publius Crassus [son of Caesar's political partner], better able to move about and see what was happening than those in the fighting line. He therefore sent up a third line to their relief. This move turned the battle once more in our favor, and the enemy's whole army broke and fled without stopping until they came to the Rhine, some fifteen miles away. A very few of the strongest tried to swim the river and a few others saved themselves by finding boats . . . but all the rest were hunted down and killed by our cavalry."

Risings in the northeast gave Caesar the pretext to proceed to the subjugation of the entire country from the Mediterranean to the Channel. He briefly visited that remote, almost mythical island, Britannia, an exploit that was militarily insignificant but was received as a huge propaganda coup back home.

Propaganda was a matter of some moment. His political opponents looked for any opportunity to criticize him and argued that the war itself was illegal on the grounds that he had not had sufficient excuse to intervene. To promote his cause, Caesar devoted great care to his dispatches to the Senate and in due course wrote them up as a history of the Gallic wars.

He was proving to be a field commander of the first rank. Pompey and Crassus were gradually coming to realize that their junior partner was growing into a serious competitor in both wealth and reputation. He was no longer the "young man" they had seen him to be in 59.

Caesar was always on the move, ready to react to the latest military threat as it arose. But wherever he was stationed, he assiduously nurtured his links with the capital. After the campaigning season he spent every winter in Italian Gaul, a vantage point from which he could keep a close eye on political developments. His newfound riches were at the disposal of anyone who would sign up (literally in many cases, with oaths and written guarantees) to protect his interests. Few applicants were turned away.

From Caesar's perspective the news from Rome in the spring of 56 could not have been worse. Clodius was running amok, Pompey and Crassus were at loggerheads, and several allies who stood for public office lost their elections. Caesar spoke bitterly at Luca about Cicero's Senate motion to nullify his second Land Reform Act. He could see that the situation was slipping out of his grasp.

Caesar's partners had long since gained all that had been covenanted when the First Triumvirate set up business: Pompey's eastern settlement had been approved, land had been found for his soldiers and, for Crassus, the tax farmers' contracts had been rewritten. Neither had any particular interest in keeping the alliance going.

With typical decisiveness and sensitivity to changing circumstances, Caesar proposed an extension to their agreement which would bring new and clearly identifiable benefits for each of them. Crassus and Pompey would stand for the Consulship in 55 and Caesar would guarantee their election by sending soldiers from his army to Rome to vote for them. Once in office the new Consuls would see to it that they were awarded new five-year special commands in Spain and Syria respectively. Crassus aimed to refresh his military laurels by leading a major expedition against the Parthian Empire, which neighbored Rome's eastern possessions. In order to ensure strict equality of treatment, Caesar's Gallic command would also be extended for an additional five years, which would give him the time he needed to complete the annexation of Gaul. After that he too would stand for a second Consulship. It was an elegant plan, with something in it for all three partners—so much so that Crassus and Pompey readily agreed to paper over their quarrels.

The agreement at Luca—especially the five-year commands—was to be kept a deep secret, at least for the time being, but it soon became clear that the alliance had hardened and that Pompey was back in Caesar's camp.

When Pompey eventually arrived in Sardinia, he looked up Quintus and warned him to rein in his brother's behavior, especially his attack on Caesar's land legislation. Quintus repeated the exchange that followed to Cicero: "Ah, just the man I want," "Very lucky our bumping into each other. Unless you have a serious talk with Marcus, you're going to have to pay up on that guarantee you gave me on his behalf." Beneath the joviality there was a new and unexpected steeliness. Pompey also sent Cicero a direct message, telling him not to take any action on the Campanian land.

Understanding at once that everything had changed, Cicero obeyed without demur and stayed away from the Senate in May when Caesar's legislation was scheduled to be discussed. As he told his brother: "On this question I am muzzled." It soon became clear that more would be asked of him than silence: the First Triumvirate was going to demand his active support. To the general amazement, Cicero showed almost instantly that he was willing to provide it.

How was this volte face to be explained? The simplest answer was that, after his brief rebellion, Cicero realized once and for all the futility of trying to maintain a freestanding political role. It was humiliating, but in the absence of effective political support from any other quarter he could see no alternative to capitulation to the First Triumvirate. But it was also true that indebtedness for a favor was a serious matter in ancient Rome; Cicero was under a heavy obligation to Caesar and Pompey for approving his return from exile, and acceding to their wishes was a way of repaying it. Finally, he remained bitter about his fellow Senators. If they would not let him into their circle, he would have to look elsewhere to maintain his position. Their flirtation with Clodius added insult to injury and made it all the more imperative that he did not remain isolated. By the end of May Cicero was helping to push through Senate proposals from Caesar which as recently as March he had called monstrous things. These engaged the Treasury to pay for four legions which Caesar had recruited without permission and on his own initiative and gave him leave to recruit ten subordinate commanders.

At the beginning of June the Senate discussed, as it was legally obliged to do, the allocation of provinces for 54. Lucius Domitius Ahenobarbus was a candidate for the Consulship of 55, and if he won the election he would be ready for a post-Consular foreign posting in January 54. He had a large client list in Transalpine Gaul, currently under Caesar's control, and wanted to take over as its governor, for by then Caesar's five-year term would have ended. This was a serious threat: if Ahenobarbus was not halted in his tracks, Caesar would be unable to have his Gallic command extended, as had been agreed at Luca.

So Cicero was enlisted to give a major address on this subject. He spoke in extravagant praise of Caesar, who (he argued) should be allowed to complete the good work he had started. He would probably need an extension of only two years and, as it was what he wanted, it should not be ruled out by allowing his provinces to be allocated at this stage. The conquest of Long-haired Gaul was vital to Italy's security and, as Caesar was in winning form, there was no doubt that it would be accomplished expeditiously. When Atticus inquired why he had not as usual received an advance copy of the speech, Cicero wrote back contritely:

> Come on! Do you really think there is anyone I would sooner have read and approve my compositions than you? So why did I send this one to anybody else first? Because the person [probably Pompey] to whom I did send it was pressing me for it and I did not have two copies. There was also the fact (I might as well stop nibbling at what has to be swallowed) that I was not exactly proud of my recantation hymn. But good night to principle, sincerity and honor!

Cicero's frame of mind shifted uneasily from one mood to another, but at heart he was depressed. He could not help despising himself for doing Caesar's bidding. Now fifty years old, he felt that his political career was over. He confided to his brother: "These years of my life which ought to be passing in the plenitude of Senatorial dignity are spent in the hurly-burly of forensic practice or rendered tolerable by my studies at home."

Over the next few years Caesar's gang of three made extensive use of Cicero's legal services as a number of friends trooped through the law courts under his care. One of them was Balbus, the rich Spaniard who had become Caesar's confidential agent and who was accused of having illegally acquired his Roman citizenship. Cicero's defense rested on the plausible proposition that the case was really intended as an indirect attack on the First Triumvirate. This was a fruitless exercise, he argued cogently, and the prosecution would be well advised to think again and let the matter drop. Cicero won the case and Balbus was acquitted.

After defending one of Pompey's supporters, Cicero complained to a friend that he was becoming disillusioned with the law. "I was weary of it even in the days when youth and ambition spurred me forward, and when moreover I was at liberty to refuse a case I did not care for. But now life is simply not worth living." His correspondence reveals his continuing uncertainty, even feelings of guilt, about his conduct. "After all, what could be more humiliating than our lives today, and especially mine?" he confided to Atticus. "For you, though you are a political animal by nature, have not actually lost your freedom. . . . But so far as I am concerned, people think I have left my senses if I speak on politics as I ought, and a powerless prisoner if I say nothing. So how am I expected to feel?"

The judgment of history has been as harsh on Cicero as he was on himself. On the face of it, his decision to go along with the wishes of the First Triumvirate was weakly self-interested. It was certainly interpreted as being so. He was much criticized and all the old charges were exhumed—the laughable epic on his Consulship, the self-important letter to Pompey in 63 and the unmanly behavior during his exile.

But it is hard to see what else Cicero could have done if he was not to retire into silence and country living. This was not his most glorious hour, but he was taking the only action likely to keep him in the game. His own view that he was uniquely placed to mediate among the conflicting forces on the political scene was not entirely unreasonable. Although the First Triumvirate had reasserted its authority in no uncertain terms, he remained convinced that the alliance would not last forever. Caesar's military successes made it increasingly clear that he and Pompey were competitors. In the long run one of them would have to give ground and yield first place. Circumstances had compelled Cicero to execute a strategic retreat and, although he has been accused through the centuries of inconsistency, his tactical maneuvers did reflect a firm underlying position.

Two years later he wrote a long, reflective letter to an aristocratic friend, designed as a public rebuttal to his critics, in which he set out a comprehensive justification of his actions. He pointed out that in politics the means can vary from time to time while the end remains the same. "I believe in moving with the times," he noted.

> Unchanging consistency of standpoint has never been considered a virtue in great statesmen. At sea it is good sailing to run before the gale, even if the ship cannot make harbor; but if she *can* make harbor by changing tack, only a fool would risk shipwreck by holding to the original course rather than change it and still reach his destination.

> Similarly, while all of us as statesmen should set before our eyes the goal of peace with honor to which I have so often pointed, it is our aim, not our language, which must always be the same.

Disappointment in public affairs drove Cicero to make the most of the comforts of private life and the consolations of literature and philosophy. With Quintus away in Sardinia, he spent time superintending the rebuilding of both his and his brother's houses.

Now that the two boys, Marcus and Cicero's nephew Quintus, were nearing their teens, their schooling had to be thought of. Cicero hired the services of a well-known Greek grammarian and literary scholar, Tyrannio of Amisus, to teach them at home. While his own nine-year-old son was an ordinary child with no exceptional talents, Quintus, who was now eleven, was impressively precocious and, according to his uncle, was "getting on famously with his lessons." Cicero was amused by his description of some wrangle between Terentia and his brother's wife, the endlessly difficult Pomponia. "Quintus (a very good boy)," he wrote to his brother in the spring of 56, "talked to me at length and in the nicest way about the disagreements between our two ladies. It was really most entertaining."

Tyrannio also helped out with a reorganization of Cicero's library, much of which must have been dispersed or destroyed by Clodius's gangs during his exile. A couple of Atticus's library clerks were borrowed to help with "gluing and other operations." The results delighted him. "Those shelves of yours are the last word in elegance, now that the labels have brightened up the volumes."

In 55 Pompey and Crassus held their prearranged Consulships and there was even less for Cicero to do. As with politicians throughout the ages, when events compel them to spend more time with their families, he made the best of things. He wrote to Atticus:

> But seriously, while all other amusements and pleasures have lost their charm because of my age and the state of the country, literature relieves and refreshes me. I would rather sit on that little seat you have beneath Aristotle's bust than in our Consuls' chairs of state, and I would rather take a stroll with you at your home than with the personage [i.e., Pompey] in whose company it appears that I am obliged to walk.

Clodius was still being troublesome. A strange "rumbling and a noise," perhaps an earth tremor, had been heard in a suburb of Rome. The Senate had referred the matter to the soothsayers, who pronounced that expiation should be offered to the gods for various offenses, including the profanation of hallowed sites and impiety in the conduct of an ancient sacrifice. Clodius ingeniously argued that the site in question was Cicero's house on the Palatine, which the College of Pontiffs had wrongly ruled never to have been consecrated at all. In a long harangue to the Senate, Cicero retorted that the mysterious sound had nothing to do with him but must be put down to Clodius's bad behavior. The house in question was not his at all but a completely different one, which Clodius had acquired after murdering its owner, and the sacrifice in question was, of course, that of the Good Goddess whose ceremonies Clodius had polluted.

Aware that his public image needed burnishing but sensing the public would not welcome any more self-praise from his own pen, Cicero tried to interest a respected historian, Lucius Lucceius, in writing a history of his Consulship, exile and return, the main purpose of which would be to expose the "perfidy, artifice and betrayal of which many were guilty towards me." He was candid about his expectations and asked Lucceius to write more enthusiastically than perhaps he felt. "Waive the laws of history for once. Do not scorn personal bias, if it urge you strongly in favor." Lucceius agreed, although for some reason the book seems never to have appeared.

A high point of the year 55 was the grand opening of Pompey's splendid new theater on the Field of Mars. Construction had started in 59 and the project was designed to show off its founder's wealth and power. It was a statement in stone and mortar that he was Rome's leading citizen.

The program included spectacular plays and shows. Cicero was unamused, writing to a friend: "What pleasure is there in having a *Clytemnestra* with six hundred mules or a *Trojan Horse* with three thousand mixing bowls?"

There were also lavish gladiatorial displays. These contests in which criminals were thrown to wild animals were among the most notorious features of Roman culture. By Cicero's day they were becoming an exotic and sadistic entertainment, but as so often with Roman customs they originated in a profound sense of tradition. For centuries, contests of hired fighters were held in honor of the glorious dead; blood flowed to slake the thirst of ancestors. It was no accident that they were usually staged in that sacred space, the Forum, with its magical fissures and chasms opening into the underworld. It was symbolically apt that gladiators waited in the subterranean tunnels beneath the pavement before coming up to fight. An ancient historian claimed that "the first gladiatorial show was given in Rome in the cattle market in the Consulship of Appius Claudius and Marcus Fulvius. It was given by Marcus and Decimus Brutus to honor their father's ashes at the funeral ceremony." For their descendants, today's Appius Claudius and Marcus Brutus, the violent deaths of armed men in the city's heart, its central square, in some vestigial but still resonant way, opened a lane to the land of the dead.

Some gladiators were slaves hired for the purpose (like the troupe trained by Atticus), others were condemned criminals. Many men enrolled as gladiators to buy themselves out of poverty. They were lodged in special barracks (one has been excavated in Pompeii). Life was tough, with whips, red-hot branding irons and iron fetters used to keep discipline.

However, successful gladiators were celebrities, like today's boxers and football stars. The gladiatorial ethos was so ingrained in the culture that in the following decade two allies, a Roman general and an African king, entered into a gladiatorial suicide pact after a lost battle. They fought a duel and when the Roman had killed his opponent he arranged for a slave to cut him down. We are told that children played gladiator games and young people discussed the form of leading fighters. Some were popular sex symbols: graffiti from the first century AD have been found on walls in Pompeii—one Thracian gladiator was "the maiden's prayer and delight" and "the doctor to cure girls." Their images appeared on pots and dishes.

Public displays attracted large crowds. A temporary stadium would be erected in the Forum. The gladiators fought with a variety of weapons and armor (some cruelly bizarre, such as the *andabatae,* whose helmets were blindfolds) and were never matched in their duels. So a naked *retiarius* was given a helmet, a net and trident and chased after a *mirmillo,* decked out in a coat of mail. Sometimes condemned criminals fought each other without armor until they were all killed. If they held back they were lashed into combat.

For his part, Cicero took little pleasure in these blood sports, at least those in which there was not a fair fight. His account of the displays with animals at Pompey's games has a flavor of modern distaste.

> What pleasure can a cultivated man get out of seeing a weak human being torn to pieces by a powerful animal or a splendid animal transfixed by a hunting spear? Anyhow, if these sights are worth seeing, you have seen them often; and we spectators saw nothing new. The last day was that for the elephants. The ordinary public showed considerable astonishment at them, but no enjoyment. There was even an impulse of compassion, a feeling that the monsters had something human about them.

However, the modern reader should not be misled that Cicero was anything other than a man of his age. Just as Dr. Johnson felt that "prize fighting made people accustomed not to be alarmed at seeing their own blood," so Cicero believed that gladiatorial contests, if well managed, were object lessons in endurance for spectators. He approved of public violence if it was a legal punishment with death as the inevitable outcome and he regretted that by his day gladiators had become professional performers whose fights, even if bloody, were exercises in virtuosity rather than courage in the face of adversity.

Pompey's theater made a great impression. During these years when competition among politicians was fierce and the profits of empire had never been so high, the city and its environs became a vast building site with leading Romans investing heavily in prestige construction projects. Caesar had ambitious plans of his own, which would more than match Pompey's and he recruited Cicero to help with the necessary land purchases. In 54 Cicero wrote to Atticus:

> Caesar's friends (I mean Oppius and myself, choke at that if you must) have thought nothing of spending 60 million sesterces on the work you used to be so enthusiastic about, to widen the Forum. . . . We couldn't settle with the owners for a smaller sum. We shall achieve something really glorious. As for the Field of Mars, we are going to build covered marble booths for the General Assembly and surround them with a high colonnade, a mile of it in all. At the same

time the Public Residence [Villa Publica, on the Field of Mars, used mainly to house foreign envoys] will be attached to our building.

During the year that Pompey and Crassus were Consuls, Gabinius, who had failed to help Cicero during his exile and was now governor of Syria, stepped into the fray and restored King Ptolemy to power in Egypt for a huge price with the help of a Roman army. In light of the prohibition in the Sibylline Books, this was a serious flouting of the law.

At about this time unusually bad weather broke the banks of the Tiber, flooding the lower levels of the city. Some people were drowned as were many animals, and houses were damaged. In the public mind the disaster was a punishment for Gabinius's invasion.

Cicero launched a blistering attack on Gabinius in the Senate. Pompey and Crassus responded in his defense. Crassus seems to have hurled the epithet "exile" at him, an insult that Cicero, who had never liked him, refused to forgive. Pompey, backed by a letter from Caesar, used his personal authority to impose an entente. The widowed Tullia, probably now about twenty years old, had recently married her second husband, Furius Crassipes, a member of an old but faded patrician family. Cicero's new son-in-law held a dinner party in the garden of his house to celebrate the apparent reconciliation with Crassus. Towards the end of the year, Crassus, paying no attention to bad omens, set off on his great expedition against the Parthians. "What a rascal he is!" Cicero observed, unrepentantly.

The three members of the First Triumvirate, or now, rather, the two, persuaded Cicero, against his better judgment, fearful that they might switch their support back to Clodius again, to give evidence on Gabinius's behalf when he faced a treason charge. The task was all the more difficult in that Cicero remained on extremely bad terms with Gabinius. He told Atticus: "Pompey is putting a lot of pressure on me for a reconciliation, but so far he has got nowhere, nor ever will if I keep a scrap of personal independence." He had even asked Cicero to undertake the defense, but that was a line Cicero absolutely refused to cross.

Cicero's finances continued to cause him anxiety. Help came at this time from a surprising source. In 54, despite what he called his own "straitened circumstances" (without for one moment expecting to be believed), Caesar agreed to make him a loan of 800,000 sesterces and offered Quintus, also hard-pressed for cash, an appointment as one of his senior officers in Gaul.

The brothers accepted the money—evidence not only of the straits in which they found themselves but of their warm personal relations with Caesar despite political disagreements. Cicero knew how deeply he was indebted. He wrote to his brother later in the year, after Quintus had joined the legions in Gaul, that he had come to regard Caesar almost as a member of the family: "In all the world Caesar is the only man who cares for me as I could wish, or (as others would have it) who wants *me* to care for *him.*" No doubt he said this with half an eye on the likelihood that Quintus would show Caesar the letter, but there is little reason to doubt the sincerity of his gratitude. Caesar was a man of great charm and was fond of the sensitive, witty advocate; of course, he was also a hardheaded calculator and had every interest in using generosity to neutralize an opponent.

The relationship between the two was helped by their shared literary interests. Somehow Caesar found time during his campaign to compose a weighty tome on Latin grammar. Well aware of Cicero's penchant for praise, he flatteringly dedicated it to Cicero, who responded by sending him another ill-advised epic he had written, this time on his exile and return. Caesar made some polite comments but evidently had reservations, and it seems the work was never published.

Quintus was a competent soldier and Caesar valued his services. At one point Quintus and his legion were besieged in their camp by a Gallic tribe, the Nervii, which had already ambushed and destroyed a Roman army. Attacks came in wave after wave. Quintus behaved coolly and bravely, as Caesar made clear in his account of the Gallic War: "Cicero himself, although in very poor health, would not rest even at night, until a crowd of soldiers actually went to him and by their remonstrances made him take care of himself." The Nervii repeated a trick they had played on the previous army and tried unsuccessfully to lure Quintus out of his camp on the promise of safe conduct.

The siege continued and messenger after messenger dispatched to Caesar was caught, tortured and killed. The Nervii invested the camp with a rampart and managed to set much of it alight with incendiary darts and red-hot molded-clay bullets. Eventually news got through to Caesar of

Quintus's plight and he marched to relieve him. He sent one of his Gallic horsemen ahead to tell him to hold out. The man was afraid to go up to the camp and enter it so he flung a javelin with a message wrapped around it into the camp. Unfortunately, the javelin happened to stick in one of the camp towers and was not noticed for a couple of days. Eventually a soldier saw it, pulled it out and took it to Quintus. By this time the smoke of burning villages warned the Romans that help was near. The camp was relieved and, in due course, the Nervii were defeated. Although on one occasion he allowed some of his troops to be surprised by a German force, there is no question that Quintus had a good war.

In Italy, his brother was still looking after his domestic interests. Quintus had bought a couple of villas near Arpinum and Cicero spent time supervising their refurbishment. In September 54 he wrote to Quintus: "Escaped from the great heat wave (I don't remember a greater), I have refreshed myself on the banks of our delightful river at Arpinum." Cicero went on to tell his brother how impressed he was by one of the new properties. He seems to have had conventional tastes in interior decor and fine art, admiring the work of Greek painters and sculptors from their heyday in the fifth and fourth centuries BC. "I was very pleased with the house, because the colonnade is a most imposing feature; it struck me only on this visit, now that its whole range is open to view and the columns have been cleared. All depends on the elegance of the stucco, and that I shall attend to. The paving seemed to be going nicely. I did not care for some of the ceilings and gave orders to alter them."

Family life was on an even keel. On October 21 he assured his brother: "Our affairs stand as follows: domestically they are as we wish. The boys are well, keen on their lessons and conscientiously taught. They love us and each other." Young Quintus seems not to have enjoyed his uncle's attempts to teach him. He preferred working with his tutor, and Cicero, not wanting his development to be held up, did not press the point and withdrew.

Civic disorder and widespread corruption continued unabated and the streets of Rome were still unsafe. The only convincing center of power, however unconstitutional, was the First Triumvirate, but fate soon played a hand in subverting Caesar's brilliant rescue operation at Luca. In June 53

Crassus and his seven legions (up to 42,000 men) invaded the Parthian Empire but came spectacularly to grief, tricked into defeat and death.

Misled by the enemy he marched his forces through barren terrain and was harried mercilessly by Parthian archers. Depressed by the death in battle of his son Publius and pressed by desperate, near-mutinous soldiers, he agreed, against his better judgment, to parley with the Parthian general, Surena. Once in his hands, Crassus was killed and his head and right hand cut off. His skull was used as a grisly prop during a performance of Euripides' *Bacchae* at the Parthian court. The legionary standards were lost, a terrible blow to Roman prestige, and thousands of soldiers were killed or captured. Only 10,000 survivors made their way back to safety. Luckily the Parthians were content with their victory and did not follow it up. Pompey's conquests in the region were left intact.

A canny businessman and an able fixer, Crassus had bulked large in the affairs of the Republic. He was a man of few obvious convictions. If his career had a keynote, it lay in his rivalry with Pompey, the immovable obstacle to his own advancement. No friend of the *optimates,* Crassus supported radicals like Catilina and Caesar, but cautiously from the wings. His death was perhaps the most influential act of his career, for it threw the spotlight on the relationship between Pompey and Caesar.

Catastrophe for Crassus brought some good to Cicero. For years he had yearned for an appointment to the College of Augurs, a board of senior Romans responsible for ascertaining the gods' opinion of intended public actions; they did this by examining the flight of birds, thunder and lightning and other signs. Cicero did not believe in augury and could see a certain illogicality in his ambition: "What an irresponsible fellow I am," he confessed to Atticus. However, when Pompey and Hortensius recommended him for the vacancy left by Crassus's dead son, Cicero was delighted. It was just the kind of honor that enhanced the standing of a distinguished elder statesman.

In August, Caesar's daughter and Pompey's wife, Julia, died in childbirth. (The infant, a boy, died a few days later.) She seems to have inherited all her father's charm and both men in their different ways were devoted to her. This personal tragedy was also a political event of great importance, for it shut down a private channel of communication which (and it is one of the great ifs of history) might have preserved their alliance.

Many people realized this at the time. Pompey intended to have Julia interred at his country estate near Alba, but during her funeral procession the crowd hijacked the corpse and buried it in the Field of Mars. This show of emotion demonstrated the impact of her death on public opinion, which respected both Caesar and Pompey and regarded Julia as the living symbol of their friendship. Caesar, absent in Gaul, was moved by the news of her funeral rites and announced the holding of gladiatorial games followed by a public banquet in her name. This was an unprecedented honor for a woman.

The year 52 got off to a gloomy start. No officeholders had been elected in the confusion of the previous year. New Year's Day fell on a market day, an unfavorable sign, and portents were reported. Wolves were seen in Rome and dogs were heard howling by night. A statue of Mars sweated. A storm with thunderbolts raged over the city, knocking down images of the gods and taking some lives. Then, on January 20, an event took place which lifted such a load of fear and loathing from Cicero's mind and gave him such pleasure that in future years he regularly celebrated the anniversary of what he called the "Battle of Bovillae."

Sometime in the early afternoon, Milo left Rome by the Appian Way. He was on his way to his hometown, where he was mayor and was due to preside at the installation of a priest on the following day. At about three o'clock he reached the small village of Bovillae a few miles outside the city when he saw Clodius coming from the opposite direction, returning to the capital from Aricia, a town a few miles farther south, where he had been addressing municipal officials. Clodius was traveling on horseback with three friends and was accompanied by about 30 slaves armed with swords.

Milo was in a carriage with his wife, Sulla's daughter, and a relative. Behind them walked a long column of slaves and some gladiators, including two stars of the arena, Eudamas and Birria, who brought up the rear. The lines passed each other without incident, but as the two ends met the gladiators started a brawl with some of Clodius's men. Clodius heard the noise and looked back menacingly. This was enough to provoke Birria, who hurled a lance at him, wounding him in the shoulder or back. More of Milo's entourage turned back and ran up to join the melee. Clodius, streaming with blood, was taken to a roadside inn, and before long most of his entourage was dead or badly injured.

When Milo heard that Clodius had been wounded, he decided it would be more dangerous to leave him alive than to finish him off in the inn. When the deed was done, Clodius's body was hauled out into the road and abandoned. By a curious coincidence, a shrine of the Great Goddess stood nearby, into whose mysteries Clodius had intruded in search of dalliance.

Milo and his wife resumed their journey, as if nothing had taken place. Sometime later in the afternoon, a passing Senator, traveling back to Rome from the country, found Clodius's corpse and had it sent on in his litter. He himself returned the way he had come, presumably wishing to avoid becoming involved in what was certain to be a major scandal.

The body arrived at Clodius's new house, centrally located off the Holy Way, a couple of minutes from the Forum. It was placed in the hallway and surrounded by distraught followers and slaves. Clodius's wife, Fulvia (not the same woman as Cicero's informant against Catilina), did not hold back her grief and showed his wounds to visitors. The following morning a crowd gathered outside the front door. Some well-connected friends, including two Tribunes, called. At their suggestion, the body was taken, naked and battered, down to the Forum, and placed on the Speakers' Platform. The Tribunes then called an informal public meeting. They persuaded the crowd to take the body to the Senate House and cremate it there, in one final act of defiance against the powers-that-be. Benches, tables and other furniture, together with the clerks' notebooks, were piled up inside the building, which was then set alight. The fire spread to the Basilica Porcia next door.

Rumors had leapt from house to house throughout the city and by then there were few doubts as to who was responsible for Clodius's murder. The crowd swept to Milo's house, but it was driven back by a hail of arrows. Crowd members grabbed the Consular *fasces* from their place of safekeeping in the grove of Libitina, goddess of the dead, and presented themselves at Pompey's garden villa, "calling on him variously as Consul and Dictator." They offered him the *fasces* as a sign of political authority. The political movement Clodius had led collapsed with his death. His power had been purely personal. After an orgy of destruction his supporters and street gangs could think of nothing better to do than ask Pompey, whom Clodius had bullied and undermined on and off for years, for justice.

That afternoon the Senate met in an emergency session and passed the

Final Act. They called on the only officeholders then in place, a Regent (*interrex,* an official appointed every five days in the absence of elected Consuls), on the Tribunes and on Pompey, with his Proconsular authority, to take steps to restore order. They authorized Pompey to raise troops.

Pompey was in no hurry to accept the Senate's commission. He wanted full powers without conditions and was eager to consult Caesar in Gaul, anxious to avoid any step that might unbalance the equal partnership agreed on at Luca. The delaying tactic worked, for the Senate, having lost whatever last vestige of control it could lay claim to, in desperation offered him what he wanted, full and complete authority. Even Cato approved, saying that any government was better than no government at all. The *optimates* cleverly arranged for Pompey to be appointed sole Consul rather than Dictator, the post he would have preferred. This was to close off any risk that he might repeat the precedent set by Sulla, who had extended his Dictatorship beyond the legal six-month limit. To make sure of Caesar's consent to the deal a sweetener was offered; all ten Tribunes put forward a bill allowing him to stand for a second-term Consulship *in absentia.* Once he was in charge, Pompey moved firmly. Troops were levied and the city was brought under control.

With characteristic managerial firmness, the sole Consul acted to restore law and order through the courts. A series of trials was undertaken of Clodius's men and Milo, for his part, was brought to justice for Clodius's murder. Cicero, the obvious choice, was asked to undertake the defense. When the case came up, troops lined the Forum. Milo knew of Cicero's tendency to be nervous at the beginning of a speech and was afraid that the presence of soldiers might alarm him. He persuaded him to come down from his home on the Palatine to the Forum in a closed litter and to wait quietly inside the litter until the jury had assembled and the court was ready. It was a good idea, but it didn't work. As soon as Cicero emerged from the litter he saw Pompey standing on high ground as if commanding a military operation and weapons flashing in the sunlight from all sides. His body shook, his voice faltered and he could hardly start his speech. This was a potential catastrophe, for, unusually, he was Milo's only advocate.

The line of defense Cicero chose was controversial. Some advised that the best thing would be to admit to the killing but to claim bluntly that it had been in the public interest. Cicero chose instead to trump the prosecution, which claimed that Milo had ambushed Clodius, with the counterargument that it was Clodius who had ambushed Milo. Of course, both accounts were wrong, for the encounter had come about by chance.

When Cicero began to speak, followers of Clodius in the square, undaunted by the presence of troops, created an uproar. He did not completely break down, but his performance fell a long way short of his usual standards. He spoke briefly and soon withdrew. It was the most embarrassing moment in his professional life.

Milo was convicted and exiled from Rome. He retired to Massilia. Cicero sent him a copy of the fully worked-up address, which he had prepared for publication. It was an accomplished piece of work. Milo sent a letter back saying that it was lucky for him that this had not been what had been said in court, for he would not now be eating such wonderful Massilian mullets.

During these years when his own career had stalled, Cicero developed an interest in nurturing the prospects of promising young men. There was Caius Trebatius Testa, a lawyer in his late twenties or early thirties, for whom he arranged a job with Caesar in Gaul. And in 53 the reprobate Curio made a reappearance, now an ardent conservative and ready for public life. Cicero recalled the good advice he had given him "in the days of your boyhood."

But perhaps the most important of Cicero's youthful correspondents in those years was his personal slave and secretary, Tiro. It is not certain when Tiro was born, but he was probably a young man at this time. His name is a Latin word (meaning "newcomer," "recruit" or "beginner") and this suggests that he may have been born in the Cicero household rather than bought at a sale. Cicero was deeply attached to him and the references in his letters present him almost as a member of the family ("a friend to us rather than a slave," Cicero wrote to Quintus). Tiro was given his freedom in 53 but, like most former slaves in Roman society, continued to work for his onetime owner.

Tiro was the man who looked after confidential financial matters. Every month he chased up debtors and pacified creditors. He checked the management accounts of the steward Eros, which were sometimes incorrect. He negotiated with moneylenders on the not infrequent occasions when Cicero found himself embarrassed for ready cash. Once he was even commissioned with the sensitive task of pursuing an aristocratic debtor for a repayment. He was also involved in superintending building works, watching over the upkeep of gardens and generally harassing workmen. He looked after Cicero's social life and organized the guest lists for dinner parties, often a delicate matter. "See about the dining room," Cicero once instructed him. "Tertia will be there—provided that Publilius is not invited."

But Tiro's main duties were secretarial and even editorial. He devised a shorthand which allowed him to write as fast as Cicero dictated. It is reported that he even helped Cicero with his writing and this is confirmed by a letter his master sent him in 53 when he was unwell. "My (or *our*) literary brainchildren have been drooping their heads missing you. . . . Pompey is staying with me as I write, enjoying himself in cheerful mood. He wants to hear my compositions, but I told him that in your absence my tongue of authorship is tied completely."

Tiro's health was poor and Cicero often had reason to be seriously worried. "Aegypta arrived today," Cicero once wrote to him solicitously. "He told me you were quite free of fever and in pretty good shape but said that you had not been able to write to me. . . . You cannot imagine how anxious I feel about your health." Cicero told Atticus that Tiro "is extraordinarily useful to me when well in all sorts of ways, both in business and in my literary work, but I hope for his recovery more because he is such a nice, modest fellow than for my own convenience." Although he was always complaining about Quintus's overdependence on his freedman, Statius, his relationship with Tiro was just as close and trusting.

Tiro seems to have been popular with other members of the family too. In the following decade, when he had saved up enough money to buy a small farm, young Marcus congratulated him in a letter that is full of affection and good humor. "Well, you are a man of landed property! You must shed your town-bred ways—you are now a Roman squire! How amusing to picture the delightful sight of you now. I imagine you buying farm tackle, talking to the bailiff, hoarding pips at dessert in your jacket pockets!"

The past few years had been deeply unsatisfactory for Cicero, who felt he had been unfairly sidelined by the rise of the First Triumvirate. He did not anticipate the future with any greater confidence. Diehards in the Senate were determined to take revenge on Caesar for the illegalities of his

Consulship. Political stability hung on the permanence of his partnership with Pompey and there were signs that this was coming under strain. In one sense, a breakdown in relations between the two men would be welcome to Cicero, for it would lift what he saw as a serious threat to the rule of law; but, from another perspective, it might transform civil discord into civil war.

8

THE IDEAL CONSTITUTION

Writing about Politics: 55–43 BC

Now that he was no longer able to play an active role in the conduct of affairs, Cicero decided to find time for another kind of political intervention. It took the form of extended critiques of the crisis facing the Republic, in which he offered his own proposals for reform. By writing books, he believed he could still influence the course of events. If he could no longer promote his cure-all for the Republic's ills, the "harmony of the classes," in the Senate House and the Forum, then he would do so from the study.

Nothing like the modern publishing industry existed in ancient Rome, of course, nor were there public libraries, until Caesar founded the first one in the 40s. Books were written out by hand on papyrus rolls (sometimes as long as thirty feet), which were then passed around to friends and acquaintances and stored on shelves. The task of copying was usually given to highly trained slaves. Atticus employed a large number and seems to have acted as a prototypical publisher, probably selling books for a profit. He had many of Cicero's speeches and books copied and distributed.

Readers had to work hard. Characters took one form only, without differentiation into capital and lowercase letters. There were no spaces between words or punctuation, and texts were unparagraphed.

Like many Romans, Cicero was a great collector of books. He was proud to acquire rare editions and enjoyed visiting other people's libraries. Despite the technical production difficulties, upper-class Romans were eager to buy the latest works of contemporary writers, which were carefully studied and much discussed. Political pamphlets were an accepted part of public life. Although copying runs must have been small, books appear to have been in plentiful supply. (According to Catullus, they could end up wrapping mackerel in fish shops.)

Cicero's literary career was checkered. The precocious teenage poet had grown into an overprolific windbag with his endless autobiographical epics. It was as an orator that he really made his reputation as a writer. He understood that a speech was a one-time, live event like an actor's performance and that, in the public eye, he would be only as good as his latest appearance. So, like other successful public speakers of his day, he took great pains to work up his speeches on paper and publish them as books. In this way, past rhetorical triumphs became permanent records of achievement.

But he had long been acknowledged as a leader, if not the leader, in this field and he sought a new, more demanding challenge. His first step was to set out his views on political education. This he did in *The Ideal Orator* (*De oratore*), a substantial work which he first mentioned to Atticus in November 55. What Cicero had in mind was a justification of rhetoric not as a technique but as an approach to the morally good life, a means of expressing and enforcing morality. Ever since his student days when he toured Greece and Asia Minor and studied both philosophy and rhetoric, he had been convinced that the two disciplines were intertwined. This was the proposition he now sought to demonstrate.

The book was written as a dialogue (following the Greeks, this was a common convention for philosophical writing) and was imagined as an actual event taking place some years earlier, in 91. The leading figures were two of the great political and legal personalities of his adolescence, Lucius Licinius Crassus and Marcus Antonius. Cicero argued for a broadly based and well-integrated liberal education in which the *discidium linguae atque cordis,* the split between word and heart, would be healed.

Modeling himself largely on Plato's *Republic,* from which there is a substantial direct quotation, he then composed another dialogue. *On the State* (*De re publica*), which he followed in due course with *On Law* (*De legibus*). Both books have only partially survived; *On the State* was discovered as late as 1820, when fragments amounting to about one third of the original were found in a palimpsest also containing St. Augustine's commentary on the Psalms. Even in truncated form, while purporting to give an account of states in general, these works provide a comprehensive analysis of the weaknesses of the Roman constitution and proposals for its reform.

As we have already seen, Cicero did not fully appreciate the gravity of the political situation. In his judgment no more was required than a return to tried and tested traditions. "When we inherited the Republic from our forebears," he wrote, "it was like a beautiful painting whose colors were fading with age. We have failed to restore its original colors and have not taken the trouble to preserve its overall composition or even its general features." Cicero probably started *On the State* in May 54 and it was published about 51. Its subject, he told Quintus, was "the ideal constitution and the ideal citizen." He found the work hard going, for it entailed a good deal of research both in the Greek authorities and in the history of Rome's political development.

He chose to set the dialogue safely in a more glorious and perhaps more authoritative past, making his main speaker Publius Cornelius Scipio Aemilianus Africanus, the adopted grandson of the great Africanus, who had defeated Hannibal at Zama outside Carthage in 204. He was a generous patron of the arts and letters and a Hellenophile. The action opens one morning during a public holiday in 129, not long before Scipio's death at the end of a long life. This timing was not accidental, for the stormy career of Tiberius Gracchus was recent history. Cicero believed that his Tribuneship, which "divided one people into two factions," had introduced the long constitutional crisis which now was coming to a head.

The scene is Scipio's country estate, where the old man is found in his bedroom receiving callers. The conversation touches on the reported sighting of two suns in the sky. More visitors arrive, including his lifelong friend Laelius, whose *cognomen, Sapiens,* is a tribute to his scholarship and philosophical attainments. Scipio rises from his couch, dresses and puts on his shoes. The company moves to a portico of the house, where the talk turns away from the physical nature of the universe, on the grounds that it is unknowable, to the nature of good governance, about which truths can be ascertained.

Scipio's thesis, which can be supposed to be Cicero's, is that there are three basic systems of government: monarchy, aristocracy and democracy. Each has its strengths and weaknesses and it is the unique distinction of Rome to have devised a constitution which combines elements of all three. Scipio's personal preference is for the good king, father to his subjects, but the tendency towards tyranny is hard to eradicate. So "a moderate and well-balanced form of government which is a combination of the three simple good forms is preferable even to monarchy." A substantial part of the book is devoted to a constitutional history of the early days of Rome and, through Scipio's words, Cicero nostalgically evokes the Republic in its primitive, pure and thoroughly oligarchical form.

> The government was so administered by the Senate that, though the People were free, few political acts were performed by them, practically everything being done by the authority of the Senate and in accordance with its established customs, and the Consuls held a power which, though only of one year's duration, was truly regal in general character and in legal sanction. Another principle that was most important to the retention of the power by the aristocracy was also strictly maintained—namely, that no act of a popular assembly should be valid unless ordered by the Senate.

This theory of the mixed constitution had a great influence on the development of European political thought during the Middle Ages and the Renaissance. It retained its appeal until the eighteenth century and the emergence of modern democracy. However, it did not fit the circumstances of the last hundred years of the Republic as neatly as Cicero argued it did. For one thing, it took no account of the political significance of the *equites,* the business class. His ideas also ignored the unpalatable fact that the last attempt to reestablish the mixed constitution, Sulla's reforms, had been dismantled soon after his death and had, in fact, been guaranteed by another power which receives little attention in *On the State,* military force.

Cicero was an acute observer of his times and it seems strange that the book does not reflect a more accurate perception of what was really happening. His analysis was cultural rather than political. Like most of his contemporaries, he saw politics fundamentally in personal rather than ideological or structural terms. There had been a decline in moral standards and a corruption of old habits of responsibility in public life. All would be well if only there were a return to traditional values, a rediscovery of the "ideal" statesman and citizen. The constitution itself, properly interpreted, was perfect.

On the State seems to have been an immediate success with the reading public. It contains some of Cicero's most majestic prose. In the sixth book Scipio recalls a dream in which he met the shade of the long-dead Africanus. A virtuous life, Africanus told him,

> "is the highway to heaven, to that assembly of all those who have ended their terrestrial lives and been freed from the flesh. They live in that place over there which you now see" (it was the round of light that blazed brightest of all the fires in the sky), "which you mortals, borrowing a Greek term, call the Milky Circle." When I looked all around me from that point, everything else appeared extraordinarily beautiful. There were stars invisible from earth, all larger than we have ever conceived. The smallest was the most distant and the one closest to the earth shone with a reflected light. The starry orbs were much larger than the earth. In fact, the earth itself seemed so small that I felt scornful of our empire, which is only a kind of dot. . . . Beneath the Moon there is nothing that is not mortal and doomed to decay, except for the souls which, by the grace of the gods, have been conferred on humankind. But above the Moon everything is eternal.

As a literary call to order, the appearance of *On the State* was timely. But it made little or no impact on the political situation.

The book's sequel, *On Law,* also inspired by Plato, was started in 52. Yet Cicero was unable to finish it, if indeed he ever did, until the last year of his life. Only three volumes survive of what may have been intended to be, or were, at least five.

The book is a dialogue, set in the countryside on Cicero's estate at Arpinum, and the speakers are Quintus, Atticus and the author. The conversation opens with a general debate in which Cicero argues that law is inherent in the workings of the universe. Human law is merely a version, and an imperfect one at that, of the wisdom of the natural order. "Law is the highest reason," he says, "implanted in nature, which commands what ought to be done and forbids the opposite. This reason, when firmly fixed and fully developed in the human mind, is Law. And so . . . Law is intelligence whose natural function it is to command right conduct and forbid wrongdoing." Later he summarizes: "Virtue is reason completely developed."

A familiar Ciceronian theme reappears: the moral force of oratory. An important means of fostering virtue is through the art of explanation and persuasion—the "science of distinguishing the true from the false [and] the art of understanding the consequences and opposites of every statement." The mind "must employ not merely the customary subtle method of debate but also the more copious continuous style, considering, for example, how to rule nations, establish laws, punish the wicked, protect the good, honor those who excel [and] publish to fellow citizens precepts conducive to their well-being and credit, so designed as to win their acceptance." This is necessary, for it is abundantly clear to Cicero that the actual legislation of states is not necessarily consistent with natural law. "The most foolish notion of all is the belief that everything is just which is found in the customs or laws of nations."

Volumes two and three proceed to outline in detail a legal code for an ideal state. Unsurprisingly, it has a close resemblance to the Roman constitution, with its more obvious flaws (as seen by Cicero) ironed out. So, for example, he recommends "two officeholders with royal powers," very similar to the Consuls, but insists that they should not hold office again except after a ten-year interval, a Roman convention more honored in the breach than in the observance. Elsewhere in his writings, Cicero's skepticism shows that his cast of mind was rational rather than religious and that he gave little credit to the validity of soothsaying and the like, but here he regards religious observance, ritual, the role of priests as the interpreters and controllers of prodigies and ancestral rites as the foundation of governance.

In closing, Cicero examines the functions and powers of public officials. His object, as ever, is to assert his concept of the mixed constitution with rights for the People but with the Senate predominant. Thus, according to one of his proposed laws concerning suffrage, the ballot should be open to all citizens but the votes cast should be scrutinized by the "traditional leaders of the state." His line is that senior figures in the state should be able to monitor how citizens vote on the grounds that "everyone knows that laws which provide secret ballots have deprived the aristocracy of all influence."

Cicero's constitutional writings reveal a humane conservatism. It says a great deal for his intellectual tenacity that he maintained his beliefs during the years when Caesar's astonishing career reached its climax and the pillars of the Republic finally came crashing down.

9

THE DRIFT TO CIVIL WAR

52–50 BC

During his sole Consulship in 52, Pompey put through a range of reforms. Some were sensibly designed to correct administrative abuses, but others were purely political and suggested that he was considering whether to align himself with Caesar, now within sight of the end of his labors in Gaul, or with the Senate. On the face of it, he still supported Caesar. Despite the displeasure of the *optimates,* he had arranged for legislation which gave Caesar permission to stand for a second Consulship *in absentia.* Caesar intended to hold office in 48—very properly observing the convention that a second Consulship could not take place until ten years had elapsed since the first.

The law that had appointed Caesar as governor of Gaul did not allow the Senate to discuss his successor before March of 50. The allocation of provinces for a given year was decided in advance, before the Consuls and Praetors who would receive them were elected. This meant that Caesar could be replaced only by the senior officeholders of 49. Although it was technically feasible for a Consul to take up a governorship while still in office, it was unusual and so in all probability Caesar could count on remaining in his post until the beginning of 48, by which time he could expect to be Consul.

It was essential that he be able to stay in his province until then. If any interval of time arose between the end of his governorship and the start of his Consular term, and if he were compelled to come to Rome and campaign in person, his legal immunity would lapse and his enemies in the Senate, led by Cato, would undoubtedly bring him to trial for alleged breaches of the law during his first Consulship in 59. If he was found guilty, his career would be brought to a rapid premature conclusion. So Pompey's new law was vital for his political survival. Yet even if Caesar lost his immunity, few believed that he would actually appear in court. More probably, the matter would be settled by force: he would lead his legions into Italy.

Meanwhile, Pompey was still governor of Spain. (In fact, he had had his appointment renewed, although he never left Italy and sent out deputies to administer the province in his place.) So he would be in a position, if the Senate asked, to fight an invading Caesar. The terrible truth was dawning on intelligent people that the days of Sulla and Marius could be returning.

Having provided a guarantee for Caesar with one hand, Pompey apparently withdrew it with the other. As part of a package of measures designed to clean up public life, he promoted a law providing that candidates for office should canvass in person. When Caesar's friends pointed out that this blatantly contradicted the previous law excusing him from this very obligation, the Consul brushed the matter aside. The new legislation was not aimed at Caesar, Pompey claimed, and, to prove it, he added a codicil excluding him by name. But he did so on his own authority and the exception probably did not have legal validity.

A decision taken in Pompey's private life had equally unfriendly implications. After Julia's death, Caesar had hoped that his son-in-law would marry a young relative of his. Instead, Pompey chose a member of the Metellus clan, Cornelia, the daughter of a leading conservative, Quintus Caecilius Metellus Pius Scipio Nasica. He arranged for his new father-in-law to become his fellow Consul during the last months of his sole term. This demonstrated in the most obvious fashion his rapprochement with the Senate and distancing from Caesar.

At about the same time, Pompey enacted another seemingly innocuous law, which imposed a five-year gap between the holding of a senior office and a subsequent governorship. Candidates for office frequently laid out huge bribes knowing that they could recoup the expenditure a year later by extorting money from their provinces. An immediate payback was now made impossible. In itself, this was a good reform, but it had unpleasant implications for Caesar. When the Senate came to discuss provincial appointments on the due date of March 50, they would not be allowed to choose from the senior officeholders of 49. They could select anyone who had held the Consulship five or more years previously, and their candidate would thus be free to take over the governorship at once rather than wait till the end of 49. The dangerous gap when Caesar would have no official post and so be liable for criminal prosecution had suddenly reappeared. The only escape from the trap was for Caesar to persuade a Tribune to veto any Senatorial decision to accelerate the appointment process in this way—something which in due course he managed to do. From now on he would have to be more vigilant.

What were the real causes of the coming conflict? Plutarch saw the question as essentially one of personal relationships. According to him:

> Caesar had long ago decided that he must get rid of Pompey—just as Pompey, of course, had decided to get rid of Caesar. Crassus had been waiting for the outcome of this contest and intended to take on the winner himself, but he had died in Parthia. It was now left for the man who wanted the top position to remove the one who occupied it and for the man who occupied the top position to dispose of his feared rival. In fact, it was only recently that Pompey had come to fear Caesar. Previously he had despised him, feeling that it would be a simple task to put down the man he had raised up. But Caesar had laid his plans from the beginning. . . . In the wars in Gaul he had trained his troops and increased his reputation, reaching a height of success from which he was able to compete with Pompey's past achievements.

There is truth in this account, but it is too simply described. It is uncertain when Pompey made his final choice between loyalty to Caesar and joining the *optimates* to thwart him. This is because he was seldom clear, one suspects even to himself, about his true political intentions. He had a way of getting himself into morally uncomfortable positions from which he hoped to extricate himself without anyone noticing. As a result it was often hard to know what he wanted and he pleased nobody. Caesar's readiness to test the constitution to its limits, and even beyond them, disconcerted the former general. The sole Consulship had enabled Pompey to reassert himself and had given him an opportunity to edge slyly away from Caesar into the arms of the Senate.

As for Caesar, his aims and the precise nature of his relationship with Pompey were equally difficult to fathom. His public line was that he was simply claiming his rights and he used studiedly moderate language in putting them forward. He must have realized that his new preeminence would inevitably lead to a clash with Pompey, but it would seem he anticipated this rather than sought it. What is uncertain is whether the repeated attempts he made at compromise were public relations (that is, he knew they would fail) or whether he genuinely hoped for a peaceful solution.

Of course, there was much more to the origins of the civil war than a clash of individual wills, important as that was. Its inception can be traced much farther back to the long struggle between the *optimates* and the *populares* which opened with the attempted reforms of Tiberius Gracchus almost a century before: between those who saw the need to modernize the Republic and those who stood for the established order of things. Marius, Sulla, even Catilina in his desperate way had tried to resolve matters, but they had all failed. Sooner or later a final decision between the contending sides had to be reached.

The new rules on governorships were a tedious irritation to Cicero. Former Consuls were being dragged out of retirement to run the empire. One of these was Cicero and much against his will he accepted the governorship of Cilicia in present-day southern Turkey. He made it clear he would do so for the minimum time possible, twelve months; he would resist any idea of an extension. "My one consolation for this colossal bore," he told Atticus, "is that I expect it will only last a year."

Despite his irritation Cicero rose to the challenge. As during his Quaestorship in Sicily many years before, he was an able, hardworking and fair-minded administrator. Following Crassus's defeat and death, the region was uneasily anticipating incursions, perhaps a full-scale invasion, by the aroused and victorious Parthians. Since he himself had practically no military experience, he made sure that his Legates, or deputies, did.

One of these was his brother, Quintus, whose background both as a governor and as a general in Gaul would make him an invaluable adviser and aide. Another was the able Caius Pomptinus, who had led the ambush at the Milvian Bridge during Cicero's Consulship and had later efficiently put down a revolt of the Allobroges in Gaul in the wake of Catilina's conspiracy.

On the domestic as well as the political front, the two brothers were leaving trouble behind them. They spent the May Day holiday, a time of symbolic misrule when servants and slaves were waited on by their masters, at Quintus's hideaway farm near Arpinum. Pomponia decided to stage a monumental sulk. Her *casus belli* was Quintus's continuing fondness for his freedman, Statius—a subject on which in principle she and her brother-in-law agreed. Cicero told Atticus, Pomponia's brother, what had happened:

> When we arrived, Quintus said in the kindest way: "Pomponia, will you ask the women in and I'll get the boys? [i.e., the slaves and servants]." Both what he said and his intention and manner were perfectly pleasant, at least it seemed so to me. Pomponia however answered in our hearing, "I am a guest here myself." That, I imagine, was because Statius had gone ahead of us to see to our luncheon. Quintus said to me: "There! This is the sort of thing I have to put up with all the time." You'll say, "What is there in that, pray?" A good deal. I myself was quite shocked. Her words and manner were gratuitously rude. I concealed my feelings, painful as they were, and we all took our places except the lady. Quintus however had some food sent to her, which she refused. In a word, I felt my brother could not have been more forbearing nor your sister ruder. . . . [Quintus] came over to see me the following day. He told me that Pomponia had refused to spend the night with him and that her attitude when she said good-bye was just as I had seen it. You may tell her to her face that in my judgment her manners that day left something to be desired.

Tullia, now probably in her mid- to late twenties, presented another difficulty. The marriage with her second husband, Crassipes, had not been a success and about this time they were divorced. Cicero was worried about Tullia's future marital prospects, although—or perhaps because—she appears to have been quite a strong-minded young woman.

Leaving his domestic affairs in Terentia's hands, Cicero and his entourage made their leisurely way south to the port of Brundisium, where they were to take a ship for Athens and the east. Marcus and young Quintus, who were in their early and middle teens, were old enough to accompany their fathers and joined the expedition. Cicero called in at his villa at Cumae, where he was gratified to receive a visit from his old rival Hortensius, who had come a long way to see him despite being in poor health. Cicero pressed him to do all he could to prevent an extension of his Cilician penance, if anyone were unkind enough to propose such a thing in the Senate.

Cicero found widespread anxiety about the future among all he met. No chief political players had shown their hands. Cicero's own view remained much as it had always been; he preached moderation, compromise and reconciliation. He was pleased to have the chance to talk things over with Pompey in the few days he spent with him at his villa outside the Greek city of Tarentum and was relieved to find that he understood where his duty lay. "I leave him in the most patriotic frame of mind," he told Atticus, "fully prepared to be a bulwark against the dangers threatening."

For all his reservations about the die-hard *optimates,* Cicero's deepest instincts were to support the Senate against Caesar. But he was seriously embarrassed by the fact that he had allowed himself to yield to Caesar's blandishments; he owed him many favors and, worst of all, the large loan of 800,000 sesterces Caesar had made him in 54 had yet to be liquidated. He was desperate to return the money to Caesar, but it was an awkward moment to have to do so. His personal finances were coming under additional strain, for his outlay as governor promised to be high and he would not be earning any money while he was absent.

It was the worst possible time to be away from Rome and Cicero made sure that he was kept fully up-to-date about the latest developments. He arranged for Marcus Caelius to be his political correspondent. Despite Caelius's rascally past, when he had been a friend of Clodius and a lover of his sister Clodia, Cicero had always had a soft spot for him. Even if he exercised little judgment over his own life, he was an amusing and well-informed commentator on the actions and motives of others. Caelius accepted the commission with boyish enthusiasm. Once he realized that what Cicero wanted was not gossip, rumors or even news stories but intelligent commentary, he proceeded to offer just that. He was candid as well as witty. When Cicero told him he would be meeting Pompey at Tarentum, Caelius warned him with unkind accuracy that Pompey "is apt to say one thing and think another, but is not clever enough to keep his real aims out of sight."

Caelius was not the kind of man to forgo his expectation of a return for his services. He had a tendency to pester Cicero with inappropriate requests, at one time asking him to dedicate a book to him. Elected Aedile for 50, he was keen to stage some impressive games (one of an Aedile's main duties) and asked Cicero to send him some Cilician leopards. This would have entailed exactly the kind of abuse of office which Cicero denounced in others and disapproved of. Pressed into a corner, Cicero claimed to have engaged hunters to find some. This was probably a white lie and he told a joke to extricate himself. "The creatures are in remarkably short supply, and those we have are complaining bitterly because they are the only beings in my province who have to fear designs against their safety. So they are reported to have decided to leave the province and emigrate to Caria."

After a long journey which included stopovers in Athens and the island of Delos, Cicero set foot in his province on July 31, 51, exactly three months after his departure from Rome. He was in a gloomy frame of mind and felt homesick. "When all's said," he wrote to Atticus, "this isn't the kind of thing I'm pining for, it's the world, the Forum, Rome, my house, my friends. But I'll stick it out as best I can so long as it's only for a year."

Cilicia was a large mixed bag of a territory stretching along the southern coast of Asia Minor to the Amanus Mountains, which provided a natural frontier with Syria. It also included the island of Cyprus which Cato had annexed a few years previously. (There had been no very obvious reason for this, except, presumably, that the island was too small to qualify as a province in its own right and someone had to look after it.) In western Cilicia mountains ran down to the sea and an abundance of wood made it a center for shipbuilding. In the lawless years after the decline of the Seleucid Empire, the region became a base for the pirate fleets which had disrupted trade and commerce for more than a century until Pompey solved the pirate problem once and for all in 67. He had acted with comparative leniency and settled some of the former buccaneers in the Cilician town of Soli. In the east of the province lay its main city, the port of Tarsus, and a fertile coastal plain crisscrossed by rivers. Not far to the south was the site of the battle of Issus, one of Alexander the Great's victories over the Persians.

Cicero insisted from the outset that he meant to run a clean administration. He did his best to make sure that no provincial had to spend money entertaining him and his staff. He opened his own quarters to local people (or at least to those "whom he found agreeable"), where he offered generous if not lavish hospitality. There was no gatekeeper at his official residence to deter visitors and Cicero had a habit of rising early so that he was ready at first light to greet those who came to pay their respects. Following the advice he had once given Quintus during his governorship, he kept his temper in public and was careful not to inflict insulting punishments. He avoided traditional brutalities such as beating offenders with rods or stripping them of their clothes. As he intended, this behavior had a powerful effect on local opinion, and Cicero made sure that the political world in Rome knew of it too. He was keenly aware of the damage done to Roman interests by bad government and meant to set an example for others to follow.

He also wanted to draw the sharpest possible distinction between his regime and that of his predecessor, Clodius's brother, Appius Claudius Pulcher. (It must sometimes have seemed to Cicero that, wherever he turned, he could not escape this domineering and hostile family.) Appius's policy as governor had been simply to enrich himself. Cicero was shocked when he saw the consequences. Writing while on the road, he described a "forlorn and, without exaggeration, permanently ruined province." Local communities had been forced to sell prospective tax revenues to tax farmers in order to meet Appius's rapacity for cash. "In a phrase, these people are absolutely tired of their lives."

However, Cicero had no intention of broaching these issues directly with Appius, to whom he wrote before his arrival with scrupulous politeness. He had learned from bitter experience that one baited a Claudius at one's peril. He tried to arrange a meeting for a debriefing, but Appius seems to have done his best to avoid Cicero and showed signs of a reluctance to lay down his authority. While knowing perfectly well that the new governor had arrived at one end of the province, he continued to hold assizes at the other.

Cicero's patience was sorely tried and eventually he wrote to Appius in terms of firm but courteously indirect protest. He also inquired nervously of the whereabouts of three military cohorts.

> Malicious persons . . . said you were holding assizes in Tarsus, making both administrative and judicial decisions, although you had reason to think that your successor had arrived. . . . Their talk had no effect on me. . . . But I must own candidly that I am disturbed to find three cohorts missing from my exiguous force, and those the most nearly up to strength, and to be ignorant of their whereabouts.

Cicero was right to be worried about the state of the armed forces at his disposal. Persistent reports were coming in that the Parthians were on the move and he would be expected to do what he could to resist them. The allied kingdoms, which Pompey had arranged as buffer states in his eastern settlement, looked increasingly unreliable.

Cicero urgently needed to lay his hands on the missing soldiers. Cilicia was garrisoned with two legions, but both were under strength. Some had been mutinous, although Appius had eventually pacified them by settling their arrears of pay. When campaigning abroad, the Romans usually employed as soldiers only their own citizens and relied on local levies for cavalry and lightly armed soldiers; but Cilicia was a recent acquisition and had no tradition of supplying troops to the Romans. Recruitment promised to be difficult. Caelius in Rome was just as worried about the military situation as Cicero was, but he warned that there would be little sympathy back home for his predicament. "Your army is hardly capable of defending a single pass. Unfortunately nobody allows for this: a man holding public office is expected to cope with any emergency, as though every item in complete preparedness had been put at his disposal."

Cicero joined his army and did his best to enlist locals. As a precaution, he sent the boys, Marcus and Quintus, north to the friendly kingdom of Galatia (in modern-day Turkey), where he hoped they would be out of harm's way at the court of its ruler, Deiotarus. Deiotarus sent him a Roman-style legion of Galatians, who turned out to be surprisingly good soldiers.

As the autumn came on, the news grew worse. The Parthians were reported to have crossed the Euphrates and there was talk that the King of Armenia was planning to invade Cappadocia, an allied kingdom to the northeast of Cilicia, in support. No word had come from the nearest province, Syria, where the new governor was the stubborn and luckless Bibulus, Caesar's fellow Consul in 59. In fact, it was not even clear if he had arrived yet to take up his duties. Cicero commented dryly: "My best resource is winter." He positioned his troops in the Taurus Mountains, from where he could either march north to meet a threat to Cappadocia or descend into the flatlands of eastern Cilicia near the Syrian border. In a dispatch to the Senate in mid-September he urgently appealed for more troops.

The young King of Cappadocia, Ariobarzanes, who styled himself "the Pious and Pro-Roman," came to see the new Roman governor in a highly nervous state. He had recently inherited the throne after his father's assassination and told Cicero that he had uncovered a plot against his own life. The idea was to install his brother, who would take an anti-Roman line. The Queen Mother was implicated and a semi-independent principality was on the point of open rebellion. Cicero advised him to take strong measures to punish the conspirators. But although Ariobarzanes asked for troops, none could be spared. It was agreed that the king could threaten their use, if necessary. As so often with young men, Cicero got on well with Ariobarzanes and when they were not talking politics they found time to discuss the differences between the Roman and Galatian systems of augury.

Hearing that the Parthian force was some way off, Cicero led his army, which he now thought "tolerably well provided," forward towards the Syrian frontier. His cavalry fought off a brief and probably exploratory Parthian incursion. By the time he arrived at the Syrian border he heard that Caius Cassius Longinus had beaten the enemy at Antioch on the other side of the Amanus Mountains. A dour character, Cassius, Marcus Junius Brutus's brother-in-law, was a good soldier and had taken charge of Syria after disaster had befallen Crassus at Carrhae.

Cicero learned that Bibulus had at last arrived in Syria. He later claimed (to some derision) that it had been his own presence close by that had emboldened Cassius to act. With the Parthian threat blunted at least for the time being, Cicero then led a punitive expedition against the Free

Cilicians, mountain communities that had never fully acknowledged the rule of Rome. He did not take himself seriously as a general but knew that enough fighting to warrant a Triumph (or, as he called it lightheartedly, "a sprig of laurel") would enhance his prestige in Rome.

The brief campaign was a success. His soldiers hailed him in the field as *imperator,* or Commander-in-Chief, an honor given to a general for leading his army to victory in person, which its recipient could use after his name (as Cicero later did when writing to Caesar). From the account he gave Atticus, it looks as if the leading role was played by Pomptinus. "On October 13 we made a great slaughter of the enemy, carrying and burning places of great strength, Pomptinus coming up at night and myself in the morning. For a few days we were encamped near Issus in the very spot where Alexander, a considerably better general than either you or I, pitched his camp against Darius." He was not altogether displeased to hear that Bibulus had attempted some fighting of his own on the Syrian side of the mountains, out of jealousy he suspected, and come to grief, losing an entire cohort.

Cicero then moved against the well-defended Free Cilician fortress of Pindenissum and a full-scale siege ensued, which lasted some weeks. A moat was dug and a huge mound with a high siege tower and penthouses was erected. Siege artillery was deployed and many archers. Eventually, on or about December 17, the town fell with no Roman loss of life and all the plunder was handed over to the army. "A merry Saturnalia was had by all," Cicero told Atticus, referring to the Christmas-like winter festival which took place at this time. The campaigning season now ended and the gratified and probably grateful *imperator* handed over his army to Quintus, who marched it away to winter quarters. Even if he was not awarded a Triumph, he could reasonably hope for a consolation prize, the lesser victory celebration called an Ovation.

Cicero's vow to govern evenhandedly was severely tested in the coming months. He had set out what he believed to be the principles of good administration in the letter of guidance he had sent his brother during his governorship of Asia from 61 to 59; we may conjecture that Quintus was watching closely to see if Cicero would live up to his own precepts.

One of the most common complaints by provincials was the tax burden. Here Cicero had no sympathy with them, for in his view taxes were a payment for peace and tranquillity and for the rule of law. A more embarrassing problem, as Cicero well knew, was caused by the way public dues were collected. In the absence of a civil service, Rome sold the right to collect taxes to the highest bidder. Tax farmers often colluded with governors to make exorbitant profits. This was a subject where Cicero had to tread carefully, for he had built his career in part as a spokesman for businessmen and traders, and the local tax farmers were expecting favorable treatment.

Cicero knew that some form of compromise would be necessary. He disguised his determination to see fair play by assiduous politeness. The tax farmers complained that people would not pay what they owed, and the provincials said that they could not. The governor insisted that debts must be settled, but he allowed plenty of time for repayment and set interest rates at the legal maximum (often breached) of 1 percent per month. The provincials found this to be fair. And the tax farmers were happy enough too, for they were now sure to get their money, even if at a lower rate of return than they had originally expected. To smooth the path, Cicero buttered them up, asking them to dinner parties and doing all he could to flatter their self-esteem. At the same time he did his best to keep his staff under control, somewhat to their annoyance as they had to forgo customary pickings. He also took venal local officials aside and persuaded them quietly to repay funds they had acquired illegally.

Throughout his governorship he was never too busy to attend to developments in Rome. The *optimates* were pursuing their single, simple and disastrous policy of preventing Caesar from moving seamlessly from his Gallic posting to a second Consulship. They made repeated attempts to have the question of his successor discussed in the Senate, but these came to nothing, as they were invariably vetoed by one or more Tribunes in Caesar's interest (and pay). Pompey let it be known that he felt it would be unfair to consider the question of Caesar's replacement before March of the following year, the date when it would be legally permissible to do so. The disgruntled Faction, as Caesar nicknamed the *optimates,* had to settle for that. In an endless stream of letters Cicero pressed for compromise, but absence had weakened his influence. Caelius became Aedile in January 50, and concentrated on putting down fraud in the administration of the water supply (on which dry subject he published a well-received pamphlet). But he still found the time and energy to write to Cicero, who read his reports with mounting anxiety.

As often happens when cataclysm approaches, a fruitlessly busy inertia paralyzed the political community. Caelius wrote in February:

> Our Consuls are paragons of conscientiousness—to date they have not succeeded in getting a single decree through the Senate except about fixing the date of the Latin Festival. . . . The stagnation of everything here is indescribable. If I didn't have a battle on with the shopkeepers and inspectors of conduits, a coma would have seized the community. Unless the Parthians liven you up a bit over there, we are as dead as dormice.

Caelius had high expectations for his and Cicero's mutual friend, Curio, who became a Tribune in 50. He stood for election on a fiercely anti-Caesar platform and even threatened to raise again the issue of the Campanian lands, which had landed Cicero in such trouble with Caesar a few years previously. His efforts, however, were ineffective. The reason for this became clear only later: Caesar was secretly negotiating with him to change sides in return for settling his colossal debts. Curio cleverly created a smoke screen to cover his shift of allegiance and, although he soon began defending Caesar's interest, it was a while before anyone realized that he was taking instructions from Gaul.

Military operations having been satisfactorily completed, Cicero turned his attention to administrative matters. Nothing that Appius could do or say surprised him, but he was greatly taken aback when he uncovered a financial scam that he eventually traced back to Marcus Brutus, the son of Servilia, Cato's half-sister and at one time Caesar's mistress. Brutus had a reputation for honesty and austerity. An intellectual devoted to Greek philosophy, he was, at thirty-four, the diametrical opposite of disreputable contemporaries such as Curio or Caelius. He modeled himself to some extent on his uncompromisingly virtuous half-uncle, Cato, and like him did not believe in half-measures. Caesar (whom gossip wrongly whispered was his natural father) once said acutely of Brutus: "What he wants is hard to say, but when he wants it, he wants it badly."

Brutus had won the Quaestorship in 54 and served in Cilicia under Appius Claudius. Cicero was astonished to discover that this paragon of integrity, through some front men, had loaned a large sum of money to the town of Salamis in Cyprus at the extortionate interest rate of 4 percent a month (i.e., 60 percent compound interest over a year). That "very impecunious monarch" Deiotarus of Galatia was also in Brutus's debt and finding it almost impossible to keep up his repayments. This was all the more shocking given that Senators were, in theory at least, barred from moneylending.

When Brutus asked Cicero to help his agents enforce the debts, the governor's first reaction was to refuse to use his public authority for private ends. He reminded Brutus of his decision to set a 1 percent interest rate for loans in Cilicia. Privately he found the situation very awkward. "I shall be sorry to have incurred his displeasure," Cicero told Atticus in February, "but far sorrier to find that he is not the man I took him for." Matters were not helped by Brutus's unwillingness to give any ground. "He is apt in his letters to me to take a brusque, arrogant, ungracious tone even when asking a favor."

It was indeed a scandalous business: at one point Brutus's people had used the cavalry to barricade the Senate of Salamis in their Senate House, as a result of which five Senators had starved to death. Cicero could not get the affair out of his mind and it dominated his correspondence with Atticus, at wearisome length. Atticus was a part of the problem, for he took Brutus's side and, in a rare note of criticism of his friend, Cicero wrote: "My dearest Atticus, you have really cared too much for Brutus in this matter and not enough for me."

The quick passage of time saved Cicero from having to take definitive action and he bequeathed the problem to his successor. We can guess that the outcome was unsatisfactory for the Salaminians, for Brutus accompanied the succeeding governor as one of his deputies.

With the waning of the Parthian threat, Marcus and young Quintus returned from Cappadocia and continued their education under a short-tempered tutor. In his father's absence, marooned in the snowy Taurus Mountains with the army, young Quintus was proving a handful, but, his uncle told Atticus, "I shall keep him on a tighter rein." It seems that the two got on badly and, to judge by later developments, efforts to discipline the teenager failed. On March 17, Cicero conducted the sixteen-year-old Quintus's coming-of-age ceremony in his father's absence.

Separation had done little to improve the elder Quintus's marriage. The quarrel at Arpinum had had deep roots and Quintus was now meditating on divorce from Pomponia, Atticus's difficult sister. He confided this to his freedman, Statius, who went around saying that Cicero approved (perhaps he was getting his own back on Pomponia, who cordially disliked him for his closeness to her husband). Cicero was furious and assured Atticus that this was the last thing he wanted. "Let me say only one thing: so far from wishing the bond between us to be in any way relaxed, I should welcome as many and as intimate links with you as possible," he wrote to Atticus, "though those of affection, and of the closest, exist already. As for Quintus, I have often found that he is apt to speak rather harshly in these matters, and again I have often mollified his irritation. I think you know this. During this foreign trip or rather service of ours I have repeatedly seen him flare up and calm down again. What he may have written to Statius I cannot say. Whatever step he proposed to take in such a matter he ought not to have written to a freedman."

The impact of these marital difficulties was greatest on young Quintus, who was very close to his mother and seems to have taken her side. While he was away Cicero allowed him to open his father's mail, in case it contained anything that needed urgent attention, and one day the boy stumbled on a reference to the possible divorce. He broke down in tears. His growing estrangement from his family in the coming years may have been partly caused by the difficulty of any talented boy growing up in the shadow of a famous relative, but perhaps a more pressing motive lay in what he saw as the ill treatment of a much-loved mother.

A worried Cicero wrote to Atticus: "He does seem very fond of his mother, as he should be, and extraordinarily fond of you. But the boy's nature, though gifted, is complex and I have plenty to do in guiding it." With Cicero's encouragement, Quintus played a part in helping to reconcile his parents. The divorce did not take place.

Serious trouble was also brewing closer to home. In June 50 Cicero broached a highly sensitive topic with Atticus, writing in veiled terms and in Greek. Terentia had sent him out to Cilicia to see Cicero and his behavior had been strange. "There's something else about which I must write to you *en langue voilée,* and you must lay your nose to the scent. From the confused and incoherent way he talked the other day, I formed the impression that my wife's freedman (you know to whom I refer) has cooked the accounts regarding [a property purchase]. I am afraid that something—you'll take my meaning. Please look into it. . . . I can't put all I fear into words." The implication is that his wife was somehow involved.

The divorced Tullia had now settled on a new husband and she could hardly have made a more unsatisfactory choice. Her eye had fallen on a handsome young aristocrat, Publius Cornelius Lentulus Dolabella. A reckless and womanizing playboy, he was not at all the match Cicero had been hoping for.

Tullia seems usually to have gotten her way with her indulgent father, and on this occasion he knew little of what was afoot until she and her mother presented him with a fait accompli. He made the best of a bad situation, although the marriage placed him in Appius Claudius's bad books just when he thought he had gotten out of them. As luck would have it, Dolabella was in the process of bringing Appius to trial on a treason charge. "Here I am in my province paying Appius all kinds of compliment, when out of the blue I find his prosecutor becoming my son-in-law!"

In the summer of 50, much to his relief, Cicero had reached the end of his posting and set off for Rome, despite the brief threat of another Parthian invasion. On the journey home he had plenty of time to think about the political situation he was going to find on his return. He called at Rhodes and Athens and wrote an affectionate letter to his "darling and much-longed-for Terentia," complimenting her on her letters to him, which "covered all items most carefully," and asking her to come and meet him in Brundisium if her health allowed. He reached the port in late November at the same time as his wife arrived at the city gates: they met in the market square. The suspicions he had raised with Atticus had evidently been lulled, at least for the time being. He was also coming to terms with Tullia's new husband, the playboy Dolabella. "We all find him charming, Tullia, Terentia, myself," he told Atticus. "He is as clever and agreeable as you please. Other characteristics, of which you are aware, we must put up with."

Cicero was in no hurry to reach Rome and did not arrive there until early January 49. He would need to retain his governor's *imperium* until he crossed the city boundary, if he were to be awarded a Triumph or an Ovation, and so he stayed at Pompey's grand country house outside the capital, accompanied by his official guard of lictors, their axes now wreathed in laurel because of his title of *imperator.* Cicero was back where he felt he belonged, and he did not intend to be inactive.

10

"A STRANGE MADNESS"

The Battle for the Republic: 50–48 BC

In the great impending crisis Cicero cast himself in the role of a disinterested mediator and bent all his efforts towards reconciling the parties. Looking back a few weeks later, he told Tiro: "From the day I arrived in Rome all my views, words and actions were unceasingly directed towards peace. But a strange madness was abroad."

Caelius reported in June that "Pompey the Great's digestion is now in such a poor way that he has trouble finding anything to suit him." This may have been the preliminary symptom of a serious illness that struck him down in the summer. For a time his life was thought to be in danger. Prayers were offered for him across Italy and when he recovered, festivals were staged in towns and cities in his honor. This led Pompey to believe that he would have overwhelming public support against Caesar in the event of a conflict. "I have only to stamp my foot on the ground anywhere in Italy and armies of infantry and armies of cavalry will rise up," Plutarch reports him as saying. But his popularity was wide rather than deep, for most people preferred peace to war. When Pompey reemerged into public life he seemed to have lost some of his old energy. Cicero noticed his lack of spirit and wondered about his future health.

Writing to Cicero in August 50, Caelius foresaw "great quarrels ahead in which strength and steel will be arbiters." He claimed to be uncertain which way to jump; he had obligations to Caesar and his circle and, as for the *optimates,* he "loved the cause but hated the men." Caelius was preparing to change sides and follow Curio onto Caesar's payroll, but his relationship with Cicero does not seem to have suffered.

The Senate ordered both Pompey and Caesar to contribute a legion each for an expeditionary force against the Parthians to avenge Crassus. Pompey ungenerously decided that his legion would be the one he had loaned to Caesar sometime before for his Gallic campaigns, which meant that Caesar would have to give up two. The officers sent to fetch these legions reported, so inaccurately that one has to wonder if they acted with conscious warmongering deceit, much disaffection and low morale among Caesar's troops.

Cicero was deeply depressed by the direction of events, which he tended to see in personal terms. In a letter to Atticus written from Athens, the first of many such, he agonized as to how he should react.

> There looms ahead a tremendous contest between them. Each counts me as his man, unless by any chance one of them is pretending—for Pompey has no doubts, judging correctly that I strongly approve of his present politics [that is, his rapprochement with the Senate]. What is more, I received letters from both of them at the same time as yours, conveying the impression that neither has a friend in the world he values more than myself. But what am I to do? I don't mean in the last resort, for if war is to decide the issue, I am clear that defeat with one is better than victory with the other. What I mean are the practical steps that will be taken when I get back to prevent [Caesar's] candidacy *in absentia* [for the Consulship] and to make him give up his army. . . . There is no room for fence-sitting.

When he asserted his preference for Pompey, Cicero was being truthful. For all his ditherings in the months and years ahead, his first priority was and remained the salvation of the Republic and, it followed, opposition to Caesar. In this he remained unalterable. However, fence-sit he did. He did not have the temperament for war and was not physically courageous—a failing to which he half-admitted: "While I am not cowardly in facing dangers, I am in guarding against them."

His personal relations with the *optimates* continued to be unsatisfactory. Cato objected to Cicero's request for a Triumph. It is hard to understand why he took this line, at a time when it was self-evidently in the *optimates'* interest to ensure that Cicero was on their side. Perhaps Cato simply assumed this was the case, but, aware of Cicero's instinct for compromise and reconciliation, preferred to keep him at arm's length from the Senatorial leadership. Caesar immediately noticed the error of judgment and wrote to Cicero, sympathizing and offering his support.

Cicero was highly critical in private of Pompey and the Senate's handling of affairs. It was an old complaint. Caesar had not been stopped during his Consulship. He, Cicero, had been betrayed into exile. Resistance to the First Triumvirate had been feeble. The shortsighted extremism of Cato and his friends was inappropriate when dealing with "a man who fears nothing and is ready for everything." Cicero was even beginning to wonder how the *optimates* would behave in the future if they were victorious. On Atticus's advice, he stayed away from Rome, using as convenient cover the need to maintain his *imperium* in case he won his Triumph.

In Cicero's opinion, peace was the only rational policy and to obtain it would mean compromise. In this he was in tune with public opinion and with the majority of Senators. On December 1, in his last coup as Tribune, Curio persuaded the Senate to vote on his proposal that both Caesar and Pompey should resign their commands and disband their armies. This ingenious motion was designed to expose the true state of feeling in the chamber. It was carried by 370 votes to 22. Curio went straight to a meeting of the General Assembly, where he was cheered and garlanded. The crowd pelted him with flowers. He had won the day: there would be no war.

This put the *optimates* in an awkward position. If they did not act quickly it would be too late. After a night's reflection, the presiding Consul, Caius Claudius Marcellus, supported by the Consuls-Elect, but with no Senate authorization (nor that of the other Consul, Lucius Aemilius Paulus, whom Caesar had bought with a bribe of 9 million denarii) went to Pompey, handed him a sword and asked him to take command of the Italian legions. His task was to save the Republic. Pompey accepted the invitation.

Curio's Tribuneship ended on December 12 and his place was taken by his longtime friend Mark Antony. The movement for peace was still flowing strongly and Caesar, partly for reasons of public relations but also because he may have preferred a negotiated solution, put forward some compromise proposals, well calculated to appeal to the Senatorial majority.

Events now accelerated beyond anyone's power to control them. Pompey went to Campania to raise troops and met Cicero by chance on a country road. They went together to Formiae and talked from two in the afternoon until evening. Pompey almost persuaded Cicero that a firm approach was the right one; if challenged, Caesar would probably step back and, if not, the forces of the Republic under his leadership would easily defeat him. A couple days later a gloomy Cicero sent Atticus a well-reasoned statement of possible outcomes. His prognosis included the one that actually occurred—a surprise attack by Caesar before the Senate and Pompey were ready to fight him. Cicero even wondered whether it would be possible to hold Rome.

The Faction shared Pompey's optimism. At the time and later they have been represented as hell-bent on war. This was probably not the case, for it would have meant handing over control of events to their general, and they did not trust him enough to want to see that happen. They calculated that an ultimatum backed by force would deter Caesar from seeking the Consulship that summer. This would have been a rational policy if the balance of military power had been clearly in the Senate's favor. It was not. As early as August, Caelius had seen that, although Pompey had access in the medium term to far greater resources both by sea and land, Caesar's "army is incomparably superior." It is telling that once hostilities actually started, Cato altered his tune and told the Senate that even slavery was preferable to war. Clearly he too could see where the real balance of power lay.

Cicero stayed for a time at Formiae and then made his way to Rome for consultations. The Senate appeared to be willing to give him his Triumph after all and so he lodged at Pompey's villa outside the city. The Senate's mood (or at any rate that of those who attended its meetings) had hardened so far as the political situation was concerned. On January 1, 49, the incoming Consuls won a large majority for an ultimatum instructing Caesar to disband his legions on pain of outlawry.

Cicero had not given up hope of a compromise and was determined to exploit the widespread antiwar sentiment. Three days later he attended an informal meeting at Pompey's villa and once again argued for a peaceful solution. According to Plutarch, he supported an offer by Caesar to give up Gaul and most of his army in exchange for retaining Illyricum and two legions while waiting for his second Consulship. When Caesar's supporters suggested he would even be satisfied with one legion, Pompey wavered. But Cato shouted that he was making a fool of himself again and letting himself be taken in. The proposal was dropped. On January 7 the Senate passed the Final Act. Mark Antony and a fellow Tribune, who had been tirelessly wielding their veto on Caesar's behalf and making themselves highly unpopular in the process, were warned to leave town. They fled from Rome, together with Curio and Caelius, and arrived three days later at Caesar's camp in Italian Gaul.

Although he continued to make peace offers, Caesar knew that it was time for action. He moved with all his famous "celerity." Most of his army was on the other side of the Alps and he had only a single legion with him in Italian Gaul, where he was waiting near the frontier for news. Suetonius gives a vivid account of Caesar's next move.

> He at once sent a few troops ahead with all secrecy, and disarmed suspicion by himself attending a theatrical performance, inspecting the plans of a school for gladiators which he proposed to build and dining as usual among a crowd of guests. But at dusk he borrowed a pair of mules from a bakery near headquarters, harnessed them to a gig and set off quietly with a few of his staff. His lights went out, he lost his way and the party wandered about aimlessly for some hours; but at dawn found a guide who led them on foot along narrow lanes, until they came to the right road. Caesar overtook his advanced guard at the river Rubicon, which formed the frontier between Italian Gaul and Italy. Well aware how critical decision confronted him, he turned to his staff, remarking: "We may still draw back but, across that little bridge, we will have to fight it out."

When Caesar crossed the river, he quoted a phrase from the Greek comic playwright Menander, "Let the die be cast," and rushed south towards Rome. He had long been known for his luck and he would need it now.

It is to Caesar's credit as a leader that his soldiers and their officers loyally followed him. Only one senior commander defected, Titus Labienus, who had helped him with the Rabirius trial in 63 and been the most able of his deputies in Gaul. They went back a long way together and it must have been a personal blow.

Caesar's troops met no resistance and town after town fell to him. In Rome discussions were under way on recruitment and the distribution of provinces. The news of Caesar's rapid advance brought them to an abrupt halt. Pompey declared, to widespread amazement and dismay, that the government should evacuate Rome. Plutarch's account captures the fevered atmosphere:

> Since nearly all Italy was in confusion it was hard to understand the course of events. Refugees from outside the city poured in from all directions, while its inhabitants were rushing out of it and abandoning the city. Conditions were so stormy and disordered that the better class of person could exert little control and insubordinate elements were strong and very difficult for the authorities to keep in check. It was impossible to check the panic. No one would allow Pompey to follow his own judgment and everyone bombarded him with their own experiences—whether of fear, distress or perplexity. As a result contradictory decisions were made on one and the same day and it was impossible for Pompey to get accurate intelligence about the enemy since many people reported to him whatever they happened to hear and were upset when he did not believe them. In these circumstances Pompey issued a decree declaring a state of civil war. He ordered all Senators to follow him and announced that he would regard anybody who stayed behind as being on Caesar's side. Late in the evening he left Rome.

On January 17 large numbers of Senators and magistrates accompanied him en route to Campania, abandoning the city so hurriedly that they forgot to take the contents of the Treasury with them. A few days later, Caesar entered Rome.

Cicero met Pompey just before his departure and recalled a couple of months later that he had found him "thoroughly cowed. Nothing he did after that was to my liking. He went on blundering now here now there." Cicero was shocked as much by the incompetence and rashness of the *optimates* as by the catastrophe itself. On January 18 he wrote to Atticus from the outskirts of Rome: "I have decided on the spur of the moment to leave before daybreak so as to avoid looks or talk, especially with these laureled lictors. As for what is to follow, I really don't know what I am doing or going to do, I am so confounded by our crazy way of going on." He retreated to his villa at Formiae, where he could watch developments in safety and consider his next move. A few days later he accepted Pompey's request that he take responsibility for northern Campania and the seacoast. He could not decently refuse, but he assumed his duties without enthusiasm.

Cicero was naturally worried about his family's safety. His imagination ran riot as he thought of what the "barbarians" might do to Terentia and Tullia when they took Rome. Perhaps, he suggested to Atticus, the boys should be sent to Greece where they would be out of the way. His fears were in part allayed by Tullia's new husband, Dolabella; he was a passionate Caesarian and would guarantee the safety of Terentia and the others. Cicero arranged for the house on the Palatine to be properly barricaded and guarded; but he soon decided that the family, including (it seems) Quintus and his son, should join him at Formiae. He was greatly put out when he learned that the boys' tutor, Dionysius, refused to come with them. A few weeks later he remarked: "He scorns me in my present plight. It is disgusting. I hate the fellow and always shall. I wish I could punish him. But his own character will do that." Typically, Cicero could not stay angry for long and there was a reconciliation in due course, if a grudging one.

As for the nonpolitical Atticus, his friend had few anxieties. "It looks to me as though you yourself and Sextus [an intimate friend of Atticus] can properly stay on in Rome. You certainly have little cause to love our friend Pompey. Nobody has ever knocked so much off property values in town. I still have my joke, you see."

Cicero condemned Pompey's abandonment of Rome and was afraid that the Commander-in-Chief was thinking of evacuating Italy, for Greece or perhaps Spain, where there were loyal legions. There can be little doubt that Pompey had been knocked off balance. He had exaggerated his personal popularity and was depressed both by the easy progress Caesar was making and by his own difficulties of recruitment. The psychological impact of the evacuation of Rome had been tremendous. The damage to public opinion if Pompey now abandoned Italy would be even greater. Yet there was strategic sense in basing himself in Greece, where he would have all the resources of Asia Minor at his back. With the army of Spain in the west, commanded by Lucius Afranius, the reputed dancer, and Marcus Petreius, Caesar would then be gripped in a vise. Once he had mustered his full strength, Pompey would descend on Italy, as Sulla had done, and meet Caesar with overwhelming force. In addition he controlled a large fleet and had unchallenged mastery of the seas. Unfortunately this plan left out of account the fact that it handed the initiative to Caesar.

Cicero had still not given up all hopes of peace. His disgust at the conduct of the war made him reluctant to join Pompey as an active supporter. More important, he felt that his hand as an intermediary would be strengthened if he could present himself as (more or less) neutral. His motives were mixed, but he was right to believe that it was in his and the Republic's interest to play a lone hand. His stance became increasingly untenable as it became clear that the war was going to continue. Unfriendly voices were already criticizing him for not joining the rest of the evacuees in Campania. His mood became volatile and edgy. It was not helped by a painful bout of ophthalmia, which lasted until May. He was finding it hard to sleep. He relied more and more on Atticus, whom he showered with letters, often daily, appealing for advice.

> I am sure you find daily letters a bore, especially as I give you no news and indeed can no longer think of any new theme to write about. But while it would certainly be silly of me to send you special couriers with empty letters and for no reason, I can't bring myself not to give a line for you to those who are going anyway, especially if they are fond of the family, and at the same time I do, believe me, find a modicum of relaxation in these miseries when I am as it were talking to you, much more still when I am reading your letters.

The military situation did not improve. Towards the middle of February Cicero visited Pompey at his headquarters in Capua before he moved his forces farther south to avoid being cornered by the enemy. What he found deepened his pessimism. The recruiting officers were afraid to do their work; the Consuls were hopeless and, as for Pompey, "How utterly down he is! No courage, no plan, no forces, no energy." Cicero resigned his Campanian commission, saying he could do nothing without troops and money. Letters came from Caesar full of kind words and peace proposals and so did curt missives from Pompey asking Cicero to join him. Balbus and Oppius, Caesar's confidential agents, were in constant touch. To these correspondents Cicero responded with fair words and no commitments.

Caesar was briefly delayed at the town of Corfinium where a reckless aristocrat, Lucius Domitius Ahenobarbus made a vain stand. He was acting against the instructions of Pompey, who refused to come to his aid. When the town fell Caesar found about fifty Senators and *equites* in it, all of whom he immediately released on condition that they not take arms against him again—an assurance many of them swiftly broke. This act of clemency had a huge impact on public opinion, which began to swing in his direction, and a number of *optimates* returned to Rome. Caesar maintained this policy of leniency for the rest of his life. He intended it as vivid proof that he was no Sulla, set on the armed overthrow of the state.

Meanwhile Pompey continued to rebuff Caesar's offers of peace and decided to extricate himself and his legions from Italy. He marched to Brundisium, where he intended to leave for Greece. Caesar followed him at top speed. On February 20 Pompey dispatched an abrupt note to "M. Cicero Imperator," telling him to meet him at Brundisium. Cicero wrote a long, detailed reply in which he explained why it was unsafe and impractical for him to do so. He also set out a justification of his role as peacemaker, adding oblique criticisms of Pompey's performance and failure to inform him of his plans. The truth was, as Cicero admitted to Atticus, he had not yet made up his mind what to do. He was coming to believe that there was less to choose between the opposing sides than he had originally thought. The constitution would probably be destroyed whoever won the impending struggle.

> Our Cnaeus is marvelously covetous of despotism on Sullan lines. *Experto crede;* he has been as open about it as he ever was about anything. . . . The plan is first to strangle Rome and Italy with hunger, then to carry fire and sword through the countryside and dip into the pockets of the rich. But since I fear the same from *this* [i.e., Caesar's] quarter, if I did not have an obligation to repay in the other I should think it better to take whatever may come at home.

On March 9 Caesar arrived outside Brundisium, but it was too late. The Consuls had already left with part of the army to set up headquarters in Greece. Pompey was still in town, but towards nightfall on March 17 he followed after them, evading Caesar's attempt at a blockade with few losses and escaping with the remainder of his troops. Caesar was left fuming outside the walls, from which vantage point he could see the fleet's sails grow smaller in the darkening light.

"I was made anxious before . . . by my inability to think of any solution," Cicero told Atticus, who was comfortably settled in Rome. "But now that Pompey and the Consuls have left Italy, I am not merely distressed, I am consumed with grief." He wrote in the language of a disconsolate lover: "Nothing in [Pompey's] conduct seemed to deserve that I should join him as his companion in flight. But now my affection comes to the surface, the sense of loss is unbearable, books, writing, philosophy are all to no purpose." The presence of his brother doubled his anxiety: Quintus, having spent some years fighting under Caesar in Gaul, owed much more to his old commander than Cicero did and could expect to suffer the severest consequences if he defected. Nevertheless, he told Cicero that he would follow his lead.

Now that a long war was more or less certain, Caesar's interest in Cicero shifted from his potentially useful role as mediator to his value as a propaganda asset. He wanted to attract as many senior figures to his side as possible, in order to legitimize his authority, and Cicero would be a great prize. Stressing his policy of clemency and their ties of *amicitia* (it is not known whether Cicero had yet been able to pay back Caesar's loan), he tried to persuade the reluctant statesman to come to Rome. Caesar's plan was to visit the city briefly to meet the remnants of the Senate, after which he would go to Spain and deal with Pompey's legions there. On March 28, on his journey back from Brundisium, Caesar stopped off at Formiae for an encounter which Cicero had been dreading for some time.

Caesar was not in an accommodating mood. He complained that Cicero was passing judgment against him and that "the others would be slower to come over" to his side if he refused to do so. Cicero replied that they were in a different position. A long discussion followed, which Cicero recorded for Atticus. It went badly.

"Come along then [to a Senate meeting called for April 1] and work for peace," Caesar said.

"At my own discretion?"

"Naturally, who am I to lay down the rules for you?"

"Well, I shall take the line that the Senate does not approve of an expedition to Spain or of the transport of armies into Greece, and I shall have much to say in commiseration of Pompey."

"This is not the kind of thing I want said."

"So I supposed, but that is just why I don't want to be present. Either I must speak in that strain or stay away—and much else besides which I could not possibly suppress if I was there."

Caesar closed the conversation by asking Cicero to think matters over. He added menacingly as he left: "If I cannot make use of your advice, I will take it where I can find it. I will stop at nothing." He meant that if moderates like Cicero would not work with him, his only alternative would be to seek help from revolutionaries.

The encounter was decisive, for both parties. Caesar must have realized that he could not push an obviously unhappy man any further. He now proceeded to Rome, where he spent a few uncomfortable days in discussion with a reluctant and much-thinned Senate. He broke into the Treasury at the Temple of Saturn and removed its contents: 15,000 bars of gold, 30,000 of silver and 30 million sesterces—a move for which he paid with the total collapse of his popularity. Then he hurried away to fight in Spain, leaving the Tribune Mark Antony in charge of Italy and Marcus Aemilius Lepidus in charge of Rome.

As for Cicero, the conversation and the behavior of Caesar's raffish entourage—he nicknamed them the "underworld"—persuaded him that, for all his reservations, he had to side with those who were (if only ostensibly) fighting for the Republic. He could do this only by leaving Italy. But when should he set off and how? And where should he go? He thought of Athens or, somewhere completely off the beaten track, Malta. Soon he realized he was being watched by Caesar's spies.

The time had come for Marcus's coming-of-age ceremony and the family moved to the ancestral home of Arpinum for the purpose. It was a melancholy trip: everyone they met was in low spirits and, as a result of Caesar's levies, men were being led off to winter quarters. On his return to Formiae, Cicero made a most unpalatable discovery. Quintus, now seventeen, had made off to Rome, claiming that he wanted to see his mother.

He had written to Caesar and perhaps even obtained an interview with him (or one of his lieutenants), in which he revealed that his uncle was disaffected and intended to leave the country. The elder Quintus was beside himself with misery. In a hierarchical society where a *paterfamilias* had theoretically unlimited power over his children, it was an almost unbelievable betrayal. Although Cicero was upset, he seems to have taken the affair in stride. After a few days he calmed down, deciding that the boy had acted out of greed rather than hatred. The runaway was brought back, and his uncle decided that "severity" was the best policy.

Curio called. Caesar had given him a commission to secure the corn supply in Sicily (where he was to face, and face down, Cato) before going on to the province of Africa. He hurried off on political business before returning, on the following day, for a longer conversation.

In the following weeks, Cicero referred from time to time to a mysterious, top-secret plan which he code-named "Caelius." It is not known what he had in mind, but there has been speculation that it might have been a scheme to take over Africa and use it as a base from which to launch a new peace initiative. Caelius can hardly have been involved himself since he was with Caesar in Spain and perhaps the name was employed jokily for what was fundamentally a madcap project. One wonders if it originated in the lengthy discussions with Curio. If Curio was complicit, it would suggest either that he was willing to detach himself from Caesar or, more deviously, that the "Caelian business" could have been a device to lure Cicero away from Greece and Pompey into a safely Caesarian zone of influence. In that case, Cicero was lucky that he did not proceed with the matter, for the militarily inexperienced Curio quickly fell afoul of King Juba of Numidia, an ally of Pompey, was routed in battle and killed with the loss of all his forces. The project, whatever it was, soon vanishes from the correspondence.

It did not call for great acumen on anyone's part to sense Cicero's misery and to guess at his intention to escape from Italy. During April and early May pressure was brought to bear on him from all sides, advising him not to leave the country but to stay where he was. Caesar wrote to him from Massilia making the point. It would appear, he observed, that "you have disapproved some action of mine, which is the worst blow you could deal me. I appeal to you in the name of our friendship not to do this." On

May 1 Mark Antony sent him a warning letter whose surface cordiality concealed menace. "I cannot believe that you mean to go abroad, considering how fond you are of Dolabella and that most admirable young lady your daughter and how fond we all are of you. . . . I have specially sent Calpurnius, my intimate friend, so that you may know how deeply I care for your personal safety and position." Caelius also argued strongly that he should not stir, writing that Caesar's clemency would not last. If he abandoned Italy, Caelius said, Cicero would be risking ruin for himself and his family, not to mention blighting the careers of friends such as himself and Dolabella.

Members of his family also disapproved of his apparent determination to leave the country. Young Marcus and Quintus were in tears, if we can believe Cicero, when they read Caelius's letter. The heavily pregnant Tullia (she gave birth prematurely a few weeks later to a sickly child who did not survive) begged him to await the result of the Spanish campaign before making up his mind.

Cicero appealed to Mark Antony to give him formal permission to leave the country and received a cool, brief response, in which he was advised to ask Caesar directly. He wrote to Atticus in May:

> Do you think that if Spain is lost, Pompey will drop his weapons? No, his entire plan is Themistoclean [Themistocles was the Athenian statesman who had defeated the invading Persians by abandoning Athens and fighting at sea]. He reckons that whoever holds the sea is sure to be master. For that reason he was never interested in holding the Spanish provinces for their own sake; his main concern was always to outfit a navy. So when the time comes, he will put to sea with huge fleets and land in Italy.

What was somewhat less obvious was the nature of Cicero's likely contribution to the Republican cause once in Greece. His military advice would not be wanted. All that he could offer would be the publicity of his name. Moderate public opinion, however, would be impressed by his choice of sides.

To discourage speculation about his imminent departure, Cicero decided to spend a few days at his elegant town house in Pompeii. As soon as he arrived, though, he received an embarrassing surprise. Centurions from the three cohorts stationed there invited him to take charge of the soldiers and occupy the town. What use were three cohorts? he asked himself. Anyway, it could be a trap. Unnerved, he left the town secretly before dawn and returned home.

Quietly, the necessary travel arrangements were made and a reliable ship was found. "I hope my plan won't involve any risk," Cicero remarked, as ever nervous of physical danger and travel by sea. Bad weather caused a delay but on June 7 he was on board and writing a farewell letter to Terentia. At long last, he set sail for Greece with Marcus, his dissident nephew and the inevitable lictors. At this point the correspondence with Atticus ends and is not resumed for a year, either because communications were impossible or because it was too risky to write frankly. For a time Cicero recedes into the background—a powerless, disconsolate figure almost lost among tremendous events.

Cicero arrived at Pompey's camp at the port of Dyrrachium in Greece to find that the Commander-in-Chief had retained all his organizational skills and had spent the interval while Caesar was in Spain gathering his forces. Nine legions were assembled, five of which had been brought across from Italy and the others from various parts of the Empire. (Cicero's two understrength Cilician legions were among them, now merged into a single unit.) He had also recruited archers and a 7,000-strong force of cavalry. Through his large fleet, he maintained command of the seas, although the lack of senior military talent at his disposal is illustrated by the fact that he appointed Bibulus his admiral.

To his relief, Cicero, who made a large loan to Pompey to boost his war chest, was greeted warmly on his arrival and an effort was made to put him at ease. At the outset, although wracked with worry and in poor health, he was hopeful of the future. He wrote to Atticus: "You ask me about the war news. You will be able to learn it from Isidorus [the letter carrier]. It looks as if what remains won't be too difficult. Do please see to what you know I have most at heart [Terentia was in financial difficulty], as you say you will do and are doing. I am eaten up with anxiety, which has made me seriously ill. When I am better, I shall join the man in charge who is full of optimism." However, with typical contrariness, Cato took Cicero aside and said that his coming to Greece was a bad mistake. He would be much more use to his country and his friends if he stayed at home and reacted to events as they occurred. As he had agonized over his decision, this was the last thing Cicero wanted to hear and he was distinctly put out. He had expected the standard-bearer of constitutionalism to praise him. Not only had Cato not done so, but he gave the impression of having little confidence in Pompey's prospects.

After being nearly trapped by floods, Caesar brilliantly outmaneuvered his opponents in Spain and in August 49 enforced a surrender without bloodshed in a campaign that lasted only forty days. In his absence he arranged for a Praetor to have him appointed Dictator, which would empower him to hold elections. He hurried back to Italy where he confronted a mutiny among his troops, which he settled with bold inflexibility.

During this second flying visit to Rome he was elected to the second Consulship for which he had spent so many years struggling and intriguing. The onset of civil war had brought financial activity in Italy to an almost complete standstill and a debt crisis was creating serious social unease. Throughout the century revolutionaries such as Catilina had promoted a policy of total cancellation of debts and many expected that this was what Caesar would do. But he was too intelligent and responsible a politician not to realize that this cure would be far worse than the disease. He issued a well-considered decree which obliged creditors to accept land at prewar values as repayment and allowed up to a quarter of the value of a debt to be set off against previous interest payments.

It was on this issue that Caelius surprisingly broke with his new master in the following year. Praetor for 48, he tried to bounce an uncertain and edgy government into more radical measures after Caesar left Rome again for Greece in pursuit of Pompey. In January 48 he was in a cocky frame of mind when he wrote his final surviving letter to Cicero. Critical of Pompey's strategy of masterly inactivity in Greece, he promised that his own dash and drive would rescue the Republican cause. "I'll make you win in spite of yourselves. Cato and company will be smiling on me yet. You lot are fast asleep." However, he was quickly dismissed from office and driven to taking up arms. He called Cicero's old friend Milo back to Italy because he owned some gladiators he could make use of. Also, unforgivably in Roman eyes, he armed some slaves. But the revolt was easily quashed by Caesar's troops and both Caelius and Milo were killed.

Brilliant, amusing and attractive, Caelius was disabled by a refusal to take serious things seriously. He threw his life away pointlessly. By opposing Caesar this late in the game, he ignored the advice he had himself given Cicero. "To go against him now in the hour of his victory . . . is the acme of folly," he had said. So it was.

Caesar joined his army at Brundisium at the end of the year. He was determined to retain the initiative and had no intention of waiting for Pompey to invade Italy. Despite the fact that it was now winter, when sailing was unsafe, he decided to cross over to Greece as soon as possible, whatever the risk. On January 4, 48, he sailed unobserved to the coast of Epirus with part of his army, evading Bibulus's naval blockade. However, bad weather and Bibulus's unwillingness to be caught napping a second time meant that it was not until early April that his remaining troops under Mark Antony were able to join him. For a while Caesar had had too few forces to match Pompey and had been in serious danger, but now he went on the offensive. At the same time, in a continuing effort to retain the moral high ground, he launched another abortive peace initiative, but his opponents, filled with optimism, were having none of it.

Caesar decided to surround Pompey's camp near Dyrrachium with a fifteen-mile fortified line and besiege him. Pompey responded by building his own fortifications and then launched a major breakout. For a moment Caesar faced total defeat, but the advantage was not followed through. Caesar observed dismissively of his opponent: "He has no idea how to win a war." Short of supplies, Caesar cut his losses and marched away south to the more fertile region of Thessaly, with the enemy in pursuit.

It was typical of his tirelessness and attention to detail that, in the press of business, he remembered Cicero. In May he asked Dolabella, who was on his staff, to write a friendly letter to his father-in-law, which he duly did. After itemizing the humiliations and reverses that Pompey had suffered, he advised: "Consult your own best interests and at long last be your own friend rather than anybody else's." If there was anything Caesar could do to protect and maintain Cicero's *dignitas,* his honor or status, he had only to ask.

This was a well-aimed, and possibly well-informed, intervention. Cicero was not at all happy with his present circumstances. Could Cato have been right, after all? He made little secret of the fact that he now regretted having come to Greece. He could not resist making sarcastic comments and jokes about his colleagues and companions in arms and wandered about the camp looking so glum that he became something of a figure of fun. He criticized Pompey's plans behind his back and ridiculed the faith he and his supporters placed in prophecies and oracles. Above all, he went on arguing for peace and believed he might have won Pompey over if his confidence had not been boosted by the success at Dyrrachium.

Looking back a couple of years afterwards he summed up his opinions:

> I came to regret my action, not so much because of the risk to my personal safety as of the appalling situation which confronted me on arrival. To begin with, our forces were too small and had poor morale. Second, with the exception of the Commander-in-Chief and a handful of others (I am talking about the leading figures), everyone was greedy to profit from the war itself and their conversation was so bloodthirsty that I shuddered at the prospect of victory. What's more, people of the highest rank were up to their ears in debt. In a word, nothing was right except the cause we were fighting for.

There was talk of a proscription and, shockingly, Atticus had been marked down, perhaps because of his wealth, as a candidate for liquidation.

The climax of the campaign took place on August 9 on a plain near the town of Pharsalus in central Greece. Against his better judgment, although his army was much the larger of the two (perhaps 50,000 strong as compared with Caesar's force of about 30,000), Pompey at last offered battle. His plan was to outflank and roll up Caesar's right wing with a strong troop of horses, but Caesar guessed his intentions and placed some cohorts out of sight behind his center. His wing retreated in good order, as it had been instructed to do, and Pompey's onrushing cavalry was attacked from the side and routed. It was now Caesar's turn to outflank the enemy center and the rest of the engagement was a massacre. Pompey's soldiers stood their ground and died patiently, but the non-Roman allies put up no resistance and fled, shouting, "We've lost." Caesar recorded 200 fatalities while some 15,000 of Pompey's men were killed and 23,000 captured.

When Pompey saw how the battle was going, he withdrew to his camp where he sat speechless and stunned. Nothing in his long, cloudless career had prepared him for such a disaster. He changed out of his uniform and made his escape on horseback. His camp presented a remarkable spectacle. In his history of the war, Caesar described what he found: "[There] could be seen artificial arbors, a great weight of silver plate laid out, tents spread with fresh turf, those of Lucius Lentulus and several others covered with ivy, and many other indications of extravagant indulgence and confidence in victory." Inspecting the corpses on the battlefield, he remarked bitterly of the *optimates:* "They insisted on it."

Cicero was not present at Pharsalus, although it is possible that Quintus was, together with the seventeen-year-old Marcus, who had been given command of a troop of horses in Pompey's army and was doubtless enjoying the break from his studies in Athens. Being in poor health (whether genuinely or expediently), Cicero stayed behind at Dyrrachium with Cato, who commanded the town's garrison. Cicero was as annoyingly sarcastic as ever. When someone said optimistically that there was hope yet, for they had seven Eagles left (the legionary standards), he joked bitterly: "Excellent, if we were fighting jackdaws."

Caesar knew that if the war was to be brought to a rapid conclusion, it was of the utmost importance to capture his defeated rival; so he set off in pursuit of Pompey as he made his way eastwards, destination unknown. Meanwhile the leading survivors of Pharsalus gathered together and sailed the fleet to Corcyra, where they pondered their next move. Caesar's victory was a devastating blow to the Republicans and it looked as if the war were over. However, this was not necessarily so: Pompey's fleet still controlled the seas. The province of Africa had been in friendly hands since Curio's defeat and death. If the defeated Commander-in-Chief managed to elude Caesar, he might well be able to raise another army in Asia Minor.

Cato had not fought at Pharsalus and was unwilling to accept its verdict. The first decision to be made was who should take over from Pompey as Commander-in-Chief. Surprisingly Cato suggested that the commission be offered to Cicero as the senior Roman official present. It is hard to believe that Cato made the invitation other than for form's sake; even he would have seen something absurd in the distinctly unmilitary orator challenging the greatest general of his day.

Cicero rejected the idea out of hand and explained that he wanted to have nothing further to do with the war. His defeatist attitude enraged Pompey's eldest son, Cnaeus, who had a short and cruel temper. Apparently Cnaeus and his friends drew their swords and would have cut Cicero down on the spot if Cato had not intervened and, with some difficulty, hustled the elderly statesman out of the camp—and, as it turned out, the war.

Most of the remaining *optimates* decided that their best course of action was to make their way to the province of Africa. There they gathered—Afranius and Petreius, defeated in Spain, Pompey's two sons, other flotsam of Caesar's earlier victories and Cato himself, the moral standard-bearer of resistance. Many of them had been pardoned once and could expect no mercy if they fell into Caesar's hands a second time. Labienus, Caesar's old comrade-in-arms who had defected from him after the crossing of the Rubicon, also went to Africa. Their plan was to muster their forces and prepare for an invasion of Italy, a short sail away.

Some fugitives from the catastrophe decided to end their resistance. Chief among them was Marcus Brutus, now about thirty years old. Despite the financial scandal in which he had been involved during Cicero's governorship of Cilicia a couple of years before, he was in some respects a principled and serious-minded young man who thought long and hard about which side to fight for in the civil war. He had a strong family reason for going over to Caesar, as the youthful Pompey had had his father put to death during the wars of Sulla. However, in his considered opinion Pompey was more in the right than Caesar and Brutus decided that it was his duty to put the public good above his personal interests. Not for nothing was he Cato's nephew.

After joining the Republican army in Greece, Brutus spent much of his time in camp reading books till late in the evening and writing a digest of the Greek historian Polybius. He took part in the battle at Pharsalus, but came to no harm. There was a reason for this. Caesar was very fond of him, perhaps due to his continuing affection for his former mistress and Brutus's mother, Servilia, and gave instructions to his officers that he should not be killed. If Brutus gave himself up his life should be spared, and if he resisted he should be left alone. After the rout Brutus managed to escape through a marsh to safety. He traveled by night to the town of Larissa and immediately wrote to Caesar, who was delighted to learn that he was safe and asked Brutus to join him. According to Plutarch, he had no qualms about advising Caesar, correctly as it would turn out, that Pompey would likely flee to Egypt.

Brutus's motives as a collaborator defy interpretation. Up to this point in his life his actions appear to have been governed by self-interest. It may be that his reputation for high-mindedness and probity derived from his somewhat un-Roman bookishness and his addiction to literature and philosophy rather than from his actual behavior. Possibly, he felt that he had done enough for his family enemy and was now within his rights to switch to Caesar. One way or another, Brutus quickly became a favorite and a few months later was put in charge of Italian Gaul. He was a popular and apparently incorruptible governor.

So far as Cicero was concerned, hostilities were now definitely at an end. He took himself off to Patrae, the Greek port from where he would be able to catch a boat for Brundisium. Here a final misfortune awaited him, as he confided to Atticus a week or so later. He and his brother had a serious disagreement. By following Cicero's star, Quintus had lost everything. He had sacrificed his excellent relationship with Caesar, under whose command in Gaul he had for once been his own man. There may have been financial problems, too, nagging both men. For all their lives Quintus had willingly played second fiddle to his older and more famous brother. Perhaps resentment had so long been growing below the surface—all those years of patronizing advice, of interference in his domestic affairs—that it boiled over all the more violently when the break came.

The upshot was that Quintus and his son followed after Caesar, with whom they intended to make their peace. Meanwhile, Cicero had nowhere to go but back to Italy. Worn down by his adventures and broken by the collapse of both his public and domestic worlds, he set off once again, without pause for second thoughts, to Brundisium and home.

11

PACIFYING CAESAR

The Last Gasps of Republican Rome: 48–45 BC

This time arrival in Brundisium was a melancholy affair. There was no Terentia or Tullia waiting when he sailed into port in mid-October 48. Tullia was ill, perhaps recovering from her miscarriage, and Cicero was at his wits' end with worry. Ready money was in short supply, for while in Greece he had made over to Pompey all the funds he had brought with him. The payment of Tullia's dowry to her new husband, Dolabella, was a touchy issue.

Cicero's lictors were still with him, an expensive and embarrassing nuisance. He was nervous about his reception as he walked into the town and made them mingle discreetly with the crowd so that he would not be noticed. He could not disband them because, although his successor in Cilicia had been nominated, Caesar, now in charge of the government in Rome, refused to accept the appointment. (This meant, interestingly, that Cicero recognized, however reluctantly and implicitly, Caesar's legitimacy.)

Cicero was not sure what to do next. Atticus advised him to go nearer to Rome, traveling by night, but he did not relish the thought. He didn't have enough stopping places at his disposal, so what would he do in the daytime? Also, there was no pressing reason to move on, for his old enemy, Vatinius, was in charge of Brundisium and was now both hospitable and friendly. Cicero always found it hard to keep a feud going and was prone to be fond of anyone who showed him affection, whatever he really thought of them and their politics.

Balbus and Oppius, busy managing Caesar's affairs behind the scenes, wrote to Cicero telling him not to worry. His position would be protected, if not enhanced. Dolabella let him know that Caesar had authorized him to invite his father-in-law to come back to Italy. This good news was soon contradicted by Mark Antony, once again responsible for governing Italy in Caesar's absence, who sent Cicero a copy of a letter he had received from Caesar which stated that no Pompeians would be allowed back into the country until he had reviewed their cases individually. "He expressed himself pretty strongly on these points," Cicero informed Atticus gloomily. He settled down miserably in Brundisium to await Caesar's return.

At the end of November he learned of Pompey's fate. After Pharsalus, the general had made his way eastwards, with Caesar in hot pursuit. His destination had been Egypt; he thought he could make a stand there and raise another army by recruiting in Asia Minor. For many years he had been the incarnation of Roman authority in the region and he expected that his writ would still hold. Also he was the Senate-appointed guardian of the boy Pharaoh.

But the royal advisers to the Pharaoh had no intention of welcoming a loser. Imagining that they would ingratiate themselves with Caesar, they lured Pompey from his ship and had him killed before he had even reached land. Not long afterwards Caesar arrived in Alexandria and was presented with Pompey's severed and pickled head; when he was given his old brother-in-law's signet ring, he is said to have wept.

Success came early to Pompey and gave him a reputation he had to work to deserve. His portraits show a frowning, worried expression and suggest a man not entirely at ease with himself. His contemporaries overrated his military abilities, and as a politician he was hesitant, devious and clumsy. Yet he had his qualities: he was a first-rate organizer and, if only the Roman constitution had allowed it, could have spent a happy career as an imperial administrator. His private life was exemplary: his two marriages were arranged for political reasons, but he seems to have loved his wives and won their loyalty.

Cicero was saddened by Pompey's death but not surprised. The two men had been on good terms, but Pompey had kept his feelings to himself and, despite their surface affection, had been happy to manipulate and on occasion deceive his sometimes gullible friend. Cicero offered Atticus his own cool but generous epitaph: "As to Pompey's end I never had any doubt, for all rulers and peoples had become so thoroughly persuaded of the hopelessness of his case that wherever he went I expected this to happen. I cannot but grieve for his fate. I knew him for a man of good character, clean life and serious principle."

There was further news from the east, which Cicero took much more deeply to heart. Following the quarrel at Patrae, Quintus had sent his son ahead of him to find Caesar and make his excuses, hoping to be taken back into favor. Thinking that his own salvation depended on throwing Cicero to the wolves, he heaped all the blame for his own behavior on his elder brother. In addition, the younger Quintus was reported to have used scandalous language about his uncle in public. Cicero was deeply upset by these betrayals: "It is the most unbelievable thing that has ever happened to me," he told Atticus, "and the bitterest of my present woes."

In early January 47 a package of letters arrived from the elder Quintus for various addressees, including Vatinius and another person in Brundisium. Cicero had the local ones sent on at once. In no time the two recipients turned up on his doorstep, furious at what they had read. Apparently the letters contained malicious and inaccurate information about him. Cicero wondered what was in the rest of the correspondence, so he opened all the other letters and found much more in the same vein. He forwarded them all to Atticus for his opinion, telling him that Pomponia had a seal to replace the imprints he had broken.

Perhaps Cicero felt guilty for having taken his brother too much for granted; in any case, he wrote to Caesar accepting all responsibility for the decision to go to Greece and join Pompey: his brother had been "the companion of my journey, not the guide." This gesture of generosity was well judged. Cicero knew Caesar well and might have guessed that treachery of this kind would not endear Quintus to a man who valued personal loyalty above almost all things. As part of his reconciliation policy, Caesar had had all of Pompey's correspondence burned unread after Pharsalus. It would hardly have been in character for him to pay attention to the self-interested information, or disinformation, which Quintus was purveying about his brother.

Meanwhile Dolabella, who was Tribune that year, was stirring up trouble in Rome. He picked up the baton Caelius had let fall and, in opposition to government policy, was campaigning for a cancellation of debts. Caesar's financial settlement in Italy was faltering and discontent spread through the country, even contaminating veteran legions stationed not far away in Campania. Antony was forced to go to the troops to pacify them, leaving the city to Dolabella and disorder. Dolabella's agitations seriously reduced his value to Cicero as an insurance policy with the new regime.

All in all, the behavior of his relatives added private misery to Cicero's public misfortune. What was worse, he did not dare to draw attention to himself by leaving Brundisium, and there was little he could do so far from Rome except brood on an uncertain future.

Caesar now unexpectedly disappeared from view and nothing was heard from him for months. Between December 23, 48, and June of the following year he sent no dispatches to Rome. He had become embroiled, with too few troops at his back, in a bitter little war with the Egyptian court and at one stage was blockaded inside the royal palace in Alexandria. One of the daughters of the late Pharaoh, Ptolemy, was Cleopatra, now in her late teens. This young woman was to become one of the most celebrated and enigmatic figures in ancient history, mysterious in part because her memory is filtered through the malicious accounts of her enemies. Cleopatra was unable to offer her own version of the momentous events of her time; sex and politics are interwoven so closely in her career that her motives are hard to disentangle. *Raison d'état* led her into the bedrooms of two famous Romans—first Caesar, and later Mark Antony. To what extent did physical attraction or love also play a part? We do not know.

Cleopatra was not, it seems, particularly good-looking, but she had a bewitching personality. "Her own beauty, so we are told, was not of that incomparable kind which instantly captivates the beholder," Plutarch avers. "But the charm of her presence was irresistible: and there was an attractiveness in her person and talk, together with a peculiar force of character which pervaded her every word and action, and laid all who associated with her under its spell. It was delight merely to hear the sound of her voice."

At the time of her first meeting with Caesar, Cleopatra and a younger half-brother were joint Pharaohs (and, according to Egyptian custom for royal families, were probably married). She had no intention of sharing her authority with her brother for a minute longer than was necessary. The arrival of Rome's leading general was an opportunity for her, if only she could win him over to her cause.

The Queen had herself smuggled into Caesar's presence wrapped in a carpet or bedroll and they soon began an affair. She quickly persuaded him to take her side in the struggle for power with her brother. Caesar defeated the Egyptian army at the end of March 47 and Cleopatra's annoying little brother was drowned while trying to escape by boat from the battlefield. She wasted no time in marrying yet another boy sibling. Unaccountably, Caesar did not leave the country until June. He seems to have spent some of this time on a lavish and leisurely excursion up the Nile.

This was risky, if not irresponsible behavior, for it undermined the apparently decisive result of Pharsalus. What remained of Pompey's fleet was scoring successes in the Adriatic and the *optimates* in Africa were raising substantial forces. Antony was not doing well at governing Italy and failed to calm the mutinous soldiery. Caesar, cut off from the rest of the world, did not learn of these developments until later, but he could have foreseen that his absence would lead to problems. It was no time for him to quit the helm.

While Rome was distracted with its internal quarrels and Caesar was indulging in his Egyptian interlude, Mithridates' son Pharnaces seized his chance, recovering his kingdom of Pontus and defeating a Roman army. Asia Minor was on the point of disintegration. It looked as if the chain of eastern provinces along the Mediterranean seaboard and the protective buffer zone of client kingdoms inland could be lost—a high price to pay for the luxury of a civil war.

It is hard to find a convincing political explanation for Caesar's behavior. He may have thought that securing Egypt, with the kingdom's vast wealth and inexhaustible corn supplies, was of high importance. Ensuring that the young and inexperienced queen was firmly established on the throne took time. In addition, he could have simply felt he needed a holiday in the company of his charming new mistress. This is posterity's favorite explanation, and there may be truth in it.

In any event, he finally left Egypt a few weeks before the birth of Cleopatra's son, named Caesarion and almost certainly the product of their affair. His first task, which he accomplished with remarkable rapidity, was to deal with Pharnaces. In a lightning five-day campaign, he annihilated the king's army at Zela in Cappadocia. "Came, saw, conquered," he remarked. He added acidly that Pompey was lucky to have been considered a great general if this was the kind of opposition he had had to face.

Meanwhile Cicero remained isolated in Brundisium, unable to move until Caesar reappeared and ruled on his case. Quintus, badgered by Atticus, sent his brother a grudging letter of apology, which as far as Cicero was concerned only made matters worse. Young Quintus also wrote to him "most offensively." In the summer Cicero learned that his nephew had been given an interview with Caesar and that he and his father had been forgiven. He was pleased, with the reservation that concessions of this sort, "from a master to slaves," could be revoked at will. Except for the occasional explosion, his anger with both Quintuses gradually subsided.

Then, as if he didn't have enough domestic problems, relations with Terentia came under increasing strain. The details are clouded, but she was "doing some wicked things" regarding her will. Cicero remained very worried about the financial prospects of Marcus and Tullia and he must have believed that his wife was in some way imperiling their interests. But he still depended on her for advice and trusted her judgment on how to handle relations with Dolabella. Tullia's marriage was turning out to be an unhappy one. Dolabella was rumored to have had a number of sexual escapades and was conducting an affair with a respectable married woman from the Metellus clan. To add insult to injury, he was proposing to erect a statue of Clodius, of all people. Divorce was being considered, but the timing was important. Was Dolabella too powerful to offend just at the moment?

In June 47 Tullia took the long and uncomfortable journey south to visit her father. He was touched and delighted, even if her presence made him feel guilty. "Her own courage, thoughtfulness and affection," he wrote to Atticus, "far from giving me the pleasure I ought to take in such a paragon of daughters, grieve me beyond measure when I consider the unhappy lot in which so admirable a nature is cast, not through any misconduct of hers but by grave fault on my part." In the absence of cash, Cicero begged Atticus to gather up his movables—plate, furniture, fabrics—and hide them away somewhere; they could be sold later as minimal provision for his children.

By now Cicero was desperate to leave Brundisium. He wrote to Antony, to Balbus and to Oppius, and finally he appealed to Atticus: "I must ask *you* to get me out of here. Any punishment is better than staying on in this place." At long last, in August he received a letter directly from Caesar, who had emerged from his Egyptian imbroglio. It was "quite a handsome one," he conceded to Terentia. We may assume that it indicated a pardon for Cicero, or at least the prospect of one, and Caesar seems to have proposed a meeting on his return to Italy. Athough welcome, this created yet another dilemma. Should he go to meet the returning victor halfway or wait where he was? He took the latter option, perhaps because it seemed less like a decision.

Caesar was in a hurry, for his first, urgent priority on regaining Italy was to meet his soldiers and quash the still simmering mutiny. In early October 47 he landed at Tarentum and made a detour to Brundisium, where Cicero was nervously waiting on the road outside the town, ashamed to be testing his personal status in front of so many witnesses. He stood alone ahead of other dignitaries. As soon as he saw him Caesar dismounted from his horse and embraced him. Then, in signal evidence of favor, he walked along with him and they talked in private for a considerable distance. The content of their conversation is not known, but from what happened next it can be surmised that Cicero received permission to live or go wherever he wanted. He was probably also allowed to dismiss his lictors, much to his relief, for they had become an embarrassingly visible reminder of a time when Cicero counted for something in the world.

Cicero set out for home at once, after dashing off a note to Terentia. It was curt to the point of rudeness. "Kindly see that everything is ready. I may have a number of people with me and shall probably make a fairly long stay there [Tusculum]. If there is no tub in the bathroom, get one put in; likewise whatever else is necessary for health and subsistence. Goodbye." If she detected a decisive coolness between the lines, she was not wrong. Soon after his return, Cicero divorced her. The marriage, which ended in 46, had lasted more than thirty years.

His complaints, as itemized by Plutarch, were chiefly thoughtlessness and financial mismanagement. Also, she did not trouble to go to meet him at Brundisium in all the months of his exile there, and, when Tullia did, she failed to provide her daughter with a proper escort and enough money for her expenses. Finally, she had stripped Cicero's house of its contents and incurred a large number of debts. These faults do not quite justify Cicero's sudden determination to get rid of Terentia. As a rule, his emotions were changeable and he had forgiven Quintus and his nephew for seemingly far greater crimes. However, for whatever reason, he was now implacable.

Terentia's defense against the charges, if she had one, cannot now be reconstructed. But it is clear that Cicero was not good at handling money, or at least that his finances were insecure: as his affairs went from bad to worse during the civil war, she might well have tried to protect what she could of the family's or of her own fortune. She was a strong-minded woman and perhaps felt she had to take decisive action if something were to be saved from the wreckage.

Even if Cicero was entirely in the right, the episode leaves an unpleasant aftertaste, suggesting a surprising emotional coldness at the heart of his domestic life. One is left wondering what Tullia and Marcus made of their mother's being sent away. As for Terentia, she was tough enough to rebuild her life. She later remarried: she is reported to have chosen Caius Sallustius Crispus—the historian Sallust, whose books include, ironically, a study of the Catilinarian conspiracy, the occasion of her first husband's greatest triumph. For his part, Cicero did not intend to remain single and discussed possible new wives with Atticus, though he made no immediate choice.

Caesar's successes had not in fact decided the outcome of the war. The Italy to which he returned after an absence of a year and a half was in crisis. Antony, armed with a Final Act, had put down Dolabella's insurrectionary debt campaign by storming the Forum with troops, an operation that led to a bloodbath with 800 citizens dead. He lost all political credibility and Caesar dropped him for the next two years. Curiously, though, Caesar retained his confidence in Dolabella and on his arrival in Rome further tightened the constraints on creditors.

The veterans waiting in Campania presented a much more serious challenge. They had had their fill of fighting and were agitating to be demobilized with their arrears paid up in full. The state was approaching bankruptcy and Caesar did not have the money to settle the account. In any case, he needed every sesterce he could lay his hands on to continue the war against the Republicans in Africa. A succession of senior figures had made the pilgrimage from Rome to parley with the veterans and been chased out of the camp. Finally Caesar promised a hefty bonus, but to no avail. The soldiers began to move on Rome. Their general had no choice but to confront them in person. He put on a bravura performance and called their bluff. He addressed them icily as "civilians," as if they had already discharged themselves by their actions. Of course, he would let them go, he said. He would pay them later, once he had won the African campaign—with *other* soldiers.

The veterans' defiance collapsed. It had not occurred to them that they would simply be dismissed. As Caesar well knew, most of them loved and trusted him and for all their grievances could not bear the thought that he no longer needed them and would turn them away. The mood of the meeting was transformed. Men crowded up to the speaker's dais, begging Caesar to change his mind and take them to Africa after all. With simulated reluctance he allowed himself to be won over.

After making some essential administrative arrangements in Rome, Caesar left the city for Africa in December 47. Once more he would be fighting a winter campaign against superior forces, for Cato and the Republicans had mustered ten legions. Also, despite the fact that it was a scandalous thing to encourage foreigners to fight against Romans, they had allied themselves with King Juba of Mauritania, who brought four legions with him. Rome was left on tenterhooks again. For once, Cicero reacted calmly to uncertainty. While waiting for news, he stayed in Rome to be near his friends. He wrote to a correspondent: "I think the victory of either will amount to pretty much the same thing."

In April 46 Caesar won a decisive victory at Thapsus, despite the fact that at the outset of the battle he suffered from what sounds like an epileptic fit. The author of the history of the campaign, who was probably an officer on Caesar's staff, referred to it as "his usual malady." Caesar's hectic and energetic life was catching up with him, and these attacks increased in frequency in his remaining years. He then marched on the North African port of Utica, where Cato and the few remaining Republican forces were based. It would be a great propaganda coup if he could extend his clemency to this obdurate upholder of Republican values. Cato understood this too and was determined to prevent him.

The Republican armies had been defeated and the war appeared to be over. All who wanted to leave by ship were allowed to do so, but Cato refused to let a delegation be sent to sue for peace. "I decline to be under an obligation to the tyrant for his illegal acts," he said. "He is acting against the law when he pardons people over whom he has no authority, as if he owned them."

A few nights later, after a bath and supper, there was some pleasant conversation over wine. Among the topics discussed was a paradox from Stoic philosophy: whatever his circumstances, the good man is free and only the bad man is a slave. Cato spoke so vehemently in favor of this proposition that his listeners guessed his intention. He then retired to bed and read Plato's *Phaedo,* the famous dialogue on the nature of death and the immortality of the soul. His son had removed his sword from his room, much to Cato's anger. He was so upset when he noticed its absence that he hit a slave on the mouth and hurt his hand. When the weapon was brought back, he said: "Now I am my own master." He took up his book again, which he read through twice before falling into an unusually deep sleep. In the morning he asked for news and dozed.

Then, when he was alone, he stabbed himself in the stomach, but, owing to his now inflamed hand, failed to strike home. He fell off his bed and knocked over a geometrical abacus standing nearby, which clattered to the floor, making a loud noise. His son and the servants ran in and found Cato unconscious, covered with blood and with his bowels protruding from his stomach. A doctor tried to replace them and sew up the wound. Cato came to and realized what was happening. He pushed the doctor away, tore open the incision and pulled his bowels out again, after which he soon died. He was 48 years old.

The impact of this event on Roman opinion was enormous; indeed, it has echoed down the ages. A century later the poet Lucan saw in the dead constitutionalist a pattern of heroic virtue, which he summed up with a famous epigram in *Pharsalia,* his epic on the civil war: "The gods favored the winning side, but Cato the one that lost" (*Victrix causa diis placuit, sed victa Catoni*).

Cato's suicide was extremely damaging to Caesar's reputation. At the beginning of the civil war, many educated Romans saw the struggle between Pompey and Caesar as no more than a competition between two overmighty generals and chose sides according to their personal and political loyalties. Inevitably, one or other of them would win. While some regarded Caesar's whole career as a conspiracy against the state, the less pessimistic assumed that once hostilities were over political life would resume more or less as normal. There might be a bloodbath and a proscription. There would be pain and personal tragedies, but, as with Sulla, the constitution would eventually be restored in some broadly recognizable form. It would be the victor's duty to ensure that this was done.

Although it began to look over time as if this might not, after all, be the final outcome, it was still possible at this stage to give Caesar the benefit of the doubt. So all-embracing and deeply rooted was the idea of the constitution's permanence that it took a year or two before suspicions of his revolutionary intentions hardened into certainty that the days of the Republic were over for good. In the meantime Cato's final act of defiance, his deliberate rejection of Caesar's tyranny and by extension of all political servitude, harshly dramatized half-spoken fears.

Cicero was greatly moved by Cato's death. He had found him an unbearable nuisance who bore no little responsibility for the slide into civil war. But his suicide burned away the inessentials of his character, leaving him as the symbol of pure principles and of a lost time for which he mourned. In May 46, shortly after the news from Utica had arrived in Rome, he was brooding on the possibility, indeed the desirability, of writing some kind of panegyric for the martyr, much more dangerous dead than alive. Brutus, whom Caesar had forgiven for fighting against him at Pharsalus and who was serving this year as governor of Italian Gaul, had been close to Cato and had given Cicero the idea. (They were now on good terms, the Cyprus moneylending scandal having been forgotten or forgiven.)

But how would Cicero be able to speak his mind without getting into trouble with the authorities? "It's a problem for Archimedes," he told Atticus. However, he was determined to find a solution and spent much of the summer at Tusculum writing his encomium, which he finished by August. The work has not survived, but it seems to have praised Cato's strength of character and pointed out how he had predicted the political crisis, fought to prevent it and laid down his life so that he did not have to witness its consequences.

The Rome that Cicero found on return from Brundisium was a very different place from the one he had left, and in many ways he found that he was a stranger there. Politics had become the possession of a regime, not an establishment, and there was no role for him, unless he were somehow to create a new one. Many familiar faces were missing—dead, in exile or still fighting in distant corners of the empire. They had been largely replaced by the "underworld," some of them members of the Catullan and Clodian counterculture of the early 60s and 50s, who had always rejected the old solid Roman virtues of duty and loyalty to tradition.

Cicero, now sixty years old, an old man in Roman eyes, had to find another way of leading his life. Depressed as he was, he still had reserves of energy and of social zest, and he set about making new friends. One of these was Marcus Terentius Varro, a distinguished and encyclopedic scholar. Varro had fought in the first Spanish campaign against Caesar, but after Pharsalus he had abandoned the Republican cause and was appointed to run a new project Caesar was planning, the creation of Rome's first public library. The two men had not previously been close, and while Cicero admired his work, he did not think much of Varro's prose style. They came together because of their mutual isolation: the surviving *optimates* despised them for coming to terms with the enemy and the victors classed them among the defeated. "As for our present times," Cicero judged, "if our friends had won the day they would have acted very immoderately. They were infuriated with us." The two agreed that the way out, or at least the way forward, was to concentrate on their writing. In April 46 Cicero advised Varro: "Like the learned men of old, we must serve the state in our libraries, if we cannot in the Senate House and Forum, and pursue our researches into custom and law."

Cicero enjoyed the necessary solitude of a writer's life and spent a good deal of time in his country villas, mainly at Tusculum, from where he made frequent forays to Rome, and later at Astura, which he loved for its remoteness. However, he was psychologically unable to devote himself entirely to decorous retirement. So although there was little legal work for him in Rome, he started giving private classes in public speaking to senior personalities in the government. "I have set up as schoolmaster, as it were, now that the courts are abolished and my forensic kingdom lost." Cicero was exaggerating somewhat: although it may well be that the legal system was suspended from time to time during the civil war, it still functioned and indeed was reformed by Caesar. (The civil code was revised and simplified and jury membership altered.) In any event Cicero felt that teaching public speaking was good for his health since he had given up his rhetorical exercises; also, his oratorical talent would wither without practice.

In addition, there were plenty of invitations to dinner. He began to accept them, fairly indiscriminately. He was happy to dine with the enemy. Leading figures in the government were on cordial terms and Balbus and Oppius were unvaryingly attentive and thoughtful. He confessed to his friend Lucius Papirius Paetus: "Hirtius [a close colleague of Caesar's who wrote the last chapter of *The Conquest of Gaul,* which its preoccupied author had left unfinished] and Dolabella are my pupils in oratory but my masters in gastronomy. I expect you have heard, if all news travels to Naples, that they practice making speeches in my house, and I practice dining at theirs."

Cicero kept company he would once have thought unacceptable. At one meal he was surprised to see that the guests included Antony's mistress Cytheris, who, against the rules of etiquette, was given a couch rather than a chair. Writing on the spot while waiting for the food, he noted to a friend: "I assure you I had no idea *she* would be there." He held some dinner parties of his own. "I even had the audacity to give a dinner to Hirtius (think of it!)—no peacock though. At that meal nothing proved beyond my cook's powers of imitation except the hot sauce."

The government was alarmed at the growth of conspicuous expenditure in Rome and passed sumptuary laws to control it. The most expensive foods were banned and, as a result, chefs began to experiment with innovative vegetarian recipes. This put a strain on Cicero's digestion, as he confessed ruefully to a friend in winter 46:

> Our *bons vivants,* in their efforts to bring into fashion products of the soil exempted under the statute, make the most appetizing dishes out of fungi, potherbs and grasses of all sorts. Happening on some of these at an inaugural dinner at Lentulus's house, I was seized with a violent diarrhea, which has only today begun (I think) to check its flow. So: oysters and eels I used to resist well enough, but here I lie caught in the nets of *mesdames* Turnip and Mallow! Well, I shall be more careful in future.

Caesar returned from Africa towards the end of July 46. His first weeks were spent organizing four Triumphs, which took place in late September and lasted an unheard-of eleven days. They marked his victories in Gaul and Egypt and over Pharnaces in Asia Minor and Juba in Africa. The number of enemies killed, excluding citizens, was claimed to be 1,992,000. Money to the value of 65,000 talents was carried in the parade. Games and shows were also staged. As a personal tribute Caesar promoted a gladiatorial display in memory of his still much-missed daughter, Julia, and a public banquet with 22,000 tables. It was ill omened to triumph over Roman citizens and Pharsalus was passed by in silence, but the crowds showed their disapproval of painted representations of the deaths of the Republican leaders in Africa: Cato was depicted tearing himself apart like a wild animal. There were groans as the images passed along the streets. The all-conquering war leader had not yet registered how long a shadow Cato was to cast. Another incident alarmed superstitious Romans: the axle on Caesar's chariot broke just opposite, of all places, the Temple of Fortune. As atonement for the portent, he climbed the steps of the Capitol on his knees.

The public mood was unsettled. There were complaints about the amount of blood shed at the Games and the soldiery, annoyed by the extravagance, rioted. Caesar reacted with extraordinary fury: he grabbed one man with his own hands and had him executed. Two other soldiers were sacrificed by priests to Mars and the heads displayed outside his official residence, the State House. This was highly unusual: the most recent previous human sacrifice was reported to have been conducted by Catilina in the 60s to bind his fellow conspirators to his cause and before that one had to go back to the darkest days of the war against Hannibal more than one and a half centuries earlier. Perhaps the threat of a mutiny in the center of Rome was such a serious matter that the most extreme measures were required: alternatively, the soldiers' offense may have broken some religious taboo. One way or the other the disinterested observer might have wondered about the stability of the regime.

The Forum of Julius, which had been under construction on the far side of the Senate House at Caesar's expense since 54, was officially opened. It put the old Forum somewhat in the shade and eclipsed, both by its location and its extent, Pompeius's theater beyond the *pomoerium* on the Field of Mars. Controversially, a gold statue of Cleopatra was erected next to one of Venus, whose temple was one of the Forum's key features. About this time the Egyptian queen appeared in Rome in person with her court and her brother and co-Pharaoh, the thirteen-year-old Ptolemy XIV. Her motives for leaving her kingdom for what turned out to be an eighteen-month stay were probably mixed. She and Caesar no doubt wanted to continue their affair, but she also knew that her throne depended on her lover and the favor of Rome's ruling class. Egypt was the last great imperial prize for the all-conquering Republic, and the danger of annexation was real. Cleopatra was prepared to devote all her personal charms to maintaining her country's independence.

She also brought Caesarion with her, whose name drew scandalous attention to her liaison with the Dictator. She stayed in a garden villa of Caesar's on the far side of the Tiber, where she must have held court with Egyptian splendor. Caesar was probably too busy to spend much time with her. She seems to have mixed on social terms with leading Romans, although she cannot have had much sympathy with antiauthoritarian attitudes. Cicero had some dealings with her and soon came to dislike her.

The Senate voted Caesar unprecedented honors, the most important of these extending his Dictatorship for ten years and the Controllership of Morals for three years and according him the right of nominating officeholders for election.

In the past, the Senate had been more or less a gentleman's club, with a few New Men like Marius or Cicero added to the mixture from time to time. Caesar, wisely acknowledging the multicultural composition of both the Empire and the city of Rome itself, resumed the old custom of opening citizenship and power to defeated and annexed peoples. More radically, he enlarged the Senate, recruiting from the provinces and the Italian communities. Cicero was shocked to find himself sitting next to trousered Gauls, bankers, industrialists and farmers. Worse than that, former centurions and sons of freedmen were appointed to the Senate.

Caesar enacted at great speed a number of important and well-judged reforms. To many people's surprise he acted evenhandedly and favored neither radical nor conservative causes, making decisions on the merits of a case. His first priority concerned the social problems of Rome and Italy. An exact census of the city's population was conducted; the free distribution of corn (Rome's equivalent of social security or unemployment payments) was limited; many of the urban proletariat were settled in citizen "colonies" overseas; special privileges were given to the fathers of large families in an attempt to increase the birth rate and so eventually replace the heavy casualties of war. In order to discourage the replacement of jobs for citizens by slave labor in the countryside, at least one third of the cattlemen on Italy's large ranches had to be freeborn.

From January 1, 45, the calendar was sensibly extended to 365 days. Previously the year had had ten fewer days, necessitating occasional intercalary months and every other year the College of Pontiffs had usually inserted an additional month to keep the calendar in time with the sun. During the years running up to the civil war, this procedure had been neglected and the result was that the calendar was more than two months ahead of itself (this meant that when, for example, Cicero returned to Italy after the battle of Pharsalus in mid-October 48 according to contemporary dating, the real date was sometime in August). To effect the transition, Caesar inserted 67 days between November and December 46 and introduced the solar year of 365¼ days. In an acid reference to the new calendar, Cicero refused to be pleased with an autocrat's decisions, however benign. When someone remarked that the constellation Lyra was due to rise on the following night, he replied: "Of course. It will be following orders."

Apart from such sour wisecracks, Cicero had little to say about all this legislation, at least in the extant correspondence. (There are no long runs of letters from this period.) He was silent in the Senate and his attendance record does not survive. His general disenchantment, though, can be deduced from a letter to a friend towards the end of the year. He wrote: "I used to sit in the poop, you see, with the helm in my hands. But now I hardly have a place in the bilge."

In order to be able to govern effectively, Caesar assembled a personal cabinet drawn from trusted lieutenants of his in Gaul, who worked alongside the official magistrates. He also seems to have laid the foundations of what eventually became the imperial civil service. Balbus was one of its key members and spent much of his time drafting decrees. Every now and then Cicero's name was borrowed without prior consultation as having proposed an edict. "Don't think I am joking," he remarked. "Let me tell you I have had letters delivered to me from monarchs at the other end of the earth thanking me for my motion to give them the royal title, when I for my part was unaware of their existence, let alone of their elevation to royalty."

For anyone with eyes to see, the old, level arena where equal competitors could contend had disappeared. Members of the ruling class who had survived the civil war were no longer genuinely elected to office but became functionaries whose *imperium* was not theirs but was on loan from the Dictator.

For all his active social life, it would be wrong to regard the Cicero of these years as merely a dilettante and socialite. The creative and organizational energies he had once devoted to politics and the law were still running strongly and sought an outlet. He became very active in persuading Caesar to pardon leading opponents who were still in exile. Paradoxically, although he was profoundly out of sympathy with the new regime, his personal relations with Caesar had never been warmer. After the Dictator's death, he admitted that "for some reason he was extraordinarily patient where I was concerned."

The busy head of state enjoyed Cicero's sense of humor and received daily reports of his latest sallies, even if some of them were at his expense. Different cultures have different senses of humor. Cicero specialized in the brutal put-down, as when he met a man with three ugly daughters and quoted the verse "Apollo never meant him to beget." At one trial a young man accused of having given his father a poisoned cake said he wanted to give Cicero a piece of his mind. Cicero replied: "I would prefer that to a piece of your cake." Only a few of Cicero's jokes still raise a smile, but his contemporaries delighted in them.

Cicero told his friend Paetus in July 46:

> I hear that, having in his day compiled volumes of *bons mots,* Caesar will reject any specimen offered him as mine which is not authentic. He does this all the more because his intimates are in my company almost every day. Talk of this and that produces many casual remarks which perhaps strike these people when I say them as not deficient in polish and point. They are conveyed to him with the rest of the day's news, according to his express instructions.

In December one of the Dictator's staff published a collection of these assiduously collected witticisms.

Cicero tirelessly exploited his Caesarian connections on behalf of defeated *optimates.* His motives for using his good offices in this way were predictably mixed. The unpatronizing tone and thoughtfulness of his correspondence with those he was helping suggest that natural kindliness was one of them. However, he would have been less than human not to take pleasure in offering a valuable service to the grandees who had scorned the New Man from Arpinum. He wanted to show them that, however much they criticized him, he bore no malice and was more than willing to help them.

By far the most important factor driving Cicero, though, was the hope that after all, at the eleventh hour and defying all probability, the "mixed constitution" for which he had argued in *On the State* and which had been Rome's glory might be reinstated. Working closely with the Dictator on reconciliation was an essential precondition if the new political order was to be truly inclusive.

For Quintus Ligarius, a former opponent of whom the Dictator had a poor opinion, Cicero offered a personal plea, as he described in a letter to him: "On November 26 [46], at your brothers' request, I paid Caesar a morning visit. I had to put up with all the humiliating and wearisome preliminaries of obtaining admission and interview. Your brothers and relations knelt at his feet, while I spoke in terms appropriate to your case and circumstances." The meeting appeared to go well, but Caesar reserved an announcement of his decision for a more public occasion: while he was genuinely unvindictive, he did not want his clemency to be hidden under a bushel. So, according to an anecdote in Plutarch, Cicero agreed to speak in Ligarius's defense at a formal hearing in the Forum. Caesar, who was presiding, was apparently so moved by what he heard, especially when Cicero touched on the battle of Pharsalus, that his body shook and he dropped the papers in his hand. Ligarius was duly acquitted and allowed to come back to Italy. Some scholars have discounted the story, but it is plausible enough as an instance of adept news management.

The most distinguished surviving Republican for whom Cicero spoke was Marcus Claudius Marcellus, the Consul for 51, a steady but not diehard opponent of Caesar who had retired to the island of Lesbos after Pharsalus. When the matter of his recall was raised at a Senate meeting, the Senate rose to its feet *en masse* to plead for clemency. Caesar, after complaining of Marcellus's "acerbity," suddenly and unexpectedly gave way. Cicero was delighted to see "some semblance of reviving constitutional freedom." The story ended sadly, for Marcellus was murdered by a friend at a dinner party before returning home.

The decision to pardon Marcellus persuaded the orator to break his long silence in the Senate. He delivered a brilliant speech of thanks, which reached the boundary of flattery but did not quite cross it. With psychological acuteness, he appealed to the Dictator's desire for glory. Caesar had recently said in reference to a reported plot against him: "Whether for nature or for glory I have lived long enough." This was unacceptable, Cicero argued: Caesar was the only person who could reunite past enemies and bring back Rome's traditional institutions—the rule of law, the freedom of the Senate, in a word everything that Cicero meant to convey by his slogan "harmony of the classes." The Dictator should legislate a constitutional settlement that would outlast him. Cicero was not being inconsistent here: in *On the State,* published six years previously, he had been explicit that on occasion a Dictator was needed to restore order.

It is interesting to observe from the tone of Cicero's correspondence at this time that he did not suffer the agonizing doubts of the early months of the civil war. He had come to a settled view which he maintained without great mental or emotional anxiety, until it became clear that the Dictator either would not or could not live up to his expectations.

Cicero's book on Cato was published towards the end of the year and attracted much attention. Although it argued that Cato had been an exemplar of all that was best in Roman culture, this was apparently not good enough for its dedicatee, Brutus, who went on to produce his own eulogy. The appearance of Cicero's *Cato* probably undid any good that might have been achieved by the Marcellus speech. Caesar was enraged. It was not just that he objected to the canonization of a man whom he regarded as a blundering reactionary. More seriously, it was a reminder that, to Cicero and the political class for which he stood, reform and renewal meant returning to a failed model of governance rather than inventing a new one. He was so upset that he asked Hirtius to write a refutation. (It was a flop, which Cicero delightedly asked Atticus to distribute as widely as possible, on the grounds that it could only further enhance Cato's reputation.)

In due course, the Dictator regained his equanimity. The following summer he praised Cicero's writing style and commented wryly that reading and rereading his *Cato* improved his powers of expression, whereas after reading Brutus's account he began to fancy himself as a writer. The political damage of all this furor about Cato called for his personal attention. Caesar composed his own rebuttal, the *Anti-Cato* (also lost). The pamphlet drew an unflattering portrait of a drunkard and miser. Cicero himself was complimented for his oratory but indirectly criticized as a political weathercock. This lack of moderation disturbed opinion in Rome and cast some doubt on the genuineness of Caesar's clemency. For the first time since the civil war began he had incautiously allowed it to be seen that an offense had wounded him personally.

The *Anti-Cato* was written while Caesar was on the march again, for it turned out that despite his African victory the civil war was not quite over after all. Having escaped from Thapsus, Pompey's two sons, Cnaeus and Sextus, went to Spain, where they raised the standard of rebellion again. Caesar appointed commanders to manage the campaign against them, but they made little headway. In November 46 he decided that the situation required his personal attention and he suddenly left Rome for the battlefront. It was to be the final confrontation.

Young Quintus joined Caesar's army and Marcus, nervous of approaching his father directly and working through Atticus, sought permission to go too. And while he was asking for favors, he would also be grateful for a decent allowance. The second request presented no great difficulty, but Cicero told his son that, as for going to Spain, it was enough for the family to have abandoned one side without joining the other. He warned him that he might not enjoy being in the shade of his older and more influential cousin. Although his father did not formally refuse to give his permission, Marcus was a docile boy and no more is heard of the project.

The exchange was a reminder that some thought needed to be given to the twenty-year-old's future. He had practical rather than academic abilities and had inherited little of his father's literary talent. Nevertheless, in the following year it was decided that he should continue his studies in Athens. He seems not to have been the most diligent of students. In a handful of letters to Tiro from 44, he apologized for being a dilatory correspondent and promised to work harder. He wanted the freedman to put in a good word for him with his father and be his "publicity agent." He also dropped a hint about his "meager allowance" and asked Tiro to get a clerk sent out to him, preferably a Greek. "I waste a lot of time copying out my notes." On Cicero's explicit instructions, Marcus dropped the company of Gorgias, a rhetorician who was encouraging the young man to overspend and to drink too much, and began to study with a distinguished Aristotelian philosopher. Marcus was good-natured, lazy and fond of a good time. He was too much in awe of his father to stand up to him directly and had the diffidence of the child who knows he is not a favorite.

Cicero now made a disastrous move in his personal life. In 46 he at last found the wife he had been looking for, but his selection, a wealthy teenage ward of his, Publilia, was unfortunate. Terentia, sniping from the sidelines, accused him of an old man's infatuation. Cicero did not help his case by responding to criticism with a tasteless joke. When someone reproached him on the eve of the wedding for marrying a mere girl, he retorted: "She'll be a woman tomorrow."

Little is known about Cicero's relations with the opposite sex. He claims that he made a point of not being promiscuous in his youth and seems to have endured separations from Terentia even early on in their marriage with equanimity. Accounts of the political support she gave him during his Consulship suggest a businesslike relationship and strong mutual loyalty. What remains of their correspondence was written when they were both middle-aged and conveys little more than routine affection.

The only woman with whom Cicero's emotions seem to have been powerfully engaged was Tullia. This was noticed by his contemporaries. In an age when political invective made a great deal out of opponents' sexual peccadilloes, the only serious (but completely unconvincing) charge against him was that he had committed incest with his daughter.

Although Roman upper-class women had considerable social freedom and could sometimes exert political influence behind the scenes, it was a male world and the socially conservative Cicero mainly enjoyed the company of men. There is mention of one elderly woman friend, although unfortunately there is very little information about her. This was Caerullia, who was ten or more years older than Cicero and had philosophical interests. They were very close towards the end of his life and their correspondence (now lost) was said to have been somewhat risqué.

Tiro disagreed with Terentia about Cicero's motives for marrying Publilia. Many years later he claimed that friends and relatives pressed

Cicero to make the match in order to settle his large debts. The only comment Cicero has left behind was matter-of-fact and says more about Terentia than Publilia. He wrote to a friend:

> As for your congratulations on the step I have taken, I am sure your wishes are sincere. But I should not have taken any new decision at so sad a time, if on my return I had not found my household affairs in as bad a state as the country's. In my own house, I knew no security, had no refuge from intrigue, because of the villainy of those to whom my welfare and estate should have been most precious in view of the signal kindnesses I had showered on them. So I thought it advisable to fortify myself by the loyalty of new connections against the treachery of old ones.

A month or two after the marriage Cicero was struck by the most terrible blow he had ever experienced in his life. For the first time since his exile his mental equilibrium was threatened. Tullia died.

In January 45, she gave birth to a son, "little Lentulus," as Cicero called him after one of his father's names. The lying-in apparently took place at Dolabella's house, although the couple was now divorced. The mother failed to recover, surviving for only a few weeks, and the child died some months later. Tullia is a shadowy figure, who never speaks for herself and is glimpsed only through her father's loving comments. We can guess that she was intelligent and amusing (as well as being self-willed and with a pronounced tendency to fall for unsuitable men).

Cicero was devastated. Tusculum and his house on the Palatine were too full of memories and for a time he stayed with Atticus, reading everything he could find in his library that the Greek philosophers had to say about grief. Then, having gained leave of absence from his public duties, he fled the city. He went to Astura, a property he had recently bought on the coast south of Antium, a wooded and remote spot where he could hide away and grieve. The Romans disapproved of extravagant mourning, especially over a woman, and Cicero did his best to control or at least to conceal his emotions. He asked Atticus to attribute his absence from Rome to ill health.

Reading did not help, so he picked up his pen and wrote a *Self-Consolation,* one of the most celebrated works of antiquity, although now lost. Consolatory texts were a recognized genre, but he was, he thought, the first man to write one for himself. He assembled every relevant text he could find and "threw them all into one attempt at consolation," he wrote to Atticus, "for my soul was in a feverish state and I attempted every means of curing its condition." He worked quickly and finished the book by early March, when he promised a copy to Atticus (with whom he was corresponding daily). "I write all day long, not that I do myself any real good, but just for the time being it distracts me—not enough, for grief is powerful and importunate; still it brings a respite." He suspected that his anguish was changing his personality and was afraid that Atticus would no longer feel towards him as in the past. "The things you like in me are gone for good."

He found that he could not stop crying and spent most of his time on his own out-of-doors. "In this lonely place I don't talk to a soul. Early in the day I hide myself in a thick, thorny wood, and don't emerge till evening. When I am alone all my conversation is with books; it is interrupted by fits of weeping, against which I struggle as best I can. But so far it is an unequal fight."

When contrasted with the self-indulgent and sometimes slightly formulaic expressions of grief of his letters from exile, Cicero's state of mind during this crisis reveals a new intensity of feeling, too raw and too astonishing to be publicized. He showed little self-pity; his pain was so fierce as almost to be physical. This was a true breakdown and he recognized it. He withdrew from the world like a sick animal and fought as hard as he could for recovery, for the regaining of his life.

Tullia's death spelled the end of Cicero's brief marriage to Publilia. She was said to be pleased that someone she had seen as a rival had been removed from the scene, and Cicero could not forgive this. Even if the story was false, his bereavement pushed her to the far periphery of his concerns. Publilia was not allowed to visit him and he asked for Atticus's support in preventing either her or her relatives from seeking him out. "I want you to find out just how long I can stay here [at Astura] without getting caught." His mind was set on divorce and before long the baffled and relieved teenager was out of his life for good.

Letters of condolence for Tullia's death poured in, among them from Brutus and from Caesar in Spain, who knew well the agony of grief for a dead daughter. His friend the jurist Servius Sulpicius Rufus wrote a long, touching epistle that brought home to Cicero the mutability of human affairs.

> I want to tell you of something which has brought *me* no small comfort, in the hope that perhaps it may have some power to lighten your sorrow too. As I was on my way back from Asia [to Rome on changing sides after Pharsalus], sailing from Aegina towards Megara, I began to gaze at the landscape around me. There behind me was Aegina, in front of me Megara, to the right Piraeus, to the left Corinth; once flourishing towns, now lying low in ruins before one's eyes. [These cities had not recovered from the Roman annexation of Greece in the middle of the previous century: Corinth had been sacked.] I began to think to myself: "Ah, how can we little creatures wax indignant if one of us dies or is killed, ephemeral beings as we are, when the corpses of so many towns lie abandoned in a single spot? Check yourself, Servius, and remember that you were born a mortal man." That thought, I do assure you, strengthened me not a little. If I may suggest it, picture the same spectacle to yourself. Not long ago so many great men died at one time, the Roman Empire was so gravely impaired, all its provinces shaken to pieces; can you be so greatly moved by the loss of one poor little woman's frail spirit?

Slowly Cicero began to get better. With an effort of will he returned to Tusculum towards the end of May. One good sign was that he transposed his emotions onto an external project. He conceived the idea of erecting a shrine to Tullia's memory. This would give her immortality of a sort, for it would celebrate her "glory." The Greeks and Romans believed that in exceptional cases a bridge could be built between the human and the divine. In Asia Minor there was an established tradition of worshiping great men and according divine status to rulers. Cicero was not going as far as that, but he wanted his daughter's remarkable qualities to receive a permanent memorial. In a fragment from the *Self-Consolation* he wrote that if it had been appropriate for heroes of Greek mythology to be raised to heaven, "surely she too deserves the same honor and devotion, and I shall give it to her."

Atticus thought the scheme eccentric, but he went patiently along with his friend and for some months they discussed various possible sites Cicero might purchase. It was important that the monument should not be off the beaten track, so perhaps somewhere in the suburbs of Rome would be best. Price was not an object, for Cicero would happily sacrifice some of his luxuries or even one of his villas to raise the necessary funds. He considered a wide range of properties, including one belonging to one of Clodius's sisters.

By the summer the project was abandoned. Cicero's engagement with and curiosity about the world around him were returning. He wrote a new will to take account of his short-lived grandson and Terentia made a nuisance of herself about it. He paid increasingly affectionate attention to Atticus's daughter, who was born around 51. Although she was only about five or six years old, she already had a tutor. She had a tendency towards fevers and Cicero was always asking after the little girl. She was no replacement for Tullia, but she took his mind off his loss.

On March 17, 45, Caesar won the battle of Munda against an army led by Pompey's son Cnaeus. His victory, although total, was narrowly achieved. Afterwards he admitted: "Today, for the first time, I fought for my life." His old comrade-in-arms, Labienus, who had deserted him at the start of the civil war, lay among 30,000 Republican dead. Cnaeus was caught and killed in flight.

Caesar remained for a few months in Spain reorganizing the provincial administration before setting out for home. Exhausted and unwell, he did not go to the capital immediately but spent some time on one of his country estates. There he wrote his will, which he deposited in September with the Vestal Virgins, as custom dictated. This was a personal, not a political, testament and disposed of his immense private fortune; however, when it was published after his death, it was to change the course of Roman history.

The civil war was conclusively over. The human price had been high, for it has been estimated that 100,000 Roman citizens had lost their lives since the opening of hostilities in 49. No one was left in the field for Caesar to fight. His leading opponents were dead. The Republic was dead too: he had become the state.

By agreement with Balbus and Oppius, Atticus suggested that Cicero write a letter of advice to Caesar, in which he could return to the theme of the restoration of the constitution. Cicero obediently attempted a draft and, out of courtesy and caution, showed it to the two confidential agents before sending it off. They thought it too outspoken and counseled a revision. On May 25, Cicero informed Atticus that it would be better not to write anything. He was relieved to have extricated himself because it now occurred to him that Caesar would interpret the letter as an apology for the *Cato.* But Atticus would not give in and continued to badger him. On the following day, Cicero came to a final decision. He announced that he was simply unable to write the letter, not so much because he would be ashamed of its contents as because he could not think of anything else to say.

Cicero no longer entertained hopes that the Republic would be restored and moved gradually from collaboration to opposition. It was becoming common knowledge in the Dictator's circle that, despite the end of the war, he had no intention of settling permanently in Rome; he had decided that the continuing Parthian threat should be addressed once and for all. So he would soon be marching off on another military campaign. Clearly he was uninterested in addressing constitutional issues.

Also, perhaps, the deep depression from which Cicero was emerging had hardened him and made him less inclined to compromise. Tullia's death and the quarrels in his family circle meant that old ties had loosened and that he could follow his own wishes.

A by-product of this more explicit disillusionment with the present state of affairs was the cooling of Cicero's friendship with Brutus. He had already been irritated by an inaccurate and less than generous account of his Consulship in 63 in Brutus's book on Cato. "Brutus reports that Caesar has joined the honest men," he wrote sardonically to Atticus. "Good news! But where is he going to find them—unless he hangs himself? As for Brutus, he knows which side his bread is buttered."

In June, Dolabella, with whom Cicero was still friendly, paid a visit and reported some new scandal concerning young Quintus. "Dolabella came this morning," Cicero wrote to Atticus. "We got on to Quintus. I heard of much that is too bad for utterance or narration, and one thing of such a kind that if the whole army did not know of it I should not dare to put it on paper myself, let alone dictate it to Tiro." The nature of this thing is not disclosed, for at this point the letter has been cut, probably by Atticus when he began to allow his friends to read his collection of Cicero's correspondence. It is hard to conceive of what new offense the young man could have committed.

In August Quintus, now back in Italy after the Spanish campaign, fell out with his mother. For this reason he needed to have a house of his own and his father wondered whether to vacate his own home to make room for him. But Quintus was still doing his best to blacken his uncle's reputation and was now busy criticizing his father as well. Cicero told Atticus that, according to Hirtius, he "is at it constantly, especially at dinner parties. When he finishes with me he comes back to his father, his most plausible line being that we are thoroughly hostile to Caesar and are not to be trusted."

The two brothers were on rather better terms than they had been and the problematic youth may have helped bring them back together. Cicero was in the money again—he had just learned of a substantial legacy from a wealthy banker—and, after settling his own debts, he planned to make over the surplus, apparently as a loan, to his brother. This was a remarkably generous gesture after their bitter quarrel and a further illustration of Cicero's inability to bear a grudge. That year Quintus finally divorced Pomponia. The aging siblings now had only each other as the remaining pillars of a dispersed family.

When Atticus had an idea he seldom let it rest. He continued to press his friend to write to Caesar and at last Cicero yielded. Cicero had told Balbus and Oppius that he had been impressed by the *Anti-Cato* (untrue; he may have admired it for stylistic reasons, but he later called it an "impudent" work). They mentioned this to the Dictator and in August Cicero agreed to write a discursive letter about the book. He had them vet the text as usual, and this time they cleared it enthusiastically. They had "never read anything better."

A gap in the correspondence with Atticus follows for nearly three months, but it seems that Cicero was on superficially good terms with Caesar again. The Dictator was back in Rome in October to celebrate a Triumph for the Spanish war. He had been elected sole Consul, but had had himself replaced for the last three months of the year by two other Senators.

Towards the end of the year Cicero made a short speech on behalf of Deiotarus, King of Galatia, who was alleged to have plotted Caesar's assassination during the civil war. The case was heard in the accused's absence behind closed doors in the Dictator's house. Caesar cast himself as judge and jury. Cicero combined compliment with candor (he commented adversely on the irregularity of the judicial procedure), a mixture that usually pleased his listener. It would appear that the Dictator found against him, but, if Cicero in a later tirade against Mark Antony is to be trusted, Antony restored the King's lost territories to him after Caesar's death.

In December, Caesar toured Campania, perhaps visiting veteran colonies, and called on Cicero at his house in the seaside resort of Puteoli. What was intended as a friendly gesture was, in fact, a massive inconvenience for a reluctant host. The Dictator turned up on December 18 with no fewer than 2,000 soldiers, who camped out in the open. He stayed the night at a neighbor's villa. The house was so crowded with soldiers that there was hardly a spare room for Caesar to dine in. Cicero was "a good deal perturbed" about what would happen the following day with so many troops wandering around. Fortunately an officer agreed to post sentries.

Caesar spent the morning alone till one o'clock, apparently working on accounts with Balbus. Then he went for a walk on the beach and took a bath an hour later. Some bad news about his Prefect of Engineers was brought in, but the expression on Caesar's face did not change. Once his skin had been oiled at the end of his bath (as was the custom), he took his place at Cicero's dinner table. The occasion throws an attractive light on Caesar's personality; although, or possibly because, he was encumbered by the cares and paraphernalia of state, he wanted a short break from work, relaxing in good company and engaging in agreeable conversation. Cicero reluctantly conceded that he too had had a pleasant time. "It really was a fine, elegantly served meal," he reported to Atticus.

> His entourage was lavishly entertained in three other dining rooms. The humbler freedmen and slaves had all they wanted—the smarter ones I entertained in style. In a word, I showed I knew how to do things. But my guest was not the kind of person to whom one says, "Do come again when you are next in the neighborhood." Once is enough. We talked of nothing serious, but a good deal on literary matters. All in all, he was pleased and enjoyed himself.

The year was ending on a modestly contented note. Not only was Cicero's relationship with Caesar ostensibly in good repair, but harmony of a sort was breaking out on the domestic front. Some days after the Dictator's visit, young Quintus paid his uncle a visit. He intended to accompany Caesar on the Parthian expedition and wanted to mend some bridges.

Cicero noted the conversation for Atticus.

"Why do you have to go?" Cicero asked.

"Debt—I haven't even enough to pay my traveling expenses."

Cicero, discreet for once, held his tongue.

"What upsets me most is my uncle, Atticus."

"Why do you let him be annoyed—I prefer to say 'let' rather than 'make'?"

"I won't anymore. I'll get rid of the reason."

"Excellent. But if you don't mind my asking, I would be interested to know what the reason is."

"It's because I couldn't make up my mind whom to marry. My mother was cross with me, and so as a result was he. Now I don't care what I do to put things right. I'll do what they want."

"Well, good luck, and congratulations on your decision."

It seemed that the difficult, hostile teenager was beginning to settle down into an ordinary Roman young-man-about-town with debts, who realized that it would be in his interest to be on good terms again with his disappointed family. Whether or not Quintus acted as he said he would is unknown, but there is no subsequent reference to a wife in the fragmentary surviving documentation. One thing is certain, though: he did not accompany the legions to Parthia, for the expedition never took place. He must have found some alternative solution to the problem of his debts.

By now, Cicero had become less volatile than he had been in the past. He met the challenges and misfortunes that faced him with determination. In politics he made up his mind about the regime with fewer of his usual doubts and nervous questionings. Criticism did not bother him as much as it had once. He still reacted passionately to events and was no less self-absorbed, but he had learned to control himself. Family estrangements troubled him and he had nearly been broken by Tullia's death, but he had struggled with all his might to regain his emotional balance. Tempered by the fire, he seemed to have acquired a new, steely resolve.

12

PHILOSOPHICAL INVESTIGATIONS

Thoughts on the Nature of Things: 46–44 BC

One explanation for Cicero's new maturity lay in his phenomenal productivity as a writer. In 46, at the age of sixty, he started work on a succession of books which, taken together, represent one of Rome's most valuable legacies to posterity. At their core is a summary of the philosophical issues that had concerned thinkers and moralists from Plato to Cicero's own day. He made no claim to originality. "I only supply the words, and I have plenty of those." However, he was a popularizer of genius. With the disappearance of the Greek language in Europe during the Dark and Middle Ages, Cicero's compendium of classical thought had a huge influence on the continuing development of western philosophy.

Politics and war were the chief but not the only means by which a Roman could achieve status. Others were scholarship and literature. Leading figures such as Cicero's friend the jurist Sulpicius could maintain their prestige by achieving an unrivaled knowledge of the law. Antiquarian expertise was necessary in a polity that was heavily dependent on the interpretation of tradition; thus Atticus, who eschewed the hurly-burly of the Forum, was able to make a name for himself by writing the *Annals* (*Liber Annalis*), an authoritative chronology of Rome back to its foundation. The religious apparatus of priestly colleges demanded detailed knowledge of the forms and procedures of ceremony and divination and it was necessary for some members of the elite to acquire it.

Cicero had already found poetry (when he was a young man), philosophy and research into the art of public speaking to be useful supports to his status as a public figure. A decade previously he had been able to pick up the threads of his political career after the end of his exile, but now advancing years and Caesar's autocracy seemed to him to mean that this time there could be no recovery.

So he set about reasserting his reputation as an author. Despite all his other preoccupations, he wrote "from morning to night" (as he told Atticus), producing a flood of books and essays during the next three years. Looking back near the end of his life, he observed: "I have written more in this short time since the collapse of the Republic than I did throughout the many years while the Republic stood." He hoped his books would be of use to the young but noticed that it was the older generation which took most comfort from them. He knew that his motives for writing were as much for his personal as for the public good. "I cannot easily say how useful I shall be to others: in any case, for my terrible sorrows and all the various troubles that assail me on every side no other consolation could be found."

Atticus advised his friend to concentrate on historical subjects, but Cicero disagreed. As he saw it, the first priority was to protect his name as an orator, which was now under some threat. As early as the mid-50s members of the Catullan/Clodian counterculture had begun to react against the elaborate and ample manner of public speaking which Cicero and, even more so, his onetime rival Hortensius represented. A leading spokesman of this point of view was Catullus's closest friend, Caius Licinius Calvus. What he called the "Attic" tendency or school of oratory stressed grammatical correctness, simplicity of expression and restraint against the "Bacchic frenzy" of a speaker like Hortensius when he was in full flight. Cicero's young friend Caelius had probably been another Atticist.

Cicero felt that the time had come to rebut this fashion, partly because it contradicted his own views on oratory but also because he feared that if it got out of hand it would supersede his own achievements. In early 46 he wrote *Brutus,* a dialogue in which the speakers were Atticus, Brutus (who was an Atticist and to whom the book is dedicated) and himself. It was a history of Latin oratory with brief but telling critiques of Rome's leading speakers, including an account of his own training and early career. It aimed to be evenhanded and, for example, was highly complimentary of Caesar's stylistic purity; referring to his histories of the Gallic campaigns and the civil war, Cicero compared them "to nude figures, straight and beautiful; stripped of all ornament of style as if they had stepped out of their clothes." However, he made it clear that, by definition, public speakers had to attract the interest of the public. Here the Atticists failed because, however correct their Latin, they bored the listener. In the law courts "they are deserted not only by the crowds of bystanders, which is humiliating enough, but by their client's witnesses and legal advisers." *Brutus* was followed later in the year by the *Orator,* which took the form of a letter to Brutus. It is a technical work and is concerned with the minutiae of rhetorical theory; the focus is on diction and style, for Cicero was aiming his fire once more at the Attic style of oratory.

During the summer of 46 Cicero's mind turned to questions of philosophy. After producing a squib on the Stoic ethical system, *Stoic Paradoxes* (*Paradoxa stoicorum*), Cicero committed himself to a much more ambitious enterprise. This was nothing more nor less than an attempt to give a comprehensive account of Greek philosophy in the Latin language. For one hundred years or so there had been numerous references to Greek philosophers and their doctrines in Roman literature, but there had been few serious books on philosophical themes. Such as there were mainly concerned Epicureanism, a way of life directed at worldly happiness and associated with a materialistic explanation of reality. Cicero deeply disapproved, although he acknowledged that it had given rise to one of the masterpieces of Latin poetry, the epic *On the Nature of the Universe* (*De rerum natura*) by Titus Lucretius Carus, a younger contemporary.

In 44 when the series of books was largely complete, he set out a prospectus of what he felt he had achieved.

> In the book called *Hortensius* I advised my readers to occupy themselves with philosophy—and in the four volumes of the *Academic Treatises* I suggested the philosophical methods which seem to me to have the greatest degree of appropriate discretion, consistency and elegance. Then in *On Supreme Good and Evil* I discussed the basic problems of philosophy and covered the whole field in detail in five volumes which set out the arguments for and against every philo-

sophical system. This was followed by *Conversations at Tusculum,* also in five volumes, which expound the key issues we should bear in mind in our pursuit of happiness. The first volume deals with indifference to death, the second with how to endure pain, the third with the alleviation of distress in times of trouble and the fourth with other distractions which affect our peace of mind. Finally, the fifth book addresses the topic that is best calculated to clarify the nature of philosophy—that is, it demonstrates that moral worth alone is adequate to ensure a happy life. After that, the three volumes of *The Nature of the Gods* were finished, which cover all the relevant issues. Once that had been adequately dealt with, I started work on my current book, *Foretelling the Future.* When I have added, as I intend to do, another book, *Destiny,* the entire field will have been satisfactorily surveyed.

Cicero is explicit that this corpus was an alternative to the public life from which he was barred. In *Foretelling the Future,* he wrote: "it was through my books that I was addressing the Senate and the people. I took the view that philosophy was a substitute for political activity." He had always believed that philosophy was an essential ingredient of a training in the art of public speaking and the collapse of the Republic was evidence of the failure by statesmen to apply moral values to their conduct. To develop this long-standing theme was the last gift he could make to his country.

The purpose of the *Hortensius,* to judge from its surviving fragments, was to establish the uses of philosophy. It was cast as a debate set in the late 60s and the speakers were four leading personalities of the day, including Hortensius and Cicero himself. It contained defenses of poetry, history and oratory. Hortensius attacked the inadequacies of many philosophers and launched a vigorous onslaught on aspects of Epicureanism. Cicero responded with a powerful apologia for philosophy. The seeker after truth traveled hopefully, he said, but would never arrive. Cicero retained the skepticism about the possibility of knowledge that he acquired during his first visit to Athens. He closed with a hint of reincarnation, borrowed from the current revival of interest in the mystical ideas of the Greek sage Pythagoras. The purer a man's soul, the greater the possibility that it would escape the impending cycle of future lives.

The *Academic Treatises* (*Academica*) were started in autumn 46 and

Cicero was still working on them the following summer. They were an epistemological inquiry which examined in greater detail than the *Hortensius* different theories of knowledge. According to Pliny, writing in the following century, the dialogue was composed in Cicero's villa at Puteoli. The setting and characters were originally the same as in the *Hortensius,* but once the book was finished its author worried that "the matter did not fit the persons, who could not be supposed ever to have dreamed of such abstrusities." The problem was solved when he learned that his new friend Varro wanted a part in one of his dialogues, although he was not altogether sure he would take kindly to representing ideas that Cicero would go on to refute. So the work was brought up to the present day and he and Atticus were added as the other speakers. Only one volume of the first version survives (now called *Lucullus*), along with a fragment of the second.

The *Academic Treatises* gave an extended account of the evolution of the doctrines of the Academy, the school of philosophy founded by Plato and developed over the centuries by his successors. What was called the New Academy flourished in Cicero's time. In the second century BC, its leading figure, Carneades, adopted a skeptical position, which emphasized probability as against certainty. Cicero gave himself the task of defending this point of view.

He also took the opportunity to justify his overall project by responding to two criticisms he put into Varro's mouth: first, anyone seriously interested in Greek philosophy could look up the original authors and, second, the Latin language lacked the necessary technical terminology. To counter these objections, Cicero argued that Latin poetry was read and appreciated even though it was heavily dependent on Greek models. Latin was a richer language than Greek; but it was true that an accepted philosophical terminology was needed. This was precisely what he intended to produce.

Posterity has largely justified this defense. While Latin has disadvantages (the lack of a definite article, for one), to some extent Cicero succeeded in widening its range. Some of the terms he coined have had a long afterlife—*qualitas, moralis* and *essentia,* for example, are the antecedents of "quality," "moral" and "essence."

The next dialogue in the series, *On Supreme Good and Evil* (*De finibus bonorum et malorum*), was composed more or less at the same time as the *Academic Treatises.* In the preface, Cicero makes the point that he is not a mere translator but is trying to express in his own words what lies at the heart of his subject. It is a justifiable claim. He is, indeed, more than a transcriber or even a high-quality journalist. He has read philosophy all his life and feels at ease with it. What he offers is a mature synthesis in which other people's ideas grow in the field of his own experience of life. His expositions are not only thought but deeply felt.

The different chapters of the book, which has survived in its entirety, are given roughly contemporary settings: Cicero's villa at Cumae in 50; Tusculum in 52; and then Athens during his grand tour in 79. Epicureanism and Stoicism are examined and rejected. To the Epicurean who asserts that the chief good is pleasure in the sense of an absence of pain and advocates a simple, virtuous and detached life, Cicero replies that what he is talking about is not pleasure in any customary sense. Also he rejects as disgraceful the notion that the man who measures his desires by utilitarian criteria has the firmest grasp on happiness.

If Epicureans say "it is good because it is pleasant," Stoics answer that "it is pleasant because it is good." Cato is now given the task of representing the Stoic view that virtue is what we naturally desire, which Cicero rebuts as not taking into sufficient account humanity's lower faculties. Cicero argues that virtue will not necessarily produce happiness, if, as is admitted, pain is an evil. *On Supreme Good and Evil* ends on a cautiously optimistic note; virtue outweighs everything and even if the good man is not supremely happy, he is *on balance* happy.

The *Conversations at Tusculum* (*Tusculanae disputationes*) were written in the summer of 45 when Cicero had begun to recover somewhat from Tullia's death. Again the form is a dialogue set in Cicero's beloved villa at Tusculum. The two speakers are identified only by the initials M and A, standing either for Marcus and Atticus or *Magister* (master) and *Adulescens* (young man). Either way it is M who does most of the talking and the book is a series of essays rather than debates.

Having examined the nature of the good life in the previous books of the cycle, Cicero now turns to practicalities. How is the good life to be lived? He answers the question by citing many instances of human behavior both from the past and from his own time. He mentions the deaths of Cato and Pompey and hints at his feelings for Tullia, while acknowledging that grief is useless and should be put aside. His underlying purpose is to show that right attitudes and a philosophical cast of mind can alleviate misfortune and suffering. Death, he argues, is not an evil, being either a change of place for the soul or annihilation. Physical suffering is of no real importance and can be borne with fortitude. Mental suffering and distress, whether caused by mourning, envy, compassion, vexation or despondency, are acts of the will and can be eliminated by thoughtfulness, courage and self-control. The same may be said for excessive delight, lust and fear. The way forward, Cicero wrote, was to distance oneself from the cares and desires of life.

> The whole life of the philosopher, Plato said, is a preparation for death. For what else do we do when we remove the soul from pleasure—that is to say, from the body, from private property (the body's agent and servant), from public affairs and from every kind of private business: what, I repeat, do we do except call the soul into its own presence and cancel its allegiance to the body? And is separating the soul from the body anything else than learning how to die? So let us, believe me, study to dissociate ourselves from our bodies—that is, to acclimatize ourselves to the idea of death. While we are still alive, this will be an imitation of heavenly life: once we are free from our chains here, our souls will run their race less slowly. For those who have always been shackled to the flesh make slower progress even when they are released. It is as if they have spent many years in manacles. Once we have arrived at the other place, and only then, shall we live. For this life is truly death and I could, if I would, weep for it.

The discipline of the gladiator and the self-sacrifice of the Indian widow who commits *suttee* and joins her husband on the funeral pyre demonstrate that virtue can transcend pain. In this conclusion Cicero endorses Stoicism in a way that he felt unable to do in *On Supreme Good and Evil,* written a few months earlier, for he could now see, as the full intensity of his mourning subsided, how he had dragged himself from the brink of breakdown through firmness of mind.

The Nature of the Gods (*De deorum natura*), *Foretelling the Future* (*De divinatione*) and *Destiny* (*De fato*) address religious and theological themes. Collectively, they ridicule the anthropomorphic conception of God, or the gods, and propose that Epicurus, who speculated that the gods lived happily but impotently and had no effect on human affairs, was a crypto-atheist. Cicero tends to a Stoic pantheism (which gives him the opportunity to celebrate the physical universe in passages of great poetic grandeur). He criticizes superstition—dreams, portents, astrology and the like—and is particularly incensed by the Stoics' commitment to the art, or pseudoscience, of divination, by which investigation into the future can make it possible to avoid unpleasant events. Either the future is subject to chance—in which case nobody, not even a god, can affect it one way or the other—or it is predestined, in which case foreknowledge cannot avert it. As he had been appointed an Augur in 53, it is not surprising to find that Cicero recognizes, even if he does not believe in, the art of augury but thinks it should be maintained for reasons of public expediency rather than accuracy. While external factors may influence our actions, they cannot control them, for that would be to negate free will. To say "what will be, will be" is not to imply that the future is predetermined.

Cicero's last major work is *Duties* (*De officiis*); written in autumn 44, it takes the form of a letter to Marcus, who was making heavy weather of his philosophical studies in Athens at this time. Complementing the theoretical discussions in *On Supreme Good and Evil*, it is based on the work of a Stoic philosopher, Panaetius, who was a member of the circle of Scipio Aemilianus, Cicero's great hero from the second century (and the protagonist of his dialogue *On the State*). It has a practical cast and reflects the experience of the author's own lifetime. Composed at a time when Cicero was returning to public life, it condemns citizens who abstain from political activity.

The work opens with a discussion of the cardinal virtues—wisdom, justice, fortitude and temperance—and goes on to set out the specific duties that follow from adherence to them. Cicero's central concern is the contradiction between virtue and the inevitable expediencies that divert human agents from the path of right conduct. Giving many examples from Roman history, he argues that often the contradiction is only apparent, although sometimes it is difficult to establish what is really right. The primary duty, transcending all others, is loyalty to the state and Cicero takes the opportunity to review the record of his contemporaries. The behavior of various politicians of his day—the avaricious Crassus and Caesar, who has gone to the lengths of destroying the state—is compared with this principle and found wanting.

This body of work kept Cicero's name in the public eye for the brief remainder of his lifetime as a man of principle and thoughtful reflection. For posterity it became a primary vehicle by which the achievements of Greco-Roman philosophy were communicated to the early Christian Church, which regarded him as a virtuous pagan, and offered essential models to the thinkers and poets of the Renaissance and those who in the following centuries were concerned with the revival of Republican ideas of governance and the reassertion of humanistic principles.

Caesar may well have laughed with everyone else when all those years ago the boastful ex-Consul had written the much-ridiculed sentence "*Cedant arma togae,*" "Let the soldier yield precedence to the civilian." But now, with his customary clarity and generosity of mind, he well understood the nature of the "glory" Cicero had won for himself. Sometime towards the end of his life, Caesar remarked that Cicero had won greater laurels than those worn by a general in his Triumph, for it meant more to have extended the frontiers of Roman genius than of its empire.

13

"WHY, THIS IS VIOLENCE!"

Plots and Conspiracies: January–March 44 BC

From the moment the civil war finally ended in 45, respectable opinion agreed that Caesar's duty was to restore the constitution. From his policy of pardoning his enemies whenever they fell into his hands and recruiting former Pompeians to his government it looked, in the early days of victory, as if this was what he would do. His clemency had few precedents, for previous generals who had used military force to take over the state had massacred their opponents. Most people thought it meant that Caesar had a clear vision of a reconciled society after his victory.

He probably did. But he was also convinced that a strong executive authority should replace the incompetent competitive cockpit of Senatorial government. He had the means with which to impose his will. However, minimum cooperation from the political class was necessary if any solution he devised was to last. To begin with, he thought that he had gained it. But former enemies—such as Marcus Junius Brutus, the dead Cato's son-in-law and half-nephew, and Caius Cassius Longinus, Praetor for 44 and hungry for a senior military command that Caesar never gave him—were willing to work with him only as long as they believed that he would bring back the Republic. As it became clear he had no intention of doing so, they lost confidence in him and withdrew their support. The more powerful he became, the more isolated he felt.

Despite the smiles and adulation, the Dictator knew he was unpopular in leading circles. Once, when Cicero called to see him but was not shown in at once, he remarked: "I should be an idiot to suppose that even so easy-going an individual as Cicero is my friend when he has to sit waiting for my convenience all this time."

The first signs of the conspiracy against Caesar can be detected almost exactly one year before the Ides of March 44—after the last battle of the civil war at Munda. As soon as news reached Rome of the outcome of the battle, all kinds of people—entrepreneurs, politicians and young men on the make—left Rome to meet the returning army en route and catch the eye of the Republic's undisputed master. At Narbo in Transalpine Gaul, Mark Antony, one of Caesar's principal lieutenants, fell in with another of his supporters, who had recently been a governor in Spain, Caius Trebonius.

Trebonius had a very curious deal to propose. He wanted to know if Antony would join a plot to kill Caesar. Antony did not respond to the tentative sounding. What was sinister about the conversation was less that it took place than that Antony did not report it. The fact that Caesar's closest political partner saw no cause to warn him is strong evidence of the disaffection of the ruling class.

Nothing came of this démarche, but at some point in the months that followed individuals began meeting in small groups in one another's houses and discussed various ideas of how and where the murder should be committed. Perhaps he could be attacked on the Holy Way, the street that led into the Forum. Or he could be ambushed during an election on the Field of Mars. Voters had to pass along a narrow bridge over a stream where the ballots were counted. Perhaps Caesar could be pushed off the bridge and pounced upon. The trouble with these schemes was that they would take place in public and there was always a risk that the assassins would themselves be assaulted or killed. For the time being these quiet conversations led nowhere and were overshadowed by the hyperactivity of the regime.

One of the leading conspirators was Caius Cassius Longinus. As Quaestor he had taken charge of Syria after Crassus met his end at Carrhae and had scored a military success against the Parthians in 51, when Cicero had been governor of the neighboring province of Cilicia. An irascible man, he did not easily forget a grudge and fell out for a time with Brutus when the latter won a promotion at his expense. His contemporaries took the view that he opposed Caesar for personal reasons rather than on principle. According to Plutarch, he was furious when, during the civil war, Caesar came across a number of lions Cassius had acquired for use at some Games he was due to stage in Rome and confiscated them for his own purposes.

Yet there is also evidence that Cassius had a long-standing deeply felt aversion to arbitrary government: as a boy he had gone to the same school as Sulla's son, Faustus. When Faustus bragged about his all-powerful father, Cassius lost his temper and beat him up. The two boys were questioned about the matter by Pompey, at the time one of Sulla's lieutenants, and Cassius is reported to have been unrepentant. He said to Faustus: "Come on, Faustus, you dare repeat in front of this man what you said before, which made me angry, and I'll smash your face in again!"

Gradually more and more people were drawn into the plot against Caesar and by the end at least sixty were involved. Their motives varied. While masquerading as principled tyrannicides or, as they called themselves, Freedom Fighters (*liberatores*), some in fact resented the deaths of family and friends in the civil war. For a few, the Dictator's clemency and generosity was too much to bear, too insulting to their sense of dignity. Others were impressed by the political and social status of the leading conspirators; in particular Marcus Brutus, one of whose ancestors had led a celebrated uprising against the monarchy centuries before, was extremely influential in giving the enterprise respectability. And then there were those who had worked for Caesar a long time and felt they had not been adequately rewarded.

Meanwhile, the regime continued to entrench itself. Honors were poured on Caesar and statues of him began appearing all over the city. His ivory image was carried in the procession at the Games alongside those of the gods. Another was set up in the Temple of Romulus, the first King of Rome, in the Forum with the dedication "To the Invincible God." His effigy was also placed on the Capitol, Rome's citadel, next to those of the former kings of Rome.

As an expression of the new spirit of harmony that he wished to project, Caesar re-erected statues of Pompey and other onetime political opponents in their old places. Cicero had the *mot* for the moment: "By his generous action, he has not just set up Pompey's statues but ensured that his own remain safely in place." Towards the end of 45 a final batch of honors was granted, in effect announcing Caesar's deification on lines uncomfortably similar to those of the Hellenistic monarchs of Asia Minor, for whom self-conferred divine status was a long-standing convention.

Plans for the huge expeditionary force of sixteen legions that Caesar had decided to lead against the Parthian Empire to avenge the defeat and death of Crassus in 53 were approaching completion. He would set off in mid-March 44 and might be away from Rome for as long as three years. He arranged for the advance election of all the Consuls who would hold office during his absence. The Dictator's lack of interest in domestic politics and the renewal of Republican institutions could hardly have been more clearly demonstrated.

On December 31 one of the Consuls died and, as elections for some other officeholders were being held at the time, Caesar forced the immediate election of a certain Caius Caninius Rebilus, a New Man who had served under him in Gaul, to be his successor for a few hours. This was using the Consulship as a cheap reward for a supporter. Public opinion was outraged. When a crowd of followers prepared to escort the new Consul down to the Forum, Cicero remarked: "We'd better get a move on, or he'll be out of office before we get there."

As the new year dawned the mood in the city was darkening. Many damaging rumors were being assiduously spread—that Caesar was going to establish Egypt as the seat of his Empire where he would rule with his mistress, Queen Cleopatra of Egypt, now living just outside the capital in opulent, un-Roman style; or, even more implausibly, that Troy was to be the new capital of the Empire. These tales were little more than distorted reflections of a perfectly rational anxiety about how Rome would be ruled during Caesar's absence in Asia Minor.

Caesar may have begun to suspect that among the fawning Senators there were those who recommended more and more fantastic honors with the conscious aim of setting opinion against him. He hesitated over whether or not to assume the title of Dictator for Life, eventually deciding to do so in the early days of February. This caused a good deal of angry comment, since the Dictatorship was traditionally a strictly temporary appointment that gave the officeholder supreme power for a short time, seldom more than six months, in order to cope with a state emergency.

Caesar's decision was seen as a very bad sign by Republicans, an obvious first step to a formal monarchy. Some of the conspirators, wanting to stir up bad feeling, began saluting him as king in public. They secretly placed a diadem (a ribbon worn around the head, denoting royalty) on one of his statues. Two Tribunes removed it, apparently to Caesar's annoyance. A little later when he was riding in from attending a festival on the Alban Mount, some men again hailed him as king. "My name is Caesar, not King," he remarked. The same Tribunes brought a suit against the first man who had shouted the word out. This infuriated Caesar and, when the Tribunes then issued a statement that their freedom of speech was under threat, they were unceremoniously deposed from office. The incident could suggest that Caesar really did want to establish a monarchy. However, there is another more plausible and less sinister interpretation, which an event a few days later seems to confirm.

On February 15, 44, the festival of the Lupercalia was held—a strange ritual which symbolized the renewal of civil order near the year's beginning. The Luperci were a college of priests, young men of good family who every year on this day ran through the city naked except for goatskin loincloths. They represented wolf-men living in a primal community held together by violence.

Caesar attended this exotic event, watching it from his gilded chair on the Speakers' Platform in the Forum. The ceremony opened with the sacrifice of goats and a dog, whose blood was smeared on the foreheads of two young men. The blood was then wiped off with milk-soaked wool, after which the Luperci dressed themselves in the bloodstained skins of the victims. They ate and drank heavily before running around the Palatine Hill to purify a grotto there which was sacred to the Luperci. They brandished strips of freshly flayed animal skin and lashed out with them at childless women, who placed themselves in their way in the belief that a touch of the whip would relieve them of their infertility.

Antony, now in his late thirties and a little old for the part, was among the runners, but instead of carrying a thong he held a diadem in his hand, twined around a laurel wreath. Some of his fellow runners lifted him up so that he could place it at Caesar's feet. Voices in the crowd shouted that Caesar should be crowned with it. Cassius with another of the conspirators, Publius Servilius Casca, picked up the diadem and put it on Caesar's knee. The Dictator made a gesture of refusal and there were cheers from the crowd. Then Antony ran up again, presumably onto the Speakers' Platform itself, and put the diadem on Caesar's head. Antony said, "The people offer this to you through me," and Caesar replied, "Jupiter alone is King of the Romans." He immediately took it off and flung it into the crowd; those at the back clapped, but in the front rows people shouted that he should accept it and not resist the will of the People. An early source says that this "pantomime" went on for some time with applause ringing out with every refusal. Looking thoroughly put out, Caesar stood up and opened the front of his toga and said that anyone who wanted to cut his throat might do so.

Eventually Antony retrieved the diadem and had it sent to the Temple of Jupiter on the Capitol. The official record in the archives for the Lupercalia of that year read: "To Caius Caesar, Life Dictator, Mark Antony the Consul, by command of the People, offered the kingship: Caesar was unwilling."

The episode betrays every sign of having been premeditated. As Cicero pointed out later to Antony: "Where did the diadem come from? It is not the sort of thing you pick up in the street. You had brought it from home." It is highly unlikely that Antony would have dared to improvise or stage an ambush of this kind without Caesar's knowledge and it seems equally implausible that the government was unaware of the real state of public feeling.

In all probability Caesar decided that the growing rush of rumors needed to be stemmed. Perhaps he had become wise to the unwisdom of accepting so many honors. Almost on the eve of the Parthian expedition, the feverish political climate needed to be calmed. The Lupercalia offered a high-profile opportunity to stage a "spontaneous" request and then have it decisively turned down. It is fascinating to observe (according to one of the earliest sources, Nicolaus of Damascus, who at one point in his life was a tutor in the household of Antony and Cleopatra) the active involvement of two known or presumed critics of the regime (and conspirators) in the charade. Their presence at the scene may imply an intention to involve a wide range of political opinion in a spectacle that was meant to quash the rumors once and for all.

The maneuver failed. What if the crowd's applause had supported rather than refused the "crowning"? skeptics wondered. Could suspicious and cynical constitutionalists be sure what would have happened then? So far as the conspirators were concerned the Lupercalia did nothing to lull their fears. If anything, it focused their minds and hurried them up. What was probably an inchoate group, or groupings, of malcontents came together as a clearly defined plot. It was probably at this point that Cassius was able to recruit the conspiracy's most celebrated member, Marcus Brutus.

Attacking Antony in a speech almost exactly a year later, Cicero said, "You, you, assassinated him at the Lupercalia." This colorful overstatement contained a germ of truth: the public offer of kingship was in a sense Caesar's death warrant.

About this time, an apparently unimportant misunderstanding also left a bad impression. Caesar was sitting in the vestibule of the Temple of Venus in his newly opened Julian Forum deciding various construction contracts. A Senatorial delegation appeared on the scene with a commission to present him with a formal record of all the honors he had been voted. Unfortunately, the Dictator was not looking in their direction and seems not to have noticed them. He went on conducting business until someone pointed out their presence. It was only then that he put aside his papers and received the Senators but, as an added discourtesy, failed to rise to his feet. He evidently realized this was a gaffe, for his friends soon put it around that he had been unable to stand up because of an attack of diarrhea.

What were Caesar's real political intentions for the future? It is hard to be certain today, and even contemporaries struggled to find an answer to the question. This may well be because Caesar himself was unsure of the way forward. In all probability he recognized that the formal assertion of monarchy was out of the question. The Dictatorship for Life gave him what he wanted while staying, more or less, inside constitutional norms. He was quoted as saying: "I would prefer to hold the Consulship legally rather than a kingship illegally"; the same principle could be applied to the Dictatorship and this was probably his genuine view on the subject.

Caesar's personal mood was depressed. His health was deteriorating. (As he got older, it is reported, his epileptic fits became more frequent and he suffered from headaches and nightmares.) He became aware of plots against him and secret nocturnal meetings but took no action except to announce that he knew of them. Warned that Brutus was plotting against him, Caesar touched his body and said: "Brutus will wait for this piece of skin." On another occasion, though, he took a less sanguine view. When Dolabella and Antony were reported to be plotting revolution, he replied: "It's not fat, longhaired fellows that worry me but those pale, thin ones"—by whom he meant Brutus and Cassius.

The Dictator dispensed with a troop of armed Spaniards that was his permanent escort, as well as a bodyguard of Senators that had been voted to him. He mingled publicly and unprotected among all comers. When advised to rehire the Spaniards, he said: "There is no fate worse than being continuously under guard, for it means you are always afraid." His decision was probably as much motivated by scorn for the opposition as by a desire to bid for popularity. "It is more important for Rome than for me that I should survive," he said on more than one occasion. "If anything happens to me, Rome will enjoy no peace. A new civil war will break out under far worse conditions than the last one." Those close to him felt he had lost the desire to live much longer.

Caesar's reluctance to show any signs of compromise and his refusal to share power with others explain the remarkable fact that so many leading members of the government joined the conspiracy to put an end to their leader. Besides Cassius and the much-trusted Marcus Brutus, who were both Praetors, there was Decimus Junius Brutus (a distant relative of Marcus), who was to be Consul in 42. The continuing silence of Mark Antony, now Consul, about his conversation with Trebonius speaks louder than words. As the final plans for the assassination were laid, the conspirators spent some time pondering what to do about Antony. The fact that he was seen as a potential sympathizer was a reason for not making him a target alongside Caesar. However, Cassius argued that he should be killed along with Caesar: he was a physically strong man and might intervene to help the Dictator. Also, he and Caesar were Consuls and he would be the senior official after the assassination. If he were out of the way, Brutus and Cassius, as Praetors, would be able to take charge of the government legally. Brutus disagreed: it was one thing, he said, to kill a tyrant but quite another to kill a lawfully appointed Consul. It was finally agreed that Trebonius would isolate Antony at the crucial moment by intercepting him before the meeting and holding him in conversation.

During the first three months of 44 a great simplification of Roman politics took place. On the one hand, Caesar finally came to see that he had failed to reconcile the *optimates* to his dominance and further consolidated his authority. On the other, the *optimates* finally came to despair of a restoration of the Republic. Neither side could see a way out of the impasse except by Caesar's removal from the scene—permanent, so far as Brutus and Cassius were concerned, and temporary from Caesar's perspective. The Parthian expedition was, in its own way, a recognition of Caesar's failure. However it was to be achieved, he had to go.

The precise decision as to where to conduct the assassination was made on short notice, when a meeting of the Senate was convened for the unlucky date of March 15 at Pompey's theater. This would be a controlled environment and, when the deed was done, the conspirators would be able to explain themselves at once to their peers.

As the chosen date was a holiday, a gladiatorial display was due to take place later in the day in the theater. Brutus, as Praetor, was in charge of the gladiators, who could be useful in the aftermath of the assassination if anything went wrong. A strong detachment of gladiators was assembled, which could be brought into the theater precincts on the pretext of a rehearsal or a training exercise. There was good reason for this precaution. Just outside the city limits on a small island on the Tiber, an army loyal to Caesar under the command of Marcus Aemilius Lepidus, who as Master of the House was the Dictator's official deputy, was encamped. A stone bridge connected the island to the city and, although soldiers were forbidden to enter Rome, it was perfectly possible that Lepidus would march in to put down any trouble.

By March 15 information about the conspiracy was leaking out. Almost as soon as Caesar left the State House in the morning a member of his household who had heard something of what was going on came running into the building to report what he had gleaned. As he did not know the date and time of the attempt, he simply told Caesar's third wife, Calpurnia, that he needed to see him on urgent business. He sat down to await his return.

While Brutus and Cassius were standing around with the other Senators waiting for Caesar's arrival, a certain Popilius Laenas came up to them. "I join you in praying for the accomplishment of what you have in mind," he said. "I urge you not to delay, for people are talking about it." At the last moment, a philosophy teacher, Artemidorus, pushed his way forward as Caesar was making his way into the meeting hall. A former tutor of Brutus and still one of his friends, he knew all the details of the conspiracy. He had written down a short summary of the plan to kill the Dictator and was determined to reveal what was afoot. Artemidorus was only one among a crowd of petitioners and he noticed that while Caesar accepted every paper that was thrust into his hands, he immediately handed it over to one of his aides. According to Plutarch, Artemidorus pleaded: "Read this one, Caesar, and read it quickly and by yourself. I promise you it's important and concerns you personally."

Caesar took the document and several times appeared to be on the point of looking through it, but was prevented from doing so by all the people who came up to talk with him. It was the only paper he was holding when he finally walked through the doorway to join the Senate. The success of the assassination was a close-run thing.

There was an understanding that, as a sign of their commitment and solidarity, all the conspirators should try to stab their victim. As a result, many wounded each other accidentally in the scrum and few had a good chance to strike home. An autopsy later showed that only one wound had been fatal—the second, which Publius Servilius Casca's brother had delivered to the flank.

Having witnessed the flurried, bloodied melee, none of the audience of Senators was in a mood to linger. Although one Senator remained long enough to say, "There has been enough kowtowing to a tyrant," there was a noisy rush to the doors while Brutus, brandishing his dagger at the center of the hall, shouted his congratulations to Cicero "on the recovery of freedom." Cicero was among those making their escape.

Antony, in conversation with Trebonius in the colonnade outside, quickly realized what had happened. (Perhaps Trebonius told him.) He changed into a slave's clothes and went to ground. Appian reports that even Caesar's official lictors ran away, and soon the dead Dictator was alone. His body lay undisturbed for some hours.

The assassins wound their togas around their arms to serve as shields and, with bloodstained swords in their hands, ran out into the open, shouting that they had destroyed a tyrant and a king. One of them carried a freedom cap (a skullcap worn by freed slaves) on a spear. They were joined by a handful of Senators, who decided to seize the hour. Among them was the youthful Dolabella, Deputy Consul to the Dictator and now, he supposed, Consul. (He was wrong in this, for his appointment needed formal approval, which was given later.)

It did not take long for panic to ensue. Members of the public, stampeding from the theater and its environs, shouted: "Run! Bolt your doors. Bolt your doors." The conspirators, followed by their gladiators and some servants, made their way through the Field of Mars to the Forum, still shouting for Cicero. News of what had happened, or at least that something terrible had happened, spread quickly. Nicolaus, commented: "The city looked as if it had been captured by an enemy."

Brutus and those with him tried their best to calm the crowds in the Forum, but there was little they could do and so they climbed up the Capitoline Hill, where they could beat off any attackers. They were able to catch their breath and plan their next move. Looking down later in the day, they would have been able to see a small, sad procession cross the Forum. Three slave boys, the only members of Caesar's entourage not to have fled, had loaded the dead body into the Dictator's litter and were carrying it home. As it passed through the streets it was greeted with cries of lamentation from people standing on housetops. The curtains of the litter were drawn back; the dead man's face could be seen covered in blood and his arms were hanging down. When the body arrived in the Forum and was taken to the State House at the far end of the square from the Capitol, Calpurnia and a crowd of wailing women and slaves came out to meet it.

Slowly the public mood quieted, as it became clear that no further deaths were taking place and that there would be no looting. In the afternoon Brutus came down into the Forum to address the People. Before he did so, arrangements were made to ensure that a suitably friendly audience was recruited. This did not prove difficult, for much of the urban population was unemployed and attendance could be bought. Also, Rome was full of demobilized veterans, camped in temple precincts and sanctuaries, who were waiting for transport to the new colonies Caesar had founded in Italy and abroad. They were not averse to making a few sesterces on the side.

Despite the fact that many of those in the Forum had been bribed, they lacked the courage to show their approval of what had been done. There was still a widespread mood of shock and uncertainty. However, the majority calculated that its best interests lay in stability. People were willing to accept a peaceful resolution of the crisis and an amnesty for the killers.

Brutus took another precautionary measure. When he, Cassius and others arrived in the Forum, they were accompanied by Dolabella, now wearing a Consular toga and surrounded by lictors; this lent the occasion an official air and suggested that the orderly business of government was being maintained.

In their speeches, Brutus and Cassius avoided triumphalism. They said they had acted from disinterested motives. They had no intention of seizing power, for their only aim was to preserve their freedom and independence. The crowd was attentive and reasonably sympathetic. Other speakers included Dolabella and a Praetor, who unwisely launched into a passionate denunciation of Caesar. This was too much for the veterans and, according to one account, they shouted him down. Crestfallen, the conspirators withdrew to the safety of the Capitol, where they spent the night. The city was not safe enough for them to return to their homes.

14

THE HEIR

Enter Octavian: March–December 44 BC

The two years that followed Caesar's assassination are the best documented in Roman history. Even so, the actors in the story do not always betray their motives. The press of events was so confusing that even when they were sure of what they wanted they often had no idea how best to achieve it. It was difficult to sense where advantage lay. Interpretation has also been hindered by the fact that the eventual winner in the struggles that lay ahead imposed his own interpretation on the past. The losers lost more than their lives, they lost their stories.

Brutus, Cassius and the other conspirators were much criticized at the time—and have been in the two millennia that have followed—for laying no plans for the aftermath of the assassination. For them, the act of killing, echoing Rome's deep past, was less a political event than a sacred ritual. Just as soldiers traditionally purified their weapons in March, so the Republic had cleansed itself. The man who dressed in a king's robes had suffered a king's death. Tactical details could wait for later.

The Dictator had maintained, if only in form, the constitutional proprieties and Brutus and his friends judged that, once he had been removed, nobody would seriously try to prevent the Republic from slipping back into gear. Their assumption was that the constitution would simply and automatically resume its functions. The Senate would have little difficulty in taking over the reins of power. This was not an unreasonable analysis and was confirmed in the event—for the time being.

A great deal hung on how Antony behaved. It was a question of character and here opinions varied. Cicero's assessment was much the same as it had been when he had had to prise the teenage rebel out of Curio's life: he was an unscrupulous and immoral rascal. Although he did not say so at once, Cicero took the view in April that "the Ides of March was a fine deed, but half done." That is, Antony should have been killed along with his master. Later he remarked to Cassius: "A pity you didn't invite me to dinner on the Ides of March! Let me tell you, there would have been no leftovers."

Against Cassius's advice, Brutus had refused to have Antony killed. By implication, he must have judged that Antony was unlikely to seek to step into the Dictator's shoes. Brutus was probably right. Antony did not have the prestige, the ability or the application to be a Caesar. An acute observer remarked: "If a man of Caesar's genius could find no way out [of Rome's problems], who will find one now?" Antony certainly had no solution.

Now in his late thirties, Antony was a handsome man, built like a bull and, according to Cicero, "as strong as a gladiator." He was sexually promiscuous and hard drinking and retained the taste he had acquired as a young man for bad company: actors and prostitutes. A good soldier, he was popular with his men. He could summon up great resources of stamina and energy, but only when occasion demanded. His patchy record when he was in charge of Italy during the Dictator's absences suggested a lack of aptitude for civilian administration. His style was straightforward, and when he said something he tended to mean it.

In all likelihood, Antony genuinely endorsed a return to constitutional methods and, if he had a future career path in mind, might have found in Pompey a safer model than in Caesar. A five-year governorship after his Consulship would establish him as the leading figure in the Republic. He could become the first man in Rome, as Pompey had been, without challenging the very foundations of Roman tradition and its familiar balanced rivalries.

Two important groups felt very differently. For the moment they were powerless because leaderless, but their minds were set on revenge and they waited for their opportunity. The first of these groups was the army. Tens of thousands of men were still armed—two legions in Italian Gaul, three in Transalpine Gaul and six in Macedonia, waiting for the now aborted Parthian expedition. There were six legions in Spain, and more troops in Africa and Asia Minor. So far as those who had served under Caesar were concerned, relations with their Commander-in-Chief had sometimes been stormy, but they had adored him. They wanted blood for blood.

Second, the aides and civil servants whom the Dictator had hired had lost their jobs. They were able and dedicated. At their head were Balbus and Oppius: everything they had been working for would be lost forever if they could not find a way of subverting the newly restored Republic. They soon realized that Antony was going to be of no use. But they had another unsuspected card in their hand, and in due course they would play it.

By contrast, Cicero was thrilled by the dramatic turn of events. A hurried note he wrote to one of the conspirators probably refers to the assassination. "Congratulations. For myself, I am delighted. You can count on my affection and active concern for your interests. I hope I have *your* affection and want to hear what you are doing and what is going on."

He did not have to wait long for a briefing. During the evening of March 15 he visited the conspirators at the Capitol. He believed they should seize the initiative. With Antony's disappearance, Brutus and Cassius were the senior officeholders and Cicero advised them to call a Senate meeting immediately for the following day. Proceduralists to the core, they preferred to wait and send a delegation to find the Consul. It was a bad mistake—and Cicero never let them forget it.

Realizing that his life was not in danger, Antony spent the night taking steps to secure his position. Lepidus led his legion from the island in the Tiber into the city and secured the Forum. Fires were lit to illuminate the streets and friends or associates of the conspirators were revealed scurrying to and from Senators' houses in search of support. Antony went to the State House, where the widowed Calpurnia, with the help of Caesar's secretary, handed over all the Dictator's papers and a large sum of money. He announced that, in his capacity as Consul, he would convene the Senate at a temple near his house on March 17.

Antony also met with Balbus and the following year's designated Consul, the gourmet and writer Hirtius. The former argued, unsurprisingly, for the severest measures against the assassins, the latter for caution. This disagreement boded ill for the dead Dictator's party: it revealed a split which constitutionalists hurried to exploit.

On March 16 Brutus addressed a large gathering at the Capitol, but he made little impression. He was a plain, unemotional speaker and his performance more than justified Cicero's low opinion of the Attic style of oratory. He let it be known that, had *he* been asked to give an address, he would have spoken much more passionately.

The conspirators stayed away from the Senate on the following day, although they were invited to attend. Die-hard Caesarians were a minority, but a lively debate started as to whether to declare Caesar a tyrant and give immunity to the assassins. Antony interrupted and went straight to the point. He ruled that if Caesar was condemned, it followed that his appointments would be illegal. Was this what the Senate wanted? Self-interest immediately concentrated minds. Senators jumped up and protested against having to go through another round of elections. Dolabella, so strong in his denunciation of the Dictator and all his works the previous day, was first among them, for he knew that his own position as Consul would be at risk.

Privately Cicero would have much preferred to have drawn a line under the past and agreed on a new start. But with veterans surrounding the meeting and Senators fearful of losing their offices and provincial commands, that was out of the question. So he spoke strongly in favor of Antony's proposal. A compromise was found: all Caesar's official acts were to be approved and, in return, the conspirators would not be punished. The formal decision was taken at a Senate meeting on March 18. A few weeks later Cicero justified himself to Atticus: "What else could we have done? By that time we were long sunk."

One of the important results of the Senate's ruling was the protection it gave to the leading conspirators. In addition to deciding the Consulships for the coming three years, Caesar had allocated provincial governorships. Brutus and Cassius were to have Macedonia and Asia in 43. Decimus Brutus was confirmed in the current year for Italian Gaul, where he would be the first conspirator to take charge of an army, for two legions were stationed there. If trouble arose, these provinces would provide power bases where the conspirators could legitimately establish themselves.

As the Senate was about to break up, a noisy discussion broke out over

Caesar's will. His father-in-law, Lucius Calpurnius Piso Caesoninus, was asked not to announce its contents or conduct a public funeral for fear of disturbances. He angrily refused and, after renewed debate, permission was granted.

When published, the will inflamed opinion on the street, for it bequeathed Caesar's gardens on the far side of the Tiber as a public park and left 300 sesterces to every Roman citizen. Popular with the masses, it was not calculated to please Antony, for it also disclosed that the chief heir to the Dictator's fortune was Caius Octavianus (in English, Octavian), his eighteen-year-old grandnephew. He was also designated as his adoptive son; from now on his formal name would be Caius Julius Caesar Octavianus. The news came as a complete surprise to everyone, including its young beneficiary. The will concerned his personal estate and did not mean that Caesar was giving him the Republic. Antony saw himself as the inheritor of Caesar's political legacy and that was how he meant it to remain. He did not anticipate a teenage boy to be a serious threat.

The funeral on March 20 promised to be a very grand affair on the Field of Mars and was to be preceded by speeches in the Forum before the bier. Brutus and the other conspirators foresaw trouble and locked themselves in their houses. A funeral pyre was built on the Field of Mars and, because the traditional procession of mourners bringing funeral gifts would have taken all day to file past, everyone was invited to come there by whatever route he pleased and without order of precedence.

In the Forum, an ivory couch stood on the Speakers' Platform, draped in an embroidered gold-and-purple pall. In front a temporary chapel had been erected, modeled on the Temple of Venus in Caesar's new Forum. Piso brought the body, clothed in the purple gown the Dictator had been wearing when killed, into the square, laid it on the couch and posted a large group of armed men to guard it. There were loud cries of mourning and the men clashed their weapons.

Antony, in his capacity as mourner, friend and kinsman (his mother was a member of the Julius clan) of the dead Dictator, delivered the funeral oration. There are two accounts of what happened. According to the historian Suetonius, writing about a century and half later but with access to the imperial archives, Antony dispensed with the usual speech and asked a herald to read out the recent decree voting Caesar "all divine and human honors" and the oath by which the Senate had vowed to watch over his safety. He then added a few comments.

Appian, writing in the second century AD, has it that Antony spoke with passion about the dead man's achievements and criticized the recent amnesty for the assassins. Standing close to the bier as though he were on stage, he hitched up his toga to free his hands. He bent over the body and, swept by emotion, pulled off Caesar's gown, bloodstained and torn, and waved it about on a pole. Choirs then sang formal dirges, again stating the dead man's achievements and bewailing his fate. At some point in these lamentations Caesar was imagined as listing by name those enemies of his whom he had helped and saying in amazement: "To think I saved the lives of the people who were to be my murderers."

It is possible that in their memory of this extraordinary day people mixed up the contents of Antony's opening presentation and the dirges. It was not obviously to the Consul's advantage to foment general disorder and Suetonius's account may be the right one. Whatever the truth of the matter, the ceremony made a tremendous impact on the crowd. The climax came when a wax effigy of Caesar (the corpse itself was lying out of sight on the bier) was lifted up. It was turned around in all directions by a mechanical device and twenty-three wounds could be seen, on every part of the body and on the face.

This was too much for many to bear. In a repetition of the outpouring of grief and rage at the death of Clodius, the mob went berserk. They burned down the Senate House, not long rebuilt after its previous incineration. Furniture and wood were pulled out of shops to create an impromptu pyre in the Forum not far from the Temple of the Castors. Musicians and performers who had been hired for the funeral threw their costumes onto it. It was reported that two young men with swords and javelins lit the pyre and subsequent mythmaking or ingenious stage management on the day suggested they were the divine brothers Castor and Pollux, who had a legendary record of guarding over Rome and making an appearance at moments of crisis. Caesar was cremated then and there.

It is hard to believe that whoever designed the funeral ceremony was unaware of the effect it was likely to have. If Antony was not responsible, it must have been Caesar's family, perhaps advised by his clever aides, Balbus and Oppius. After all, it was in their interest to subvert the attempts by Republicans and moderate Caesarians to create a peaceful transition to a new political order.

The conspirators realized it was impossible for them to remain in Rome and withdrew to their country estates. This left Antony master of the situation. He acted with restraint, discouraged an unofficial cult of Caesar and was deferential to leading Senators. A well-received law was passed abolishing the office of Dictator. Antony was scrupulously polite to Cicero, who in early April decided that he was "more concerned about the composition of his menus than about planning any mischief."

This was a misjudgment of the situation, for the Consul was still intent on securing his power base. To this end he used Caesar's papers for his own purposes, forging documents to reward his supporters and enrich himself. His main aim was to ensure that the compromise settlement of March 17 stuck. The main threat to him lay in the future behavior of the conspirators when they went abroad to take over their allotted provinces and armies. Decimus Brutus, soon to set off for Italian Gaul, already looked threatening and in the summer two other conspirators left for commands in Asia Minor.

In some ways Cicero found himself in the same uncomfortable position that he had been in at the beginning of the civil war. This time, though, he had absolutely no doubt whose side he was on and had no intention of putting himself forward as mediator again. However, there was a problem of competence. He admired the conspirators for their heroism on the Ides of March but felt that everything they had done afterwards had been ill-conceived and poorly planned. He believed that Antony's venality and willingness to act arbitrarily was the prelude to a new autocracy. Realizing that he was not being taken seriously, he became cross with everybody and left the city. He confessed wryly to Atticus that he ought to reread his own essay *On Growing Old.* "Advancing years are making me cantankerous," he remarked in May. "Everything annoys me. But I have had my time. Let the young ones worry."

Cicero kept restlessly on the move from one villa to another, often sleeping in one place for only one night. He wrote to Atticus almost every day. He also seems to have revised the savage *Secret History* he had started working on in 59, in the bitter aftermath of his Consulship.

Marcus was getting on reasonably well in Athens. Atticus, presumably in Greece, was helping out with his cash flow. The boy was poor at keeping in touch, but when in June he did eventually write home his father was pleased to see that his literary style showed signs of improvement. Meanwhile, Quintus fell out with his son and was having difficulty repaying Pomponia's dowry. Young Quintus was as politically unsatisfactory as ever, having now attached himself to Antony.

Balbus and Hirtius took care to keep in touch with Cicero. He received a very civil letter from Antony asking him to agree to the recall of one of Clodius's followers from exile; this unpleasant reminder of the past annoyed him, but he made no objection. He was delighted when "my wonderful Dolabella" put down some pro-Caesar riots and demolished a commemorative pillar and altar where the Dictator had been cremated in the Forum. An agitator, falsely claiming to be Marius's grandson, was arrested and executed.

Cicero noted the hurried departure of Cleopatra from Rome. "The Queen's flight does not distress me," he wrote coolly. Well endowed with regal ways, Cleopatra appears not to have been a popular figure in Rome, and the death of her protector meant that there was nothing left to keep her in Italy. She may have hoped that Caesar would have recognized their son, but there had been no mention of Caesarion in his will. This may have been a disappointment, but at least she was able to leave with a renewed treaty of friendship between Rome and Egypt.

A month later, on May 11 Cicero noted cryptically: "I hope it's true about the Queen and that Caesar of hers." A week or so later, he made further references to some rumor about her. It is hard to know what to make of this, but it has been conjectured that Cleopatra had become pregnant a second time and that she had been reported to have miscarried on the journey home. "That Caesar" would have been a dismissive reference to the dead fetus.

Towards the end of April Caesar's youthful heir arrived in Italy. Octavian had been born during Cicero's Consulship in 63 and came from a respectable provincial family in the country town of Velitrae in the Alban Hills south of Rome. His ambitious father had married Atia, Caesar's niece, but he had died when Octavian was four. The widowed Atia had married again, choosing Lucius Marcius Philippus, who was Consul in 56.

Octavian grew up to be a short, slight, attractive young man with curly yellowish hair and clear, bright eyes. A weakness in his left leg sometimes gave him the appearance of having a limp. His health was delicate, but he was an industrious student. Although he had a gift for speaking extempore, he worked hard at improving his rhetorical technique.

In 45, despite being in a state of semiconvalescence after a serious illness, Octavian had followed Caesar to Spain, where he was fighting the last campaign of the civil war. After surviving a shipwreck, he had traveled with a small escort along roads held by the enemy. His great-uncle had been delighted and impressed by his energy and formed a high estimation of his character. Doubtless this was why he had decided to make the boy his heir.

After the battle of Munda, Octavian had been sent to the coastal town of Apollonia, across the Adriatic Sea in Macedonia. Caesar wanted him on the Parthian campaign and told him to wait there with the assembled legions until he joined them. In the meantime he was to pursue his education and receive military training.

When the terrible news arrived in Apollonia, Octavian's first nervous instinct was to stay with the army, whose senior officers offered to look after him. But his mother and stepfather suggested that it would be safer if he came quietly and without fuss to Rome. Shortly afterwards Octavian was informed of his dangerous inheritance. His family thought he should renounce it, but he disagreed. Crossing the sea to Brundisium, he made contact with the troops there, who received him enthusiastically as Caesar's son. He decided, as instructed, to assume his great-uncle's name. He liked to be addressed as Caesar, although this was not to his stepfather Philippus's liking, and for a time Cicero insisted on calling him Octavius and later by his *cognomen* after adoption, Octavianus.

In taking these actions, Octavian was publicly asserting himself as the Dictator's *political,* not merely personal, heir. He felt able to do so because he realized that Antony's compromise settlement with the Senate did not take the feelings of the army into full account. It was a remarkably bold step and calls for explanation. Is it reasonable to believe that an inexperienced teenager would have seized the initiative in this way without prompting? It is of course a possibility, for his later career revealed very considerable political ability. It is much more plausible, however, that Balbus and other members of the Dictator's staff, disenchanted with Antony's policy of reconciliation, judged that the young man, carefully handled and advised, was well placed to assume the leadership of the Caesarian cause. The boy would be a focus for the simmering resentments among the Roman masses, the disbanded veterans and the standing legions, and that Antonius would be outmaneuvered and put on the defensive.

The long-term plan, shadowy in outline at this stage and not publicly emphasized, would be to turn the tables on the conspirators and take revenge for the assassination. What the Caesarians had in mind was, in essence, a plot to overthrow a restored Republic. When Caesar foresaw that a new civil war would break out if he was removed from the scene, he can hardly have guessed that it would be his heir who fulfilled his prediction.

On his journey north from Brundisium, Octavian was welcomed by large numbers of people, many of them soldiers or the Dictator's former slaves and freedmen. Perhaps some of these demonstrations on the road were engineered, but they revealed a deep well of support for the young pretender. In Naples he was met by Balbus and went on to his stepfather's villa at Puteoli. Cicero happened to be on hand when he arrived, for Philippus was his neighbor. (It was at their two villas that they had entertained Caesar the previous December.) Always prone to like young men and take them under his wing, Cicero may have been tempted by the prospect of another *protégé* to groom. On the following day he received a visit from Octavian and, writing to Atticus in his presence, insisted that gratified vanity did not mean he had been taken in. "Octavian is with me here—most respectful and friendly," he noted. "My judgment is that he cannot be a good citizen. There are too many around him. They threaten death to our friends and call the present state of affairs intolerable. . . . I long to be away."

During recent weeks Cicero had been thinking of leaving the country for a few months and he arranged for a special leave of absence from the Consuls. He intended to be in Rome for a Senate meeting on June 1 but afterwards there would be no reason to linger. His idea was to go to his beloved Athens and check in person how Marcus was getting along.

Young Octavian's appearance on the scene turned the political situation on its head. His growing popularity with the army and the Roman masses had the effect, as intended, of detaching Antony from the Senate, for it compelled him to outbid his new rival as a loyal supporter of Caesar's memory. This in turn meant that Brutus's and Cassius's strategy of sitting around quietly in their country houses, on the assumption that politics were gradually returning to normal, was pointless. All sums had to be recalculated.

For the time being the newcomer was little more than a nuisance and the Consul called him dismissively a "boy who owes everything to his name." However, the popularity of that name in the army and among the urban masses soon made him a force to be reckoned with. If he meant to remain at the head of affairs, Antony would sooner or later be driven to align himself against the constitutionalists (and so fulfill Cicero's originally misplaced suspicions). To begin with, though, he bided his time.

When Octavian asked Antony to make over the moneys promised in the Dictator's will so that he could pay out the various bequests, the Consul coolly responded that the funds belonged to the state and had, in any event, been spent. With a sharp eye on public relations, Octavian simply raised the necessary funds from his family and by loans.

The atmosphere in Rome grew tense and uneasy. Antony's popularity slid and he enlisted the services of veterans to keep public order. The Consuls, who had been squabbling, were now friends, for Dolabella, bribed (or so Cicero thought) by Antony, had changed sides and abandoned the constitutionalists. They had already dispossessed Brutus and Cassius of their original provincial allocations, with Antony taking over Macedonia and Dolabella Syria. But this was no longer enough for Antony, who decided that it was time to tackle Decimus Brutus head-on in Italian Gaul. With the help of the General Assembly, Antony engineered a further switch of his Consular province from Macedonia (taking the army there with him) to the two Gauls. This was an unusual maneuver, for according to convention it was the Senate that decided provincial appointments, and the move was seen as a blatant attempt to undermine Decimus Brutus. A land-distribution bill was also passed, which would please the demobilized soldiery. In place of their original provincial commands, Brutus and Cassius were given insultingly unimportant commissions to purchase corn, respectively, in Asia and Sicily.

Many moderates in the Caesarian camp, including the following year's Consuls-elect Hirtius and Caius Vibius Pansa Caetronianus, now agreed with Cicero that open hostilities were approaching. They did their best to stop the main players from provocations. When Hirtius heard that Brutus and Cassius were thinking of leaving Italy, to raise troops he suspected, he sent Cicero a desperate appeal to try to prevent them. "Hold them back, Cicero, I beg you, and don't let our society go down to ruin; for I swear it will be turned upside down in an orgy of looting, arson and massacre."

The conspirators' position was becoming increasingly uncomfortable and a conference was called in Antium to consider the situation. Cicero was invited to attend. He gave Atticus a long description of what was said. Those present included Brutus and Cassius, together with their wives. Brutus's mother and Julius Caesar's onetime lover, Servilia, was also in attendance. For many years this well-connected and astute matriarch had been an influential figure in Roman politics behind the scenes, and she was still in a position to pull strings when necessary.

Without revealing his source, Cicero passed on Hirtius's advice that Brutus should not leave Italy. A general conversation followed, full of recriminations about lost opportunities. Cicero remarked that he agreed with what was being said, but there was no point in crying over spilled milk. He then launched into a reprise of all his familiar views ("nothing original, only what everyone is saying all the time"): Antony should have been killed alongside Julius Caesar, the Senate should have met immediately after the assassination and so forth. He was doing exactly what he had just criticized the others for, and no doubt at much greater length. Servilia lost her temper. "Really, I've never heard anything like it!" This silenced Cicero and the gathering went on to debate, with little success, what should be done next. The only firm decision taken was that the official Games, which Brutus was financing in his capacity as Praetor, should go ahead in his absence. Servilia promised to use her good offices to get the corn commissions revoked.

"Nothing in my visit gave me any satisfaction except the consciousness of having made it," Cicero concluded. "I found the ship going to pieces, or rather its scattered fragments. No plan, no thought, no method. As a result, though I had doubts before, I am now all the more determined to escape from here, and as soon as I possibly can."

It would have been out of character if he had not delayed acting on his decision, and for the next month he nervously pondered the best route to take. The Macedonian legions being brought back to Italy by Antony would land at Brundisium, so he had better avoid the place. He worried that people might blame him for running away, but if he promised to return for the new year when Antony's Consulship would have finally ended, surely that would pacify his critics? Brutus had, after all, decided to leave the country and perhaps he would allow Cicero to accompany him. (In fact, he was not very enthusiastic.)

Despite his anxieties, Cicero insisted to Atticus that his underlying frame of mind was firm. He attributed his calmness to the "armorproofing" of philosophy and it is evidence of Cicero's creativity that he continued producing a flood of books and essays, including his treatise for Marcus, *Duties.* He monitored Octavian's activities with interest and suspicion. "Octavian, as I perceived, does not lack intelligence or spirit," he remarked to Atticus in June. "But how much faith to put in one of his years and name and heredity and education—that's a great question. . . . Still, he is to be encouraged and, if nothing else, kept away from Antony."

He found it shocking that Brutus's Games were advertised for "July," the new name in honor of Julius Caesar that had replaced the month of Quintilis. The Republican Sextus Pompey, who had survived the disaster at Munda, was running a fairly successful guerrilla war in Spain and it was thought he might march his forces to Italy against Antony. If he turned up, it would create an awkward dilemma for Cicero, for there would be no mercy for neutrals this time around. It may have come as a relief when news arrived later that Sextus Pompey had come to terms with an army led by Lepidus, the Dictator's onetime Master of the Horse.

On the domestic front, young Quintus wanted to get back into Cicero's good books. He claimed to have quarreled with Antony and to have decided to switch his allegiance to Brutus. Cicero did not believe a word of it. He asked Atticus: "How much longer are we going to be fooled?" More credibly, Quintus had apparently used his father's name without permission in some dubious financial transaction. (It may well be that shortage of funds was behind much of his political maneuvering and his efforts to regain his family's confidence.) He was still wife hunting and had found a possible candidate. His uncle was unimpressed: "I suspect he's romancing as usual."

As he was getting nowhere at a distance, Quintus decided to spend some days with Cicero at Puteoli and see what persuasion in person could achieve. He wanted an introduction to Brutus, which his embarrassed uncle could not decently refuse. Also he was anxious for a family reconciliation and Cicero wrote Atticus a dissembling letter in which he pretended to be convinced that the young man's reformation was sincere. He warned Atticus under separate cover that he had written in these terms only under pressure from Quintus and his father.

At long last, on July 17, Cicero set sail for Greece from his house in Pompeii in three ten-oared rowing boats. As he boarded, he was, of course, already having second thoughts. A long sea voyage would be fatiguing for a man of his age. (He was now 62.) The timing of his departure was unfortunate, for he was leaving peace behind him with the intention of returning when the Republic would very probably be at war. Also, he was going to miss his country estates. His financial affairs were in their usual state of disarray.

The little flotilla sailed at a comfortable speed down to Syracuse, from where it would set out west across the open sea. But a southern gale blew the boats back to the toe of Italy. Cicero stayed for a few days at a friend's villa near Regium and waited for more favorable weather. While he was there a local delegation returned from the capital on August 6 with some exciting news.

The story was that disorder on the streets of Rome and Octavian's ceaseless efforts to gain the public-relations initiative were shifting the Consul's policy again. Perhaps, after all, Antony was believed to think, his best bet would be to return to the March 17 settlement and align himself with moderate, antiwar Caesarians and the Senate. He delivered a speech in which he made some friendly references to the conspirators. A Senate meeting was called for August 1, which Brutus and Cassius begged all ex-Consuls to attend.

Cicero also learned, to his dismay, that people were commenting adversely on his absence. Atticus was having second thoughts too and, although he had endorsed Cicero's original plan to spend some time in Athens, now took him to task. Cicero decided to abandon the expedition. On his way back to Rome he met Brutus, who was in the southwest of Italy gathering ships in preparation for his departure for Macedonia. "You wouldn't believe how delighted he was at my return or rather my turning back!" Cicero told Atticus. "Everything he had held back came gushing out."

Unfortunately, the Republicans had been tempted by a false dawn. Caesar's father-in-law, Piso, who Cicero still believed had connived at his exile and whom he consequently loathed, launched a fierce attack on Antony at the August Senate meeting. He received no support, but, if a tentative rapprochement was being considered, this was enough to halt it in its tracks.

In fact, the idea had probably never been seriously viable. Octavian, or his advisers, was too canny to allow a complete breach with his competitor. Dealing with Antony was a balancing act: on the one hand the two were rivals for popularity with the army—that is, for Caesar's political succession, for whoever controlled the legions in the last analysis controlled Rome. On the other hand, it was essential not to drive the Consul back into the arms of the *optimates.* The task was to manage him, not to crush him.

At a personal level the two men had little in common. Antony, who was twenty years older than Octavian, was a playboy. He probably had no long-term strategy and seems not to have been particularly interested in avenging the Ides of March. He would react vigorously if prodded but preferred to live and let live. By contrast, Octavian had a colder personality and, although he told no one about it, intended to pursue the conspirators to the end. Yet, whether they liked it or not, the two men were obliged to cooperate. The legionnaires, aghast at their disagreements, forced a reconciliation and a special ceremony was held on the Capitoline Hill to mark the event.

Hopes of compromise dashed, Brutus and Cassius had finally made up their minds to abandon Italy, although their precise intentions after that were unclear. Servilia had evidently fulfilled her promise to work behind the scenes to get the corn commissions canceled and they had again been awarded new provinces, but they did not go to them. Instead, Brutus settled in Athens in the province of Macedonia where, hoping that the political situation would improve, he waited for as long as possible before determining whether or not to recruit an army. Cassius traveled to Syria (where he had been Quaestor in 51) with the idea of taking over the legions based in the region.

Cicero's return to Rome on August 31 echoed the excitement and applause of his return from exile thirteen years earlier. The crowds that poured out to meet him were so large that the greetings and speeches of welcome at the city gates and during his entry into the city took up most of a day. It would be wrong to exaggerate Cicero's influence, for he commanded no divisions, but his significance can also be undervalued. Perhaps he undervalued it himself; his letters show him to be much preoccupied with the preservation of his public standing, but they convey little awareness of his authority and influence.

That autumn a combination of factors conspired to give him real political influence for the first time since his Consulship. This was partly because he was one of the few senior statesmen of ability to have survived in a pollarded oligarchy. As Brutus had recognized when he called out Cicero's name at Pompey's theater, he stood for the best of the past, the old days and the old ways. People were beginning to fear a new breakdown of the fragile Republic and Cicero was the one man who had proclaimed the need for reconciliation throughout his career. His proven administrative ability and formidable skills as a public speaker were assets that few other politicians of the time could deploy.

But the most important factor was the change which seems to have taken place in his personality. He showed a new ruthlessness and clarity, as if iron had entered his soul. Perhaps it was simply that by the standards of the age Cicero was an old man and felt he had little to lose. Perhaps his immersion in philosophy had made him clearer about what was important and what could be jettisoned. In any case, step by step, he let himself be drawn towards the center of events and, to the surprise of those who knew him well, Brutus above all, showed himself willing to use unscrupulous and even unconstitutional methods to achieve his ultimate goal: the full, complete and permanent restoration of the Republic.

The day after Cicero's return Antony called a Senate meeting at which he would propose a new honor in Julius Caesar's memory. Cicero was working towards a coalition with moderate Caesarians including Hirtius and Pansa who revered the Dictator's memory. If he opposed the measure publicly he would unnecessarily offend them. So he pleaded exhaustion and kept to his bed.

Antony was furious. During the debate he launched an outspoken attack on Cicero, threatening to send housebreakers in to demolish his home on the Palatine. On September 2, in the Consul's absence, the Senate was reconvened and Cicero responded to the onslaught with the first of a series of speeches against Antony. He later nicknamed them his "Philippics" (after the Athenian orator Demosthenes' speeches against

Philip of Macedon) in a letter to Brutus, who for the time being was impressed by Cicero's new firmness and replied that they deserved the title.

Avoiding personal insults and using studiously moderate terms, he followed up Piso's criticisms a month earlier of Antony's unconstitutional activities and fraudulent use of Julius Caesar's papers. It was a well-judged address, carefully aimed at all who occupied the middle ground. The Consul well understood the threat it posed to his position and spent a couple of weeks in his country villa working up a counterblast. At a Senate meeting on September 19 he delivered a comprehensive onslaught on Cicero, who cautiously stayed away: he dissected his career, blaming him for the "murder" of Catilina's followers, the death of Clodius and the quarrel between Julius Caesar and Pompey. Antony's aim was to unite all the factions in Rome against Cicero and, above all, to show the veterans that here was the real contriver of their hero's downfall. If he failed, little in the way of a power base would be left to him in Rome and the affections of the legions would continue to slide toward Octavian. In a letter to Cassius, alluding to a tendency of Antony's to vomit in public (presumably when drunk), Cicero commented: "Everyone thought he wasn't speaking so much as spewing up."

Cicero settled safely in the countryside, where he spent the next month preparing the second of his Philippics, a lengthy, colorful but in the end unappealing invective against Antony, in which he reviewed the Consul's life episode by episode. Like the speeches against Verres, it was never delivered. He wanted it published, but Atticus doubtless advised against, and the work did not appear until after its author's death.

At about this time, Cicero learned that an old friend of his, Caius Matius, whom he nicknamed Baldy, was annoyed by some critical remarks he had reportedly made about him. Matius had been devoted to Julius Caesar and was one of the few who had worked for him without asking for any favors. He had been deeply upset by Caesar's assassination and had irritated Cicero by his constant prophecies of doom and, indeed, by the very fact of his grief.

In a carefully composed letter, Cicero defended himself but made it clear that he did think Caesar had been a despot. He dropped a broad hint that in his view the claims of freedom came before those of affection. Matius wrote a reply, so open in its emotions that it still has the power to touch the reader.

> I am well aware of the criticisms which people have leveled at me since Caesar's death. They make it a point against me that I take a friend's death so much to heart and am indignant that the man I loved has been destroyed. They say that country should come before friendship—as though they have already proved that his death was in the public interest. . . . It wasn't Caesar I followed in the civil conflict but a friend whom I did not desert, even though I didn't like what he was doing. I never approved of the civil war or indeed the origin of the conflict, which I did my very utmost to get nipped in the bud. . . . Why are they angry with me for praying that they may be sorry for what they have done? I want every man to be sorry for Caesar's death.

The letter is testimony to the magnetism of Caesar's personality. Cicero had once given in to it himself, but, as he entered this last exclusively public phase of his life, he was becoming impervious to the claims of private feeling. In *Duties,* which he was writing at the time, he made no concession to the genius of his great contemporary; he condemned the

> unscrupulous behavior of Caius Caesar who disregarded all divine and human law for the sake of the preeminence on which he had deludedly set his heart. . . . If a man insists on outcompeting everyone else, then it is hard for him to respect the most important aspect of justice: equality. Men of this type put up with no restraint by way of debate or due process; they emerge as spendthrift faction leaders, because they wish to acquire as much power as possible and would sooner gain the upper hand through force than fair dealing.

The entente between Antony and Octavian was short-lived, and the scene of action soon shifted from the Forum to the legionary camps. The Consul's rage at Cicero's first Philippic reflected a tacit acknowledgment that he could no longer depend on support from the Senate. His year of office was drawing to a close and his priority now was to establish himself in his province with a strong army. Otherwise, he would be politically marginalized. He decided to move at once to Italian Gaul, before his Consulship was over, and to seize it from Decimus Brutus, who was enlisting legions to add to the two already stationed there. For this purpose he needed soldiers and in early October he set out for Brundisium to pick up four legions he had ordered over from Macedonia.

At this point his plans faltered. While his back was turned, Octavian went to Campania and started recruiting veterans. It was completely illegal for someone who held no public office to raise a private army, although forty years previously Pompey had launched his career by doing so. Today's young adventurer, only nineteen years old, knew that unless he had troops behind him he would make no political headway. The appeal of his name and the added inducement of a hefty bribe of 2,000 sesterces per soldier was persuasive, and Octavian soon had a force of 3,000 experienced men at his disposal. The question now was what should he do with it.

Meanwhile, at Brundisium the Consul found his legions in truculent mood. He promised them only 400 sesterces for their loyalty. Aware of Octavian's much more generous offer, they booed him, left him standing while he was speaking to them and rioted. "You will learn to obey orders," was his savage response. Some judicious summary executions brought the soldiers to heel, but morale remained low.

What had been a political crisis was transforming itself into a phony war. The civilian leaders in Rome had no direct access to an army and were on the sidelines. The nearest loyal troops belonged to Decimus Brutus in Italian Gaul, but they were too few to pose an aggressive threat to anybody; he could only await the arrival of Antony, with some nervousness, behind the walls of the city of Mutina.

Between Antony and Octavian there was a standoff. The former was an experienced general and commanded a substantial force, but his soldiers would not follow him against Octavian. For its part Octavian's illegal army was growing, but he was no military match for the Consul.

Faced with this impasse, Octavian had to regularize his position somehow or he risked being marginalized by both Antony and the Senate. In all probability, Antony would march on Rome, impose a concordat of some sort and then proceed north to Italian Gaul to defeat Decimus Brutus and install himself safely in his province. In January there would be new Consuls, Hirtius and Pansa, who would be able to raise their own troops: this was unhelpful from Octavian's point of view because they were moderate Caesarians and likely to cooperate with the Senate. Meanwhile, there was no saying what Brutus and Cassius would be getting up to in Macedonia and Asia Minor. It was perfectly possible that they would raise armies and invade Italy if they thought the Republic was in danger.

So the young man and his advisers took what must have been an agonizing step, going against their deepest instincts. This was to ally themselves with the despised Republican leadership, which was only too happy to forget all about Octavian's adoptive father and had not the slightest intention of making the conspirators pay for his death. But the prize was worth the sacrifice, for, in return for helping the Senate deal with Antony, Octavian and his illegal army would receive official status.

It was at this moment that Octavian decided to approach Cicero: if he could only win over the leading personality in the Senate to his scheme, the other Republicans would follow.

At a safe distance from these alarms and excursions, Cicero continued to devote much of his time to literary pursuits. Besides *Duties,* he was working on a short dialogue, *Friendship,* dedicated to Atticus, as a complement to *Growing Old,* which he probably completed towards the end of November. In it he returned to the theme of his correspondence with Matius: the conflict between loyalty to one's friend and loyalty to the state. There was no easy answer, he decided, except that one should make sure that a friend deserved one's trust before giving it to him.

This principle was soon put to the test, for a proposal of friendship arrived from a startling source. On October 31 Cicero, who was staying in his villa at the seaside resort of Puteoli on the Bay of Naples, received a letter from Octavian in which he offered to lead the Republican cause in a war against Antony. The letter was delivered by a personal emissary, who brought the news that the Consul was marching on Rome. "He has great schemes afoot," Cicero wrote excitedly to Atticus. "So it looks to me as though in a few days' time we shall be in arms. But whom are we to follow? Think of his name; think of his age." It was an uninviting choice.

Octavian proposed a secret meeting and asked for Cicero's advice: should he anticipate the Consul, who would soon be returning from Brundisium with his troops, and march on Rome himself? In Cicero's opinion, a secret meeting was a childish idea because news of it would inevitably be leaked. He wrote back, explaining that it was neither necessary nor feasible; but he recommended that he go to the capital. He told Atticus: "I imagine he will have the city rabble behind him and respectable opinion too if he convinces them of his sincerity."

Octavian's approach was not a one-time advance; it quickly grew into a courtship. On November 4 Cicero reported that he was being pestered:

> Two letters for me from Octavian in one day. Now he wants me to return to Rome at once, says he wants to work through the Senate. I replied that the Senate could not meet before the Kalends of January, which I believe is the case. He adds "with your advice." In short, he presses and I play for time. I don't trust his age and I don't know what he's after.

The future for Republicans lay in splitting the partisans of Caesar. Moderates grouped around Hirtius and Pansa, the following year's Consuls, were likely to align themselves with Cicero and the constitutionalist majority in the Senate. In theory that would isolate Antony, increasingly desperate to find himself a safe provincial base, and Octavian, with his magical name. However, they both commanded the loyalty of the legions. Together they would be irresistible and it was essential that nothing be done to persuade them to overcome their differences and join forces.

Cooperation with Octavian would raise two difficult issues. If Cicero wanted to play this dangerous and delicate game, he would have to work with people who operated outside the constitution; he might even have to act unconstitutionally himself. However much he told himself that this would be for the greater good, dubious means might subvert virtuous ends. This was certainly the view of some of the conspirators, who were deeply suspicious of any accommodation with the new Caesar. The more immediate question was how far the young man was to be trusted. If his short-term interest was to align himself with Cicero and the Senate, what were his long-term aims? It seemed that the people around him, like Balbus and Oppius, shared the dead Dictator's belief that the Republican oligarchy was incompetent to run an empire and would have to give way to some kind of autocracy.

For the time being Cicero kept his distance. For some days he wondered nervously whether or not to join Octavian in Rome. He did not want to miss some great event; but then it might not be safe to leave the coast: Antony was approaching and Cicero could be cut off and at the Consul's mercy. On balance he felt that Octavian's project of taking his new troops to Rome was daring but ill considered. Nevertheless, he acknowledged Octavian's growing popularity and decided that he might, after all, go to the capital before January 1, as he had originally intended.

The march on Rome turned out to be the fiasco Cicero had feared. Undeterred by the absence of Senators, Octavian met the General Assembly and delivered an uncompromisingly anti-Republican speech. He gestured towards a statue of Caesar and swore under oath his determination to win his father's honors and status. But Antony was fast approaching and Octavian's troops made it clear they would not fight against him. Many deserted. His hopes dashed, he withdrew north to Arretium.

The setback was only temporary. Antony arrived in the city "in battle array" and, just as Octavian had done a few days earlier, illegally introduced troops inside the *pomoerium.* He called a Senate meeting for November 24, with the intention of charging Octavian with treason. However, for some reason the session was postponed. According to Cicero, Antony was drunk: "He was detained by a drinking bout and a feast—if you can call a blowout in a public house a feast." A more plausible explanation was that one of his legions had mutinied and transferred its allegiance to Octavian. As soon as he heard the news, the Consul rushed from Rome to confront the mutineers at a town named Alba Fucens; they would not listen to him and shot at him from the walls. Doubtless drawing on Caesar's hijacked fortune, Antony arranged a donation of 2,000 sesterces for every soldier to calm his remaining legions. He then returned to the city and reconvened the Senate, which met (against convention) by night at the Capitol.

A former Consul had been primed with a motion declaring Octavian a public enemy, but now Antony faced another disaster. The Fourth Legion also changed sides. The balance of power was shifting and Antony could no longer depend on a favorable vote in the Senate; even if he could win a majority, a Tribune would probably veto the bill. Some hurried business was pushed through: Brutus and Cassius had their latest provinces withdrawn again; a vote was passed to compliment Antony's ally Lepidus for coming to terms with Sextus Pompey, the Republic's standard-bearer in Spain; and Macedonia was allotted to Antony's brother, Caius.

After a military review the following day the Consul, who had been given a bad fright, left Rome and marched north. He still had four legions at his disposal. If he could have had his way, he would doubtless have preferred to finish off Octavian and encamped at Arretium, but he knew that his men would not have followed him. However, they were more than happy to fight any of Julius Caesar's assassins, so Antony led them to Mutina and Decimus Brutus. With the onset of winter no immediate developments were expected.

On December 9 Cicero at last made his way back to Rome from the country. Before setting off, he gave Atticus a summary of the political situation as he saw it. He was still cautious about Octavian, especially after receiving a copy of the speech he had given to the General Assembly on November 12.

> The boy is taking the steam out of Antony neatly enough for the moment, but we had best wait and see the issue. But what a speech—a copy was sent to me. Swears "by his hopes of rising to his father's honors," stretching his hand out towards the statue! Sooner destruction than this kind of a rescuer! But, as you say, the clearest test will be our friend Casca's Tribuneship. [Casca, one of the conspirators, was due to take up office on December 10 and Octavian's behavior towards him would be a test of his sincerity.] I told Oppius on that very subject, when he was pressing me to embrace the young man, not to mention his whole movement and band of veterans, that I could do nothing of the kind unless I was sure that he would be not only no enemy but a friend to the tyrannicides.

At this point the correspondence with Atticus closes. We do not know why. Atticus may have been in Rome for the rest or most of the rest of Cicero's life and so there would have been no need to write; alternatively the correspondence may in fact have continued but have been judged to be too controversial for publication and thus suppressed. As Emperor years later, Octavian may not have relished his maneuverings as Julius Caesar's heir being exposed to the public gaze.

In the absence of both Consuls (Dolabella had already left Rome for Asia, his province) a Tribune called a meeting of the Senate for December 20 to approve the appointment of an armed guard for the new Consuls,

Hirtius and Pansa, when they took up office on January 1. At first Cicero had not intended to be present, but, having read an edict by Decimus Brutus warning Antony to stay away from his province and announcing his allegiance to the Senate, he let it be known he would be there. He had encouraged Decimus Brutus to make a stand and, now that he was doing so, was determined to help him in any way he could.

There was no time to be lost. The Consul was moving as fast as he could to take over Italian Gaul before his successors could repudiate the legality of the law that had given him the province. He does not appear to have been acting unconstitutionally. After all, Decimus Brutus was soon due to hand over his powers to his successor. It should also be remembered that Antony (with his ally Dolabella) was head of the government with supreme executive powers. By the admittedly loose standards of the time he was within his rights to act as he did.

Cicero opened the debate at an unusually well-attended meeting with a powerful address, his third Philippic. He sought to demonstrate that Antony was an enemy of the state (arguably a treasonable assertion, bearing in mind that he was still Consul, if only for a few more days). He also argued that Octavian's position as the leader of a private army should be regularized. For the first time he referred to the young man not as Octavian but by his new patronymic. "Caesar on his own initiative—he had no alternative—has liberated the Republic." It sounded very much as if Cicero, despite all his misgivings, had at last decided to yield to the young man's advances and strike a deal.

The Senate accepted most of Cicero's advice but not all. It agreed that Antony was engaging in civil war but refused to outlaw him. It recognized Caesar and his army and confirmed all provincial governors in their posts until further notice, thereby overriding the following year's appointments.

In his speech Cicero made a passing reference to young Quintus. He had definitively broken with Antony, who accused him of plotting his father's and uncle's deaths. Cicero commented: "What amazing impudence, presumption and bravado! To dare to write this about a young man whose sweetness and excellence of character make my brother and me rivals in our love for him." The charge was routine slander and not to be taken seriously—but those who were aware of the dissensions inside the Cicero family will have smiled at this description of the orator's unreliable nephew.

Aware of the need to secure public opinion for the Republican side, Cicero made a point throughout this period of guiding the People through complex and confusing developments. Once the Senate meeting was over, he went on to give a rousing address (the fourth Philippic) to a packed General Assembly in the Forum, in which he said: "We have for the first time and after a long interval, on my advice and by my initiative, been fired by the hope of freedom." He compared Antony to Spartacus and, interestingly, to Catilina. As Consul in 63, Cicero had had Catilina condemned for raising a private army, but now he was using all his powers of persuasion to have a legally appointed Consul declared a public enemy and a freebooting young privateer its savior. The lifelong conservative was standing his convictions on their head. He did not notice the contradiction, or if he did thought it a matter of no consequence.

To the conspirator Trebonius, now in Asia as its governor, he wrote: "I did not mince my words, and, more by willpower than by oratorical skill, I recalled the weak and weary Senate to its old, traditional vigor. That day, my energy and the course I took, brought to the Roman People the first hope of recovering their freedom."

Without the letters to Atticus we no longer have a window into Cicero's mind, his private moods and doubts; but, so far as we can tell, the process of transformation that had begun with Cato's death was now reaching completion. Some twentieth-century historians have detected fanaticism and obsession in Cicero at this time, especially so far as his loathing of Antony is concerned. One certainly senses a coarsening of his personality, the obverse perhaps of his new decisiveness. This was the price Cicero was to pay for his return to power. Although he held no public office, the next six months saw him become the first man in Rome, with as great a dominance over the political scene as during his Consulship. The disappointments and humiliations of the intervening twenty years were behind him.

15

CICERO'S CIVIL WAR

Against Mark Antony: January–April 43 BC

January 43 opened with gales. Some tablets around the Temple of Saturn in the Forum were snapped off and scattered on the ground. An epidemic was reported across Italy and one of the new Consul's lictors fell down and died on his first day of office. A statue representing Honor was blown over and the little image of Minerva the Guardian, which Cicero had set up in the Temple of Jupiter on the Capitol before his departure for exile in 58, was shattered. These were sinister omens for the new, culminating phase of Cicero's career.

The Senate met starting on January 1 for three days to discuss the political situation. The new Consuls, Aulus Hirtius and Caius Vibius Pansa Caetronianus, took a loyally constitutionalist line, but they distrusted Cicero's extremism against Antony. Somewhat to Cicero's annoyance, Pansa, in the chair, called on his father-in-law, Quintus Fufius Calenus, to speak first. A supporter of Antony, Calenus argued for negotiation and proposed that a delegation be sent to meet the former Consul, who was now besieging Decimus Brutus at the town of Mutina in Italian Gaul. Antony's friends in Rome had been taken by surprise at the Senate meeting on December 20, but this time they had come prepared to launch a strong counterattack against their critics.

In his fifth Philippic, Cicero argued that this motion was pernicious and absurd. Antony's intentions were the reverse of peaceful and negotiations would be pointless. He went through the familiar catalog of sins. The blockade of Mutina was an act of war and he proposed that the Senate declare a state of military emergency. He then moved to another subject: honors. Votes of thanks should be passed in honor of Decimus Brutus and Lepidus and a gilt equestrian statue of Lepidus should be erected on the Speakers' Platform or elsewhere. This undistinguished but crucially placed Caesarian was now governor of Transalpine Gaul and Near Spain and commanded a substantial army; his loyalty was suspect and Cicero wanted to do all he could to bind him to the Senate.

Finally, Cicero came to Octavian, whom he called "this heaven-sent boy." Throwing constitutional proprieties to the winds, he proposed that he be coopted to the Senate and given Propraetor status (that is, as if he had served as Praetor and so was eligible for military command). "I happen to know all the young man's feelings," he claimed. "Members of the Senate, I promise, I undertake, I solemnly swear, that Caius Caesar will always be such a citizen as he is today and as we should especially wish and pray he should be."

This was a bold statement. If Cicero were not entirely convinced of Octavian's settled intentions, he would know it to be a dangerous hostage to fortune. He was too experienced a politician to have taken such a risk without having prepared the ground carefully; something must have happened in December to allay his fears and allow him to enter into a firm alliance.

Cicero had not lost his fondness for teaching and guiding young men. He had even offered his services earlier in the year as mentor to his disreputable former son-in-law, Dolabella, before his defection to Antony. Now Octavian joined the long line of these unofficial trainees and took to calling him "father." For all his early suspicions, Cicero must have been flattered by these respectful attentions.

Although he was popular with the legions, Octavian was in a weak position. The Caesarian faction, as we have seen, was split into three parts—the young man's own followers, moderates who fell into place behind the Consuls Hirtius and Pansa, and supporters of Antony—and there was little he could do to bring them back together for the moment. The agreement with Cicero and the Senate gave him official status. He would in all likelihood have calculated that if the Republicans triumphed it would be difficult, *pace* Cicero, to discard him entirely. After all, time was on his side and he could live to fight another day; if necessary he would work through the constitution rather than openly against it.

Cicero's speech was well received and he got much of what he asked for. The Senate had no difficulty in agreeing to the honors. Octavian was given Propraetorian rank and Antony's Land Reform Act was declared invalid. But the assembly agonized over whether or not to declare a state of emergency. Eventually, despite Cicero's advice to the contrary, it was agreed that a delegation would be sent to Antony. Three men were appointed to it: Piso, Philippus (Octavian's stepfather), and the distinguished, cautious jurist Servius Sulpicius. Sulpicius was terminally ill but felt that, having argued for negotiations, he was morally obliged to accept the commission. The envoys were to convey a series of demands: Antony was to submit to the Senate and People; he was to abandon the siege of Mutina; and he was to move his troops out of Italian Gaul into Italy but should not come closer than 200 miles from Rome. Their demands were more of an ultimatum than a negotiating position.

It was a sign of his growing dominance that Cicero rather than the Consuls was then summoned by a Tribune to report to the People gathered in the Forum on what had been decided. This he did in his sixth Philippic, in which he made his opposition to the delegation very clear. "I give you notice," he cried out. "I predict that Mark Antony will perform none of the commands which the envoys bring."

Cicero was now the energy and guiding force behind the government. He used all of his resources of persuasion to get his way. The Consuls were honorable men, ready to do their duty but not altogether certain what it was. In addition, Hirtius was in poor health. Nothing much was expected of them—certainly not by Quintus, who had campaigned with them in Gaul. In his usual choleric manner he told Tiro: "I know them through and through. They are riddled with lusts and languor, utter effeminates at heart." Quintus was exaggerating, for Hirtius and Pansa were soon to acquit themselves bravely on the battlefield, but in the Forum they were no match for Cicero, who liked to call them "my Consuls." The Senate contained few people of note and moderate opinion tended to follow where he led.

In addition to sending their official dispatches to the Senate, provincial governors and generals took care to inform Cicero of their activities. He spent much of his time writing them letters—chivying, cajoling, flattering, advising, briefing. He tried hard to cheer up the depressed and beleaguered Decimus Brutus. He paid particular attention to men of wavering loyalty—Titus Munatius Plancus and Lepidus in Gaul, Caius Asinius Pollio in Far Spain—and was in close touch with Brutus in Macedonia and Cassius in Asia Minor. He was not exaggerating when he told his friend Paetus: "My days and nights are passed in one sole care and occupation—the safety and freedom of my countrymen." In the same letter he showed that he still had time for private concerns and friendships. He twitted Paetus for having become rather antisocial for some reason.

> I am sorry to hear you've given up dining out. You have deprived yourself of a great deal of amusement and pleasure. Furthermore (you won't mind my being frank) I am afraid you will unlearn what little you used to know and forget how to give dinner parties. When I laid the facts before Spurinna [the *haruspex,* or official diviner of entrails, who had warned Julius Caesar of the danger of assassination] and explained to him how you used to live, he pronounced a grave danger to the supreme interests of the State unless you resume your former habits!

He was riding high but always had time to poke fun at a friend. In the middle of January it was decided that Hirtius should take command of the troops in Italy, while Pansa would be responsible for further levies. Octavian agreed to lead his army towards Mutina, where he would join forces with Hirtius. Preoccupied by their military tasks, the Consuls were not in a position to manage affairs in Rome and, despite the fact that he held no official post, Cicero acted more and more like a popular leader. There were frequent General Assemblies, at which he seems to have had remarkable success in winning support for his policies. He had arms manufactured by gathering craftsmen together and convincing them to work without pay. To finance the war he raised money and exacted heavy contributions from Antony's supporters. They in turn campaigned loudly against him, exploiting the public mood for peace and portraying him as hell-bent on a military confrontation. At a routine meeting of the Senate, Cicero took advantage of the rules of debate that allowed speakers to raise any subject they wished and launched into another Philippic (the seventh) in which he defended his record as a peacemaker but said that any compromise with Antony would be dishonorable. "I do not reject peace," he said, "but I am afraid of war disguised as peace."

Towards the end of the month the delegation to Antony returned without Sulpicius, who had died before reaching Mutina. Antony took advantage of the fact that the Senate was not treating him as an outlaw and tabled counterproposals. He would give up his claim to Italian Gaul, thus removing the threat to Decimus Brutus, but he insisted on retaining Long-haired Gaul with an army for five years. This would mean that Brutus and Cassius, who had the prospect of becoming Consuls in 41 and then being assigned post-Consular governorships, would have served their terms before he would have to lay down his arms. His political survival would be secured.

For Cicero, these terms had to be resisted, for their real consequence would be that the two leading followers of Caesar would be left in possession of armies and sooner or later might combine against the Senate. What looked like a personal obsession concealed a reasoned determination to keep the pair at loggerheads.

The Senate, under Pansa's chairmanship, rejected Antony's proposals and a motion for a second embassy was defeated. Opinion was hardening and war seemed inevitable. In a bid to ward off the greater evil, outlawry, Antony's supporters finally conceded that a state of emergency should be decreed. The following day Cicero delivered his eighth Philippic, in which he politely criticized Pansa for not having been firm enough with the opposition. Everyone knew there was a war on, he said, and it was ridiculous to suggest yet more talks. There could be no negotiations so long as Antony contrived to threaten Rome with his army. When a state of emergency was declared, all Senators except former Consuls were obliged to wear military uniform rather than their togas; despite the fact that he was excused, Cicero announced that he would follow the rule too. He proposed that anyone who switched sides from Antony to the Consuls before the Ides of March that year would be granted an amnesty and that anyone who joined him would be deemed to have acted against the interests of the state. On the following day, in his ninth Philippic, Cicero celebrated Servius Sulpicius's career and persuaded the Senate to vote him a bronze statue in the Forum.

Cicero's policy did not win universal support and he was regarded by some middle-of-the-road Senators as a warmonger, but he held to it unswervingly, seeing his critics as without energy and without principle. The prize was within grasp. He wrote to Cassius in February: "If I am not in error, the position is that the decision of the whole war depends entirely on D. Brutus. If, as we hope, he breaks out of Mutina, it seems unlikely that there will be any further fighting."

Cicero had other grounds for optimism. After Marcus Brutus left Italy the previous year he settled in Athens and gave the impression that he had abandoned politics for literary and philosophical pursuits. He attended lectures at the Academy. He was genuinely unenthusiastic for war and for a time waited and watched on events in Rome; he wanted to do nothing that would give his enemies any pretext for action.

With the situation in Italy deteriorating, however, he decided he had to act. He took possession of the province of Macedonia, which had originally been promised him by Julius Caesar and was now being claimed by Marcus Antony's brother, Caius. He was helped in this endeavor by the outgoing governor, Quintus Hortensius Hortalus, the famous orator's son and a close relative of his. Once Brutus had made up his mind, he moved with speed and efficiency and sent an agent to win over the legions based in the province. He recruited the 22-year-old Marcus Cicero, who happily abandoned his studies and accepted a military command. He intercepted the Quaestors of Asia and Syria on their homeward journey and persuaded them to hand over the tax revenues they were taking back to Rome. Caius Antonius was soon under siege in the town of Apollonia. By the end of the year Brutus was in control of most of the province.

In February he sent an official dispatch to the Senate setting out what had happened and reporting that Hortensius had handed the province over to him. This presented Cicero with a tricky problem: the allocation of governorships since Julius Caesar's assassination had been altered so many times, and on occasion with dubious legality, that it was hard to say who was entitled to what. However, Cicero had to acknowledge that one thing at least was clear: Brutus no longer had any legal right to Macedonia. Nevertheless, in the tenth Philippic he successfully persuaded the Senate to confirm Brutus in place. He argued, not unreasonably, that

Caius Antonius's allegiance would not be to the Senate but to his brother, who would use the province as his refuge if he were defeated at Mutina. Once again, Cicero was abandoning the rule of law for realpolitik.

Meanwhile, Cassius had managed to take over the troops in Syria as well as those which Julius Caesar had left behind in Egypt—in total, eleven legions. On March 7 he sent a report to this effect to Cicero, adding: "I want you to know that you and your friends and the Senate are not without powerful supports, so you can defend the state in the best of hope and courage."

Cassius would now have to deal with Dolabella, his rival claimant to Syria, who had arrived in the region. Decisive action was all the more necessary as Dolabella had recently murdered Caius Trebonius, the governor of the neighboring province of Asia (western Turkey). Dolabella had wanted to pass through Asia on his way to Syria, but Trebonius refused to let him into the port of Smyrna, where he was based. The town was only lightly defended and Dolabella broke in by night. He captured Trebonius and tortured him for two days with a whip and rack before having him beheaded. Some soldiers kicked his head around like a football.

The Senate was shocked and, with a rare unanimity, condemned the crime. Dolabella was declared a public enemy. But what could be done to arrest and punish him? Two motions were debated—one that a distinguished elder statesman should be given a special command to lead a campaign against Dolabella and the other that Hirtius and Pansa should be appointed governors of Syria and Asia for the following year. In his eleventh Philippic, Cicero opposed both proposals, saying that the matter should be left to Cassius, who was on the spot. But, as one of the leading conspirators, Cassius was a controversial figure and moderate Caesarians were offended. The Senate decided to give the Consuls the commission, once they had defeated Antony.

This was a setback for Cicero, but with cheery unconcern he wrote to Cassius advising him to act on his own initiative. This was, in fact, exactly what he did. It did not take him long to hunt Dolabella down. The clever young opportunist realized that he had run out of opportunities and, perhaps fearing he would be given the same treatment he had meted out to Trebonius, had the good sense to commit suicide before being captured. Seeing that his position was hopeless, he asked a bodyguard to cut off his head. The man who had charmed Tullia clearly knew how to win the affection of those around him, for, having obeyed the order, the soldier then turned the sword against himself.

In Italy, Antony's supporters made a last desperate attempt to avert war. In Rome, Pansa put a motion before the Senate for yet another embassy, reporting that Antony was now pessimistic about his prospects and would be willing to make concessions. Cicero agreed to join a negotiating team of five ex-Consuls, but for some reason the project was abandoned after further discussion. In his twelfth Philippic Cicero regretted having agreed to be an envoy. He told the Senate that his duty lay elsewhere. "If I may, I will remain in the city. Here is my place. Here I keep watch. Here I stand sentinel. Here is my guardhouse." The speech is interesting because it confirms that clemency was a discredited policy of the past. We learn that Antony had, in the event of victory, already decided to confiscate Cicero's property and give it to a supporter. The orator's life would almost certainly have been forfeit too. In this civil war there would be no pardons.

In late March, Lepidus and Plancus wrote letters from their provinces in Spain and Gaul urging peace. The former implied that he would join forces with Antony if his advice was not heeded. This was potentially a serious threat. On the same evening Cicero sent firm replies, and in Lepidus's case struck a distinctly brusque note. "In my opinion, you will be wiser not to meddle in a kind of peacemaking which is unacceptable to the Senate and the People—and to every patriotic citizen." However, it was important not to give needless offense. At a Senate meeting called on April 9 to discuss the letters, Cicero moved a vote of thanks for Plancus. On the following day he seconded another for Lepidus, to which a rider was attached warning the governor to leave questions of peace to the Senate. This was his thirteenth Philippic, in which he also dealt with a long dispatch which Antony had sent Hirtius and Octavian.

Antony's dispatch was a very dangerous document, for it exposed Cicero's policy of divide-and-rule with devastating clarity. It was written with passionate candor and had a ring of despair, as though Antony was at the end of his tether. He presented himself as the dead Dictator's only sincere avenger and the letter must have made (as was surely intended) uncomfortable reading for Octavian. Antony made it threateningly clear that Lepidus was his ally and Plancus

> the partner of my counsels. . . . Whichever of us is defeated, our enemies will be the beneficiaries. So far Fortune has avoided such a spectacle, not wanting to see two armies of one body fighting each other under the supervision of Cicero in his role as a trainer of gladiators. He has deceived you with the same verbal trickery he has boasted he used to deceive Julius Caesar.

Cicero took the Senate through Antony's charges one by one, using them to demonstrate his treasonable intentions. But the length and detail of his rebuttal and a certain shrillness of tone betrayed his unease. The dispatch may well have disturbed waverers, especially among moderate Caesarians. Fortunately for Cicero, events had traveled too far to be undone.

A few days later battle commenced outside Mutina. On April 14 Antony led his army to intercept Pansa's four newly recruited legions before they managed to join the other Republican forces already in the field. In order to keep these at bay he organized a simultaneous attack on their camp, not knowing that Hirtius had already sent Pansa the experienced Martian Legion the night before.

Antony laid a trap. He kept his legions hidden in a village named Forum Gallorum and showed only his cavalry. The Martian Legion and some other troops moved forward without orders, marching through marsh and woodland. Antony suddenly led his forces out of the village before Pansa could bring up his legions.

The mood among the soldiers of both sides was somber; instead of uttering their usual battle cries, they fought in grim silence. Surrounded by marshes and ditches it was difficult to charge or make flanking movements. Unable to push each other back, the two sides, as the historian Appian writes, were "locked together with their swords as if in a wrestling contest." When a man fell he was carried away and another stepped forward to take his place.

Eight cohorts of the Martian Legion repulsed Antony's left wing and advanced about half a mile, only to find their rear attacked by his cavalry. Pansa was wounded in the side by a javelin and his inexperienced army was routed. But Hirtius had anticipated Antony's tactics and, leaving Octavian to guard the camp, arrived with some veteran troops in support. They came too late to prevent the defeat, but were in time to fall on Antony's triumphant but disordered troops, on whom they inflicted heavy casualties.

A week later Hirtius, assisted by Decimus Brutus, who organized a sortie from Mutina, defeated Antony again and raised the siege of the town. Antony's only hope now was to escape north with what was left of his army to the protection of Lepidus in Gaul, assuming that that weak but canny man would be willing to associate himself with an obviously lost cause.

A false report of an Antonian victory arrived in Rome and people fled from the city. It was rumored that, to meet the crisis, Cicero intended to become Dictator, a charge he furiously denied. When the truth about the first battle became known, the city erupted in celebrations. Cicero wrote to Brutus in Macedonia:

> I reaped the richest of rewards for my many days of labor and sleepless nights—if there is any reward in true, genuine glory. The whole population of Rome thronged to my house and escorted me up to the Capitol, then set me on the Speakers' Platform amid tumultuous applause. I am not a vain man, I do not need to be; but the unison of all classes in thanks and congratulations does move me, for to be popular in serving the People's welfare is a fine thing.

Cicero had every reason to be proud of himself. The Caesarian faction was broken. Antony was out of the game and time-servers like Lepidus and Plancus would quickly come to heel. Brutus and Cassius controlled the eastern half of the empire. All that needed to be done now was some mopping up: Cicero wrote to Plancus on May 5, asking him to make sure that "not a spark of this abominable war is left alive."

The only hostile, or potentially hostile, piece left on the board was Octavian, who was locked into the Republican cause. Cicero expected trouble from him but felt he could handle it. He told Brutus: "As for the boy Caesar, his natural worth and manliness is extraordinary. I only pray that I may succeed in guiding and holding him in the fullness of honors and favor as easily as I have done hitherto. That will be more difficult, it is true, but still I do not despair."

It had been a close-run thing, but Cicero's strategy had worked: the Republic was saved.

16

DEATH AT THE SEASIDE

The End of the Republic: April–November 43 BC

As so often happens in human affairs, fate intervened at the moment of victory and destroyed the best-laid plans. It soon emerged that Hirtius had been killed in the second battle at Mutina, and Pansa died of the wound incurred in the first. This created a power vacuum at the worst possible moment. The absence of Consuls left Rome in disarray. There would have to be elections and in the meantime the Republic was without an effective executive authority. In the field Pansa's troops went over to Octavian. He stayed where he was and refused to have anything to do with Decimus Brutus, the ally for whom he had fought at Mutina and, as he had not forgotten, one of his adoptive father's assassins. He left Decimus Brutus and his forces to chase after the fleeing Antony on their own.

To Cicero's annoyance and disappointment, Decimus Brutus made little progress. He wrote in extenuation that his "apology for an army" had hardly recovered from the privations of a siege. He had no cavalry and no pack animals. He was short of money. Also, although he did not admit this to Cicero, he was alarmed by the growing strength of Octavian's military position and may not have wanted to see the young man's only effective military rival in the west destroyed for good. Soon Antony joined forces with a supporter of his who had been raising troops in central Italy on his behalf: he was now back in charge of a powerful force and made his way north with greater confidence towards Lepidus. If he could win Lepidus (and Plancus in Long-haired Gaul) to his side, the defeat of Mutina would be reversed.

It took some time for the Senate to take in the significance of the loss of its Consuls. One of Cicero's correspondents, surveying the scene at a distance, wrote wisely that those who were rejoicing at the moment "will soon be sorry when they contemplate the ruin of Italy." However, for the moment the constitutionalists could think only of victory. In his fourteenth and last Philippic, Cicero called for an official Thanksgiving to last for an unprecedented period of fifty days. Antony was finally declared a public enemy. Decimus Brutus was voted a Triumph. There were to be ceremonies and a monument to honor the fallen. Cassius was confirmed in place in Asia Minor and Sextus Pompey, still in Spain with his guerrilla forces, was given a naval command.

Careful thought should have been given to Octavian's position, but it was not. He was an ally of the Senate and had played his part, a minor one though useful for all that, in the battles at Mutina. But would he continue to obey its orders? The answer to that question depended on whether his rapprochement with Cicero was sincere or tactical. Whatever the leadership in Rome might propose, he disposed of the only significant army in Italy and was now at last in a position to act as he pleased. He could see that he was stronger than Antony—but was it really in his interest to see him swept away? If Brutus and Cassius were to come to Italy with their seventeen legions, he might wonder what his fate would be.

It would have been wise to placate him, but the Senate took the contrary view. It was reluctant to grant him the same honors as Decimus Brutus and excluded them both from membership of a commission established to distribute land allotments to the veterans who (it was presumed) would soon be demobilized. The Senate ruled that the commissioners should deal directly with the soldiers and not go through their commanders. It also reduced their promised bonuses. These were extraordinarily shortsighted measures, for they were bound to irritate rank-and-file opinion, which was fundamentally Caesarian. The Senators must have known this but presumably thought it did not matter. So far as they were concerned the war was over.

Cicero saw the dangers in this attitude and tried to have both generals appointed as commissioners, but the Senate, complacent now that the crisis was over, was less willing to do his bidding than it had used to be. He praised Octavian as highly as the other generals, despite the fact that he had played a subordinate role in the fighting. He proposed an Ovation for him, but it is not certain that the motion was passed.

Completely unexpectedly, Cicero's policy was on the verge of collapse. Critics, even friendly critics, began to speak openly of the unwisdom of his cultivation of the young Caesar. In the middle of May an anxious Marcus Brutus wrote to him from Macedonia about reports that the young man was seeking the Consulship. "I am alarmed," he commented. "I fear that your young friend Caesar may think he has climbed too high through your decrees to come down again if he is made Consul. . . . I only wish you could see into my heart, how I fear that young man."

Privately, Brutus was increasingly unhappy about his friend's behavior. He confided his feelings to Atticus, in a letter one hopes its subject never read. His judgment was that Cicero was swayed by vanity. "We're not bragging every hour of the day about the Ides of March like Cicero with his Nones of December [the date in 63 when he put down the Catilinarian conspiracy]." The kernel of Brutus's complaint was that Cicero was too eager to please.

> You may say that he is afraid even now of the remnants of the civil war. So afraid of a war that is as good as over that he sees no cause for alarm in the power of the leader of a victorious army and the rashness of a boy? Or does he do it just because he thinks the boy's greatness makes it advisable to lay everything at his feet without waiting to be asked? What a foolish thing is fear! . . . We dread death and banishment and poverty too much. For Cicero I think they are the ultimate evils. So long as he has people from whom he can get what he wants and who give him attention and flattery he does not object to servitude if only it be dignified—if there is any dignity in the sorriest depth of humiliation.

This is a powerful indictment, but it is not all there is to be said about the matter. It is true that Cicero was nervous and lacking in physical courage—but with the saving grace that he knew it, admitting that he was "susceptible to scares." He was prone to seesaws of emotion and longed for compliments, of which he felt he did not receive nearly enough. But although his connection with Octavian fed his self-esteem, it was also based on a sound analysis of the political situation. Brutus's judgment was distorted by his irritation with Cicero's personality and he failed to understand that the only card Cicero had left in his hand was his relationship with Octavian, who might otherwise join forces with Antony so that he could be strong enough to deal with any conflict that might arise with Brutus and Cassius. Somehow or other he had to be charmed into staying loyal to the Republic. This was the essential priority and whatever had to be done to achieve it, however embarrassing and disagreeable, had to be done.

If the Consuls had survived and his strategy had succeeded, as it very nearly did, Cicero's attitude towards Octavian would surely have been very different, for his usefulness to the Senate as its protector against Antony would have been at an end. In this connection it was most unfortunate that Octavian learned his "father's" true intentions. Never one to avoid careless talk if a witty remark or a pun occurred to him, Cicero had observed that "the young man must get praises, honors—and the push." The Latin is *laudandum, ornandum, tollendum;* the last word had a double meaning: to "exalt" and to "get rid of." Towards the end of May, Decimus Brutus warned Cicero that someone had reported this joke to the young man, who had been unamused, commenting tersely that he had no intention of letting that happen.

Cicero watched, exhausted, as the edifice he had laboriously constructed during the previous six months was gradually demolished. In early June he wrote to Decimus Brutus: "What is the use? Believe me, Brutus, as one not given to self-deprecation, I am a spent force. The Senate was my weapon and it has fallen to pieces." He realized that for all his struggles the constitution was dead and power lay in the hands of soldiers and their leaders.

Lepidus, claiming he had been forced into it by his men, switched allegiance to Antony and was followed by Plancus and then Pollio. The supposedly loyal army in Africa was recalled to Rome (a desperate measure, for its commander, Titus Sextius, was a Caesarian) and a legion of new recruits was formed. Frantic appeals were sent to Brutus in Macedonia to come home, but he knew better than to accede to them. He still hoped to avoid civil war; this was why he was keeping Caius Antonius alive as a hostage, despite Cicero's obdurate appeals for his execution. He knew that safety lay in joining forces with Cassius and marched off eastwards to meet him. An invasion of Italy would be practicable only with their combined forces. For the time being, the Senate was on its own.

Throughout July, Cicero bombarded Brutus fruitlessly with letters begging him to intervene. He continued bravely, or obstinately, to defend his policy. "Our only protection was this lad," he insisted. But in the end he was compelled to admit that he had failed. "Caesar's army, which used to be excellent [i.e., loyal], is not only no help but forces us to ask urgently for *your* army."

Octavian's likely defection from the Republican cause was clear enough for any intelligent observer to predict, hence the appeals for help. However, Cicero must have felt he had no choice but to assume his trustworthiness until he had definite evidence otherwise. The two men stayed in touch.

Brutus was unimpressed by Cicero's explanations and when he saw an excerpt from a letter he had written to Caesar, passed on to him by Atticus, he delivered a magisterial rebuke.

> You thank him on public grounds in such a fashion, so imploringly and humbly—I hardly know what to write. I am ashamed of the situation, of what fortune has done to us, but write I must. You commend our welfare to him. Better any death than such welfare! It is a downright declaration that there has been no abolition of despotism, only a change of despot. Read over your words again and then dare to deny that these are the pleadings of a subject to his king.

On July 25 Servilia, Brutus's mother, invited Cicero to an informal council of war and asked him for his advice as to whether they should try to persuade Brutus to return to Rome. Cicero said in the firmest terms that Brutus should "lend support to our tottering and almost collapsing commonwealth at the earliest possible moment." In his last surviving (and perhaps his last actual) letter to Brutus on July 27, he reported this conversation in a further futile attempt to change his mind. Although he tried to be positive, he was obviously dispirited and gloomy. For the first time he admitted that the solemn oath he had sworn in the Senate at the beginning of January, guaranteeing Caesar's good behavior, was no longer deliverable. "As I write I am in great distress because it hardly looks as though I can make good my promises in respect to the young man, boy almost, for whom I stood bail to the Republic."

The rumors of Octavian seeking the Consulship turned out to be well grounded. According to Appian, he no longer troubled to communicate with the Senate but dealt privately with Cicero. He invited Cicero to join him in the Consulship—an echo of the far-off days when his adoptive father had tried to recruit the orator to join the First Triumvirate. It is possible that on this occasion Cicero was tempted to say yes, although a letter of the time to Brutus indicates otherwise. He claimed that "as soon as I had an inkling of [his wish to be Consul], I wrote him letter after letter of warning and taxed those friends of his who seemed to be backing his ambition to their faces, and I did not scruple to expose the origins of these criminal designs in the Senate." The Senate was reluctant to give way to Octavian and postponed the elections. There was talk of a compromise that would allow him to stand as Praetor, but the sop was insufficient.

Not without reason, the families of the conspirators suspected that if he became Consul, the Dictator's heir would launch a proscription. People were coming to believe that his alliance with the Republicans had been a pretense. He meant to avenge his father's murder and restore his autocracy; no doubt it had been his secret policy all along.

In August, for the second time in a year, Octavian marched on Rome at the head of eight legions. He sent a flying force in advance, which entered the city and met the Senate. The soldiers made three demands: the Consulship, restoration of the bounty for the troops and, a sinister token of his future intentions, the repeal of the decree of outlawry against Antony. In the context of people's fears, this was a comparatively modest request. It looked as if there would not, after all, be a proscription.

Some Senators lost their tempers and apparently struck the soldiers. One of the soldiers fetched his sword and touched it, saying: "If you don't give Caesar the Consulship, this will." Cicero replied dryly: "If *that's* the way you ask for something, I am sure you're right."

Reluctant to face reality, the Senate would not be moved. Then, as Octavian approached, it panicked and issued a flurry of edicts, allowing him to stand for the Consulship *in absentia,* doubling the original army bonus, winding up the contentious Land Commission and transferring its powers to Octavian. But there was no stopping the young man now and he continued his advance.

With the arrival in Rome of the legions from Africa there was a flurry of resistance. The city planned for a siege, but the soldiers refused to fight and declared for the young Caesar. The next day he entered the city protected by a bodyguard. Even his opponents came out to greet him. The Urban Praetor, the Republic's senior public official following the deaths of the Consuls, killed himself; this was the only bloodshed recorded.

Cicero arranged to meet Octavian and reportedly raised the now dead question of the joint Consulship. The "heaven-sent boy" did not bother to make a direct response. He simply remarked, with mocking regret, that Cicero had been the "last of his friends" to greet him.

A flame of hope briefly flared and died down again. A rumor spread through the city that two of Octavian's legions were preparing to defect. Senators met at dawn at the Senate House with Cicero welcoming them at the door. As soon as it transpired that there was nothing to the story he slipped away on a litter. On August 19 the Consular elections were held and the youngest Consul in Rome's history took office with Quintus Pedius, a little-regarded relative of Julius Caesar, as his colleague in office. He had not reached his twentieth birthday. Now that he had power he was not slow to act. Dolabella was rehabilitated, Julius Caesar's assassination was declared a crime and a special tribunal was appointed to try the conspirators.

Cicero was given permission to stay away from Senate meetings and his last surviving written words are an unheroic fragment of a letter to the new Consul. "I am doubly delighted that you have given Philippus [his neighbor at Puteoli and Octavian's stepfather] and me leave of absence; for it implies forgiveness for the past and mercy for the future." He probably stayed at Tusculum and for the time being disappears from view. It is curious that he did not try to leave the country and escape to Brutus. Perhaps he was under surveillance. More probably he simply lost heart.

Octavian left Rome and went back north at a leisurely pace, ostensibly to campaign against Antony. However, there was to be no more fighting. Octavian's Consular colleague stayed in Rome and reversed the condemnations of Antony and Lepidus (who had also been declared a public enemy). Formal negotiations now opened to reunite the Caesarian factions which Cicero's strategy had divided.

Antony and Octavian had every reason to distrust each other, but the logic of events drove them together. To deal with the challenge from Brutus and Cassius in the east, they were obliged to pool their resources. They gingerly marched their armies towards each other and met on a small island in a river at Bononia (today's Bologna). Antony on one bank and Octavian on the other walked forward with 300 men each to bridges leading to the island. Lepidus went on ahead to conduct a search for hidden weapons and gave an all-clear by waving his cloak. The three men then met alone in talks that lasted for two or three days, working from dawn to dusk. Before sitting down they searched one another to make sure that no one had brought a dagger with him.

They agreed to appoint themselves as a three-man Constitutional Commission (which historians have called the Second Triumvirate) charged with the familiar duty of restoring the Republic. Their mandate was to last for five years. It was as if the old alliance of the First Triumvirate had returned in a new guise, but, unlike the private agreement among Pompey, Julius Caesar and Crassus in the 50s, the Commission was formally established in due course by the General Assembly and was, in effect, a triple Dictatorship. Of course, reform was the last thing on the Commissioners' minds. Antony and Octavian (with Lepidus as a junior partner) had formed a coalition of convenience. Their priorities were to allocate provincial commands to themselves and assemble the forces necessary to defeat Brutus and Cassius.

The Commissioners were short of ready cash and needed to fundraise. They also had to consider what to do with the defeated Republican opposition in Rome. There was one solution that would solve both problems: a proscription. A good deal of time on the island was spent haggling over names. More than 130 Senators (perhaps as many as 300) and an estimated 2,000 *equites* were marked down for execution and property confiscation. Huge rewards were offered for anyone who killed a proscribed man—100,000 sesterces for a free man and 40,000 sesterces for a slave.

For members of the Roman ruling class, such as remained, history seemed to be repeating itself. They knew what to expect, for some of them could recall fearfully the last proscription conducted by Sulla nearly forty years previously. However, that dark moment in the history of the Republic had at least been followed by a rapid return to (more or less) constitutional government. Few people could be confident that this time around the three Commissioners would, like Sulla, step down voluntarily and retire into private life. What looked far more likely were further years of war as the reunited Caesarians fought it out with Brutus and Cassius in the east for final mastery.

During the following weeks new names were added to the original list—some because they were genuine political opponents, but others simply because they had been a nuisance or were friends of enemies or enemies of friends or, most appositely, were known to be rich. Appian writes: "The point was reached where a person was proscribed because he had a fine town house or country estate." Verres, Cicero's old adversary, whom he had prosecuted for corruption in Sicily a quarter of a century before, was still alive and a collector of valuable Corinthian bronze artifacts; it was said that Antony had him proscribed when he refused to part with any of them.

In a thoroughly un-Roman betrayal of family loyalties and the ties of *amicitia,* each Commissioner agreed to abandon friends and relatives. Lepidus allowed his brother Paulus to be marked down, Antony an uncle of his (although both ultimately survived) and Octavian a man reported to have been his guardian. Cicero was proscribed along with the rest of his family. It was claimed that Octavian fought to keep his name off the list for two days, but the vindictive Antony insisted. This account may have been propaganda, for Octavian will not have forgotten Cicero's self-betraying remark about him, "*Laudandum, ornandum, tollendum,*" and this may have strengthened a resolve to see an end to the troublesome old man. If the last of the orator's young disciples had genuine feelings of affection for him, they probably did not run deep: with Octavian personal ties took second place to public expediency.

Cicero and his brother were at Tusculum when they heard about the proscription. They moved at once to the villa at Astura about thirty miles away on the coast (and forty miles or so from Rome), planning to sail to Macedonia and join Brutus. They were carried on their way in litters—a journey that could be accomplished in a long day. According to Plutarch, "they were quite overwhelmed with grief and on the journey would often stop and, with the litters placed side by side, would condole with each other." Quintus suddenly realized that he had brought no cash with him and Cicero too had insufficient funds for the journey. So Quintus volunteered to go back home, get what was needed and catch up with Cicero later. The brothers hugged each other and parted in tears.

The decision to return was disastrous. Bounty hunters were already on the family's trail and Quintus was betrayed by servants. His son was either with him or within reach: according to one account, he found a hiding place for his father and, when tortured to reveal its whereabouts, did not utter a syllable. As soon as Quintus was told about this, he came out into the open and gave himself up. Each man begged to be killed first. The conflicting requests were reconciled, for they were taken away to separate parties of executioners and, on an agreed signal, put to death simultaneously.

During the civil war both father and son had tried in their different ways to extricate themselves from Cicero's clouded fortunes, but they had been unable to escape his ruin. The brothers had been reconciled, at least on the surface, and, whatever their disagreements about Julius Caesar, they both unhesitatingly backed the last surviving defenders of the Republican cause. Young Quintus was a clever but unsympathetic figure. However (if we can believe the story of his last days, as recounted by late sources), it is touching to see him behave for once with courage and unselfishness.

Meanwhile, Cicero reached Astura and, presumably after waiting vainly for Quintus or having received news of his capture, found a boat. He sailed twenty miles south to the headland of Circaeum. There was a following wind and the pilots wanted to continue their journey, but Cicero insisted on disembarking and walked about twelve miles in the direction of the Appian Way, the road to Rome.

His motives are unclear. Plutarch offers various alternative explanations. One is that he was afraid of the sea. It was true that Cicero disliked sea voyages, but in the past that had not prevented him from sailing; in 44 he got as far as Syracuse on his abortive escape to Greece. Plutarch also suggests that he had not entirely lost his faith in Octavian and thought he could negotiate a pardon; and conversely, that one idea he had was to go secretly to Octavian's home, presumably in Rome or perhaps at a country villa, and kill himself on the hearthstone—this would be so grave a pollution that it would bring down a curse from heaven on its owner. Fear of being caught and tortured might have decided Cicero against this course of action. Whatever his motive, he lost his resolution, perhaps fearing he would be recognized on the Appian Way, and turned back to Astura, where he spent a sleepless night, according to Plutarch, with his mind "full of terrible thoughts and desperate plans."

He now put himself in the hands of his servants and they took him by sea to his villa about sixty miles south at Caeta, near Formiae, which in happier days he had used as a refreshing retreat in the heat of summer. In Plutarch's account, as the boat was being rowed to land, a flock of crows approached, cawing loudly. They perched on both ends of the yardarm and pecked at the ends of the ropes. Despite the fact that everyone thought this to be a bad omen, Cicero disembarked and went to the house to lie down and rest. He is reported to have said, rather grandly: "I will die in the country I have so often saved." According to Plutarch:

> Then most of the crows perched around the window, making a tremendous cawing. One of them flew down to the bed where Cicero was lying with his head all covered up, and little by little began to drag the garment away from his face with its beak. When the servants saw this they reproached themselves for standing by as spectators waiting for their master to be murdered, and doing nothing to defend him, while these wild brute creatures were helping him and caring for him in his undeserved ill fortune. So partly by entreaty and partly by force, they took him up and carried him in his litter towards the sea.

They were too late. A small party of men, led by a Military Tribune, Popilius Laenas, whom Cicero had once successfully defended in a civil case, and a centurion, Herennius, arrived at the villa. Finding the doors bolted, they broke them down, but those inside disclaimed all knowledge of their master's whereabouts.

Then a young freedman of Quintus named Philologus, whom Cicero had educated, told Popilius that Cicero's litter was being carried towards the sea along a path hidden by trees. In a flanking movement, Popilius went around to the shore where he could meet the party when it came out of the woods. Meanwhile Herennius hurried along the path. Cicero heard him coming and told his servants to put down the litter. This was the end and he was no longer going to run away.

He was reclining in a characteristic posture, with his chin resting on his left hand. He had a copy of Euripides' *Medea* with him, which he had been reading. He would have been familiar with this drama of bitter revenge, in which a woman kills her children to spite her faithless husband. His eyes may have fallen on lines near the beginning of the play: "But now everything has turned to hatred and where love was once deepest a cancer spreads."

He looked terrible: he was covered in dust, his hair was long and unkempt, his face pinched and worn with anxiety. He drew aside the curtain of his litter a little and said: "*I* am stopping here. Come here, soldier. There is nothing proper about what you are doing, but at least make sure you cut off my head *properly.*" Herennius trembled and hesitated. Cicero added, supposing that the man had already killed other victims and should by now have perfected his technique: "What if you'd come to me first?" He stretched his neck as far as he could out of the litter and Herennius slit his throat. While this was being done, most of those who were standing around covered their faces. It took three sword strokes and some sawing to detach the head and then the hands were cut off.

Popilius was very proud of his achievement. He had specifically asked Antony for the commission to execute Cicero and later set up a statue of himself wearing a wreath and seated beside his victim's severed head. Antony was greatly pleased and topped up Popilius's advertised reward with a bonus.

The surviving accounts differ in detail but they all agree on Cicero's bravery. He showed the same professionalism as the gladiators he had written about in *Conversations at Tusculum* when they received the *coup de grâce* in the arena: "Has even a mediocre fighter ever let out a groan or changed the expression on his face? Who of them has disgraced himself, I don't just mean when he was on his feet, but when falling to the ground? And, once fallen, who has drawn in his neck when ordered to submit to the sword?"

The news of Cicero's death was received variously. Antony was unreservedly delighted. His comment "*Now* we can end the proscription" exposes the depth of his frustration with, and hatred of, the man who on three occasions had intervened decisively and negatively in his life and who had led a relentless oratorical campaign against him. When he was in his late teens, his stepfather, Lentulus, had been arrested and executed at

Cicero's instigation. Cicero had advised the elder Curio how to break up Antony's close friendship with his son. And through the ferocious Philippics the orator had only just failed to derail his political career. None of these things was forgotten or forgiven.

His wife, Fulvia, also felt she had grounds for joy, for she had been married to Cicero's greatest enemy, Clodius, before graduating via Curio to the victorious Commissioner, her third and last husband. Before the dead man's head and the right hand that had written the Philippics were nailed onto the Speakers' Platform in the Forum, it is said that Fulvia took the head in her hands, spat on it and then set it on her knees, opened its mouth, pulled out the tongue and pierced it with hairpins.

We are not told of Atticus's reaction; one can assume his grief but also, one suspects, that he was too discreet to reveal it. All his energies were now devoted to getting onto the best possible terms with the new regime. Pomponia, despite the fact that she and Quintus were divorced, expressed her feelings more vigorously. Antony handed the freedman Philologus over to her; she forced him to cut off his own flesh bit by bit, roast the pieces and eat them.

These terrible stories may or may not be true. Plutarch records that Tiro, the defender of Cicero's memory, who can be presumed to have known exactly how his master died, made no reference to Philologus in his writings. However, they are not inconsistent with other recorded atrocities both at this time and on the earlier occasions during the previous century when the rule of law had broken down.

17

POSTMORTEMS

Cicero's contemporaries and historians of the period were a little cool in their assessment of him. Livy, one of the greatest of the imperial historians, wrote:

> During the long flow of success he met grave setbacks from time to time—exile, the collapse of his party, his daughter's death and his own tragic and bitter end. But of all these disasters the only one he faced as a man was his own death. . . . However, weighing his virtues against his faults, he was a great and memorable man. One would need a Cicero to sing his praises.

Pollio, the governor of Spain and later an eminent historian, who knew Cicero personally, observed sharply:

> This man's works, so many and so fine, will last forever and there is no need to comment on his great abilities and capacity for hard work. . . . However, it is a pity that he could not have been more temperate when things went well and stronger in adversity.

This view was to hold for some time. Aufidius Bassus, a historian from the next imperial generation, observed acidly: "So died Cicero, a man born to save the Republic. For a long time he defended and administered it. Then in old age it slipped from his hands, destroyed by his own mistake—his insistence that the state would only be secure if Antony were removed. He lived for sixty-three years, always on the attack or under attack. A day did not pass when it was not in someone's interest to see him dead."

In Macedonia, Brutus received the news of his friend's murder with equanimity. He said that he felt more ashamed by the cause of Cicero's death than grief at the event itself. He had been baffled by Cicero's willingness, after a lifetime of constitutional rectitude, to defend the Republic by its enemies' methods. The relationship with Octavian had been unforgivable. However, he reluctantly exacted retribution by finally accepting Cicero's advice and executing Antony's brother, Caius, whom, as coincidence would have it, young Marcus had played an active part in capturing.

These contemporary assessments do not do full justice to their subject. In our eyes Cicero was a statesman and public servant of outstanding ability. He had administrative skills of a very high order and was the preeminent orator of his age, if not of any age. In a society where politicians were also expected to be good soldiers, he was preeminently a civilian and this makes his success all the more remarkable. That his career ended in ruins and that for long years he was a bystander at great events was not due to lack of talent but to a surplus of principle. The turning point in his career was his refusal to join Julius Caesar, Pompey and Crassus in their political alliance during the 50s. He declined the invitation to do so because it would have betrayed his commitment to the Roman constitution and the rule of law. In his eyes that was totally unacceptable.

Cicero acquired a reputation for vacillation and compromise. It is true that he sometimes found it difficult to decide on a particular course of action, as his letters reveal. But his maneuvering was invariably tactical and he never sold his beliefs. His basic aim—to restore traditional political values—remained unchanged throughout his life, although in his last two years his character hardened and he became willing to adopt unconstitutional methods.

Cicero's weakness as a politician was that his principles rested on a mistaken analysis. He failed to understand the reasons for the crisis that tore apart the Roman Republic. Julius Caesar, with the pitiless insight of genius, understood that the constitution with its endless checks and balances prevented effective government, but like so many of his contemporaries Cicero regarded politics in personal rather than structural terms. For Caesar the solution lay in a completely new system of government; for Cicero it lay in finding better men to run the government and better laws to keep them in order.

His personality was insecure and nervous. This had two important consequences. First, he needed continuity and stability to thrive and it was his misfortune to live in an age of change; he was a temperamental conservative caught in the nets of a revolution. Second, he never stopped boasting of his successes. Roman politics was extremely competitive: where a man like Brutus had generations of ancestors stretching back to the foundation of the Republic with which to maintain his prestige, Cicero had only his own record. If he did not talk about it, nobody else would. His correspondence with Atticus shows that he did not take himself too seriously in private and was amused by his habit of talking up his achievements.

We know something of Cicero's domestic life, but not nearly enough to come to a firm judgment about it. His divorce of Terentia and marriage to Publilia may well have been justified, but they leave him in a rather poor light. It is hard to avoid the impression that he was insensitive to the feelings of his brother, Quintus, whom he treated as a political extension of himself rather than as an independent figure in his own right. Tullia seems to have been the only member of his family who engaged his deepest feelings; otherwise, if we may judge by the surviving evidence, his affections centered on male friendships.

If few people read his speeches today for pleasure, his philosophical writings are masterpieces of popularization and were one of the most valuable means by which the heritage of classical thought was handed down to posterity. Cicero was not an original philosopher, but all his life he read philosophy and his writings are imbued with a humane skepticism that reflects his character more than his age. In that sense, his greatest gift to European civilization was the man himself—rational, undogmatic, tolerant, law-abiding and urbane.

When Caesar was struck down and Brutus shouted out Cicero's name as the talisman of liberty regained, the conspirators supposed that the Republic would resume its interrupted course and that the civil wars were over. Cicero knew better. He was not content to remain a symbol of civic virtue. He saw what Marcus Brutus could not, that the death of one man would not save the state, and with a surprising decisiveness and energy he seized the initiative himself. As the Caesarian faction regrouped, he devised his policy of divide-and-rule and pushed it through ruthlessly. It was not because it was ill conceived or poorly executed that it failed.

Cicero did not have Julius Caesar's fabled luck. Failure, when it came, was the consequence of an unforeseeable and improbable accident: the deaths of both Consuls within a few days of each other during the two battles at Mutina. Even if Cicero had won, however, victory would have been only provisional. History admits no counterfactuals, no might-have-beens, but it is a reasonable guess that a restored Republic would have betrayed everything Cicero stood for, that at best it would have been a continuation of the violent, corrupt and unstable status quo that had lasted his lifetime, that further crises would have followed. Could he have endured the spectacle?

Under Julius Caesar's heir, history took a different course. At Philippi a year after Cicero's death the last great battle for the Republic was fought. The Republicans lost and Brutus and Cassius killed themselves. Lepidus was quickly discarded and the two remaining warlords divided the known world between them. Antony ruled the east and entered into an enduring partnership, more political than sexual, with Cleopatra. The new Caesar took the western half and stayed in Italy. The arrangement lasted uncomfortably for a decade, when war broke out again. Antony was defeated in the sea battle at Actium in 31, and in 30 he and his queen committed suicide in Alexandria. Caius Julius Caesar Octavianus was left the last man standing. With much greater patience and ingenuity than his great-uncle and adoptive father, he reformed the Republic, preserving its institutions—the Consuls, the Praetors and the other officeholders, the Senate and the General Assembly—as the medium through which an autocracy backed by military force could discreetly express itself. As the Emperor Augustus, he laid the foundations for Rome's continuing dominion.

Cicero attracted loyalty after his death as well as during his lifetime. In distinction from his brother, his slaves and servants did their best to save him from his pursuers. Despite his delicate health Tiro apparently lived a long life, spent on his smallholding in Campania, and devoted himself to his master's memory. He wrote a biography of Cicero, published the notes for his speeches and may have assembled a collection of his sayings and witticisms.

Marcus loved his father and defended his name. He fought at Philippi and served under Sextus Pompey, but then made his peace with the triumphant Commissioners. He was pardoned in 39. The drinking that had worried Cicero when Marcus was a student in Athens became a lifelong habit. He was reported to down nine or ten pints at a session and once when drunk he threw a goblet at Augustus's greatest general, Marcus Vipsanius Agrippa. Fortunately, he inherited his father's administrative competence (and, apparently, his sense of humor). Augustus seems to have liked him: he was appointed Augur (according to Appian, "by way of apology for Cicero's sacrifice") and in 30 he served as Consul. He was twice a provincial governor. Presumably he had no son, for, after him, nothing more is heard of the Tullii Cicerones.

During his Consulship, Marcus had the satisfaction of reading out in the Forum Octavian's dispatch from Alexandria announcing the death of Antony; he posted a document to that effect on the Speakers' Platform where his father's head and hands had been displayed. During the same year, the Senate took down Antony's statues, canceled all the other honors that he had been awarded and decreed that in future no member of his family should bear the name of Marcus. Plutarch commented with dry satisfaction: "In this way Heaven entrusted to the family of Cicero the final acts in the punishment of Antony."

During one of his foreign postings Marcus found himself dining with a rhetorician who was critical of his father's oratory. According to an anecdote told by Seneca the Elder in the following century:

> Nature had stolen away Marcus's memory—and anything that remained was being filched by drunkenness. He kept asking who the guest was on the bottom couch. The name Cestius was supplied a number of times, but he went on forgetting it. Finally a slave, hoping to make his memory more retentive by giving it something to hang on to, said, when his master repeated the question: "This is Cestius, who said your father didn't know his alphabet." Marcus called for whips on the double and, as was only right and proper, avenged Cicero on Cestius's skin.

Terentia lived to the great age of 103 and took a third husband.

Despite his wealth, Atticus managed to avoid being listed in the proscription, although he went into hiding for a time. He took care to be on excellent terms with both Octavian and Antony, whose family he placed under his protection in Rome. His daughter, the little girl who had so delighted Cicero, grew up to marry Agrippa; and their daughter was betrothed in her infancy to the future Emperor Tiberius. At the age of seventy-seven, Atticus was taken ill with ulcerated intestines; rather than endure a painful disease, this imperturbable disciple of Epicurus starved himself to death.

During his lifetime Atticus allowed people to read his collection of Cicero's correspondence. Probably at some time during the first century AD, this was published alongside other collections of letters to Quintus, Brutus and various other recipients (the so-called *Letters to His Friends*). Some collections—regrettably, his correspondence with Julius Caesar and his heir—have not survived.

The Emperor Augustus assiduously cultivated the memory of his adoptive father. The assembly hall in Pompey's theater was walled up, the fifteenth of March was named the Day of Parricide and the Senate resolved never to meet on that date again. However, the "heaven-sent boy" remembered with admiration one of the Dictator's greatest critics, in whose murder he had colluded. Many years later he happened to pay a visit to one of his grandsons. The lad was reading a book by Cicero and, terrified of his grandfather, tried to hide it under his cloak. Augustus noticed this and took the book from him. He stood for a long time reading the entire text. He handed it back with the words: "An eloquent man, my child, an eloquent man, and a patriot."

SOURCES

GENERAL

By classical standards the sources for the period of Cicero's life are voluminous, although many histories written within a generation or so of his time are lost. Much has been translated and, for the reader who would like to know more at firsthand about Cicero and the fall of the Roman Republic, some accessible literature is cited below. Titles of classical works are given in translation; see under Abbreviations for original Latin titles.

The most important documentary sources are Cicero's own writings (all of which are available in Latin alongside translations in the Loeb Classical Library, Harvard University Press). Many of his speeches, which he revised and issued himself, survive, as do his books on philosophy and oratory. So do about 900 letters; some were designed for publication or for judicious circulation by the recipient, but others, a large proportion of the correspondence with Atticus, were not. They are organized into a number of different collections: the so-called *Letters to His Friends* and *Letters to Brutus* and *Letters to Quintus* are mainly, but not entirely, communications to politicians and public figures; they include letters from Julius Caesar and Pompey and other politicians of the day. They were probably published before the *Letters to Atticus,* which appeared some time in the first century AD. The complete correspondence was edited and translated in the 1960s by D. R. Shackleton Bailey; he reordered the letters in one continuous sequence, which is cited first in the references below (followed by the traditional numbering).

Cicero's speeches need to be treated with caution, for he is always arguing a case. On the one major occasion where an alternative version exists to the story he is telling, his defense of Milo, we find that he is almost certainly promoting a tissue of untruths. The letters are an invaluable resource, a reliable guide to day-to-day events even if we do not always agree with their author's political analyses.

Contemporary or near-contemporary histories include the following: Sallust's two surviving monographs, *The Conspiracy of Catilina* and *The Jugurthine War,* give useful if highly colored and sometimes chronologically haphazard accounts. Caesar's lapidary, accurate but not always truthful *Conquest of Gaul* and *The Civil War* are essential reading. A short life of Atticus was published by a friend of his, Cornelius Nepos. Two sections from a *Life of Augustus* by Nicolaus of Damascus about his subject's youth (edited and translated by Jane Bellemore, Bristol Classical Press, 1984) give interesting details about Caesar's assassination. An Augustan Senator, Quintus Asconius Pedianus, wrote intelligent and well-informed commentaries on some of Cicero's speeches, in one of which he gives a detailed account of Clodius's death (*Commentaries on Five Speeches by Cicero,* ed. and trans. Simon Squires, Bristol University Press and Bochazy-Carducci Publishers, 1990).

Diodorus Siculus, a Sicilian writing in Greek, was a near-contemporary of Cicero. He wrote a history of the Mediterranean world, *Library of History,* in forty volumes from mythological times up to his own day. He is useful on his native island of Sicily. Unfortunately most of the book survives only as excerpts or paraphrases from Byzantine and medieval times. He was an uncritical compiler and only as good as his sources.

Plutarch, a Greek biographer and essayist of the second half of the first century AD, is one antiquity's most charming authors. His *Parallel Lives* include biographies of Marius, Sulla, Pompey, Cato, Crassus, Brutus, Caesar, Mark Antony and Cicero. They are full of fascinating personal detail, but he was interested in character rather than history and was indiscriminate in the use of his sources.

Suetonius was a slightly later contemporary of Plutarch and, as the Emperor Hadrian's secretary, had access to the imperial archives; this makes his short biographies of Julius Caesar and Augustus, in *The Twelve Caesars,* of particular interest, although, like Plutarch, he is no historian and concentrates his attention on his subjects' private lives. Velleius Paterculus lived during the reigns of Augustus and Tiberius and wrote a patchy *History of Rome* from earliest times to 30 AD.

Lines from Catullus, whose poetry movingly expresses the way of life of the younger set who simultaneously attracted and repelled Cicero, are quoted in Peter Whigham's translation (Penguin Classics, 1966). Further verse quotations have been made from John Davie's translation of Euripides' *Medea* (Penguin Classics, 1996) and Robert Fagles' version of the *Iliad* (Viking, 1990).

Although the Greek historian Polybius wrote in the second century BC, his history of Rome's rise to dominance of the Mediterranean world gives a well-grounded account of the workings of the Roman constitution.

General histories of the period date from later in the Empire. The best of them is by Appian, who flourished in Rome in the middle of the second century AD. He wrote a history of Rome from the arrival in Italy of Aeneas to the battle of Actium in 31 BC. Five books on the civil wars survive, of which the first two give a continuous account of events from the Tribuneship of Tiberius Gracchus to the aftermath of Caesar's assassination. For the first part of this narrative he depended on a very good source and, although his chronology is sometimes confused and his belief in the role of fate in human affairs unhelpful, Appian is invaluable.

Dio Cassius was a Greek historian, born about the middle of the second century AD, who wrote a *Roman History* from Aeneas to his own second Consulship in 229 AD. The books that survive cover the period between the second war against Mithridates and the reign of Claudius. Although he had no way of evaluating his sources, he offers a useful complement to other earlier texts.

Our knowledge of the late Republic has been enhanced by twentieth-century archaeology, especially through coins and inscriptions.

Modern literature on Cicero and the Roman Republic is multitudinous. (See Further Reading for full details of works mentioned in this and the next paragraph.) Information on further reading in English can be found in two excellent surveys, H. H. Scullard's standard textbook *From the Gracchi to Nero,* and Michael Crawford's analytical study *The Roman Republic.* Matthias Gelzer's masterpiece *Caesar, Politician and Statesman,* with full annotations, is perhaps the classic account of Caesar's life. Christian Meier's *Caesar* is authoritative and readable and, as well as giving a lively narrative of the life, offers a profound insight into the nature of Rome's constitutional crisis. Ronald Syme's great *The Roman Revolution* is forthright and challenging about Cicero's behavior. F. R. Cowell's *Cicero and the Roman Republic* is a thorough and readable account of the politics and economic and social development of ancient Rome.

Among previous books on Cicero to which the present work is indebted are the following: Gaston Boissier's delightful *Cicero and His Friends,* applying to its subject the perceptions of a nineteenth-century French man of the world, skeptical, witty and without illusions; scholarship has moved on, but this remains a convincing evocation of a vanished society. Elizabeth Rawson's *Cicero* is the last full-length biography to have been published in Britain by an English author and is both scholarly and attractively written. T. N. Mitchell's two-volume *Cicero: The Ascending Years* and *Cicero: The Senior Statesman* constitutes an authoritative and monumentally comprehensive study.

FURTHER READING

The major classical authors cited above are available in the original with English translations, in Loeb Classical Library, Harvard University Press, Cambridge, Mass.

Principal classical sources

Appian, *The Civil Wars,* trans. John Carter, Penguin Classics, 1996.

Caesar, *The Civil War,* trans. Jane F. Gardner, Penguin Classics, 1967.

———, *The Conquest of Gaul,* trans. S. A. Handford, Penguin Classics, 1951.

Catullus, *Odes,* trans. Peter Whigham, Penguin Classics, 1966.

Cicero, *Letters to Atticus and to His Friends,* ed. and trans. D. R. Shackleton Bailey, Penguin Classics, 1978.

———, *Selected Political Speeches,* trans. Michael Grant, Penguin Books, 1969.

———, *Works,* Loeb Classical Library, Harvard University Press, Cambridge, Mass.

Plutarch, *The Fall of the Roman Republic,* trans. Rex Warner, Penguin Classics, 1958.

———, *The Makers of Rome,* trans. Ian Scott-Kilvert, Penguin Classics, 1964.

———, *Parallel Lives,* Loeb Classical Library, Harvard University Press, Cambridge, Mass.

Polybius, *The Rise of the Roman Empire,* trans. Ian Scott-Kilvert, Penguin Classics, 1979.

Sallust, *The Jugurthine War; Conspiracy of Catiline,* trans. S. A. Handford, Penguin Classics, 1963.

Suetonius, *The Twelve Caesars,* trans. Robert Graves, revised Michael Grant, Penguin Classics, 1979.

Principal modern sources

Gaston Boissier, *Cicero and His Friends,* Ward, Lock, 1897, first published in France, 1865.

F. R. Cowell, *Cicero and the Roman Republic,* Penguin Books, 1948.

Michael Crawford, *The Roman Republic,* Fontana Collins, 1978.

Florence Dupont, *Daily Life in Ancient Rome,* Basil Blackwell, 1992.

Matthias Gelzer, *Caesar, Politician and Statesman,* Basil Blackwell, Oxford, with corrections 1969; first published in Germany, 1921.

Christian Meier, *Caesar,* HarperCollins, 1995, first published by Severin & Siedler, Germany, 1982.

T. N. Mitchell, *Cicero: The Ascending Years* and *Cicero: The Senior Statesman,* Yale University Press, 1979 and 1991.

Elizabeth Rawson, *Cicero,* Allen Lane, 1975.

H. H. Scullard, *From the Gracchi to Nero,* Routledge, 5th ed., 1982.

Ronald Syme, *The Roman Revolution,* Oxford University Press, 1939.

ABBREVIATIONS

ACI—Cicero, *Ad Caesarem iuniorem (frag.)* [*To the younger Caesar*]

App—Appian, *The Civil Wars*

Arch—Cicero, *For Archias (Pro Archia)*

Asc—Asconius, *Commentaries on Five Speeches by Cicero* (Bristol University Press)

Att—Cicero, *Letters to Atticus* (ed. Shackleton Bailey)

Bell civ—Caesar, *The Civil War (Commentarii de bello civili)*

Bell gall—Caesar, *The Conquest of Gaul (Commentarii de bello gallico)*

Boiss—Gaston Boissier, *Cicero and His Friends*

Brut—Cicero, *Brutus*

Brutus—Cicero, *Letters to Brutus* (ed. Shackleton Bailey)

Cael—Cicero, *In Defense of Caelius (Pro Caelio)*

Castle—E. B. Castle, *Ancient Education and Today* (Pelican, 1961)

Cat I—Cicero, *First Speech Against Catilina (In Catilinam I)*

Cat II—Cicero, *Second Speech Against Catilina*

Cat IV—Cicero, *Fourth Speech Against Catilina (In Catilinam IV)*

Catull—Catullus, *Odes (Carmina)*

Clu—Cicero, *In Defense of Cluentius (Pro Cluentio)*

Comm—Quintus Tullius Cicero, *A Short Guide to Electioneering (Commentariolum petitionis)*

Corn Nep—Cornelius Nepos, *Life of Atticus* (from *De viris illustribus*)

De inv—Cicero, *On Invention (De inventione)*

De or—Cicero, *The Ideal Orator (De oratore)*

Dio—Dio Cassius, *Roman History*

Div—Cicero, *Foretelling the Future (De divinatione)*

Dom—Cicero, *About His House (De domo sua)*
Fam—Cicero, *Letters to His Friends (Ad familiares)* (ed. Shackleton Bailey)
Harusp—Cicero, *Concerning the Response of the Soothsayers (De haruspicum responsis)*
Homer Il—Homer, *Iliad* (trans. R. Fagles, Viking, 1990)
Hor Sat—Horace, *Satires (Sermones)*
Imp Pomp—Cicero, *On Pompey's Commission (De imperio Gn. Pompeii)*
Lact—Lactantius, *Divine Institutes (Institutiones divinae)*
Leg—Cicero, *On Law (De legibus)*
Leg ag—Cicero, *On the Land Act (De lege agraria)*
Luc—Lucan, *Pharsalia* (trans. Robert Graves, Penguin Classics, 1956)
Marc—Cicero, *In Defense of Marcellus (Pro Marcello)*
Mod Dig—Modestinus, *Digest (Digesta)*
Mur—Cicero, *In Defense of Murena (Pro Murena)*
Nic—Nicolaus, *Life of Augustus*
Odf—*Orationum deperditarum fragmenta* [Fragments of Lost Speeches] (ed. I. Puccioni, Milan)
Off—Cicero, *Duties (De officiis)*
Para Stoic—Cicero, *Stoic Paradoxes (Paradoxa Stoicorum)*
Phil—Cicero, *Philippics (Orationes Philippicae)*
Planc—Cicero, *In Defense of Plancius (Pro Plancio)*
Pliny—Pliny the Elder, *Natural History (Naturalis historia)* (trans. John F. Healy, Penguin Classics)
Plut Brut—Plutarch, *Life of Brutus*
Plut Caes—Plutarch, *Life of Caesar*
Plut Cat—Plutarch, *Life of Cato*
Plut Cic—Plutarch, *Life of Cicero*
Plut Crass—Plutarch, *Life of Crassus*
Plut Pomp—Plutarch, *Life of Pompey*
Plut Sull—Plutarch, *Life of Sulla*
Post red—Cicero, *Speech to the People after His Return (Post reditum ad quirites)*
Quint—Cicero, *Letters to Quintus*
Quintil—Quintilianus, *The Education of an Orator (Institutio oratoria)*
Rab—Cicero, *In Defense of Caius Rabirius on a Charge of Treason (Pro C. Rabirio perduellionis)*
Rep—Cicero, *On the State (De republica)*
Rosc—Cicero, *In Defense of S. Roscius Amerinus (Pro S. Roscio Amerinó)*
Sall Caes—*Letter to Caesar (Epistula ad Caesarem)*
Sall Cat—Sallust, *The Conspiracy of Catilina (Bellum Catilinae)*

Sall Inv—Sallust, *Invective Against Cicero (In M. Tullium Ciceronem oratio)*
Sen—Seneca the Elder, *Suasoriae*
Sest—Cicero, *In Defence of Sestius (Pro Sestio)*
SIG—*Sylloge Inscriptionum Graecorum* [*Collection of Greek Inscriptions*] (ed. W. Dittenberger)
Suet—Suetonius, *Life of Caesar,* in *The Twelve Caesars (De vita Caesarum)*
Tac—Tacitus, *Dialogue on Orators (Dialogus de oratoribus)*
Tusc—Cicero, *Conversations at Tusculum (Tusculanae disputationes)*
Val Max—Valerius Maximus, *Memorabilia*
Vell—Velleius Paterculus, *History of Rome (Historia romana)*
Verr—Cicero, *First Speech Against Verres (In Verrem I)*

CHAPTER BY CHAPTER SOURCES

p. vii "What a triumph" Hugh Brogan, *The Penguin History of the United States* (Penguin Books, 1999), p. 191.

The opening account of Caesar's murder through Cicero's eyes is based on Appian, Dio Cassius, Plutarch (lives of Caesar and Mark Antony), Suetonius and Nicolaus.

p. 6 "You too, my son?" *Dio XLIV 19* and *Suet I 82*

Chapter 1—Fault Lines: First Century BC

Readers who wish to go beyond this summary account should read Cowell, Scullard and Crawford. Among the sources for the historical narrative from Tiberius Gracchus to Cicero's youth are Appian and Plutarch.

p. 12 "rank, position, magnificence" *Clu LVI 154*
p. 15 Tribal or General Assembly. Two other types of assembly existed, the *concilium plebis,* which had the same membership as the *comitia tributa* minus the Patricians, and the *comitia curiata,* which was largely concerned with legal approvals.
p. 17 "This was the first time" *Vell II 3 3*

Chapter 2—"Always Be the Best, My Boy, the Bravest": 106–82 BC

The description of Cicero's childhood is based on Plutarch together with the evocation of Arpinum in *On law* (*De legibus*). The section on education is indebted to E. B. Castle. The historical account draws on Appian, Plutarch, Sallust and Diodorus Siculus.

p. 21 "Whenever I can get out" *Leg II 1*
"We consider" *Leg II 5*
p. 22 "With your courage" *Leg III 16 36*
p. 23 "This is what I prayed for!" *Hor Sat 6 1*ff.
p. 24 "I am going to make my *cognomen*" *Plut Cic II 1*
p. 26 "how our mother in the old days" *Fam 351 (XVI 26)*
"We rule the world" *Val Max VI 3*
p. 28 Twelve Tables *Leg I 21 55*
p. 32 "Didn't you learn your unbridled loquacity" *Sall Inv I 2*
p. 33 "The time which others spend" *Arch VI 13*
p. 34 "Caesar and Brutus also wrote" *Tac 21*
"Our people are like Syrian slaves" *De or II 265*
"For as far as I can cast my mind back" *Arch 148*
p. 35 "I love Pomponius" *Fam 63 (XIII 1)*
p. 36 Crassus's "swan song" *De or III 2–5*
p. 40 "We are not asking you to pardon" *Plut Sull*
p. 44 "No, please, I beg you" *Corn Nep IV 1*
"He always belonged to the best party" *Boiss 137*f.
p. 45 "the proscriptions of the rich" *Para Stoic VI 2 46*
"Victories in the field" *Off I 74*
"it appeared that the whole institution of the courts" *Brut LXXXIX 306*
"Seeing that the whole state" *Plut Cic III 2*
p. 46 "that we do not recklessly and presumptuously assume" *De inv II 10*
"Always be the best" Homer Il VI 247

Chapter 3—The Forum and the Fray: 81–77 BC

The description of the Forum, as well as being based on personal visits, draws on *The Roman Forum* (Electa, 1998); and that of Rome on Florence Dupont. The accounts of the Roscius, Verres and Cluentius trials are largely drawn from the relevant speeches by Cicero. For the characters and early careers of Pompey and Crassus, Plutarch has been used.

p. 48 "planted in mountains" *Leg ag II 35 96*
"Two of my shops" *Att 363 XIV 9*

p. 57 "not (as most do) to learn my trade in the Forum" *Brut XCI 312*
"a disreputable victory" *Off II 27*
p. 58 "Personally, I am always very nervous" *Clu XVIII 51*
"Why, you always come" *Dio XLVI 7*
p. 60 "According to the custom of our ancestors" *Mod Dig XLVIII 9 9*
"He comes down from his mansion" *Rosc XLV 132–35*
p. 62 "Terentia was never at any time" *Plut Cic XX 2*
p. 64 "I was at that time very slender" *Brut XCI 313*
p. 65 "we have learned from them" *Leg II 36*
C "planned that, if he were finally deprived" *Plut Cic IV 2*
p. 66 "not only a pleader" *Brut XCI 316*

Chapter 4—Politics and Foreign Postings: 77–63 BC

The story of Cicero's early political career derives from Plutarch, his speeches and the correspondence with Atticus.

p. 67 "Just as in the music of harps" *Rep II 42*
p. 69 "When I was Quaestor" *Tusc V XXIII 64–66*
p. 70 The incident at Puteoli *Planc XXVI, XXVII*
p. 73 "his hair swept back in a kind of wave" *Plut Pomp II 1/2*
p. 79 "Today the eyes of the world" *Verr I 16 46–47*
"I am afraid I'm no good at solving riddles" *Plut Cic VII 6*
p. 80 C's jokes at the Verres trial *Plut Cic VII 4–5*
"Gentlemen of the jury" *Verr II 8 22*
p. 81 "It is the judge's responsibility" *Off II 51*
"my brother, Quintus" *Att 1 (I 5)*
p. 82 "All the pleasure" *Att 1 (I 5)*
"I am delighted with my place at Tusculum" *Att 2 (I 6)*
C's citrus table *Pliny XIII 91*
C's estimate of his income *Phil II 16*
p. 84 "You know the game I am playing" *Att 10 (I 1)*
p. 85 "Such is his unbelievable, superhuman genius" *Imp Pomp XIII 37*
"My handling of C. Macer's case" *Att 9 (I 4)*
p. 86 "both that he did not assault the standing" *Asc: Pro Cornelio argumentum*

Chapter 5—Against Catilina: 63 BC

The account of the Catilinarian conspiracy is largely based on Sallust, Cicero's Catilinarian speeches and Asconius, together with Appian and Dio Cassius for the general picture.

p. 87 "People naturally prefer you to lie" *Comm 48*
p. 89 "No one has ever had such a talent for seducing young men" *Cat II 4 5*
"debauchees, adulterers and gamblers" *Sall Cat XIV* 2ff.
"There are shouts and screams" *Off 1*
p. 90 "Catilina had many excellent qualities" *Cael V 12*
Catilina's first "conspiracy" is a mysterious affair; for further discussion see Gelzer, pp. 38ff. and S. A. Handford (Sallust, *Jugurthine War* and *Conspiracy of Catiline*), pp. 164ff.
p. 93 "We have the jury we want" *Att 11 (I 2)*
"Can any man be a friend" *Asc: In toga candida*
p. 94 "I assert" *Asc: In toga candida*
p. 98 "What I assert" *Rab XII 332–34*
"I see two bodies" *Plut Cic XIII* 4–5
p. 101 Catilina reported to sacrifice a boy, *Dio XXXVII 147/149*
p. 102 "quite overcome by the news" *Plut Cic XV* 2
p. 103 "I am able to report" *Cat I iv 8*
p. 104 "I do not intend" *Sall Cat XXXVI 1*f.
p. 105 "But I must change my tone" *Mur XXXV 74*
p. 108 "Imprisonment, [Caesar] says" *Cat IV iv 8*
"ought to distribute the accused around the towns of Italy" *App II 6*
p. 109 "sluggish of comprehension" *Plut Cat I 3*
"If we could afford" *Sall Cat LIII 4*

Chapter 6—Pretty-Boy's Revenge: 62–58 BC

The events leading to Cicero's exile are covered by various lives of Plutarch, Dio and, to a lesser extent, Appian but, increasingly, by Cicero's letters, which now begin to be available in large numbers. Cicero's speech *In Defense of Caelius* throws a brilliant light on the Clodian circle.

p. 113 "One could not attend the Senate" *Plut Cic XXIV 1–2*
"This unpleasing habit of his" *Plut Cic XXIV 2*
"a certain foolish vanity" *Att 38 (II 18)*

p. 114 "I swear to you" *Plut Cic XXIII 2*
p. 116 "This district, let me tell you, is charming" *Att 392 (XV 16a)*
p. 117 "I imagine you have heard" *Att 12 (I 12)*
p. 118 "passion for fornication" *Sall Cat XIII 3–5*
p. 119 "at the cross-roads" *Catull 58*
"You [Mark Antony] assumed a man's toga" *Phil II 18 44–45*
p. 120 *"Silver-tongued among the sons of Rome" Catull 49*
p. 121 "When the day came for the bill to be put" *Att 14 (I 14)*
"Inside a couple of days" *Att 16 (I 16)*
p. 122 Cicero's jokes at Clodius's expense *Att 16 (I 16)* and *21 (II 1)*
p. 123 "as if he were coming back from a foreign holiday" *Plut Pomp XLII 3*
p. 124 "He professes the highest regard for me" *Att 13 (I 13)*
p. 125 "Life out of uniform" *Plut Pomp XXIII 4*
"I need 25 million sesterces" *App II 8*
p. 126 "I brought the house down" *Att 14 (I 14)*
The description of Pompey's Triumph is based on Plutarch's life of him but also draws on some material from his life of Aemilius Paulus.
p. 128 "Giving up all attempts to equal Pompey" *Plut Crass VII 2*
"The demand was disgraceful" *Att 17 (I 17)*
"the dregs of the urban population" *Att 19 (I 19)*
p. 129 "As for our dear friend Cato" *Att 21 (XI 1)*
p. 130 "those conspirators of the wine table" *Att 16 (I 16)*
"had used up the entire perfume cabinet of Isocrates" *Att 21 (II 1)*
"What I most badly need at the present is a confidant" *Att 18 (I 18)*
p. 131 "I trusted and indeed convinced myself" *Att 17 (I 17)*
p. 134 *"Meantime the paths" Att 23 (II 3)*
p. 135 "When I notice how carefully arranged his hair is" *Plut Caes IV 4*
p. 136 Cato's arrest *Dio XXXVIII 2–3*
p. 137 "Let us wait then" *Plut Cic XXVI 3*
"the Queen of Bithynia" *Suet I 49*
p. 138 "I have taken so kindly to idleness" *Att 26 (II 6)*
"When I read a letter of yours" *Att 35 (II 15)*
p. 139 "I have so lost my manly spirit" *Att 34 (II 14)*
"Sampsiceramus . . . is out for trouble" *Att 37 (II 17)*
p. 140 "Dear Publius is threatening me" *Att 39 (II 19)*
"For himself he wanted a high command" *Sall Cat LIV*
p. 141 "all Catilina's forces" *Post red XIII 33*
p. 143 "the Senate met to pass a vote" *Plut Cic XXXI 1*
p. 144 "could not face seeing him" *Plut Cic XXXI 2–3*

Chapter 7—Exile: 58–52 BC

Appian and Dio Cassius continue to give the general background with Plutarch providing additional color. (Also, with Caesar's growing prominence, Suetonius's life of him begins to be useful.) Cicero's letters and speeches are the crucial resource. For Clodius's death Asconius is more to be trusted than Cicero's almost completely unreliable account in his defense of Milo. Quintus's adventures in Gaul are taken from Caesar's *Conquest of Gaul.*

p. 146 "I miss my daughter" *Quint 3 (I 3)*
"Has any man ever fallen" *Att 55 (III 10)*
p. 147 "I will only say this" *Att 54 (III 9)*
p. 149 "The Tiber was full of citizens' corpses" *Sest LVII*
p. 151 "From your letter and from the facts themselves" *Att 72 (III 27)*
"by which I did not simply return home" *Dom XVIII 75*
p. 152 "It is a sort of second life" *Att 73 (IV 1)*
"heavy with wine . . . talking with him" *Post red VI 13–14*
praise of Pompey *Post red II 5*
"The decree was read out" *Att 73 (IV 1)*
p. 154 "Those same gentlemen" *Att 74 (IV 2)*
"On November 11" *Att 75 (IV 3)*
"My heart is high" *Att 75 (IV 3)*
p. 156 "Pale with fury" *Quint 7 (II 3)*
p. 157 "My refutation" *Cael XIII 32*
p. 159 "The Germans' left was routed" *Bell gall II 2*
p. 160 "Ah, just the man I want" *Quint 20 (I 9)*
p. 162 "Come on! Do you really think" *Att 79 (IV 8)*
"These years of my life" *Quint 25 (III 5)*
"I was weary of it" *Fam 24 (VII 1)*
p. 163 "After all, what could be more humiliating" *Att 83 (IV 6)*
"I believe in moving with the times" *Fam 20 (I 9)*
p. 164 "talked to me at length" *Quint 10 (II 6)*
"Those shelves of yours" *Att 79 (IV 8)*
"But seriously, while all other amusements" *Att 84 (IV 10)*
p. 165 "perfidy, artifice and betrayal. . . . Waive the laws of history" *Fam 22 (V 12)*
"What pleasure" *Fam 24 (VII 1)*
p. 166 "the first gladiatorial show" *Val Max II 4 7*
p. 167 "What pleasure can a cultivated man" *Fam 24 (VII 1)*

"Caesar's friends" *Att 89 (IV 16)*

p. 168 "Pompey is putting a lot of pressure on me" *Quint 21 (III 1)*

p. 169 "In all the world Caesar is the only man" *Fam 25 (III 5)*
"Cicero himself, although in very poor health" *Bell gall VI 2*

p. 170 "Escaped from the great heat wave. . . . I was very pleased with the house" *Quint 21 (III 1)*
"Our affairs stand as follows" *Quint 23 (III 3)*

p. 175 "a friend to us" *Fam 44 (XVI 16)*

p. 176 "See about the dining room" *Fam 185 (XVI 22)*
"My (or *our*) literary brainchildren" *Fam 43 (XVI 10)*
"Aegypta arrived today" *Fam 42 (XVI 15)*
Tiro "is extraordinarily useful to me" *Att 128 (VII 5)*
"Well, you are a man of landed property!" *Fam 337 (XVI 21)*

Chapter 8—The Ideal Constitution: 55–43 BC

p. 180 "When we inherited the Republic" *Rep V 1 2*

p. 181 "The government was so administered" *Rep II 32 56*

p. 182 " 'is the highway to heaven' " *Rep VI 16*
"Law is the highest reason" *Leg I 6 18–19*

p. 183 "Virtue is reason completely developed" *Leg I 16 45*
"science of distinguishing." . . . The mind "must employ" *Leg I 24 62*
"The most foolish notion of all" *Leg I 15 1*
"two officeholders" *Leg III 3 8*
votes cast should be scrutinized by the "traditional leaders of the state" *Leg III 15 33*
"everyone knows that laws" *Leg III 15 34*

Chapter 9—The Drift to Civil War: 52–50 BC

This chapter relies on Cicero's correspondence with Caelius and Plutarch. Appian, Dio and the others set the larger scene. The opening discussion on the date that Caesar's Gallic governorship came to an end and his legal predicament is tracked in Matthias Gelzer and examined by John Carter in Appian, 409–10.

p. 187 "Caesar had long ago decided" *Plut Caes XXVIII 1–2*

p. 188 "My one consolation" *Att 95 (V 2)*

p. 189 "When we arrived" *Att 94 (V 1)*

p. 190 "I leave him in the most patriotic frame of mind" *Att 100 (V 7)*

p. 191 Pompey "is apt to say one thing, and think another" *Fam 77 (VIII 1)*
"The creatures are in remarkably short supply" *Fam 2 (II 11)*
"When all's said, . . . this isn't the kind of thing" *Att 108 (V 15)*

p. 192 "forlorn and, without exaggeration. . . . In a phrase" *Att 109 (V 16)*

p. 193 "Malicious persons" *Fam 69 (III 6)*
"Your army is hardly capable" *Fam 83 (VIII 5)*

p. 194 "My best resource is winter" *Att III (V 18)*

p. 195 "On October 13 we made a great slaughter" *Att 113 (V 20)*
"A merry Saturnalia was had by all" *Att 113 (V 20)*

p. 197 "Our Consuls are paragons" *Fam 88 (VIII 6)*
"What he wants" *Att 355 (XIV 1)*

p. 198 "I shall be sorry to have incurred his displeasure" *Att 115 (VI 1)*
"He is apt in his letters to me" *Att 115 (VI 1)*
"My dear Atticus" *Att 116 (VI 2)*
"I shall keep him on a tighter rein" *Att 113 (V 20)*

p. 199 "Let me say only one thing" *Att 116 (VI 2)*
"He does seem very fond of his mother" *Att 116 (VI 2)*
"There's something" *Att 118 (VI 4)*

p. 200 "Here I am in my province" *Att 121 (VI 6)*
"We all find him charming" *Att 126 (VII 3)*

Chapter 10—"A Strange Madness": 50–48 BC

The main sources for these years are Appian, Dio Cassius and Cicero's correspondence, together with Caesar, Plutarch and Suetonius.

p. 202 "From the day I arrived in Rome" *Fam 146 (XVI 12)*
"Pompey the Great's digestion" *Fam 94 (VIII 13)*
"great quarrels ahead" *Fam 97 (VIII 14)*

p. 203 "There looms ahead a tremendous contest" *Att 124 (VII 1)*
"While I am not cowardly" *Quintil XII 1 17*

p. 205 Caesar's "army is incomparably superior" *Fam 97 (VIII 14)*

p. 206 "He at once sent a few troops" *Suet I 31*

p. 207 "Since nearly all Italy" *Plut Pomp LXI 1–3*
"thoroughly cowed" *Att 177 (IX 10)*

p. 208 "I have decided on the spur of the moment" *Att 133 (VII 10)*
"He scorns me" *Att 179 (IX 12)*
"It looks to me" *Att 141 (VII 17)*

p. 209 "I am sure you find" *Att 141 (VII 17)*
"How utterly down he is" *Att 145 (VII 21)*
p. 210 "Our Cnaeus is marvelously covetous of despotism" *Att 174 (IX 7)*
p. 211 "I was made anxious before" *Att 172 (IX 6)*
"Nothing in [Pompey's] conduct" *Att 177 (IX 10)*
Cicero's meeting with Caesar *Att 187 (IX 18)*
p. 213 "you have disapproved" *Att 199B (X 83)*
p. 214 "I cannot believe that you mean to go abroad" *Att 199a (X 8a)*
"Do you think that if Spain is lost" *Att 199 (X 8)*
p. 215 "I hope my plan won't involve any risk" *Att 208 (X 16)*
"You ask me about the war news" *Att 214 (XI 4a)*
p. 216 "I'll make you win" *Fam 156 (VIII 17)*
p. 217 "To go against him now" *Fam 153 (VIII 16)*
"He has no idea how to win a war" *Suet I 36*
"Consult your own best interests" *Fam 157 (IX 9)*
p. 218 "I came to regret my action" *Fam 183 (VII 3)*
p. 219 "[There] could be seen artificial arbors" *Bell civ III 96*
"They insisted on it" *Suet I 30*
"Excellent, if we were fighting jackdaws" *Plut Cic XXXVIII 5*

Chapter 11—Pacifying Caesar: 48–45 BC

The same sources as for the preceding chapter, with the addition of speeches by Cicero.

p. 223 "He expressed himself pretty strongly on these points" *Att 218 (XI 7)*
p. 224 "As to Pompey's end" *Att 217 (XI 6)*
"It is the most unbelievable thing" *Att 219 (XI 8)*
p. 225 "Her own beauty" *Plut Ant XXVII* 2ff.
p. 227 "Came, saw, conquered" *Plut Caes L 2*
"Her own courage, thoughtfulness" *Att 228 (XI 17)*
p. 228 "I must ask *you* to get me out of here" *Att 230 (XI 18)*
"quite a handsome one" *Fam 171 (XIV 23)*
"Kindly see that everything is ready" *Fam 173 (XIV 20)*
p. 230 "I think the victory of either" *Fam 182 (V 21)*
p. 231 "I decline to be under an obligation" *Plut Cat LXVI 2*
"The gods favored the winning side" *Luc I 128*
p. 232 "It's a problem for Archimedes" *Att 240 (XII 4)*
p. 233 "As for our present times" *Fam 177 (IX 2)*

“Like the learned men of old” *Fam 177 (IX 2)*
“I have set up as schoolmaster” *Fam 191 (IX 18)*
p. 234 “Hirtius . . . and Dolabella are my pupils” *Fam 190 (IX 16)*
“I assure you I had no idea *she* would be there” *Fam 197 (IX 26)*
“I even had the audacity” *Fam 193 (IXD 20)*
“Our *bons vivants*” *Fam 210 (VII 26)*
p. 237 “Of course. It will be following orders” *Plut Caes LIX 3*
“I used to sit in the poop” *Fam 196 (IX 15)*
“Don’t think I am joking” *Fam 196 (IX 15)*
p. 238 “for some reason he was extraordinarily patient” *Att 371 (XIV 17)*
Cicero’s jokes *Plut Cic XXVI*
“I hear that, having in his day compiled volumes of *bons mots,* Caesar” *Fam 190 (IX 16)*
p. 239 “On November 26 . . . , at your brothers’ request” *Fam 228 (VI 4)*
p. 240 “some semblance of reviving constitutional freedom” *Fam 203 (IV 4)*
“Whether for nature or for glory” *Marc VII 8 21–25*
The need for a Dictator *Rep VI 12*
Caesar comments on reading Cicero’s *Cato Att 338 (XIII 46)*
p. 242 “I waste a lot of time” *Fam 337 (XVI 21)*
“She’ll be a woman tomorrow” *Quintil VI 3 75*
p. 243 “As for your congratulations” *Fam 240 (IV 14)*
p. 244 “threw them all into one attempt” *Tusc III 76*
“The things you like in me are gone for good” *Att 251 (XII 14)*
“In this lonely place” *Att 252 (XII 15)*
“I want you to find out” *Att 270 (XII 30)*
p. 245 “I want to tell you of something” *Fam 248 (IV 5)*
“surely she too deserves” *Lact I 15 18*
p. 246 “Today, for the first time” *Plut Caes LVI 3*
p. 247 “Brutus reports that Caesar” *Att 343 (XIII 40)*
“Dolabella came this morning” *Att 317 (XIII 9)*
p. 248 Young Quintus “is at it constantly” *Att 346 (XIII 37)*
Balbus and Oppius had “never read anything better” *Att 348 (XIII 50)*
p. 249 Caesar dines with Cicero *Att 353 (XIII 52)*
p. 250 Young Quintus’s conversation with Cicero *Att 354 (XIII 42)*

Chapter 12—Philosophical Investigations: 46–44 BC

p. 252 “I have written more in this short time. . . . I cannot easily say” *Off III i 4*

p. 253 "to nude figures" *Brut LXXV 262*
"they are deserted" *Brut LXXXIV 289*
"In the book called *Hortensius*" *Div II 1ff.*
p. 254 "it was through my books" *Div II 7*
p. 255 "the matter did not fit the persons" *Att 326 (XIII 19)*
p. 257 "The whole life of the philosopher" *Tusc I XXX 74–31 75*
p. 259 Caesar's praise of Cicero *Pliny VII 117*

Chapter 13—"Why, This Is Violence!": January–March 44 BC

The main sources for Caesar's assassination are various lives by Plutarch, Nicolaus and Suetonius together with Appian and the other general historians.

p. 261 "I should be an idiot" *Att 356 (XIV 2)*
p. 262 "Come on, Faustus" *Plut Brut IX 1–4*
p. 263 "By his generous action" *Plut Cic XL 5*
"We'd better get a move on" *Plut Caes LVIII 1*
p. 264 "My name is Caesar" *Dio XLIV 10 1*
p. 265 "The people offer this" *Dio XLIV 11 3*
"To Caius Caesar" *Phil II 34*
"Where did the diadem come from?" *Phil II 85*
p. 266 "You, you, assassinated him" *Phil XIII 41*
Caesar's diarrhea *Dio XLIV 8*
"I would prefer to hold the Consulship legally" *Nic XX 70*
p. 267 "Brutus will wait for this piece of skin" *Plut Brut VIII 3*
"It's not fat, longhaired fellows" *Plut Brut VIII 2*
"There is no fate worse" *App II 109*
"It is more important for Rome" *Suet I 86*
p. 269 "I join you in praying" *Plut Brut XV 4*
"There has been enough kowtowing" *Nic XXVI 96–97*
p. 270 "The city looked as if it had been captured by an enemy" *Nic XXIV 91*

Chapter 14—The Heir: March–December 44 BC

In addition to the general historians Appian and Dio together with Plutarch, Cicero's Philippics are an essential source together with his correspondence. Suetonius's life of Augustus is also used.

p. 273 "the Ides of March was a fine deed, but half done" *Att 366 (XIV 12)*
"A pity you didn't invite me to dinner" *Fam 363 (XII 14)*
"If a man of Caesar's genius" *Att 355 (XIV 1)*
p. 274 "Congratulations" *Fam 322 (VI 15)*
p. 275 Cicero criticizes Brutus's speech *Att 378 (XV 1a)*
"What else could we have done?" *Att 364 (XIV 10)*
Brutus's and Cassius's provinces. There were so many changes in the provincial allocations in 44 that it has proved hard to disentangle who received which province at what stage. The view is followed here that Julius Caesar designated Macedonia and Asia for Brutus and Cassius. A discussion of the subject can be found in Syme, 102ff.
p. 277 "To think I saved the lives" *App II 143–47*
p. 278 "more concerned about the composition of his menus" *Att 357 (XIV 3)*
"Advancing years are making me cantankerous" *Att 375 (XIV 21)*
p. 279 "The Queen's flight" *Att 362 (XIV 8)*
"I hope it's true" *Att 374 (XIV 20)*
p. 281 "Octavian is with me here" *Att 366 (XIV 12)*
p. 282 "boy who owes everything to his name" *Phil XIII 11 25*
p. 283 "Hold them back, Cicero" *Att 386 (XV 6)*
Conference with Brutus and Cassius *Att 389 (XV 11)*
p. 284 "armor-proofing" of philosophy *Fam 330 (XVI 23)*
"Octavian, as I perceived" *Att 390 (XV 12)*
"How much longer are we going to be fooled?" *Att 399 (XV 22)*
"I suspect he's romancing as usual" *Att 408 (XV 29)*
p. 285 "You wouldn't believe how delighted he was" *Att 415 (XVI 7)*
p. 288 "Everyone thought he wasn't speaking so much as spewing up" *Fam 344 (XII 2)*
p. 289 "I am well aware of the criticisms" *Fam 349 (XI 28)*
"unscrupulous behavior of Caius Caesar" *Off I 26* and *64*
p. 290 "You will learn to obey orders" *App III 43*
p. 291 "He has great schemes afoot" *Att 418 (XVI 8)*
p. 292 "I imagine he will have the city rabble behind him" *Att 418 (XVI 8)*
"Two letters for me from Octavian in one day" *Att 419 (XVI 9)*
p. 293 "He was detained by a drinking bout" *Phil III 8 20*
p. 294 "The boy is taking the steam out of Antony" *Att 426 (XVI 15)*
p. 295 "Caesar on his own initiative" *Phil III 2 5*

p. 296 "We have for the first time" *Phil IV 6 16*
"I did not mince my words" *Fam 364 (X 28)*

Chapter 15—Cicero's Civil War: January–April 43 BC

The sources are the same as for the preceding chapter.

p. 298 "this heaven-sent boy" *Phil V 16 43*
"I happen to know all the young man's feelings" *Phil V 18 51*
p. 299 "I give you notice" *Phil VI 3 5*
"I know them through and through" *Fam 352 (XVI 27)*
p. 300 "My days and nights are passed in one sole care" *Fam 362 (IX 24)*
"I am sorry to hear you've given up dining out" *Fam 362 (IX 24)*
Cicero as popular leader *App III 66*
p. 301 "I do not reject peace" *Phil VII 6 199*
p. 302 "If I am not in error" *Fam 365 (XII 5)*
p. 303 "I want you to know" *Fam 366 (XII 11)*
p. 304 "If I may, I will remain in the city" *Phil XII 10 24*
"In my opinion, you will be wiser not to meddle" *Fam 369 (X 27)*
p. 305 "the partner of my counsels" *Phil XIII 19 44* and *19 40*
"locked together with their swords" *App III 68*
p. 306 "I reaped the richest of rewards" *Brut 7 (IX or I.3)*
"not a spark of this abominable war is left alive" *Fam 384 (X 14)*
"As for the boy Caesar" *Brut 7 (IX or I.3)*

Chapter 16—Death at the Seaside: April–November 43 BC

The sources are the same as for the preceding chapter. The account of Cicero's death is based on Plutarch, Livy (quoted by Seneca the Elder) and Appian.

p. 308 those who were rejoicing at the moment "will soon be sorry" *Fam 409 (X 33)*
p. 309 "I am alarmed" *Brut 11 (XII or I.4a)*
"We're not bragging every hour of the day. . . . You may say" *Brut 17 (XXV or I.17)*
"susceptible to scares" *Fam 330 (XVI 23)*
p. 310 "the young man must get praises, honors—and the push" *Fam 401 (XI 20)*
"What is the use?" *Fam 413 (XI 14)*

p. 311 "Our only protection was this lad" *Fam (XXIII or I.15)*
"Caesar's army, which used to be excellent" *Brut 23 (XXII or I.14)*
"You thank him on public grounds in such a fashion" *Brut 25 (XXIV or I.16)*
Brutus should "lend support" *Brut 26 (XXVI or I.18)*

p. 312 "As I write I am in great distress" *Brut 26 (XXVI or I.18)*
"as soon as I had an inkling" *Brut 18 (XVIII or I.10)*
"If you don't give Caesar the Consulship" *Dio XLVI 43*

p. 313 "I am doubly delighted" *ACI 23B Watt*

p. 315 "The point was reached where a person was proscribed" *App IV 5*
The fate of Verres *Pliny XXXIV 6*
"they were quite overwhelmed" *Plut Cic XLVII 1*

p. 317 "I will die in the country I have so often saved" *Sen VI 17*
"Then most of the crows" *Plut Cic XLVII 6*

p. 318 "*I* am stopping here. . . . What if you'd come to me first?" *Sen VI 19*
"Has even a mediocre fighter ever let out a groan" *Tusc II 17 41*
"*Now* we can end the proscription" *Plut Cic XLIX 1*

p. 319 Fulvia and Cicero's head *Dio XLVII 8 4*

Chapter 17—Postmortems

p. 320 "During the long flow of success" *Sen VI 22*
"This man's works" *Sen VI 24*
"So died Cicero" *Sen VI 23*

p. 324 Marcus throws a goblet at Agrippa *Pliny XIV 147*
Marcus appointed Augur "by way of apology" *App IV 51*
"In this way Heaven entrusted to the family of Cicero" *Plut Cic XLIX 4*
"Nature had stolen away Marcus's memory" *Sen VII 14*

p. 325 Augustus and his grandson *Plut Cic XLIX 4*

ACKNOWLEDGMENTS

This book would not have seen the light of day without the advice and support of Christopher Sinclair-Stevenson and the generous temerity of Grant McIntyre at John Murray in taking on a greenhorn. A special debt of gratitude goes to Antony Wood, with whose kindly but ruthless editorial support a shapeless bundle of pages was put into good order, and to Joy de Menil of Random House, whose sharp-eyed enthusiasm refocused the biography for the American reader. However, whatever is flawed in my study of Cicero is nobody's responsibility but my own.

I am deeply indebted to D. R. Shackleton Bailey for permission to reproduce passages from his translation of *Cicero: Letters to Atticus and to His Friends* in the Penguin Classics edition.

I am grateful to the Publishers and Trustees of the Loeb Classical Library for their kind permission to reprint passages from *Cicero,* vol. XVI, Loeb Classical Library Volume L213, translated by Clinton Walker Keyes, pp. 167, 245, 317, 345, 347, 361, 367, 373, 375, 499, 503, Cambridge, Mass.: Harvard University Press, 1928. (The Loeb Classical Library is a registered trademark of the President and Fellows of Harvard College.)

I should also like to thank Penguin Books, Ltd., for permission to reproduce passages from the following translations of works by Cicero which appeared in Penguin Classics: *Letters to Atticus and to His Friends,* Copyright © D. R. Shackleton Bailey, 1978; *Selected Political Speeches,* Copyright © Michael Grant Publications, Ltd., 1969; Sallust, *The Jugurthine War; Conspiracy of Catiline,* Copyright © the Estate of S. A. Handford, 1963; and Plutarch, *Fall of the Roman Republic,* Copyright © Rex Warner, 1958.

For the illustrated reconstruction of the Roman Forum, I am indebted to John E. Stambaugh, *The Ancient Roman City,* p. 112. © 1988 [Copyright holder]. Reprinted with permission of the Johns Hopkins University Press.

INDEX

Page numbers in *italics* refer to illustrations.

About the Author

ANTHONY EVERITT's fascination with ancient Rome began when he studied classics in school and has persisted ever since. He read English literature at Cambridge University and served four years as secretary general of the Arts Council for Great Britain. A visiting professor of arts and cultural policy at Nottingham Trent University and City University, Everitt has written extensively on European culture and development and has contributed to the *Guardian* and *Financial Times* since 1994. *Cicero,* his first biography, was chosen by both Allan Massie and Andrew Roberts as the best book of the year in the United Kingdom. Anthony Everitt lives near Colchester, England's first recorded town, founded by the Romans, and is working on a biography of Augustus.

About the Type

This book was set in Garamond, a typeface designed by the French printer Jean Jannon. It is styled after Garamond's original models. The face is dignified, and is light but without fragile lines. The italic is modeled after a font of Granjon, which was probably cut in the middle of the sixteenth century.